John Baxter

John Baxter is a film critic, novelist, biographer and broadcaster, whose books on the cinema include *The Hollywood Exiles*, *The Cinema of Josef von Sternberg*, *The Cinema of John Ford*, and biographies of Ken Russell (*An Appalling Talent*), Fellini and Buñuel. He was born and brought up in Australia, has worked in London and taught in the United States, and now lives in Paris with his wife Marie-Dominique Montel. His latest book is a biography of Stanley Kubrick.

Further reviews for *Steven Spielberg*:

'Diligent, perceptive and with every available anecdote'

SIMON HATTENSTONE, *Guardian*

'riveting . . . retains a healthy objectivity throughout his enthralling account' PENELOPE DENING, *Irish Times*

'. . . a film-lover's book, a review of a remarkable era, an exhaustive filmography – a movie about the evolution of Hollywood, with Spielberg as the central character' JEREMY LESTER, *Jewish Chronicle*

'Baxter may have a blockbuster on his hands.'

RICHARD E. GRANT, *Sunday Times*

'highly entertaining, packed with interesting information. If you want to know how a Spielberg film was made, what shenanigans went on during the making, or who fell out with whom, it is all here.'

WILLIAM RUSSELL, *The Herald* (Glasgow)

'Its usefulness lies in Baxter's shrewd assessment of Spielberg's relationship with the wider context of the entertainment industry in general and Hollywood power-politics . . . the account of Spielberg's unsettled early years . . . is illuminating in terms of his later preoccupations.' HUGO DAVENPORT, *Sunday Telegraph*

'Baxter is quietly professional . . . and makes good use of the copious interviews Spielberg has given throughout his career.'

ANTHONY QUINN, The *Observer*

'A very valuable book . . . the thing that most impresses in his book is the calm, careful and nearly gentle way in which it builds up our disquiet that the movie kingdom and our society as a whole should be so ordered that Steven Spielberg is its Gatsby, its Kane, and such a shining young example . . . it is Baxter's most intriguing point that Spielberg not only caters to youthfulness, but extends and preserves it . . . What is so clever, I think, is Baxter's sense of a man too narrowly focused to amount to a villain . . . Baxter's success is beyond question.'   DAVID THOMSON, *Independent on Sunday*

'An impeccably professional film-biographer (he's already done Buñuel, Fellini, Ford and is now working on Kubrick), Baxter leaves no document unrifled, no fact unchecked, no anecdote untold.'

Sight and Sound

' . . . a full, frank and readable account of a man who the public regards as one of the greatest enchanters in the history of film.'

STUART GILLES, *Manchester Evening News*

STEVEN SPIELBERG

The Unauthorised Biography

STEVEN SPIELBERG

JOHN BAXTER

HarperCollins*Publishers*

HarperCollins*Publishers*
77–85 Fulham Palace Road,
Hammersmith, London W6 8JB

This paperback edition 1997
3 5 7 9 8 6 4 2

First published in Great Britain by
HarperCollins*Publishers* 1996

Copyright © John Baxter 1996

ISBN 0 00 638444 7

Set in Berkeley Book

Printed and bound in Great Britain by
Caledonian International Book Manufacturing Ltd, Glasgow

Contents

Illustrations

Hooper and Spielberg collaborate to recreate Spielberg's childhood nightmare as a sentient tree tries to devour Oliver Robbins in *Poltergeist*.

John Williams with Spielberg during the scoring of *Close Encounters*.

John Milius directing *Red Dawn*. *(Author's collection)*

Matthew Robbins, co-writer of *The Sugarland Express* and uncredited script consultant on most Spielberg screenplays.

Paul Schrader, first screenplay writer of *Close Encounters*. *(Author's collection)*

Spielberg with Frank Marshall during *Poltergeist*.

Spielberg with long-time editor Michael Kahn.

On the set of *Temple of Doom*, Spielberg's mood is lightened by a visit from Kate Capshaw.

Spielberg with Kate Capshaw in 1988.

Spielberg directs David Yip in the opening sequence of *Indiana Jones and the Temple of Doom*.

Spielberg films Yip dying in Harrison Ford's arms.

Spielberg with Barry Levinson on the set of *Young Sherlock Holmes*. *(Author's collection)*

Spielberg and Joe Dante at the time of *Gremlins*. *(Author's collection)*

Spielberg and George Lucas immortalise themselves in cement in front of Mann's Chinese Theater, 1984.

Robert Zemeckis, Spielberg protégé and director of *Back to the Future* and *Forrest Gump*. *(Author's collection)*

Spielberg and children: with Cary Guffey on *Close Encounters*, Henry Thomas on *E.T.*, Raj Singh on *Temple of Doom* and Christian Bale on *Empire of the Sun*.

Spielberg directs Whoopi Goldberg in *The Color Purple*.

Richard Dreyfuss watches Holly Hunter with Brad Johnson in *Always*.

Kevork Malikyan with Alison Doody in *The Last Crusade*.

Emily Richard with Christian Bale and Rupert Frazer during the Shanghai location shooting of *Empire of the Sun*.

Stan Winston's animatronic tyrannosaurus rex contemplates dinner from a can in *Jurassic Park*.

Liam Neeson as Oskar Schindler.

Spielberg, in a White House baseball cap, directs *Schindler's List*.

Acknowledgements

In 1971, with great kindness, Jack Arnold, director of *The Incredible Shrinking Man* and *It Came from Outer Space*, showed me, a young critic on a first visit to Hollywood, around Universal Studios, bought me lunch in the commissary and introduced me to the company chairman, Lew Wasserman. Distantly, this book springs from that first encounter.

Somewhere in the black tower that marks out Universal's empire, Steven Spielberg was gearing up to make his professional debut in movies. He and I must have gone to some of the same previews at Universal during the weeks I spent in Hollywood on that trip. We definitely knew some of the same people, in particular Carey Loftin, the veteran stunt man who nearly killed himself on the climactic scene of Spielberg's first theatrical success, *Duel*.

Like most critics, I've watched, listened to and briefly met Spielberg as he moved around the world over the last twenty years, promoting his movies. He declined, however, to be interviewed for this book. 'He has never authorised a book about himself or his career,' his colleague Marvin Levy told me when I approached Amblin for assistance – admittedly with little expectation of success. 'It is possible one day he will do one himself.'

Fortunately Spielberg is one of the most widely interviewed of all contemporary artists. There is almost no corner of his life, professional or private, which he has not illuminated over the years. He is, in fact, almost obsessive about revealing himself to the public. His has been a career lived in the most unsparing of lights, that of the cinema screen. I've drawn on scores of these interviews, many of them unpublished, for this book. They have been extensively augmented by conversations with people who know or who have worked with Spielberg. Some of these cannot be named, since Amblin Entertainment insists on employees signing a lifetime confidentiality agreement. I'm grateful to those who felt they could speak to me, while respecting their wish to remain off the record.

Among those prepared to be quoted, I'm particularly grateful to J. G. Ballard, who spoke at length about his experiences on *Empire of the Sun*, Joe Dante about the making of *The Twilight Zone* and *Gremlins*, and his long experience of working with Spielberg, and Mick Garris about the production of *Amazing Stories*. Paul Freeman, Julian Glover, Kevork Malikyan, David Yip, Emily Richard and Bill Hootkins provided graphic and vivid memories of acting for Spielberg in *Raiders of the Lost Ark*, *Empire of the Sun* and *Indiana Jones and the Temple of Doom*. In the course of an extraordinary morning, Gordon Stainforth brought an unaccustomed drama to the staid premises of the Royal Geographical Society with his description of Spielberg's encounter with snakes and Stanley Kubrick on *Raiders*. Sir David Puttnam illuminated Spielberg's corporate significance, while Tom Stoppard battled the 'flu to tell me about their association. And I'm more than usually grateful to Jackie and Patrick Morreau, this time for introducing me to Jerry Goldsmith, not only for his memories of long days and white nights with Spielberg, but the unforgettable experience of hearing him conduct Alex North's *Streetcar Named Desire* music on a wet Soho Sunday.

Adrian Turner reminisced about presenting Spielberg at the National Film Theatre and kindly supplied a tape of his lecture there. Professor John Lincoln was cordial in recalling details of California State University, Long Beach, and Michael Lucas of the St James's Club in enlightening me about Spielberg's domestic arrangements. Pat McGilligan recalled his meetings with Spielberg on the set of *Jaws* and *1941*, only one of many kindnesses.

Bill Warren interviewed a number of people in Los Angeles on my behalf. I've consulted, and in some cases quoted from, my own interviews with Terry Hayes and Byron Kennedy, Carey Loftin, Denholm Elliot, Jack Arnold, Ray Bradbury, Forrest J. Ackerman, Robert Zemeckis, Hal Needham, François Truffaut, Richard Franklin and Raymond Burr, none of whom knew they would one day be contributing to this book.

Alex McGregor in Los Angeles and Mary Troath in London worked tirelessly to sift the mountain of clippings about Spielberg and his films. In Paris, the staff of the American Library and of the Bibliothèque Andre Malraux were extremely helpful. Maggie Brammall and John Brosnan also provided background material. In Sydney, Simon Taaffe searched out additional research documents, and in Melbourne Lucy Sussex sieved the Internet for the tracks of Thomas Keneally. Louise Swan and Mark Burman performed a similiar service for the BBC Archives, and David Thompson of *Omnibus* was kind enough to supply me with some of the rarest filmed interviews of Spielberg, John Milius and others. At the Museum of Modern Art in New York, Charles Silver and Ron Magliozzi were, as usual, courteous and helpful. Kevin Jackson, Richard Johnson and Rebecca Levin also provided help and encouragement.

Finally, to Pat McGilligan, Bill Warren and John Brosnan, for their incisive, if often abrasive comments on the manuscript, the most heartfelt of thanks.

John Baxter
Paris, 1996

If personality is an unbroken series of successful gestures, then there was something gorgeous about him, some heightened sensitivity to the promises of life, as if he were related to one of those intricate machines that register earthquakes ten thousand miles away. This responsiveness had nothing to do with that flabby impressionability which is dignified under the name of the 'creative temperament' – it was an extraordinary gift for hope, a romantic readiness such as I have never found in any other person and which it is not likely I shall ever find again.

F. Scott Fitzgerald, *The Great Gatsby*

The truth is, Charlie, you just don't care about anything except you. You just want to convince people that you love them so much that they should love you back. Only you want love on your own terms. It's something to be played your way – according to your rules. And if anything goes wrong and you're hurt – then the game stops, and you've got to be soothed and nursed, no matter what else is happening – and no matter who else is hurt.

Joseph Cotten in *Citizen Kane*. Herman J. Mankiewicz and Orson Welles

STEVEN SPIELBERG

Pre-Credit Sequence

The Sandcastle

Everyone's lost but me.

I N MAY 1977, two men sat on the beach in front of the Mauna Kea Hotel in Hawaii and built a sandcastle.

One was a stringy thirty-year-old with untrimmed beard and hair, round metal-rimmed Armani spectacles and nails bitten to the quick. His friend, three years older, had a beard too, but it was trimmed, as was his curly hair. Even in the heat of Hawaii, however, he wore gloves and a wide hat, to protect the skin of his face and hands, permanently sensitised by sunburn.

Watching them mould and buttress the walls of their castle, nobody would have guessed the two men were Steven Spielberg and George Lucas, the world's most successful creators of mass entertainment. They looked more like college teaching assistants on a weekend getaway. Only the scale of their construction hinted at their imagination. This wasn't *a* sandcastle but, as befitted their vision, *the* sandcastle, the size of a bathroom.

Lucas had yet to launch his career as a major Hollywood player. Spielberg, however, was already rich. His 1975 film of Peter Benchley's shark thriller *Jaws* had grossed $458 million in worldwide sales, $260 million of that in American domestic box-office alone. His share, though only a fraction of the sum retained by the producing studio, Universal, had made him a multi-millionaire. His percentage of the film he had just finished, *Close Encounters of the Third Kind*, would bring his personal fortune close to $200 million. Yet while Hollywood film-makers less wealthy than he routinely swept around town in Cadillac stretch limousines, owned sprawling Bel Air houses, dined at fashionable restaurants like Ma Maison, Spago or Le Dôme, Spielberg lived frugally, drove a rented car and still dressed in baseball cap, trainers, jeans and a checked shirt open at the throat.

The shooting of *Close Encounters* had taken him from Mobile, Alabama, to Madras in India, from the Mojave Desert to, at least in imagination, the Gobi in Mongolia, and from suburban Indiana to the fringes of outer space. At the end of what he wearily called 'two blood-letting years of effects shooting and optical compositing', however, he'd broken down. Through hours of shooting at clay pigeons with his friend, the director John Milius, he'd contracted the hearing dysfunction tinnitus. In the middle of dubbing the sound tracks, he lost, he said, his 'sense of judgment and objectivity, but continued to make decisions, not all of them the right ones'. His devoted but distracted crew, preoccupied with getting the film finished for the November release date imposed by Columbia, suggested as diplomatically as possible that he take a holiday.

Spielberg joined Lucas in Hawaii, where he and his wife Marcia had retreated to wait for news of his new film, *Star Wars*, which had just opened. The trade paper *Variety* assured everyone that this juvenile space opera would flop. Instead, the audience figures phoned through daily to Lucas soon showed that it was the hit of the year, if not the decade. Enviously, his sometime mentor and now rival Francis Ford Coppola, chronically impoverished despite his success with *The Godfather*, cabled from San Francisco: 'Send Money. Francis.'

Lucas and Spielberg chatted as they worked – mostly about future projects. Instinctively, Spielberg deferred to the older man. Lucas's interest in history, his monkish temperament and long silences had earned him the reputation of a guru among the rowdy group of young directors journalists were already calling 'New Hollywood'.

Heaping more sand on the walls of the castle, Spielberg wondered aloud if he might not attempt something mindless and undemanding next; an action adventure movie, like a James Bond film. He didn't tell Lucas he'd already tried to win a commission from the British-based producer of the series, Albert 'Cubby' Broccoli, and been turned down.

'I've got a better film than that,' Lucas said. 'Have you ever heard of the lost Ark of the Covenant?'

'Noah's Ark?'

'No, no, no, no, no, not Noah's Ark,' Lucas muttered, adding a battlement. He explained about the Ark, the casket in which the Israelites carried the two tablets of the Ten Commandments given to Moses by God, Aaron's rod, and a pot of the manna that had sustained them in the wilderness. In truth, it was almost as new to Lucas as to Spielberg. Bay Area writer/director Phil Kaufman, with whom he'd developed the idea, had suggested it. Kaufman's orthodontist had told him about the Ark when he was nine years old, and the story left an indelible impression.

As the tide rolled in, Spielberg dug a moat. The castle won another twenty minutes of life. In that time Lucas outlined a plot for a movie he'd had simmering for almost four years.

The trigger had been an old poster of a movie hero jumping from a horse to a truck. It reminded him of the serial cliffhangers of the thirties and forties. 'I started out by asking myself, "Gee, when I was a kid, what did I really like?"' Lucas said later. His musings, and some brainstorming with Kaufman, had produced an archetype, a rapscallion archaeologist in a snap-brim fedora, leather jacket and three-day beard who carried a bullwhip and roamed the world, searching for lost cities and hidden treasure. In the film Lucas envisaged, the archaeologist would never be off the screen. Anybody else in the story – a buddy, a girl – would exist only for comic relief, or to provide someone for him to rescue. In a world where movie characters usually had feet of clay and convictions to match, this man would be an old-fashioned hero, faithful only to his own quirky code of honour. He christened the archaeologist 'Indiana', after his wife's pet Alaskan Malamute. For a surname, he favoured something less exotic, like 'Smith'.

Lucas had five plots on file. In the first, his hero would be hunting the Ark of the Covenant and trying to keep it from an occult-obsessed Hitler. Something stirred in Spielberg as he listened. He didn't much like serials, but he could name a dozen films of the thirties and forties where stars like Robert Mitchum, Clark Gable or his personal hero,

Spencer Tracy, appeared as a soldier of fortune in a leather jacket and greasy felt. Charlton Heston had worn an almost identical outfit in *The Greatest Show on Earth*, the first film he'd ever seen. On the set, Spielberg often wore a hat like Indiana's himself.

More important, however, his internal barometer sensed a shrewd career move. With James Bond, he would be covering old ground. What Lucas suggested was, despite its roots in Old Hollywood, fresh, untouched. It was a risk, but a small one: the success of *Star Wars* had endorsed Lucas's instincts.

'I'd love to do that,' Spielberg said carefully, 'if you decide not to.'

'I'm working with Phil Kaufman on this,' Lucas replied, 'but if you like, it's yours.' To Spielberg's surprise, he added, 'I'm not directing any more. I've retired.' The success of *Star Wars* had inspired Lucas to make radical changes in his life and career. He was already planning a three-thousand-acre hideaway in a valley in rural Marin County, in northern California, near where he'd been born. Within this idealised nineteenth-century village, named Skywalker Ranch after his *Star Wars* hero Luke Skywalker, and protected from the modern world by prowling security guards, he could devote himself to reading history and the great Russian novels, experimenting with film technique, and producing films for others to direct. If he wanted company, he could buy it. He and Marcia were already planning to adopt a child. After they divorced, Lucas would adopt two more as a single parent.

As they continued to talk, the tide washed in from the Pacific, eroding their castle as New Hollywood was eroding the old. But its foundations, metaphorically, survived and endured. A month after the beach meeting, Spielberg had the film. In imitation of serials like *Adventures of the Flying Cadets* and *King of the Rocket Men*, they called it *Raiders of the Lost Ark*. It, and the innovative deal Lucas and Spielberg negotiated to fund it, became the cutting edge of a revolution in international entertainment and leisure, the effects of which have still fully to be assessed.

1

The Man Who Fell to Earth

Yesterday, upon the stair,
I met a man who wasn't there.
He wasn't there again today.
I wish that man would go away.

Traditional rhyme

THE FORCE of American popular art lies in its directness, its simplicity,
its economy of means and of scale. Analysis may uncover cultural
and autobiographical references, sophistications of technique, even pro-
fundity of intellect, but the first appeal of a George Gershwin song, a
Walt Disney cartoon, a Norman Rockwell painting is, and must be,
commonplace delight.

Steven Spielberg embodies this tradition. His films, even the sombre
Schindler's List, are machines for delighting us. Almost always they succeed in doing so. It's not hard to see why. He traffics in what authors of
science fiction, his preferred form, call 'a sense of wonder', a heightened
apprehension of physical possibilities. It has been said that the universe
is not only stranger than we know but stranger than we *can* know.
Spielberg dispels this idea. His vision, like that of the best science fiction
writers, is of a welcoming, explicable place.

Writing about Ray Bradbury, whose books like *The Martian Chronicles*
and *Something Wicked this Way Comes* share Spielberg's simplicity of
vision and sureness of technique, the critic Damon Knight, in a passage
that could well refer to Spielberg, remarked:

To Bradbury, as to most people, radar and rocket ships and atomic
power are big, frightening, meaningless names; a fact which, no

doubt, has something to do with his popular success, but which does not touch the root of the matter. Bradbury's strength lies in the fact that he writes about the things that are really important to us: not the things we pretend we are interested in – science, marriage, sports, politics, crime – but the fundamental pre-rational fears and longings and desires; the rage at being born; the will to be loved; the longing to communicate; the hatred of parents and siblings; the fear of things that are not self . . .

People who talk about Bradbury's imagination miss the point. His imagination is mediocre; he borrows nearly all his backgrounds and props, and distorts them badly; wherever he is required to invent anything – a planet, a Martian, a machine – the image is flat and unconvincing. Bradbury's Mars, where it is not as bare as a Chinese stage setting, is a mass of inconsistencies; his spaceships are a joke; his people have no faces. The vivid images in his work are not imagined; they are *remembered*.

In 1987, cartoonist Jules Feiffer drew a panel for the magazine *Village Voice*. A writing professor lauds a student for his 'Joycean gift of language coupled with a Hemingwayesque spareness'. He goes on to compare him with Fitzgerald, Bellow, Updike, Styron, Mailer, then asks him what he's working on. 'A screenplay for Spielberg,' the boy says airily. The professor is suddenly a beaming enthusiast. 'Do you know him?' he demands. 'What's he really like?'

The public urge to know what Spielberg is *really* like has never abated. His personality and appearance are so unremarkable, his public statements so bland, that everyone feels there must be a secret Spielberg hidden under the ramshackle exterior.

If you were to ask *Spielberg* what he is really like, he would probably reply that he is just like his audience. He is like everyone. But the image of Just Plain Steve is simply one aspect of his public persona. Examine that persona, and it fragments into a jigsaw puzzle where real memories slot into fabricated ones, and where childhood enthusiasms jostle for space with the structures of corporate power.

Spielberg's indifferent communication skills don't help to explain him to his public. His voice has never quite lost the self-absorbed gabble and stammer of the teenager drunk on ideas. 'He has all the virtues – and defects – of a sixteen-year-old,' one colleague remarks. Over the years he's learned to smile and to pause occasionally for others to speak, but the interpersonal still daunts him. He communicates best from behind a protective grille of technology. On that level, he radiates competence. Everyone notices it. The novelist Martin Amis almost mistook him for the man who'd come to fix the Coke machine. Someone else described his image as 'chemistry-student-next-door'. Both Amis and actor Tom Hanks compared him to the high school audio-visual assistant who alone understood 16mm projectors. (Spielberg worked his way through three years of college, in part by projecting classroom films.)

His mastery of cinema technology, what critic Pauline Kael called 'a film sense', is innate and effortless, his innocent flair and enjoyment disguising the complexities of what he does. 'I got the feeling,' said Julian Glover, who acted for him in *Indiana Jones and the Last Crusade*, 'that, if he wanted to, he could have built the set. He knew as much about lighting as [director of photography] Douglas Slocombe. And he operated the camera himself.' The worst sin for a Spielberg collaborator is to fail in technique. When that happens, Spielberg can be scathing. 'There is no, "Nice try, guys – better luck next time,"' complained one crew member. 'He says things like, "You didn't get it right. Think about *that* when you go to bed."'

Partly by chance but increasingly by design, Spielberg has immured himself in the prison of his facility. It is the central irony of his life that the more he is driven to employ his skills, the more they destroy the very spontaneity he strives to capture. The audience which follows him, and which he helped create, is perfectly happy, however, with technique. To them, not understanding his systematic methods, his ability to engineer entertainment machines like *Jurassic Park* can seem almost miraculous, and it's to a god that many of them compare him. Or an alien. When *American Premiere* magazine entitled one article about *E.T.* and its maker 'Steven Spielberg in his Adventures on Earth', they articulated a sense shared by many that he does not belong here. With his prodigies of imagination undermined by physical fragility and social clumsiness, he recalled the soft-spoken extra-terrestrial played by Michael Rennie in Robert Wise's *The Day the Earth Stood Still*, or David Bowie's Martian, fragile as a stick insect, in Nicolas Roeg's 1976 film *The Man Who Fell to Earth*.

Spielberg makes a credible alien. He's most comfortable with those who live in private worlds. When stories of eccentric habits and lifestyle accreted around Michael Jackson, Spielberg, who planned to film *Peter Pan* with the singer and spent hours playing games with him at his Disneyland-like estate, remarked wistfully, 'It's a nice place Michael comes from. I wish we could all spend some time in his world.'

Spielberg's need for protection and distance has its roots in a genuine fragility. Since he was four years old, he's bitten his fingernails. Despite his technical ease, he was for most of his early adulthood a white-knuckle flier who had nosebleeds at high altitudes. For many years he so disliked elevators that he'd walk up half a dozen flights of stairs rather than enter one. The man who terrified the world with *Jaws* also hated and feared the ocean, and the director of that archetypal night-time film *Close Encounters of the Third Kind* admits, 'I'm scared of the dark except in a motion picture theatre.'

It is only in the welcoming darkness of the cinema that Spielberg truly feels at home – and only with the myths of the movies that he is intellectually comfortable. Increasingly, it has been through and by myths that he has chosen to define himself. Admirers have been quick to add their own manufactured myths that confirm his role as an Honorary Outsider, and just another misunderstood teenager, like them; a Peter Pan of movies, the Boy Who Wouldn't Grow Up, but who invested hugely in preserving himself in artificial adolescence. As early as *Jaws* in 1974, rumour claimed – erroneously – that Spielberg's jeans with their multitude of zipped pockets were specially made for him at $250 a pair. Even his pet Cavalier King Charles spaniels were pressed into the fantasy. Some people felt the turnover in dogs was curiously high. As Zalman succeeded Elmer, Chauncey succeeded Zalman and Halloween followed Chauncey, rumours grew that Elmer/Zalman/Chauncey/Halloween wasn't a dog but a role: when the incumbent lost its puppy cuteness, another replaced it. Friends insist this is untrue. However, Spielberg's reclusiveness fanned the story, and others like it.

Although Spielberg's career is entwined with that of George Lucas, the two men are cultural and psychological opposites. Lucas, short, slight, seems habitually curled in on himself, arms often folded across his body. Spielberg, at five feet eight inches and 151 pounds, is fractionally taller, but contrasting body language exaggerates the difference. 'Some people look at the ground when they walk,' he says. 'Others look straight ahead. I always look upward, at the sky.'

Lucas's expressionless face and low, toneless voice emphasise the mask effect of his beard and moustache. Director John Badham calls him 'a painfully shy person who hates dealing with people'. Writer Willard Huyck, another student friend, said, 'George made a few friends at [the University of Southern California Film School], and decided that's about all he needed for the rest of his life.'

As a director, he communicates even less. 'George Lucas,' confided a *Star Wars* actor, 'is the worst director in the world. *Never* takes his nose out of the newspaper.' The conventional view of film as a collaborative art – or an art of any kind, for that matter – isn't his.

Lucas's childhood in Modesto, California, was suffused with Methodism and German Lutheranism. He reacted against it in adulthood by creating a laid-back, feel-good home life. This 'redwood tub mentality' amused Spielberg, who joked about 'LucasLand'. Spielberg himself is a product of the east coast suburbs, the rural midwest and the high desert of Arizona, but culturally he is archetypally Jewish; Thomas Keneally, author of *Schindler's List*, talks of his 'classic Central European map-of-Poland face'. His first memory is of being taken to a synagogue at six months, and he learned numbers from those tattooed on the arm of a relative who survived Auschwitz. Though he'd been bar mitzvahed, he didn't practise his religion until well into adulthood. Long before that, however, he went out of his way to introduce a Jewish dimension into his films. In both *Jaws* and *Close Encounters of the Third Kind*, characters written as gentile were redesigned to accommodate Richard Dreyfuss, an actor proudly and obviously Jewish. It wasn't until Spielberg's second marriage, to the actress Kate Capshaw, that he integrated his cultural heritage into any system of belief, but since childhood, Judaism exercised a powerful influence of which even he wasn't fully aware.

Being born Jewish also gave Spielberg an entrée to Hollywood which gentiles – and this included most of the USC group – could never possess. Along with Lucas, the film-makers who came to be known as New Hollywood included Brian De Palma (*Carrie*, *Sisters*), John Milius (*Big Wednesday*), the slightly older Francis Coppola (the *Godfather* trilogy, *Apocalypse Now*), husband and wife producers Michael and Julia Phillips (*The Sting*) and a group of lesser talents like writers Hal Barwood, Matthew Robbins, Willard Huyck and Gloria Katz, composer Basil Poledouris and cameraman/director Carroll Ballard.

Most emerged from that sixties phenomenon, the university film school, and elected to work inside the studio system rather than in the underground. Christened 'Movie Brats' by Michael Pye and Lynda Myles in their 1979 book *The Movie Brats: How the Film Generation Took Over Hollywood*, they rushed into the vacuum created when the US Justice Department forced the studios to shed their theatre chains and embrace the free market.

Old Hollywood had served the post-war baby boomers, now entering their thirties and looking for a Nice Night's Entertainment. New Hollywood targeted their children, the teens and pre-teens in Nike and Adidas trainers, stone-washed Levis and New York Yankees caps, who spent homework time reading EC Comics' *Tales from the Crypt* or watching reruns of the TV series *Twilight Zone*, and queued every weekend outside multiplex cinemas across the country.

Spielberg's technique to win this audience was to scavenge Hollywood's scrapyard, salvaging genres and recycling them in widescreen, colour and stereo sound. His ability to resuscitate moribund material was unique. His approach to the shark of *Jaws*, to Puck, the 'Little Green Man' of *E.T.*, *Jurassic Park*'s velociraptor dinosaurs and the Nazis of *Schindler's List* was identical. In each case, he animated a cliché by showing that even cardboard thinks and feels. Not for nothing was he an admirer of Disney's *Pinocchio*, in which a puppet is brought to life.

As an added guarantee that the audience would embrace his work, Spielberg preferred never to instigate an idea. The tendency of Lucas and Scorsese to push ahead with their visions, bulldozing all in their path, could produce successes, but Spielberg fed on consensus, not confrontation. Most of his films would be years in gestation, and would often begin with another director. *Jaws* had been Dick Richards's film. *Close Encounters of the Third Kind* originated with Paul Schrader. Phil Kaufman would start as the director of *Raiders*, John Milius developed *1941*, Tobe Hooper *Poltergeist*, and Hooper, with John Sayles, did the preliminary work on *E.T. Empire of the Sun* was intended for David Lean. Even *Schindler's List* was at one point a Martin Scorsese project.

Just as Spielberg is anything but the common man, he's also anything but the common artist. His vision is closer to that of a politician or a corporate CEO than to a film-maker. *Newsday* critic Jack Matthews articulated the truth that had been dawning for some time on the film-makers with whom Spielberg had grown up in the industry, but whom he is now leaving further and further behind: 'His contemporaries in the Hollywood firmament are not Scorsese and Coppola, they're studio execs Jeffrey Katzenberg, Mark Canton, Peter Guber, Joe Roth and the other fortysomething crowd controlling the power.' The critic Peter Biskind has pointed out how closely Spielberg's and Lucas's business philosophies conformed to those of Ronald Reagan, who served as president from 1981 to 1989, throughout the period of their greatest success. Reagan, says Biskind, 'was the strong father Lucas and Spielberg didn't know they were looking for, the ideal president for the age of *Star Wars*'. In temperament, Spielberg has more in common with the Democrats like John F. Kennedy who saw it as their role to make a world fit for baby boomers to live in. Arthur Schlesinger Jr speaks of Kennedy as 'a realist and an ironist, a man of sardonic wit and impenetrable reserve who sought to apply reason to the problems of state'. One senses some of the same cool estimate of cause and effect in Spielberg. 'His direct and unfettered mind,' Schlesinger continued of Kennedy, 'freed him to con-template a diversity of possible courses. At the same time, he was a careful judge of those possibilities and was disinclined to make heavy investments in losing causes . . . He once described himself to Jacqueline as "an idealist without illusions". ' Spielberg shares many of these characteristics, albeit in diluted form. He's even closer, however, to the philanthropic industrialists of a century ago like Carnegie and Frick.

In person, he appears diffident, nervous, unsure, eager to be liked and to have his work approved by the audience, but a frosty stare at moments of threat reveals him as a man who understands power and expects to be obeyed. On the set, he's fast, focused, saying little to his crew, even less to his cast. He's animated, however, when talking business. If he is truly an artist, his art is the deal. No Edison or Ford, perhaps – but Federico Fellini was right to say, as he did to Francis Coppola, 'Spielberg is a tycoon, like Rockefeller.' When historians assess the 1970s and eighties, during which entertainment and audio-visual media began to dominate large segments of the world economy, Spielberg, along with innovators like Microsoft's Bill Gates, may well emerge as a major architect of the change.

Millions would be astonished to hear Spielberg called, as he sometimes is, 'the most hated man in Hollywood'. Admittedly, 'hate' is a term so contaminated by self-interest as to be meaningless in show business. The gibe 'You'll never work in this town again – unless we need you' embodies so much conventional wisdom that nobody sees it as a joke. After Spielberg allied with ex-Disney studio head Jeffrey Katzenberg and record producer David Geffen in 1994 as DreamWorks SKG, David Letterman, master of ceremonies of the 1995 Oscar broadcast, joked that the alliance was a time saver; instead of waiting for them to fail separately, Hollywood could now wait for them to fail as a group.

However, even if one replaces 'hated' with 'resented' or 'envied', a residue of genuine dislike remains. Friends and colleagues agree; Steven Spielberg is hard to like. Geffen called him, according to Julia Phillips, 'selfish, self-centred, egomaniacal, and worst of all – greedy'. Geffen denied the quote, but there are plenty in Hollywood prepared to endorse it, if not for the record. Spielberg can be remote, grasping, sulky, narrow.

In his office, he seldom acknowledges anyone except to raise some technical point. He 'lacked social graces', one colleague said of his rapport, or lack of it, with his employees. 'He never asked anybody about their personal lives. His only subject of conversation is the movies.'

But Spielberg shares these characteristics with many – perhaps most – great directors. Fellini, Buñuel and Welles all drew the same criticism. Likewise many of his own contemporaries in New Hollywood. Film-making is an art learned in decades alone in the dark with other people's dreams, and pursued in an environment of inflated egos and expectations, sudden-death deadlines and Brobdingnagian profits and losses. As the matador respects the bull more than the crowd which gathers to see one of them die, directors come to love films more than they love the audience.

During the seventies and eighties, while he was finding his feet, Spielberg was famously approachable. While other directors retired to their trailers between takes and had lunch sent in, he schmoozed with the actors, ate in the commissary and hosted evening screenings of his favourite old movies to which the entire cast and crew were invited. He always entertained his cast at dinner just before shooting, and greeted each of them, 'Welcome to the family.' Lucas simply sent a basket of fruit to their rooms.

All this, however, may simply have been more a technique of manipulation than a sign of interest in other people. 'Directing is 80 per cent communication and 20 per cent know-how,' Spielberg says. 'Because if you can communicate to the people who know how to edit, know how to light, and know how to act – if you can communicate what you want . . . and what you feel, that's my definition of a good director.' One of the warmer stories about him describes him winning over ageing star Joan Crawford on his first job by presenting her each day with a rose in a Pepsi-Cola bottle: Crawford was the widow of Pepsi's chairman. At an American Film Institute seminar, however, Spielberg recollected cynically: 'I put the day of the week on the Pepsi bottle, and each day I'd give her one. She didn't know it was a countdown. I couldn't wait to get off the picture. Oh yeah, I did a lot of that bullshit.'

What sort of man prefers to be seen as a cunning manipulator than a charming collaborator? The same kind who will get up early on a film set to bake *matzoh* for 150 people? With Spielberg, it is safer to suspect the easy answers. He is stranger than we know – perhaps stranger than we *can* know.

2

The Boy Who Swallowed a Transistor

We belong to the last generation that could relate to adults.

Joan Didion

H E WAS short and thin. His ears stuck out, and his narrow face seemed to elongate towards the chin, making his mouth V-shaped, and pulling the lower lip out and down, so that his mouth would never seem quite closed. He looked like an inquisitive bird, with a beaky nose he found so embarrassing in childhood that he stuck tape to the tip of it and to his forehead, praying it would develop a tilt. The beak was matched by a bird's gaze, motionless, eerily unblinking. If he disliked something, as adult or child, he just stared it out of existence. A bird's voice, too, high, fast, uninflected. And he moved in an avian way, darting and stopping, darting and stopping, his actions apparently unmediated by intellect. When teams were chosen for any game, he would always be the last one picked. Nobody wanted jerky little Steven. Adolescence would bring not muscles but acne, freckles and even greater gawkiness. His thin arms so embarrassed him that it wasn't until the production of *Close Encounters of the Third Kind* in 1976 that he dared take off his shirt in public.

Spielberg's birth almost coincided with the first sightings of UFOs over the United States. On 24 June 1947, Idaho businessman Kenneth Arnold, flying his two-seater plane over the Yakima Indian Reservation in Washington state, reported nine shallow dish-like objects heading towards the Cascade Range. They looked to him like skipping stones, but he estimated their speed at 1200 m.p.h. Over the next two weeks

'flying saucers' were seen in thirty states, after which sightings settled
down to fifty a month.

For many years it was believed that Spielberg was born a few months
after this, at the Jewish Hospital in Cincinnati, Ohio. In fact, his mother
Leah Posner Spielberg gave birth to him a year earlier, on 18 December
1946, a date Spielberg systematically obscured during his early adulthood. He was followed within the next few years by three sisters, Anne,
Sue and Nancy. Spielberg would complain that he spent his childhood
in a house with three screaming younger sisters and a mother who played
concert piano with seven other women. Elliott's little sister Gertie in
E.T., inclined to sudden squeals and conversational irrelevancies, was,
Spielberg claimed, an amalgamation of his three 'terrifying' siblings.

Leah Posner was small, agile and nervous, like her son. She hated to
fly, a trait he inherited. She'd trained as a pianist, but given it up as a
possible career when she married Arnold Spielberg, another locally-born
Cincinnatian whose parents, like hers, had come from Poland and Austria
in the century's first wave of immigrants. Almost immediately after their
marriage, Arnold enlisted in the Air Force, flying as a B-25 radio operator
in Burma with a squadron nicknamed the 'Burma Bridgebusters'. Demob-
ilised, he stayed with electronics, which had fascinated him since he was
eight or nine. In 1948, Bell Telephone engineers John Bardeen, Walter
Brattain and William Shockley invented the transistor, the tiny ger-
manium diode that would replace vacuum tubes and make miniaturised
electronics possible. Arnold found a job with the Burroughs business
machine company, working on the beginnings of computers. An obsessive tinkerer, he would bring home bits of equipment, or drag the family
off in the middle of the night to observe some natural wonder. His son
thought him inflexible and workaholic. Richard Dreyfuss's character Roy
Neary in *Close Encounters* is a not entirely affectionate portrait of him.

Arnold read the science fiction magazines that proliferated after the
war as publishing stumbled on a middle-class audience newly sophisticated in technology and interested in its potential. John W. Campbell
built the monthly *Astounding Science Fiction* into the premiere sf magazine,
discreetly alternating fiction with technical articles and the occasional
outright piece of charlatanism, like *Dianetics: A New Science of the Mind*,

in which L. Ron Hubbard, one of Campbell's most successful pre-war fiction writers, expounded his pseudoscientific religion, Scientology. Sensing a shift in his readership towards technology, Campbell changed the title in 1960 to *Analog Science Fiction/Science Fact* and began publishing more thoughtful material, typified by Frank Herbert's ecological saga *Dune*. Arnold Spielberg, an *Analog* fan, piled copies behind the lavatory cistern in the bathroom where he could read them in comfort and privacy.

Broadcast media permeated Spielberg's childhood. When he was four or five, his father built him a crystal set. He would lie in his room at night, listening through an earpiece – and sometimes, he insists, through his teeth. 'I remember one day, without the radio, hearing some music and then hearing this voice I was familiar with from the radio. It was the comedy programme *Beulah*.'

'There are certain young directors, like Steven Spielberg,' says film editor Ralph Rosenblum, 'who were raised in the age of television and seem to have an intuitive sense of film rhythm and film possibilities.' Spielberg agreed. 'I did begin by reading comics. I did see too many movies. I did, still do, watch too much television. I feel the lack of having been raised on good literature and the written word.' As critic David Denby would say later of him and his generation of directors, 'Cartoons exert a greater influence than literature on his tastes and assumptions.' For the rest of his life, Spielberg would apologise for lacking the intellectual discipline to deal with print. 'I don't like reading. I'm a very slow reader. I have not read for pleasure in many, many years. And that's sort of a shame. I think I am really part of the Eisenhower generation of television.'

TV had just begun to pervade America. 1952 saw the debut of the prototypical cop series, *Dragnet*, the celebrity tribute programme *This is Your Life*, *The Jackie Gleason Show*, with Gleason as a New York bus driver with delusions of grandeur and Art Carney as his dutiful sewer-worker friend, and *Our Miss Brooks*, one of many series to give a new career to a Hollywood character performer, in this case Eve Arden as an acerbic unmarried middle-aged schoolteacher.

It was *The Adventures of Ozzie and Harriet*, however, which exerted the greatest influence over Spielberg's generation. Band leader Ozzie Nelson transferred his situation comedy from radio, and with it his real-life family, including son Eric, known as Ricky, whom the series made into a pop star. TV cloned the Nelsons into a multitude, among them the Cleavers of *Leave it to Beaver* and the white-bread Andersons of *Father Knows Best*, led by another Hollywood retread, Robert Young, whom Spielberg would find himself directing. As David Halberstam says, the sitcoms celebrated

> a wonderfully antiseptic world, of idealised homes in an idealised, unflawed America. There were no economic crises, no class divisions or resentments, no ethnic tensions . . . Dads were good dads whose worst sin was that they did not know their way around the house or could not find common household objects or that they were prone to give lectures about how much tougher things had been when they were boys . . . Moms and dads never raised their voices at each other in anger . . . This was a peaceable kingdom. There were no drugs. Keeping a family car out late at night seemed to be the height of insubordination . . . Moms and dads never stopped loving one another. Sibling love was always greater than sibling rivalry. No child was favoured, no child was stunted.

The reality was very different. In 1955 teenage pregnancies reached a level unsurpassed even in the nineties, and one in every three marriages ended in divorce.

It was into this real world that Spielberg descended from TV's fantasies of domestic perfection. Leah and Arnold Spielberg were no Ozzie and Harriet. Leah was frustrated in her musical ambitions, Arnold harassed by the need to keep up in a competitive new industry. 'He left home at 7 a.m.,' Spielberg recalled, 'and sometimes didn't get home until 9 or 10 p.m. I missed him to the point of resenting him.' Their children roved the emotional no man's land between them. '[My mother] would have chamber concerts in the living room with her friends who played the viola and the violin and the harp. While that was happening in another room, my father would be conferring with nine or ten men about computers, graphs and charts and oscilloscopes and transistors.' Sometimes the conflict degenerated into domestic arguments. When these started, the four children huddled together, listening to the marriage fall apart.

Steven learned to tune out the rage and fear. He'd go into his room, close the door and, stuffing towels under it, immerse himself in building model planes from Airfix hobby kits. 'For many years I had a real Lost Boy attitude about parents,' he said. 'Who needs them?' He carried his defence mechanism into adult life. When an employee of Spielberg's told Leah she'd quit Amblin Entertainment, Leah laughed and asked, 'Have you ceased to exist yet?'

'She knew the deal,' said the employee. 'That's his childlike personality. If you do something a baby doesn't like, he just shuts you out.'

Television became at once Steven's educational medium and security blanket. Leah and Arnold didn't allow him to watch anything as violent as *Dragnet*, but he absorbed almost everything else, in particular the old movies which were TV's cheapest and most reliable fodder. For him, as for many of his contemporaries who became directors in the seventies and eighties, TV was his film school.

It gave him a taste for Hollywood films of the thirties, in particular the A-pictures of MGM, which often featured an actor who, to him, was the epitome of fathers, Spencer Tracy. Tracy's appearance in MGM's 1937 adaptation of Kipling's *Captains Courageous*, about a spoiled rich kid who, falling overboard from an ocean liner, is rescued by a Portuguese fisherman and educated and civilised by him, profoundly affected Spielberg. It, and Tracy, would provide the key to his version of *Empire of the Sun*, just as another Tracy film, *Adam's Rib*, in which Tracy and Katharine Hepburn play married lawyers who represent opposite sides in a domestic violence case, would inspire scenes in *Indiana Jones and the Last Crusade* and in *Raiders of the Lost Ark*, where Harrison Ford coaxing kisses from Karen Allen parallels Tracy doing the same with Hepburn.

Spielberg was drawn even more to the fantasies of the period. His parents barred him from horror films – which, in any event, were not extensively programmed at the time – but he saw most of Hollywood's imaginative classics, including *Lost Horizon*. The virtuoso first third of Frank Capra's 1937 film of James Hilton's novel, with the small group of refugees carried across the roof of the world in a montage of maps, mountainscapes, bantering dialogue, high-plateau refuelling stops and a final spectacular special effects crash, would be replicated in the *Indiana Jones* movies.

Mobs interested Capra. Nobody was more skilful at orchestrating crowds in motion, cutting between a few significant cameos as detonators to drive a screen filled with people into surging movement, and Spielberg learned his lesson well. He was influenced in particular by *It's a Wonderful Life*. Offered by Capra and James Stewart as an affirmation to post-war America of everything it had fought to preserve, the fantasy of a savings and loan manager in rural Bedford Falls who sacrifices everything for his neighbours, only to lose faith, then regain it when an angel reveals the hell his town would have been without his contribution, the film endorsed everything Spielberg most needed to believe in: family, community, suburbia.

Steven's first memory was a visual one, of being taken to a Hassidic Jewish temple in Cincinnati by his father. Still in his stroller, he stared in wonder as he was rolled down a dark corridor into a room filled with men wearing long beards and black hats. He only had eyes, however, for the blaze of red light flowing from the sanctuary where, in imitation of the biblical Ark of the Covenant, the rolls of the holy torah were kept. The impression was indelible. 'I've always loved what I call "God Lights",' he says, 'shafts coming out of the sky, or out of a spaceship, or coming through a doorway.' Asked to define the central image of his work, he nominated the scene from *Close Encounters* where six-year-old Cary Guffey, about to be kidnapped by aliens, stands in the open kitchen door; 'the little boy ... standing in that beautiful yet awful light, just like fire coming through the doorway. And he's very small, and it's a very large door, and there's a lot of promise or danger outside that door.'

The blank TV screen exercised a similar fascination. When Spielberg's parents went out, they draped the set with a blanket and booby-trapped it with strategically placed hairs to reveal if Steven was viewing surreptitiously. He learned to note the position of the hairs and replace them. Then he would turn on the set and watch it, even if nothing was being transmitted. He was fascinated by the hissing 'snow', and the ghosts of faraway stations. Pressing his face to the tube, he would pursue them as they drifted in and out of range.

Sensory overload became Spielberg's preferred state of mind, and remained so for decades. He functioned best, he told a journalist, in a soup of received impressions: radio and television blaring, record player going, dogs barking, doorbell ringing – all while he answered a telephone call. Directing *Hook* in 1990, he would sit on the camera crane between shots, playing with a Game Boy and at the same time eavesdropping with earphones on flight controllers at LA International Airport.

As a child, alone in his room, he induced an aesthetic frenzy by a sort of optical masturbation, throwing hand shadows on the ceiling and scaring himself with them. Seeing himself as both artist and medium encouraged a schizophrenic division of personality. Until he was fourteen, he would stare into the mirror for five minutes at a time, hypnotising himself with his own reflection. As an adult, he would reach for a camera at moments of stress and photograph his tearful face in a mirror, the film-maker dispassionately recording the stranger inside him.

Insecurity bred fantasies of domestic disaster. He imagined creatures living under his bed, monsters lurking in the closet, waiting to suck him in. At night, he would lie shivering under the blankets, fancying that the furniture had feet, and that tables and chairs were scuttling about in the dark. 'There was a crack in the wall by my bed that I stared at all the time,' he said, 'imagining little friendly people living in the crack and coming out to talk to me. One day while I was staring at the crack it suddenly widened. It opened about five inches and little pieces fell out of it. I screamed a silent scream. I couldn't get anything out. I was frozen ... I was afraid of trees, clouds, the wind, the dark ... I liked being scared. It was very stimulating.'

*   *   *

In 1952 Arnold introduced Steven to two phenomena that fundamentally affected his life.

> My dad woke me in the middle of the night and rushed me into our car in my night clothes. I didn't know what was happening. It was frightening. My mom wasn't with me. So I thought, 'What's happening here?' He had a thermos of coffee and had brought blankets and we drove for about half an hour. We finally pulled over to the side of the road, and there were a couple of hundred people, lying on their backs in the middle of the night, looking up at the sky. My dad found a place, and we both lay down. He pointed to the sky, and there was a magnificent meteor shower. All these incredible points of light were criss-crossing the sky. It was a phenomenal display, apparently announced in advance by the weather bureau . . . Years later we got a telescope and I was into stargazing.

To memorialise this incident, Spielberg has incorporated a shooting star in all his films.

The other event of 1952 was his first experience of a movie theatre. Again it was Arnold who took him, after carefully explaining what they were going to see. Not carefully enough, however, since Steven thought Cecil B. DeMille's film about a circus, *The Greatest Show on Earth*, was a real circus and not one on film. The circus interested him, since his mother had told him how an uncle had run away with one as a boy; the same uncle, it seems, who had been in the black market, and had hidden contraband watches under the family bed.

DeMille's film conflated all the fantasies of circus life: the clown, played by James Stewart, whose permanent make-up hides his tragic past as a surgeon; sadistic animal trainer Lyle Bettger; French trapeze artist Cornel Wilde ('Ze Great Sebastian'); tough boss Charlton Heston, and all-American love interest in the person of raucous blonde Betty Hutton, all culminating in the collision of two trains where Stewart's long-suppressed skills are called upon.

Arnold told Steven, 'It's going to be bigger than you are, but that's all right. The people in it are going to be up on the screen and they can't get out at you.' (This is a common fantasy of suggestible children. Stephen King shared it, and as an adult persuaded his children not to sit too close to the screen by telling them that people who did so fell into the picture and became the extras visible behind the stars.) Spielberg recalls:

> So we stood in line for an hour and a half, and we go into this big cavernous hall and there's nothing but chairs and they're all facing up, they're not bleachers, they're chairs. I was thinking: something is up, something is fishy. So the curtain is open and I expect to see elephants and there's nothing but a flat piece of white cardboard, a canvas ... I retained three things from the experience: the train wreck, the lions and Jimmy Stewart as the clown.

As soon as he had a train set, Spielberg repeatedly recreated the crash, and shadows of DeMille's cardboard characters drift through many of his films. Indiana Jones has something of Heston, while Betty Hutton is the model for Willie, the shrill nightclub singer heroine of *Indiana Jones and the Temple of Doom*. Above all, DeMille's showmanship left an indelible impression. 'I guess ever since then I've wanted to try to involve the audience as much as I can,' said Spielberg, 'so they no longer think they're sitting in an audience.'

He continued to find movies, unlike television, emotionally overwhelming. Especially Disney cartoons. At eight, he said, he 'came screaming home from *Snow White* ...' – in some interviews he's eleven, and the film is *Bambi* – 'and tried to hide under the covers. My parents didn't understand it, because Walt Disney movies are not supposed to scare but to delight and enthral. Between *Snow White*, *Fantasia* and *Bambi*, I was a basket case of neurosis.' Though he was allowed to watch the *Wonderful World of Disney* TV shows, with their compilations of cartoons and behind-the-scenes documentaries about Disney films in production, his parents tried to keep him away from the feature cartoons. It gave them a glamorous sense of the forbidden they never lost.

*   *   *

One price of Arnold's job in a sunrise industry like electronics was the occasional moves in search of work or promotion. In 1950 the Spielbergs had relocated in Haddonfield, New Jersey, when he joined RCA. In 1953 he took a job with General Electric in Scottsdale, Arizona, then a dormitory town east of Phoenix, but now a suburb. They were to spend eleven years there. The move wrenched Steven, and instilled his lifelong sense of dislocation and loneliness. 'Just as I'd become accustomed to a school and a teacher and a best friend,' he complained, 'the FOR SALE sign would dig into the front lawn and we'd be packing. And it would always be that inevitable goodbye scene, in the train station or at the carport, packing up the car to drive somewhere, or at the airport. Where all my friends would be there and we'd say goodbye to each other and I would leave. And the older I got the harder it got.' Among the first phrases he learned to say was 'looking forward to'. His grandparents would occasionally come from New Jersey to Ohio to visit, and he loved it when his mother said it was something to look forward to.

His mother had been no less anguished. 'I was hysterical,' she recalled. 'I mean, in 1955 what nice Jewish girl moved to Arizona? I looked in an encyclopedia – it was published in 1920, but I didn't notice at the time – and it said: "Arizona is a barren wasteland." I went there kicking and screaming. I had to promise Steve a horse, because he didn't want to go either. I never made good on that promise, and he still reminds me of it today.' Phoenix, as Jodie Foster was famously to remark in Martin Scorsese's *Alice Doesn't Live Here Any More*, is 'weird'. Scottsdale, described by one visitor as 'suburbia on steroids', itself mixed mass-produced bungalows of the kind in which the Spielbergs lived with sprawling ranch-type houses set in gardens of sand, rock, spiky yucca and twenty-foot-high saguro cactuses. The desert around Scottsdale attracted more than its fair share of visionaries who exploited its open spaces and frontier manners to experiment. Frank Lloyd Wright started building his winter home Taliesin West just north-east of the town in 1937. Despite the discomfort of the fieldstone building, it became a centre for his students from Wisconsin, and after his death in 1959 metamorphosed into an arts centre and museum. One of Wright's students, Paolo Soleri, chose another spot outside Scottsdale to build Arcosanti, his 'arcology', a community of futuristic shell-like buildings integrated into the desert environment.

Spielberg seems never to have visited either Taliesin West or Arcosanti. The visions offered him nothing. He enrolled in Scottsdale's Arcadia High School but, whatever school meant to him, it wasn't higher education. He's always avoided discussing classes or his academic record, which, in common with most of the Movie Brats, was dismal. A survey of America's twelve most influential media personalities in the nineties found that more than half never finished college. Three of them, including Ted Turner, were dyslexic. Spielberg has always had to struggle with the written word. There are no extant Spielberg letters, no diaries, and he never brings a script on set, preferring to memorise the shots beforehand. 'He wasn't a good student,' Leah says. 'He was less than mediocre. He needed tutors in French and math.' Asked to dissect a frog in biology class, he threw up, an incident recycled in *E.T.* His sole reference to English class is a memory of turning a copy of Nathaniel Hawthorne's *The Scarlet Letter* into a flip book by drawing cartoon characters on the corner of each page.

More important than anything that happened in class were the friendships and alliances of the playground. Like any sensitive child Spielberg loathed new places and people but, once accepted, he embraced them with jealous fervour. The metaphor of the new school remained with him for life. When he encountered George Lucas's tight team, he found it like changing schools. He felt, he said, as if he'd moved into Lucas's eighth-grade class.

At Arcadia High School he signed up with the Boy Scouts, and was admitted to its honour society, the Order of the Arrow. He began to study the clarinet too, and to march in the school band. Leah's preoccupation with her piano prejudiced him against the classical repertoire, and he would never warm to pop or rock. His ideal was movie music, of which he soon had an encyclopaedic recall. Once he began making his own amateur films, he would noodle tunes on his clarinet, but only for Leah to transcribe for piano and record as soundtracks.

Shorn of friends and relations by the move to Arizona, and hungry for acceptance, Spielberg took refuge increasingly in showmanship. 'I began wanting to make people happy from the beginning of my life. As a kid, I had puppet shows – I wanted people to like my puppet shows when I was eight years old.' For the rest of his life, displays of virtuoso invention would alternate with attempts to create the suburban content-ment for which he envied others.

Physical awkwardness remained his greatest humiliation. In a school footrace, he once found himself second last, only just ahead of an even slower handicapped boy. It was this boy the crowd cheered on, yelling, 'C'mon, John, you can beat Spielberg!' With the compulsion to win but also to satisfy the expectations of an audience that became characteristic of him as an adult, Spielberg contrived to trip so that the other boy could pass him. Then, once the other was well ahead, he threw himself into almost catching up, coming in a close last. John was carried off in triumph, while Spielberg, winner and loser at the same time, stood on the field and cried for five minutes. 'I'd never felt better and I'd never felt worse in my whole life.'

In adulthood, Spielberg's ideal social and intellectual level remained that of his life as a suburban schoolboy in the late 1950s. George Lucas was to have Luke Skywalker say of provincial Tatooine in *Star Wars*, 'If there is a bright centre to the universe, this is the place it is furthest from.' But for Spielberg, suburbia would always radiate a prelapsarian glow. He came to revere middle-class virtues. Richard Dreyfuss says Spielberg has 'a love affair with the suburban middle class. I don't share his fascination, but Steven could do whole movies about block parties if he wanted to.' If he'd been making *All the President's Men*, Spielberg said, he would have concentrated on the White House typists rather than the reporters. His favourite painter was, and remained, Norman Rockwell, whose covers for the *Saturday Evening Post* showing scenes of gentle whimsy, often set in churches, soda fountains and domestic interiors, exemplified a sunny vision of America as God's Country.

A later writer was to sum up Rockwell's style in terms that make clear Spielberg's affinity for the artist: 'At his peak, Rockwell reflected an American dream which did not at the time seem ridiculous or unobtainable – the dream of international power, domestic pleasure and civil tranquillity. Rockwell's arcadia was peopled by clever kids, indulgent grandparents, bourgeois shopkeepers, shy courting couples and pious schoolteachers – all painted in a style which was a strange blend of fairy-tale, cinematic still and comic strip.' Another critic wrote: 'To be feeling good at home is the secret and desire of the world Rockwell narrates. "Home" is also his narrative horizon and his project. Having a comfortable, solid, lived-in home, being confident in oneself and one's values, are everyday and prosaic values which are obvious, lived and shared. It is art for, and about, Joe Sixpack. It plays very well in Peoria.' Spielberg's lifelong fascination with Rockwell culminated in him becoming a collector of his works, and a trustee and major financial contributor to the Rockwell Museum.

Unlike the Haddonfield house, which was surrounded by trees, and in particular a large one just outside his window on which Spielberg focused his scarier fantasies, the house in Scottsdale was part of a modern development sprawling over flat semi-desert. Spielberg loved its sense of community, the way one could look into the kitchen windows of the families on either side. 'You always knew what your neighbours were cooking because you could see them preparing dinner and you could smell it. There were no fences, no problems.' In the nineties, ensconced in a mansion in Los Angeles' luxurious suburb of Pacific Palisades, he still felt the same affection. 'I live in a different kind of suburbia, but it still is. There are houses next door and across the street, and you can walk, and there are street lamps on the street and sidewalks, and it's very nice.'

The Spielberg household placed a premium on work and hobbies. Leah would invite her musician friends for musical evenings. Steven was encouraged to have pets. He filled his room with eight free-flying parakeets which perched on the curtain rod and left their droppings underneath. He would continue to keep them as an adult, naming them serially, as he had as a child. In the seventies he still had a pair, called Schmuck I and Schmuck II. On holidays, his parents drove as far as the White

Mountains and the Grand Canyon, pitching their tent and, particularly in Leah's case, throwing themselves into serious hiking and nature study. One of Spielberg's most vivid memories is of his mother on a mountaintop, whirling in ecstasy, and while shooting *Raiders* in Tunisia he reminisced of scorpion hunts with his father in the Arizona desert.

His first encounter with a movie camera sprang from these camping trips. Leah gave Arnold an 8mm Kodak for Father's Day. He hosepiped like any amateur until Steven, sensitised by prolonged viewing of movies on TV, became impatient. After being criticised repeatedly by his son for shaky camera movements and bad exposure, Arnold handed over the camera. After that, holidays were never the same. His mother recalled:

> My earliest recollection of Steven with a camera was when my husband and I were leaving on vacation and we told him to take a shot of the camper leaving the driveway. He got down on his belly and was aiming at the hubcap. We were exasperated, yelling at him, 'Come on! We have to leave. Hurry up.' But he just kept on doing his thing, and when we saw the finished results, he was able to pull back so that this hubcap spinning around became the whole camper – my first glimpse of the Spielbergian touch, and a hint of things to come.

A hundred yards before they arrived, Steven jumped out and filmed them driving through the campsite gate. After that, every part of the trip was recorded. 'Father Chopping Wood. Mother Digging Latrine. Young Sister Removing Fishhook From Right Eye – my first horror film. And a scary little picture called *Bear in the Bushes*.'

1959 was a year of significance for Spielberg. References to it riddle his films. It was the year he was bar mitzvahed, only managing to mumble through his ill-memorised extract from the torah with the help of the old men in the front row, who muttered along with him. This was also the year he began actively to resent his father's obsession with work, and his insistence on precision and order. His father brought home a transistor, and told him, 'Son, this is the future.' Spielberg grabbed it and swallowed it.

Detroit's disastrous attempt at manipulating the American public by designing cars according to theories of subliminal sexual symbolism reached fruition in 1959 with the Ford Edsel. Spielberg used one of these doomed gas-guzzlers with its calculatedly vaginal front grille in his first film, *Amblin'*. One of the year's big hits, Jerome Kern's 'Smoke Gets in Your Eyes', revived by the black singing group The Platters, provided the theme of *Always*.

More important, CBS premiered a new half-hour TV series in October. An anthology of quirky science fiction or fantasy stories, each with an ironic trick ending, it was introduced each week, and often written by, its creator, TV writer Rod Serling, already well-known for original dramas like *Requiem for a Heavyweight*. In his dark suit and with his crooked smile and off-handedly intellectual comments, Serling, like Arnold Spielberg, was an ex-GI with a revisionist view of the America Fit For Heroes To Live In. Through the window of *The Twilight Zone*, he invited his audience to spy on a puzzling future with more than a hint of threat.

The Twilight Zone influenced not only Spielberg but a whole generation of film directors-in-waiting. Like them, he came running at the sound of Marius Constant's theme, which he compared to a bugle call drawing one to the TV set. The tune inspired the five-note alien signature of *Close Encounters*. Spielberg would also attempt, unsuccessfully, to replicate the series, first in a film version, then on TV in the ill-fated *Amazing Stories*.

The family camera admitted Spielberg to his first real life of the mind. Here his skill was not in doubt. It gave him absolute control of a world. While other kids were involved in a Little League baseball team or in music, he was watching TV and, his phrase, 'drowning in little home movies'. Once he exhausted the technical possibilities of the little Kodak's single lens, flip-up viewfinder and thirty-five-second clockwork motor, he persuaded his father to buy a better model with a three-lens turret. Being able to cut from long shot through medium shot to close-up widened his horizons.

Over the years, his versions of his debut in narrative film have varied. Initially, he went off alone during a camping trip and experimented with shooting something other than the family. 'The first film I ever made was . . . about an experience in unseen horror, a walk through the forest. The whole thing was a seven-hundred-foot dolly shot and lasted fourteen minutes.' Story films quickly followed. 'My first . . . I made when I was twelve,' he says, 'for the Boy Scouts.' For the Photo Proficiency badge, he had to tell a story in a series of still photographs. Spielberg went one better with a movie, variously remembered as *Gun Smoke* or *The Last Gun*. A 3½-minute western about a showdown between homesteaders and a land baron, it cost $8.50, which he raised by whitewashing the trunks of neighbours' citrus trees at 75c a tree. Fellow Scouts with plastic revolvers played all the characters, and Spielberg persuaded a man with a cigarette to puff into the barrel of a gun so that the film could end on the sheriff's smoking pistol shoved back into his holster. The Scouts loved his movie, and Spielberg got his badge. 'In that moment,' he said, 'I knew what I wanted to do with the rest of my life.'

The instant gratification of story film influenced Spielberg against abstraction. 'I think if I had made a different kind of movie, if that film had been maybe a study of raindrops coming out of a gutter and forming a puddle in your back yard, I think if I had shown that film to the Boy Scouts and they had sat there and said, "Wow, that's really beautiful, really interesting. Look at the patterns in the water. Look at the interesting camera angle" – I mean, if I had done that, I might have been a different kind of film-maker.'

Until then, his record in the Scouts had been as undistinguished as that in high school. He couldn't cook, was so hamfisted he never learned to tie knots well, and enlivened a demonstration of sharpening an axe by cutting his finger open in front of five hundred Scouts at a summer jamboree. He avoided weekend camps, which robbed him of his only chance to see a UFO; other Scouts returned from a camp in the desert with stories of a strange glow in the sky. But movies made him, if not popular, then at least accepted. He freely acknowledged that his first films were exercises in ingratiation. They gave him, he said, 'a reason for living after school hours'. The school bully could also be placated by putting him in a film. He rented *Davy Crockett, King of the Wild Frontier* and *War of the Worlds* on 8mm, and showed them at 25c a head in the family den. As well, he sold popcorn and soda – an integral part of the film experience for him. The proceeds went to charity. The point, then as later in his career, wasn't profit but popularity.

Over the next four years he made about fifteen story films. Old enough now to be allowed to see almost anything at his local cinema, the Kiva, he plundered Hollywood for ideas. Some of the lessons of *The Great Locomotive Chase*, Disney's version of the Civil War raid on which Buster Keaton had based his classic 1926 comedy *The General*, were put into effect in *Duel*, and parts of Henry Levin's version of Jules Verne's *Journey to the Centre of the Earth* would be restaged for *Raiders of the Lost Ark*. One of the first films he saw which was not straight escapism was *The Searchers*. John Ford's story of racist loner John Wayne searching for the niece kidnapped by Indians opened his eyes to the poetic possibilities of landscape. 'I wasn't raised in a big city,' Spielberg says. 'I lived under the sky all through those formative years, from third grade right through high school. That's my knowledge of a sort of lifestyle.' Ford, brought up on the imagery of Catholic paintings and 'holy pictures', instinctively employed aspects of the natural world as metaphors for mental and moral states. Dust represented dissolution; rivers a sense of peace and cleansing; silhouettes presaged death. Certain landscapes, like Monument Valley, were for him intellectual universes in miniature. Those weathered towers of limestone rising from the desert against a vast sky became the unalterable precepts by which honourable men must live. Spielberg would make his own pilgrimage to them in *Indiana Jones and the Last Crusade*, one of many films to exhibit a Fordian vision of the American west.

Frank Capra also returned to the screen in 1959 after eight years in the wilderness to direct *A Hole in the Head*, though neither it, nor the film that followed, *A Pocketful of Miracles*, a remake of his 1933 *Lady for a Day*, in which sentimental gangsters transform an impoverished street-corner apple seller into a socialite so that her daughter can make an advantageous marriage, rivalled *Mr Deeds Goes to Town* or *Mr Smith Goes to Washington*.

While his future colleagues in the New Hollywood like Brian De Palma were surrendering to the moral intricacies and multiple deceptions of Alfred Hitchcock or, in the case of Martin Scorsese, relishing the social disquiet behind Sam Fuller's tabloid cinema and the pastel melodramas of Douglas Sirk and Nicholas Ray, Spielberg made Ford and Capra his models. Lacking a strong moral structure of his own, he absorbed theirs, populist, sentimental, reverent and patriotic. Never comfortable talking to actors, he adopted their technique too, employing landscape and weather as symbols of character, and developing a fluid camera style and skill in directing masses of people that swept his audiences past fragile narratives and sketchy characters. 'Film for me is totally pictorial,' he says. 'I'm more attracted to doing things with pictures and atmospheres – the idea of the visual telling the story.'

In this state of mind, Spielberg also dabbled in theatre:

> I was probably the only student director at Arcadia High School in Arizona who was allowed to control and put together a show. I did *Guys and Dolls* and brought the action, especially the brawl in the Hot Box, into the audience. I guess that's kind of commonplace in today's theatre, but then it was very strange to have people running up and down the aisles singing and acting. I got killed for it! Every critic in Arizona who could write said, 'How dare he open up the proscenium and do this drivel in the audience. *Guys and Dolls* is meant to be on stage.' I did the standards – *Arsenic and Old Lace*, *I Remember Mama* – everything you were allowed to do then.

Like many directors destined to work in sf and fantasy, Spielberg discovered the quirky magazine *Famous Monsters of Filmland*. Edited by Forrest J Ackerman, self-styled 'Mr Sci Fi', whose Los Angeles home contained the world's largest collection of sf movie memorabilia, it celebrated horror film and its techniques with jocular reverence.

The wave of cheap science fiction films that was Hollywood's response to the sf publishing boom washed through American cinemas throughout 1959 and 1960. Spielberg was banned from seeing the 1958 *I Married a Monster from Outer Space*, a relatively modest and reticent film despite its gaudy title, but went anyway, and was racked by nightmares. In particular he came to admire the work of Jack Arnold, who directed *The Incredible Shrinking Man*, *It Came from Outer Space*, *The Space Children* and *The Creature from the Black Lagoon*. The catchpenny titles disguised thoughtful exercises in imagination and suspense which made evocative use of natural surroundings and domestic interiors. The shrinking man in Richard Matheson's story, exposed to fallout from an atomic test, dwindles away in an ordinary suburban home; the film's menaces are a cat and a spider. In *It Came from Outer Space*, written by Ray Bradbury, aliens arrive outside a small desert township. The man who first makes contact with them, John Putnam, is an archetypal Spielberg character, an unassuming Jeffersonian natural philosopher and amateur astronomer who muses about the nature of the universe and the desert, to both of which he has a gently mystical attitude.

Spielberg shared the general enthusiasm for *The Thing (from Another World)*, a rare example of a major director, Howard Hawks, dealing with an sf subject. The script also had an important pedigree. It was based on a story called 'Who Goes There?' written by John W. Campbell before he became editor of *Analog*. Like most of Campbell's work, it is refreshingly iconoclastic. A crashed alien ravages an Arctic research station, smashing down the scientist who tries to befriend it. It's left to a few tough professional airmen to kill it off and save the world. At the end, a reporter broadcasts the story, warning his listeners, 'Watch the skies. Keep watching the skies.'

For all the film's flair, however, Hawks's right-wing paranoia always jarred. It's to Arnold's films (and Bradbury's script for *Outer Space*) that much of Spielberg's later work is traceable. After *Close Encounters of the Third Kind* was released, Spielberg asked Bradbury, 'Well, how did you like your film?' and explained he'd been inspired by *It Came from Outer Space*. Bradbury and Arnold's idea, that alien visitors may be benign, and concerned mainly to return home as quickly and quietly as possible, would surface in both *Close Encounters* and *E.T.* The fathers of the 'space children' who discover an alien in a beachside Californian cave work on a nearby scientific project and share the dislocated life Spielberg knew well, and which he evoked in *The Goonies*. And while the Black Lagoon may only have been in a corner of the Universal backlot lake, the under-water footage shot in the crystal springs of a Florida park played so effec-tively on the sense of 'something' lurking below us where we swim that the aquaphobic Spielberg paid it homage in the opening scenes of *Jaws*.

From the start, it wasn't the atmosphere of fantasy films Spielberg enjoyed so much as their depiction of alternative realities through model work, special effects and elaborate make-up. His sisters, resented because of the attention they drew from his mother, and thus away from him, became victims of his exercises in imagination. He would scare them by building his face into a horror mask with *papier mâché* made from wet green toilet paper, or would lurk outside the window of Anne, the youngest, and groan 'I am the moooooon' until she became hysterical. He convinced them that the bedroom closet hid the decomposing body of a World War II airman, then left it to their curiosity to peek in at the plastic skull he'd hidden there, with goggles over the eyes and a flashlight inside. After they had been terrified by William Cameron Menzies' *Invaders from Mars*, which featured the disembodied head of the Martian super-mind, played by an actress with green-painted face, fringed with tentacles, in a glass bubble, he locked them in the closet, this time with an empty fishbowl within which, he said, the head would materialise. All these domestic horrors and more would be recycled in *Poltergeist*.

War films could be just as interesting as science fiction, providing there were elaborate uniforms, and plenty of buildings were blown up. Firms like Castle Films sold World War II documentaries on 8mm, and Spielberg used some of these as stock footage for a flying story called *Fighter Squadron*. Arnold persuaded Skyharbor airport in Phoenix to let Steven shoot a friend in the cockpit of a P-51. In 1960, inspired by his father's purchase of a war-surplus Jeep, Spielberg made the forty-minute *Escape to Nowhere*, about a World War II American platoon evading a Nazi army in the Libyan desert. He found a few fake German helmets, put them on friends and had them walk slowly past the camera, passing the helmets back down the line so that it looked like an army. Leah drove the Jeep and created uniforms in Wehrmacht grey in which Steven costumed his sisters and friends, who were then machine-gunned and forced repeatedly to roll down a hill in the desert which stood in for North Africa.

'There was always a camera in his hands,' Leah says. 'Once he took a big cardboard carton from the supermarket and cut windows and doors and took it in the back alley and set it on fire to film it. When we saw it, it looked like a real building burning. These are things that in retrospect you try to figure out, but at the time it just seemed normal. He was my first child, and having no prior experience I thought all kids played like that.'

Escape to Nowhere won a prize at the Canyon Film Festival – a 16mm camera. Knowing he couldn't afford 16mm film processing, Spielberg traded it for a more sophisticated H8 8mm Bolex. At the same time, with a little help from his father, he got a Bolex Sonorizer, with which he could put a soundtrack on his magnetically striped film.

He began to have friends, nerds like himself with over-active imaginations. During the run of the dinosaur film *The Lost World* in 1960, he and friends mixed white bread, Parmesan cheese, milk, creamed corn and peas in a paper bag and smuggled it into the Kiva. Then they made vomiting sounds and dripped the mixture from the balcony. It started a chain reaction of vomiting. The film was stopped and the lights went up as the malefactors escaped down the fire stairs.

Other attempts at sophistication didn't work. 'I'll never forget the time I discovered girls,' he says. 'I was in the fifth grade. My father took me to a drive-in movie with a little girlfriend of mine. This girl had her head on my arm, and the next day my parents lectured me about being promiscuous at an early age. My growing up was like a sitcom ABC buys for a season before they drop it.' Never passion's plaything, except where movies were concerned, Spielberg would have a chequered emotional life that headed inexorably towards a marriage Ozzie and Harriet Nelson would have envied.

*   *   *

By the early sixties, Arnold and Leah's marriage was failing. Spielberg recalled Arnold storming out of the house, shouting, 'I'm not the head of the family, yet I am the man of the family' – a line he would recycle in *Duel*. Steven fled from the cold silences of the house to the cinema's warmth. In 1962, he saw the film that was to inspire him above all others. David Lean had spent years in the desert making *Lawrence of Arabia*, a truly epic picture of a larger-than-life historical character whose acts were mirrored and amplified by the landscapes in which they took place. Robert Bolt's dialogue was minimal – indeed minimalist; aphorisms, orders, insults, seldom more than a sentence long. This was Ford crossed with Capra, but mediated by Lean. For the rest of his life, Spielberg would rate *Lawrence* as the one true classic of his early film-going. 'I really kicked into high gear,' he said of seeing it, 'and thought, "This I gotta do. I gotta make movies."'

Single-minded as ever, Spielberg set out to make his first feature, a science fiction adventure called *Firelight*. He wrote the first draft of the script in a night; the story of scientists who, investigating lights in space, provoke an alien invasion during which the visitors steal an entire city from earth and reassemble it on another planet.

Every weekend for a year, Spielberg worked on the film with anyone he could cajole or bully into helping. No girl, no football games, no summer jobs diverted him. His enthusiasm and persistence were infectious. When he needed someone exploded in the living room, Leah opened cans of cherries and stood by as her son balanced them on one end of a board and had someone jump on the other. She never got the stains off the furniture. Once again the airport closed a runway for him. A local hospital where he had worked as a volunteer in his holidays lent its corridors for a shot, though Spielberg found the experience disconcerting. 'I saw things that were so horrifying that I had to fantasise that there were lights, props, make-up men, just to avoid vomiting.'

Once he was finished, Spielberg edited the film to 140 minutes. Actors had come and gone over the year, but he persuaded students at the nearby University of Arizona to post-synchronise the speaking parts as he ran the film on a sheet stretched over one end of the den. The Arcadia school band recorded some music for it.

The result, though he now deprecates it as 'one of the five worst films ever made', was good enough to screen for an audience. He persuaded his father, who had already invested $300 in the project, to gamble another $400 for the hire of a local cinema. Spielberg rented a limousine to bring him to the theatre with Leah, who had cudgelled enough friends, relatives of the actors, ex-Boy Scouts and local film fans to fill the seats. Most stayed to the end, and Arnold pocketed $100 profit.

Spielberg's entry into the cinema was also his exit from childhood and Phoenix. Arnold had decided on another move, this time to join IBM at Saratoga, ten miles from San Jose, near San Francisco. Almost immediately, they packed up, and set out for California.

3

Amblin' Towards Bethlehem

Show business is high school plus money.

Hollywood saying

AFTER THE parched landscape of Arizona, Spielberg loved the hills and vineyards of Saratoga. But this move finally wrecked the rickety marriage of Leah and Arnold Spielberg. Arnold had barely finished sketching a design for the house he hoped to build when the couple separated. Leah returned to Phoenix and started divorce proceedings. The separation wrenched Steven, who developed insecurities about marriage and a sense of loss that would be reflected in his films, which are filled with sons seeking fathers and children deprived of their families.

Saratoga also exposed him to anti-Semitism for the first time. Unlike her parents, Leah hadn't kept a devout household. Spielberg called their style of Judaism 'storefront Kosher'. When the rabbi called, the *mezuzah* was put on the door frame and the *menorah* on the mantel, and removed after he left. Spielberg understood vaguely that his mother's family fled from Odessa to escape pogroms. His first memory of numbers is of a man, one of a group his grandmother was tutoring in English, trying to entertain him by displaying his concentration camp tattoo, and illustrating by turning his arm to show how 6 upside-down became 9.

As a boy, Spielberg was embarrassed by his heritage. 'My grandfather would come to the porch when I was playing football with my friends and call out my name in Hebrew. "Schmeul! Schmeul! Dinner's ready." They would say, "Isn't that your place? Who's this Shmoo?" I'd say, "I don't know. It's not me he's calling."' To anyone who asked, his name was German. He resisted the pressure from his grandmother to conform to what he called 'the Orthodox mould', but at the same time the religion's emphasis on family values fed his need to belong. As an adult, he became a classic Jewish father – and, sometimes, mother. Though no enthusiast for cooking, he would prepare Leah's recipes at home, and occasionally get up early on location to make *matzoh* for 150 people, an almost sacramental act that reaffirmed the production unit as his surrogate family.

The America in which Spielberg grew up accepted racial discrimination as a fact of life. Medical and law schools operated quotas for Jewish students, and colleges had Jewish fraternities. One still occasionally encountered a discreet 'Christian Only' in 'Positions Vacant' ads. Many golf clubs operated a racial ban. Realtors wouldn't sell houses in certain districts to Jewish families. 'Neighbourhoods for [a Jew],' wrote William Manchester, 'like his summer camps and winter cruises, would advertise "Dietary rules strictly enforced."'

In Phoenix, even as one of only five Jewish children in his school, Spielberg hadn't stood out, but Saratoga was actively anti-Semitic. Pennies were tossed at him in study hall, and he was mocked so much in gym that he gave up sports altogether; admittedly no great sacrifice for him. The Spielberg house, the only one not to display lights at Christmas, was just a walk away from the school, but after he'd been bullied on the way home, Steven insisted Leah pick him up each day. Once, in fury at the slurs of a neighbouring family, he smeared their windows with peanut butter. Explaining his decision to film Alice Walker's book *The Color Purple*, rather than choosing a black director, he would say, 'I felt I was qualified because of my own kind of cultural Armageddon, even though as a child I exaggerated the pain – as all children will do – and I became the only person discriminated against in history as a child.'

Because of this discrimination, but from a lack of academic interest as well, Spielberg's grades, never high, sagged still further in Saratoga. When he graduated from high school with a dismal C average, it was in the knowledge that no major college would accept him. And not being in college meant that he was eligible for the draft. 'I would have done anything to stay out of Vietnam,' he said. But this wish dovetailed so neatly with his ambition to become a film director, ideally before he was twenty-one, that they soon fused in his mind.

*   *   *

The moment the 1963 summer vacation commenced, Steven persuaded Arnold to let him spend it with an uncle in Canoga Park, a suburb of Los Angeles. His uncle lent him his 1957 Plymouth convertible, but only on the understanding he stayed in the slow lane, going no faster than forty-five m.p.h. Since the speed limit in the fast lane in those days was sixty-five, other cars rocketed by, but Spielberg didn't care. He was in heaven. Disneyland had opened in 1955, and he made the first of many long drives to the suburb of Anaheim where Walt Disney had built his fantasy world.

Los Angeles, a horizontal city defined by freeways, opened Spielberg's eyes to linear motion. The boy who was uncomfortable with the written word discovered in movement a handwriting he could read and in which he could, he sensed, become fluent. 'Looking at most modern cities involves seeing a lot of buildings,' writes the architectural historian Charles Moore. 'Looking at Los Angeles involves experiencing a lot of rides . . . Even the strictly architectural sights of Los Angeles are experienced more than seen, often in carefully controlled time . . . They are theatre as much as architecture.' The concept of the ride became central to Spielberg's cinematic vision. He designed rides for Disneyland and the Universal Studios tour, and in 1994 an LA journalist writing of the Dive! 'total experience' restaurants he opened with Jeffrey Katzenberg would comment that Spielberg 'does not so much create movies as he assembles theme-park rides in the shape of movies'.

There are no good years to enter the film industry, but 1963 was worse than many. Hollywood was drastically reorganising. Since just after World War I, it had been dominated by the major studios: MGM, Paramount, Twentieth Century-Fox, Columbia, Universal and United Artists. However, the Federal Justice Department had decided that companies which controlled every step in the production of film, from conception to marketing, were in restraint of free trade, and forced the studios to shed their theatres, and open production to independent filmmakers.

Shorn of the power to control production and distribution, the studios re-inserted themselves into the equation in a different role, lending the independents money, renting them office and production space, and organising promotion and distribution. The charges they levied for their help were often extortionate. Spielberg's fees for *Jaws* and his percentage of its profits, known in the trade as 'points', would give him a personal fortune in the millions, but it was Universal and Columbia who really profited. Of *Star Wars*' $200 million US domestic income, George Lucas would complain that he personally received, after taxes, less than $20 million.

Even by milking the film-makers, however, the studios still could not defeat television. Throughout the fifties and early sixties, desperate for novelties to win back their audience, they exhumed and relaunched all the technical improvements which had been developed over the previous half century but abandoned for lack of investment or interest: 70mm, CinemaScope, 3-D, VistaVision, even Aromarama, smellovision, and the tricks popularised by William Castle; seats wired with electric buzzers and plastic skeletons falling from the ceiling.

None slowed the inexorable trend towards home entertainment at the expense of the cinema experience. Many studios saw this as the writing on the wall, and hurried to cut their losses. The accumulated movies of fifty years were sold off to TV. Everywhere, backlots were bulldozed and the land redeveloped for office buildings. By the end of the sixties, MGM and Twentieth Century-Fox, rather than retain large warehouses of costumes and props and the staff to service them, would sell everything at auction: Garbo's gowns, Judy Garland's ruby slippers from *The Wizard of Oz*, Charles Foster Kane's Rosebud sled from *Citizen Kane* – the patrimony of Spielberg's dreams, fragments of which he would later pay a fortune to retrieve.

Some of the most attractive real estate in greater Los Angeles belonged to Universal Studios. Its 374-acre studio and backlot was the first thing a visitor saw as he topped the Cahuenga Pass out of Los Angeles and slid onto the wide flat floor of the San Fernando Valley, the dormitory suburb of greater LA. Universal's chairman, Lew Wasserman, was a cunning and stubborn negotiator with a reputation for seeing further than many. As head of the MCA talent agency he'd pioneered package and profit-sharing deals under which stars deferred salary in favour of a share of income. The first such deal he negotiated, for James Stewart, made the actor a multi-millionaire. MCA had bought Universal Studios to guarantee work to its clients and a supply of television product to the networks and advertising agencies with which it enjoyed production deals. In 1962, however, forced by the Justice Department to decide whether it was an agency or a film producer, MCA shed the former and went into film-making full time.

To mark his territory, Wasserman commissioned an office block from the prestigious Chicago firm of Skidmore, Owings and Merrill, an opaque stub of anodised aluminium and black glass. Inside, according to rumour, the dividing walls were movable. An executive in disfavour might arrive one morning to find his office subtly more cramped than when he left the night before.

From his seventeenth-floor executive suite, Wasserman squinted out over his fiefdom, and wondered how to make money with it. From high on the hill, the half-scale Gothic mansion from Hitchcock's *Psycho* looked down on the plaster-and-lath sets where Lon Chaney Snr made his version *of The Hunchback of Notre Dame*, and his son Lon Jr *The Wolf Man. The Invisible Man*, *Frankenstein* and *Dracula* sprang from here, as did their multitudes of sequels. Jack Arnold's films were shot on these sets and stages too. In the sixties, Ernest Borgnine and the crew were making the TV series *McHale's Navy* on the black lagoon from which the creature had crawled. Interiors for *Wagon Train* and *The Virginian* were being shot on sets where Boris Karloff had once worked. Most of Universal's income, however, was generated by a few blocks of bland shopfronts that provided a setting for modern cop shows and spy stories. Meanwhile, run-off from the hills was undermining the older sets, some of which were already collapsing.

One cost-cutting option that didn't exist was firing people. The film production and craft unions, IATSE, the International Alliance of Theatrical Stage Employees, and NABET, the National Association of Broadcast Employees and Technicians, aided by Jimmy Hoffa's corrupt Teamsters, enjoyed near-omnipotent power. 'Feather-bedding' was rife. Once you were in, you were in for life – and beyond, if, like many, you apprenticed your sons. In the same way, a handful of executives circulating from studio to studio dominated management. 'Affirmative action for family members,' acknowledged the *Los Angeles Times*, 'is an accepted practice in a town where everyone seems to be related to everyone else ... A solid education and good grades are not necessarily relevant or even desirable and are considered much less valuable than the kind of insider's knowledge acquired at the dinner table night after night.' As Hollywood had joked when David Selznick married the daughter of MGM's Louis B. Mayer, 'the son-in-law also rises.'

In the thirties, under its founder Carl Laemmle, Universal had been notorious for nepotism. His son, known simply as 'Junior', ran production, and the payroll groaned with cousins. 'Uncle Carl Laemmle,' ran the crack, 'has a very large faemmle.' In reaction, the company promulgated an anti-nepotism rule in the forties, with jobs allocated by merit and experience. But this soon hardened into a rigid roster system, with pay hikes and other benefits graded according to length of service. Walking off a film meant you lost seniority, so productions at Universal always went ahead, no matter how inept the director or crew. Despite its large complement of staff technicians, most producers preferred to hire contract crews for anything being made to a deadline.

In 1963, the MCA board was pressing Wasserman for a decision about whether or not to follow a consultant's advice and sell the backlot for hotels and condos, and lawyer Albert Dorskind was put in charge of assessing offers. Dorskind saved the studio. Shopping downtown one day in Farmers' Market, the ramshackle complex of fruit and vegetable stalls and quick-lunch counters at Fairfax and Third Street, on the fringe of Hollywood, Dorskind noticed a Gray Line bus disgorging tourists. Remembering that Universal's restaurant was losing $100,000 a year, he rang Gray Line and suggested they put Universal on their itinerary. Visitors could even lunch in the commissary – Eat With the Stars! And it would only cost Gray Line $1 a head, over and above what people ate. Gray Line jumped at it. The restaurant manager upped his prices by 20 per cent, and the commissary was soon in profit.

* * *

Spielberg stepped out of the Gray Line bus onto Universal's hallowed ground in June 1963 with the awe of a zealot entering Jerusalem. He hid until the bus left, then spent the rest of the afternoon poking around, even walking onto sound stages where TV episodes were being shot. He found his way to the cutting rooms, where editor Tony Martinelli was working on episodes of *Wagon Train*. Spielberg asked questions. Flattered, and glad of a diversion, Martinelli and the other editors were happy to reply. He told them he'd made some movies, and asked if they would take a look at them. One said, 'Bring 'em in, kid.' Dazzled, Spielberg found a phone and called his cousin to pick him up. The next day he was back with *Firelight* and his 8mm films. Almost every day for the rest of his vacation he dressed in his one suit and, carrying an empty briefcase, drove to Universal. At the gate, the guard, assuming he was just another nephew with a summer job at the studio, waved him through.

Elsewhere in Los Angeles, the people who were to become Spielberg's contemporaries in New Hollywood were gathering. Some almost didn't make it. In June 1962, George Lucas, having graduated – barely – from high school in Modesto, took his Fiat Bianchina for a drive, and wrapped it round a tree. He nearly died. Others already had movie jobs. Francis Ford Coppola was writing screenplays while working as dogsbody for Hollywood's cheapest producer, Roger Corman, and moonlighting as a director of soft-core porn. But the majority, like Spielberg, were just out of high school and wondering how to get in. Lucas, once he recovered, tried the accepted way, visiting every film production company on Ventura Boulevard, the ribbon development of low-rent two-storey office buildings and storefronts that wove along the periphery of the San Fernando Valley. He got nowhere.

Entering the business through a film school was still a novel concept. Cinema remained, in Hollywood at least, a business, not an art. Nobody anticipated the flood of film students attracted by the French New Wave, Britain's Free Cinema documentary movement, or the underground films that were boiling out of New York and San Francisco.

After his accident, Lucas spent two more years in Modesto Junior College improving his grades, and was accepted by the University of Southern California's film programme, the nation's oldest. It helped that his father was moderately well-off. USC's location on the edge of the unfashionable and dangerous downtown area belied the fact that it was a private university with high fees, whereas the plush UCLA, headquartered in well-barbered Westwood, had state funding. Despite its funky appearance, however, USC was, as one writer put it,

> a citadel of privilege. Its graduates in public administration governed Los Angeles. Its doctors and technicians governed the medical establishment. The student body – overwhelmingly white and upper-middle-class – was largely immune to the social turmoil of the sixties. The school newspaper admitted that the 'high cost of a USC education seems to screen out almost all Negroes. The notable exceptions to this rule are athletes admitted on scholarship.' [In 1967, one of the black juniors on a football scholarship was O.J. Simpson.]

USC's film programme didn't rate the attention or investment of its medical or law school, let alone the football team. Its fifty students were mostly kids from second- or third-generation industry families, picking up the rudiments of sound recording or camera operation before they took the place awaiting them in the hierarchical studio system. They studied in classrooms built from World War 1 surplus lumber, and cut their films side by side on twenty-five ancient Moviolas in a graffiti-spattered room. The university guaranteed each student the funds and equipment to make a fifteen-minute film, but learning how to do it was mostly up to them. The faculty included a few good people, like Verna Fields, who been sound editor for Fritz Lang and taught courses when she wasn't working on films like Anthony Mann's *El Cid*. But she was in the minority.

Spielberg knew none of these people until much later. After the summer of 1963, he returned to Saratoga and high school. In vacations, he made lengthy forays to Los Angeles. Unwittingly, he followed George Lucas's route along Ventura Boulevard, trying to find someone to look at his films. Everywhere, weary producers of promotional documentaries spurned them like the plague. One did agree to screen some of *Firelight*. 'I gave him two of the best reels,' says Spielberg. 'I came back a week later and he was fired. Gone! His office was cleared out and now there's a Toyota dealership where the office used to be . . . So part of *Firelight* still exists, but all the exposition is gone.'

In 1964, the decision about his immediate future was made for him. He was waiting in line at a San Jose cinema to see Stanley Kubrick's *Doctor Strangelove, Or How I Learned to Stop Worrying and Love the Bomb* when his sister and father drove up with an envelope. It was his Selective Service notice, confirming that, lacking a student exemption, he had been graded 1-A – prime cannon-fodder. He still went to the film, though he didn't enjoy it, not knowing whether to laugh or be frightened. 'I was so consumed with the possibility of going to Vietnam that I had to see it for a second time to really appreciate it.' Wars came and went, but Kubrick was eternal.

College seemed the only feasible option. USC turned him down, and there was no money to send him through junior college to raise his grades, so the family chose academically indifferent California State College at Long Beach.

A half-hour drive from Hollywood across the industrial and suburban sprawl of Los Angeles, Long Beach hardly seemed Californian. The suburb's untidy bungalows huddling along a nondescript coastline had a lacklustre, countryfied feel that reminded Spielberg of Arizona. For years, Long Beach hosted the Iowa State Picnic, attracting 150,000 midwesterners eager for a look at the Pacific. In an attempt to attract tourists and raise the tax base, the county allowed oil companies to sink wells on artificial islands just a few yards offshore, hiding the rigs inside fake apartment buildings. Entrepreneurs also moored the superannuated liner *Queen Mary* as a floating convention centre, and installed next to it Howard Hughes's gigantic and almost unairworthy 'Spruce Goose' flying boat.

Spielberg was as indifferent to the gimcrack atmosphere of Long Beach as he was to his college education. If the draft had ended earlier, he admitted, he probably wouldn't have gone to college at all. As it was, his three years at Long Beach created scarcely a ripple in his life. Since it had no film courses, the man who had turned *The Scarlet Letter* into a flip book majored in English. He worked in the cafeteria to earn pocket money, and projected classroom films. If he squeezed all his classes into two days a week, he could spend the rest of the time in Los Angeles.

What film education he gained was in Hollywood's rerun and repertory cinemas like the NuArt and the Vagabond. 'Anything not American impressed me,' he said. 'I went through a phase of seeing Ingmar Bergman films. I must have seen every Bergman movie ever made, because that's what they were showing at that theatre. The next week, you'd see Buñuel movies.' Hurriedly he added, 'Not very many.' Buñuel's ragged technique, quirky plots and rigorous Catholicism baffled him. He preferred Jacques Tati, France's master of the sight gag, whose films had no dialogue.

When he could scrape up enough money, he hired a 16mm camera and shot a film. He made five during the Long Beach years, a few of which experimented with abstraction. 'I did a picture about dreams – how disjointed they are. I made one about what happens to rain when it hits dust.' Another was 'about a man being chased by someone trying to kill him. But running becomes such a spiritual pleasure for him that he forgets who is after him.' Shooting these shorts kept his hand in, but the films were arid. He was, he knew already, a 'concept' director who made films from the general to the particular. What he needed was a big story, and the resources to deal with it as it deserved.

Spielberg's contacts at Universal continued to be the most promising route to a career, and he spent as much time at the studio as he could. To raise a little money, Wasserman rented office space to independent producers. Spielberg tracked some of them down in remote corners or in the two-storey cinder-block buildings, mostly ex-warehouses, that huddled like mushrooms outside the studio perimeter. A few were glad to see him. All of them had advice. None offered him a job.

After the profitable public tours had been running for a year, Wasserman, sensing a money-maker, invested $4 million in turning the Universal City Tour into a studio enterprise. Restrooms and concession stands were installed, and special rubber-tyred trams designed. On 4 July 1964 the tour was officially inaugurated. Students acted as guides. Among the earliest was a young man from Encino named Mike Ovitz with a sleepy, catlike smile. Thirty years later, he would be offered the running of the studio.

If only Spielberg had known it, he already possessed an advantage that would give him the inside track in Hollywood. Being Jewish meant he was born into the culture and ethos prevailing in sixties Hollywood. Had he been part of an industry family, he would have found work instantly. Instead, he was forced to prowl Universal, looking for a connection, a sponsor, a patron.

Chuck Silver (whom Spielberg has identified as head of the editing department, but whom Sidney Sheinberg remembers as the film librarian) spotted him in the corridor and asked who he was. As a young man, he stood out: other than the student guides, the only people under forty on the lot were actors, and he obviously couldn't be one of those. Tickled by Spielberg's tale of bluffing his way in, Silver wrote him a pass, and tried to introduce him to some executives, but the few that did agree to see him recoiled when he arrived with his little 8mm projector and started taking down their diplomas to make space on the wall for an impromptu screening. He learned quickly that he was competing with UCLA graduates who, thanks to Uncle Irving who ran the camera department at Warner Brothers, could boast 35mm show reels of professional quality.

Bolder now, he wandered onto sets to watch directors at work, and was thrown off Hitchcock's *Torn Curtain* and Franklin Schaffner's *The War Lord*. He had a revenge of sorts when the studio's head sound mixer, Ronnie Pierce, let him sit in on the soundtrack recording of *Torn Curtain*, and of lesser films like the Doris Day/Rock Hudson comedy *Send Me No Flowers*.

TV directors weren't as fastidious as Hitchcock about visitors, and Spielberg had no trouble crashing the set of Robert Ellis Miller, who was directing a 1964 episode of *Bob Hope Presents the Chrysler Theater* with John Cassavetes.

Noticing the pimply boy in the shadows, however, Cassavetes introduced himself. As they chatted, he asked Spielberg, 'What do you want to do?'

'I want to be a director.'

Cassavetes chewed this over. 'OK,' he said. 'After every take, you tell me what I'm doing wrong.'

The next time Miller called 'Cut!' the actor walked up to Spielberg. 'What do you think? How can I improve it? What am I doing wrong?'

Spielberg equivocated. 'Gah, it's too embarrassing right here, Mr Cassavetes. Don't ask me in front of everybody; can't we go round the corner and talk?'

But Cassavetes insisted. He probably enjoyed lighting a fire under Miller, a minor talent even by Universal standards, but Spielberg learned a valuable lesson. As François Truffaut said, 'a director is someone who answers questions.' If you came on a movie set, you had better know how to deal with anything that arose. Over the next few years, Spielberg made it his business to become expert in every aspect of film-making technique. Nobody would ever again ask him a question he couldn't answer.

The years between 1966 and 1969 are among the poorest-documented of Spielberg's career, and he has made sure they remain so. There is no consistency to the chronology he quotes in interviews. Projects which obviously occupied his time and energy for long periods are passed over in a sentence. The vagueness reflects his disillusion with Hollywood and the sense that he would never achieve his aim of directing before he was twenty-one.

He made few friends while at Long Beach, though one, Carl Gottlieb, would go on to co-write the script of *Jaws*. Another was a personable young actor named Tony Bill, who'd had a small role in Coppola's *You're a Big Boy Now* and was getting a reputation as a comedy lead. His ambitions, however, lay in production. He and Spielberg started work on a film called 'Slipstream', about a cycle race, but it was never finished. The cameraman, Serge Haigner, was assisted by a young man named Allen Daviau, someone else who would figure in Spielberg's career. John

Cassavetes also gave Spielberg a few weeks' work as gofer on his film *Faces*.

After bluffing his way into Universal, getting into USC was easy, if not as a student, then simply to crash evening screenings and hang out. At a retrospective of USC graduate films, Spielberg got to know the more social of the film students. Not, however, George Lucas, who, secretly terrified that people might think him gauche and naive, said little or nothing to anybody, and concentrated on making movies.

Spielberg's first friends there were Hal Barwood and his writing partner Matthew Robbins, from UCLA. They would write *The Sugarland Express* and go on to directorial careers, while continuing to act as his script doctors; until the early eighties, Spielberg seldom made a film without their input. He met Randal Kleiser, later director of *Grease* and *The Blue Lagoon*, Caleb Deschanel, lighting cameraman on *The Right Stuff* and director of *The Escape Artist*, Walter Murch, editor of *Julia* and *Apocalypse Now*, Howard Kazanjian, destined to be producer on *Raiders* and many other Lucas films, John Carpenter, director of *Halloween* and *The Fog*, composer Basil Poledouris, of *Conan the Barbarian* and *Big Wednesday*, and David S. Ward, writer of *The Sting* and director of *Cannery Row*.

Most important of all, he became friendly with John Milius. Massive, bearded and irascible, a war lover, surfing buff and gun freak – when he became a director, Milius demanded as part of his deal that the studio buy him a rare firearm of his choice – Milius, Hollywood's self-styled resident expert on legendary Americans, was the group's renegade, indispensable to its sense of community. When the college fired him for punching a professor, the others went on strike until he was reinstated. Milius and Robbins became like older cousins to Spielberg; people to whom he could turn in an emergency, and on whom he could rely for useful, if sometimes undiplomatically phrased, advice. Quietly, Spielberg was rebuilding the family he'd lost when his parents broke up.

In the summer of 1967, Spielberg decided to take the law into his own hands. By now he was well known around Universal, so he simply began to act as if he worked there. Quizzed later, Scotty, the studio guard who waved him through every day, admitted he took him for Lew Wasserman's son.

Independent producers came and went all the time, and there were always vacant offices in the warren at the back of the studio. Spielberg found an empty room, introduced himself to the women at the main switchboard, and told them what extension he was on. With plastic letters from a camera store, the sort used to title home movies, he listed himself on the main directory: Steven Spielberg, starring in his own production of his career.

Spielberg is vague about the amount of time he hung out at Universal. It might have been two years, or six months, or even three months. Sometimes he's seventeen, at other times twenty-one. The vagueness reflects his disillusion with Hollywood and his sense that he would never achieve his aim of directing before he was twenty-one. When it became obvious that he would not achieve this goal, fantasy took over.

Around this time, it became generally believed that Spielberg was born not in 1946 but in 1947. Undoubtedly he himself was responsible for this error, and its persistence. His driver's licence bore, and continued to bear, the date of birth 1947, as did his voter registration. In January 1981 a *Los Angeles Times* journalist noticed the discrepancy, and repeatedly tried to get a reaction from Spielberg's publicist, but without success. In January 1988, shortly after what had apparently been his fortieth birthday, the *New York Times* and many other papers would publish articles on 'Spielberg at Forty'. No attempt was made by Spielberg or Amblin to correct them. Finally confronted with the disparity in 1995, Marvin Levy, Spielberg's spokesman on publicity, told the *Los Angeles Times*, 'I'm sure there's an answer. Maybe he didn't care what people said about his age. He cares about one thing: making films.' The inference is inescapable, however, that Spielberg put back his birthday so as to maintain the illusion that he might still make his first film before he was twenty-one.

As for the usefulness of his time at Universal, Spielberg admits, 'I never made any deals, but I used the phone a lot (to call up the time) and learned how to play the game. I got fed up with the joint though, and left, and went to Long Beach College and made a short called *Amblin'*.'

The short-film route to a job in movies was a traditional one in the sixties. Some cinemas still showed a 'full supporting programme', and there were plenty of festivals interested in good new work. George Lucas had just made *Filmmaker*, a thirty-minute documentary about Francis Coppola shooting *The Rain People*. Noel Black had won his first feature with a short called *Skater Dater*, a teenage romance with skateboards shot in San Francisco.

Spielberg now understood enough of Hollywood to realise that only a 35mm film carried conviction. Fortunately, he says, 'I met someone who was as enthusiastic to make movies as I was. The difference was that he was a millionaire, Dennis Hoffman. He had a [special effects] optical company. He saw some of my 8mm and 16mm films and said he'd give me $10,000 – which to me was a bloody fortune – to make a short film, but he wanted the possessory credit. That means the films said "Dennis Hoffman's *Amblin'*". I said, "Fine." I took the money and made the film in 35mm. 1.85:1 ratio [of wide screen used by all professional cinemas]. The big time for me!'

Later Hoffman, who diversified out of the lab business into a chain called Designer Donuts, the investors in which included Spielberg, would claim that their 1968 contract covered not only *Amblin'* but a feature, to be directed for Hoffman during the next ten years. The deal was one that would come back to haunt Spielberg.

Amblin' is a twenty-four-minute story of a young couple who meet in the Mojave desert and hitchhike to the Californian coast. Amateurs Pamela McMyler and Richard Levin played the lovers. Allen Daviau shot it, delighted to be working in 35mm after long periods of documentaries. The landscape was beautiful, the cars sleek, the lovers – who had no dialogue – affectingly clean-cut and attractive. A brief love scene and a shared joint gave the film a trendy modernism. Spielberg, however, was under no illusions about the worth of *Amblin'*. It had only one function: to demonstrate his and Daviau's grasp of cinema technique and their ability to make a slick Hollywood product. He called it 'a Pepsi commercial', and joked that it had the empty decorative appeal of a piece of driftwood.

Hoffman was delighted, however, and in 1969 entered *Amblin'* in the second Atlanta Film Festival, where it won an award. Convinced that his career as a producer was assured, he threw what Spielberg remembers as 'an inflated premiere . . . to all the execs in Los Angeles. Or rather, he invited all the execs, but no one came.' Fortunately, a few 'lower-echelon studio people' saw the film. One was Chuck Silver, who took a copy to show a Universal executive named Sidney Jay Sheinberg.

Sheinberg started his working life as a law instructor at UCLA, but in 1959 Albert Dorskind hired him as an assistant; Sheinberg's father-in-law was business manager for a number of MCA executives. Courteous, even formal in manner, and intensely discreet, Sheinberg called everybody, even his juniors, 'sir', a habit he never lost. He quickly impressed the Universal hierarchy, and Jennings Lang, who ran the television division, put him in charge of long-term production planning, which included keeping an eye out for new talent.

Sheinberg remembers Chuck Silver buttonholing him one night when he'd been previewing a film in one of the studio screening rooms. 'He said there's this guy who's been hanging around the place who's made a short film,' said Sheinberg. 'So I watched it and I thought it was terrific. I liked the way he selected the performers, the relationships, the maturity and the warmth that was in that short. I told Chuck to have the guy come see me.'

Nervous that his moonlighting on the lot had been found out, Spielberg presented himself at Sheinberg's office in the Black Tower.

'Sidney is very austere. He said, "Sir, I liked your film. How would you like to go to work professionally? You sign the contract, you start in television. After TV, if you do a few good television shows and other producers on the lot like your work, you go into feature films." It wasn't that easy, but it sounded great.'

Spielberg dithered. 'But I have a year left to go in college.'

'Do you want to go to college,' Sheinberg asked, 'or do you want to direct?'

Spielberg's formal education ended in that moment. 'I left so quickly that I never even cleared out my locker,' he said. Years later, at odd moments, he'd think of the chicken salad sandwich he'd left rotting there.

As Spielberg signed his contract a few weeks later, he murmured, 'My father will never forgive me for leaving college.' It was a reaction

Sheinberg understood. Like Leah's parents, his father had emigrated to escape anti-Semitic persecution. He and his attractive young wife, the actress Lorraine Gary, were devoted to each other and to their two boys.

The contract was the standard seven-year pact for 'personal services', under which Spielberg sold every working minute to Universal to use as they pleased. The business called it 'the Death Pact'. Only the desperate – or the desperately ambitious – would sign it, and Spielberg was both. So was his *Amblin'* star, Pamela McMyler, whom Universal also put under contract. Coincidentally, John Milius was also offered the same seven-year deal, but as a writer. He turned it down.

How old was Spielberg when Universal signed him? In early versions of what was to become a legend, he claimed unashamedly that he was twenty. 'One day in 1969, when I was twenty-one . . .' he told the *Hollywood Reporter* in 1971. In another version, he says he told Sheinberg when he signed the contract, 'I just have one request, and I'd like you to give me not so much a commitment, Mr Sheinberg, as a promise. I want to direct something before I'm twenty-one. That would be very important to me.' Sheinberg, he said, agreed. Yet for Spielberg to have signed a contract as a minor would have necessitated investigation of his age, which would have brought his true date of birth to light.

The likelihood is that Sheinberg knew that Spielberg had turned twenty-one in December 1967, and was therefore twenty-two when he signed their deal, but that he went along with the illusion for publicity reasons. Already the older man sensed an affinity that would grow over the years. Some people felt the two even looked alike. As his own children failed to show any of his flair for show business, he began to regard Spielberg as a surrogate son.

4

Universal Soldier

The people who do well in the system are the people who do
films that producers like to produce, not that people want
to see.

Orson Welles

STROLLING AROUND the studio where he'd spent so much time as an
interloper, Spielberg could hardly believe his luck.

He'd rented a cramped $130 a month apartment on Laurel Canyon
and furnished it with an *ad hoc* mixture of bean bags and movie posters,
but he spent little time there. Each evening he caught whatever film was
previewing in the studio's theatres. Next day he was on the phone,
complimenting actors on their performances, directors of their direction,
producers on their acumen. Producer/writer William Link remembers
him as 'a great politician. Even then, we knew we would all be working
for him one day.'

He relished the sense of Universal as another world, sealed off from
the city of Los Angeles. Science fiction writer and sometime scenarist Ray
Bradbury, who was also, coincidentally, afflicted with some of Spielberg's
phobias, about heights, elevators and flying, shared his love of working
on a movie lot, where

> everything was clearly defined. Here there were absolutely sharp
> beginnings, and ends that were neat and irreversible. Outside, beyond
> the stages, I did not much trust life with its dreadful surprises and
> ramshackle plots. Here, walking among the alleys just at dawn or
> twilight, I could imagine I opened the studio and shut it down. It
> belonged to me because I said it was so.

The studio looked busy. The electric trolleys of the public tours with their pink-and-white candy-striped awnings and rubber wheels seemed to be everywhere. Occasionally a limo cruised by. With the new influx of visitors, security had been tightened. Scotty now rigorously checked everyone at the gate, and people with legitimate business on the backlot had to wait in the shadow of the black tower until a Teamster-driven limo arrived to take them to their meeting – another example of the union excess which was driving producers to Europe.

As the summer approached, Spielberg waited to be given a job, but nothing eventuated. It was ironic. He had an office again at Universal, yet still the phone never rang. They were paying him now, but not much. After taxes, his weekly $130 pay cheque dwindled to less than $100. With leisure to read the fine print of his contract, he found he was less employee than slave. 'I couldn't work outside Universal, couldn't look for independent financing, couldn't go underground like all my friends were doing. I was trapped in the establishment, but nobody would give me a job in the establishment.' With his birthday looming, he pressed Sheinberg to find him a directing project. 'And he twisted someone's arm – or broke it off – and got someone to give me a shot at one third of the pilot for *Night Gallery*.'

Night Gallery was a new series being prepared for NBC, and scheduled to begin in November 1969. To write and present it, Universal had hired Rod Serling, in the hope of repeating the success of *The Twilight Zone*, which he had sold outright to CBS, only to kick himself as it earned a fortune in regional reruns. Serling had grudgingly ceded all creative control to Universal. He was to write and introduce the three segments of *Night Gallery*, each hingeing on a painting with supernatural powers. In this way he hoped to fill the one-hour slot preferred by networks while conserving the sting-in-the-tail short-story format of *Twilight Zone*.

Boris Sagal and Barry Shear, both practised directors, were to share the pilot under William Sackheim, a B-movie scriptwriter who became a TV producer in his fifties. Sackheim assigned Spielberg the middle story, *Eyes*, a characteristic piece of Serling tables-turning about a ruthless blind businesswoman who yearns for a corneal transplant despite warnings by her doctor, Barry Sullivan, that she'll win at most twelve hours of sight. She plunders the eyes of a desperate Tom Bosley anyway, to find that her half-day coincides with New York's city-wide 1965 blackout.

Spielberg read the script, and immediately tried to get out of the assignment.

'Jesus, can't I do something about young people?' he begged Sheinberg.

'I'd take this if I were you,' Sheinberg said.

It was sound advice. To add class to the pilot, Universal had hired Joan Crawford. The widow of Pepsi-Cola owner Al Steele, and Oscar-winning star of wartime Hollywood's archetypal melodrama of upward mobility and guilty passion, *Mildred Pierce*, Crawford had been reduced to playing straight woman to a monster in the British horror film *Trog*. Even at sixty-three, however, she had never, despite having appeared in game shows, variety and live dramas, made a film specifically for TV. For that particular indignity she demanded, despite her millions, a fee of $50,000, 10 per cent of the pilot's total budget.

By assigning the waning but still potent Crawford to Spielberg, Sheinberg was showing his confidence in him. Nervously aware that his star had locked horns with great directors like Howard Hawks, Michael Curtiz and George Cukor, Spielberg ran some of her movies and pored over books on her career. Though only five feet four inches tall, she immediately drew the eye, even next to his hero Spencer Tracy. He set up a preliminary meeting at her Hollywood apartment.

Crawford was his introduction to the contradictory power of stars, nondescript in real life, magnetic on screen. Her magnetism, however, wasn't immediately apparent when, acutely conscious of his gawky appearance, Spielberg was ushered in, since she was standing in the middle of the room with a mask over her eyes.

'This is how a blind person walks through a room,' she explained as she groped towards him. 'I need to practise with the furniture two days before we shoot.'

Then she took off the mask and saw him for the first time.

'Actually I heard later that she had been promised a director like George Cukor,' Spielberg said, 'and had no idea that they were going to

assign an acne-ridden, sniffling-nosed, first-time-out director. I only
knew years later that she had a temper tantrum when she found out that
she had to work with me.'

There was no immediate sign of irritation. Crawford grilled him. What
had he made? No features, just a short? Was he perhaps related, she
asked drily, to someone in the Black Tower?

'No, ma'am,' he quavered. 'I'm just working my way through Universal.'

Spielberg never described the meal that followed the same way twice.
Sometimes he remembers Crawford saying, 'Steven, you and I both made
it on our own. We're going to get along just fine. C'mon, let's go out to
dinner.' In other versions, she tells him tersely, 'I don't want you sitting
with me in a restaurant. People will think you're my son, not my director.'
Given the course of their relationship, the second version seems more
probable.

On the first day of the eight-day shoot, Crawford arrived at 8.45 a.m.
precisely, swathed in mink and trailed by her personal hairdresser,
make-up man, costume lady, and three men carrying iceboxes of Pepsi,
which she handed around among the sixty-man crew. Nobody needed
cooling. Crawford's contract stipulated that the studio was chilled, as it
had been in her great days at Warner Brothers, to 55 degrees.

The week before, Spielberg had been given an audience with Serling,
daunting for someone who knew him only as the suave black-suited mc
of *The Twilight Zone*. Serling told him that, by contract, not a word of
any script could be changed without his approval. (This wasn't true.
Universal had full story approval on all its series, and didn't hesitate to
use it when ratings began to slide.) Feeling himself straitjacketed again,
Spielberg fought back, diagramming a series of jump cuts, looming
low-angle close-ups and sinuous crane shots reminiscent of those horror/
suspense series like *Thriller* and *The Outer Limits*, which were lonely
islands of German Expressionism in the ocean of Hollywood pap. Some
of these devices, like his quick cuts to a series of progressively larger
close-ups to build emotional pressure, he would use again and again

until they became fixtures of his visual style. But as he tried to explain them during Day One, traditionally spent blocking out camera movements, he found the technicians scornful. Stuff like that was regarded as an unhealthy hangover from live TV drama. The house style called for sets lit with the intensity of an electronic flash, and characters framed in umbilicus-and-up medium shot.

Undeterred, Spielberg lined up his opening, a medium close-up of the back of a large chair that swivelled at the touch of a diamond-ringed finger to reveal Joan. He had plenty more of the same: an unbandaging that owed something to Eisenstein in its swift cutting, and a climax, as Crawford stumbled to her death through a window, that recalled the overt symbolism of 1930s montage expert Slavko Vorkapich. 'I remember shooting through the baubles on chandeliers,' says Spielberg, embarrassed – though the shot of Sullivan's image inverted in distorting glass as he arrives in Crawford's office is one of the most memorable in *Eyes*.

He might have got away with it had Crawford been as malleable on set as off. Instead, she exhibited a steely stubbornness, bombarding him with questions about her character. 'Joan was climbing the walls while they were filming,' recalled Serling's wife Carol. 'She was calling Rod all the time, and he reassured her.'

Under his tan, Spielberg was in a cold sweat. Seeing him pale, Barry Sullivan took him aside and told him something he would never forget: 'Don't put yourself through this,' he said, 'unless you absolutely have to.'

Spielberg saw he had no choice but to accede to most of Crawford's demands. When she couldn't remember her lines, he printed up cue cards, at Sullivan's suggestion, with print large enough for her to read through her bandages. He agreed as well to the retakes she requested, knowing that to deny her could lead to a catastrophic confrontation in front of the crew.

With her young director under control, Crawford relaxed. She gave him cologne, and a bracelet. He responded by placing each morning, in her dressing room, a single rose in a Pepsi bottle. A loyal Pepsi drinker, Crawford belched every time she finished a bottle – a sign of enjoyment, she explained. When Spielberg told her he'd never learned how to belch, she taught him.

The price of conciliation was delay. At the end of the shoot, two days of script remained unfilmed. Sackheim stepped in and directed the last day. A few days later, Spielberg showed Sackheim his rough cut. The producer sat next to Spielberg in the editing room, groaning faintly at each new visual excess.

'We're going to have to perform major surgery on your show,' Sackheim said at the end.

'And he went in,' said Spielberg, 'and shifted the vision from my choices to his own choices.'

Exhaustion and depression forced extreme decisions. 'I was in a despondent, comatose state,' Spielberg recalled. 'I learned a lot of lessons with that show, but rather than say, "Well, I'll let that roll off my back and go on to the next show," I went to Sid Sheinberg and said, "I can't do TV any more. It's just too tough. I quit."'

Wisely, Sheinberg refused his resignation. Instead he offered a year-long leave of absence. 'So my salary was suspended and I went home and wrote for a year. All I did was write.'

Spielberg's first thought had been to break into the underground, where some of the USC group were making their reputation. 'I went to the underground to make films in 16mm – and I couldn't get in there. I could not raise $100 to make a film.'

Networking had won him a few useful contacts at Universal. One was composer John Williams. Spielberg admired his music for Mark Rydell's version of William Faulkner's *The Reivers*, folksy and ebullient by turns. Its cross-fertilisation of the American tradition with the European – 'like a combination of Aaron Copland and Debussy', Spielberg said – marked Williams as someone who shared his taste.

Another new acquaintance was Cliff Robertson. As much a victim of the TV ghetto as Spielberg was, the boyish-looking actor had starred in *The Hustler* and *Days of Wine and Roses* on TV, only to see Paul Newman and Jack Lemmon click with them in the cinema. When he appeared in *The Two Worlds of Charlie Gordon*, a teleplay based on Daniel Keyes's story 'Flowers for Algernon', about a mentally handicapped man who becomes a genius through experimental surgery, Robertson recognised a potential hit and bought the film rights himself, adapting it into the screenplay *Charly*. Seven years later, in 1968, his foresight was rewarded with an Academy Award for Best Actor.

Robertson was Spielberg's first call after he started his leave. The actor loved World War I aircraft and, after the success of *Charly*, he wrote a treatment for a flying movie called *I Shot Down the Red Baron, I Think*, which would use rare original aircraft accumulated by another fanatic in Ireland. Robertson's agent, David Begelman, sold the idea to Cinerama Corporation for $150,000, but the project bogged down in wrangles over finance, in which, to Robertson's fury, Begelman sided with Cinerama. Robertson was forced to pay $25,000 to Cinerama, with a further $25,000 if the film was ever made. In sworn depositions, he claimed Begelman 'sandbagged' and 'completely subverted' him.

Aware of this debacle, and knowing Robertson's interest in old planes, Spielberg offered him a treatment he'd written with a friend, Claudia Salter, about a World War I flyer and his son barnstorming around America in the early twenties. Robertson liked *Ace Eli and Rodger of the Skies*. He bought it, hiring Salter to write a screenplay.

After graduation from USC, Hal Barwood and Matthew Robbins had tried to sell some screenplays, but without success. Spielberg began feeding them his ideas. George Lucas was staying with the writers while he cast what would become his first studio feature, *American Graffiti*. The abstracted Lucas seldom spoke to anyone as he wandered in and out, but to him it seemed the dweeby guy with the big nose and the glasses was there almost all the time. Spielberg's voice filled the house as he leaned over the shoulders of Robbins and Barwood, suggesting lines, laughing at those they'd written, and urging them on.

One of Spielberg's ideas was a comedy he'd already tried to float at Universal, a modern *Snow White*, about seven men who run a Chinese food factory in San Francisco. Another was based on a clipping from the *Los Angeles Citizen News* about a May 1969 Texas incident when Ila Faye Dent, just released after a shoplifting conviction, persuaded her husband

Robert to break out of prison to retrieve their two-year-old daughter from court-appointed foster parents. On the way, they kidnapped state patrolman James Crone, which led to a massive car chase across the state.

From this story, Barwood and Robbins, with Spielberg's collaboration, worked up the tale of Lou Jean and Clovis Poplin's flight in search of Baby Langston. Police Captain Tanner, hamstrung by the incompetence of his men and the young couple's sentimental appeal, trails them with a motorcade as they bumble across Texas. Crowds cheer them and high school bands play them through town, while well-wishers offer free gas and chicken dinners, and fill the car with gifts. Even the vigilantes who ambush them on a used-car lot manage only to riddle the cars and do no harm to the fugitives at all. The dream dies at the end, when Clovis is killed, but until then it's a folk tale straight from *Reader's Digest*. The screenplay was called 'Carte Blanche', then 'American Express', but later it was renamed, in honour of the town towards which the Poplins were fleeing, *The Sugarland Express*.

Each decade throws up its hot writing teams, and Barwood and Robbins were to be as hot as any during the seventies. Episodic and oriented totally towards action, their work seems mechanical today, a loose stringing together of action sequences, owing more to animators like Chuck Jones, Tex Avery, Frank Tashlin and Walt Disney than to the meticulous plot- and scene-builders of the 1940s. But Spielberg called them 'geniuses' and praised their 'wonderful cartoon imagination'. Once Barwood and Robbins went on to direct their own films, he found and encouraged other partnerships like theirs. Robert Zemeckis and Bob Gale, his protégés in the eighties, were Barwood and Robbins writ large, not least in their fascination with animation.

As if to underline the comparison with Jones and Avery, Barwood, Robbins and Spielberg put Lou Jean and Clovis into an Indian Chief mobile home on a used-car lot and had them watch Chuck Jones's Road Runner evade Wile E. Coyote on the screen of a nearby drive-in cinema. Spielberg lavished all his craft on this scene when the film was finally made. *Birdus Fleetus* and *Lupus Persisticus* (Jones's cod-Latin names for his hero and villain) were his boyhood heroes, and he prevailed on

Universal to buy from Warners forty seconds of Jones's cartoon to under-line the film's most poignant moment.

His Universal contract had won Spielberg an agent. He was accepted by the prestigious International Creative Management, founded by David Begelman, a plump middle-aged man, famous as one of Hollywood's highest-betting poker players, but also well-known, because of argu-ments like that with his ex-client Cliff Robertson, as chronically unre-liable. Spielberg's first representative at ICM was Mike Medavoy, himself later a studio executive. 'Spielberg came in with . . . *Amblin*',' Medavoy recalled. 'I saw it and I said: "Terrific!"' Medavoy got him a few commer-cials, one of which featured a black actress named Margaret Avery, whom Spielberg would remember when he came to direct *The Color Purple*.

But he and Medavoy disagreed over Universal, to which Spielberg, disconsolate about the lack of work on the outside, was thinking of returning. Medavoy recalled:

> I wanted him to get out of that contract. He wanted to stay. He was right, actually, to stay. My feeling was that at Universal at that particu-lar time – this was right before *Airport* – he'd get boxed into doing garbage. And I had just gotten Phil Kaufman out of his contract. So I said, 'Listen, you should get another agent, I don't think your career is going to go anywhere if you stay there.' So I got him another agent within the same agency.

The new agent was Begelman's partner, Freddie Fields, who was decis-ively to launch Spielberg's career. During his sabbatical, Fields took him round the traditional circuit of all film-makers looking for backing. One stop was at Twentieth Century-Fox, then being run by Richard Zanuck while his father Darryl, who'd founded the company almost forty years before, enjoyed European retirement with a series of darkly dramatic French mistresses like the singer Juliette Greco.

Novelist John Gregory Dunne described Zanuck, then thirty-eight, as 'a tightly controlled man with the build of a miniaturised half-back, twelve-month tan, receding brown hair and manicured fingernails that are chewed to the quick. He has hesitant blue eyes, a quick embarrassed smile and a prominent jaw whose muscles he reflexively keeps knotting and unknotting.' The tics hid a violent temper. Around Fox, Zanuck was known as 'Little Napoleon', after Nehemiah Persoff's twitchy gang boss in Billy Wilder's *Some Like it Hot*.

David Brown, twenty years older than Zanuck, a pipe-smoker with a bushy moustache which earned him the nickname 'The Walrus', handled story operations from New York and acted as Zanuck's adviser and lieutenant. He affected a vague manner that belied his long experience as magazine writer, editor and publisher. His politeness and tact made him ideal to act as a buffer between the volatile Zanuck and the world. An odd but effective team, Zanuck and Brown had launched some of Fox's biggest hits, though their decision in 1970 to abandon the broad entertainment values of their earlier successes like *The Sound of Music*, *Hello Dolly!* and *Butch Cassidy and the Sundance Kid* for more challenging, adult films was already eroding their power with the acutely profit-conscious Fox board.

It was this pair that Fields brought Spielberg to meet. As a package, he offered *Ace Eli*, with Robertson to star and Spielberg to direct. Zanuck suspected Spielberg was a better salesman than director. 'I found him tremendously gifted, at least from a conversational point of view, but it was a highly physical and complex film, and I didn't think he had the experience to do stunt flying and all that.' They did buy the script, however, Spielberg's only sale during his absence from Universal.

Spielberg later gave the impression that he spent a year away from Universal, but, despondent with his attempt at independence, he actually returned after only four months.

'Sid,' he told Sheinberg, 'I'm ready to eat crow and pay my dues. Assign me something.'

Word of his problems on *Eyes* had spread, however, and nobody wanted him. 'I was regarded on the Universal lot as a folly, a novelty item, bric-a-brac for the mantelpiece. Something to joke about at parties.'

Fortunately, *Night Gallery* got good reviews when it went out on 8 November 1969, and NBC commissioned the rest of the series. With hindsight, Spielberg could see that he had a lot to learn, and that the best way to do so was to work. He could admit now that *Eyes* was a disaster, and that watching Sackheim eviscerate his work, however humiliating, had been a salutary display of the power of editing.

Sheinberg offered him six directing assignments. For *Marcus Welby MD*, a plodding but popular series starring Robert Young as a kindly Santa Monica physician, Spielberg directed an episode called *The Daredevil Gesture*, about a teenage haemophiliac who risks his life on a class field trip to prove his courage. Unable to instil individuality with bravura camerawork, he tried for Significance in performances. 'I was taking *Marcus Welby* seriously,' he said later, self-mockingly. '. . . and a lot of these older actors would look at me . . . wondering, "Gee, I'm doing three shows this week and this guy is acting like this is *Twelve Angry Men* with Henry Fonda." And I'm trying to flush out Marcus Welby and making an ass of myself on the set.'

He had even less success with *Make Me Laugh*, another segment of *Night Gallery*. In a variation on the Midas Touch, black comic Godfrey Cambridge is given the magic power to make people laugh – but only to laugh, even at his own death. Towards the end of shooting, in a repeat of the post-production interference of *Eyes*, Tom Bosley replaced Eddie Mayehoff in the role of Cambridge's manager, and Jeannot Szwarc, not Spielberg, was called in to direct his scenes. The episode aired on 6 January 1971.

Life as a TV director was exhausting. 'It's very, very hard to learn film-making when you're watching five-day television shows,' Spielberg said. 'People are running and shouting, and the pitch is so ear-shattering you become a neurotic before you become a movie-maker.' Even so, it taught him a lot. 'You learn to do your homework,' he said. 'TV pulled a long train, and I was the last carriage. If you didn't finish on time and under budget, they would just cut you loose.'

He had also returned at exactly the right moment. Episode drama was dying. Networks were demanding more features. Rather than abandon their popular characters and titles, Universal lengthened episodes to ninety minutes and widened their scope while keeping to the same tight schedule and budget. Despite their length, these films still had to be shot in ten days.

Among the inflated series was *The Name of the Game*. Set in the world of magazine publishing, it had a rotating roster of three leading men: Gene Barry, Anthony Franciosa and Robert Stack. In the autumn of 1970, Spielberg directed *L.A. 2017*, an episode written by Philip Wylie which aired on 15 January 1971. Barry crashes his car on the way to an environmental conference and wakes up in 2017 to find that Angelenos have taken refuge underground from smog and gang warfare. After siding with the rebels who want to overthrow big boss Barry Sullivan, he retreats to the surface and is transported back to his own time, converted overnight to clean-air legislation.

L.A. 2017 earned Spielberg minor eminence when he was invited to screen it at the World Science Fiction Convention. Most fans dismissed the long-haired young director in tailored leather jacket and open-necked flowered shirt as another psyched-up fast-talking Hollywood hype, but the experience alerted him to the existence of a growing national market for fantasy and science fiction. Unlike himself at their age, these kids had money to spend and the power to do pretty much what they pleased. They were obsessive about inside and advance information on science fiction films. Spielberg, still young enough to remember what it was like to be a fan, took note. Jeff Walker, a publicist who came to specialise in promoting films, including some of Spielberg's, to this market, comments that today 'there's an entire market segment that thrives on knowing the stuff beforehand, that was created by [Spielberg] practically, and George [Lucas], and [*Star Trek* producer Gene] Roddenberry.'

Success gave Spielberg some leverage, and Freddie Fields was able to renegotiate his terms of employment. On 28 December 1970 *Variety* noted that he'd signed a five-year exclusive contract as a producer and a six-year non-exclusive deal as director. It was his first step on the road to total control, and an early recognition that his ambitions lay less in creative film-making than in the building of a production empire.

A pecking order operated on the Universal lot. Feature directors looked down on the TV contingent as hacks, just as directors at other studios looked down on Universal's features and the bright pastel 'house style' that extended even to credits, trailers and print advertising. Instantly recognisable, a Universal film was also instantly dismissable. In the fifties, TV had launched Arthur Penn, John Frankenheimer, Sidney Lumet and Sam Peckinpah, but in the seventies it was more often a graveyard of reputations. Spielberg was the only director under thirty-five at Universal. Most of the colleagues with whom he was to share the chores of *Name of the Game* and *Night Gallery*, like Robert Collins, Daryl Duke and Robert Michael Lewis, were ten years older, and saw little in their future but more of the same.

Feature film producer/directors were an elite. The emblem of their standing was a bungalow on the lot. The prosaic word belied the lushness of these buildings. 'A sort of pseudo-English manor house,' says screenwriter David Freeman, '[they were] a bungalow the way summer houses in Newport are cottages.' Hitchcock's, the most lavish, had two levels, with a dining room, screening and editing rooms, and its own art department. Don Siegel rubbed along in something the size of a suburban house. Billy Wilder had two storeys on a hill, past which the tour trams coasted in silence to avoid disturbing him and I.A.L. Diamond, at work on *The Front Page*.

Spielberg hungered for a bungalow. Instead, he had a corner office in the Black Tower, well below the seventeenth floor where Wasserman and Sheinberg controlled his destiny. From there, he looked out on a future that contained, he was beginning to discover, nothing as solid as the films of Wilder or Hitchcock. He had plenty of ideas for features and, now that he was back on the inside, no shortage of people to pitch them to. But everywhere he met a brick wall. His career may have looked to be up and running, but it became increasingly clear that he was jogging on the spot.

Universal incorporated *Night Gallery* with *McCloud*, *San Francisco International Airport* and *The Psychiatrist* into an omnibus for NBC, *Four-in-One*. Writer/director Jerrold Freedman was in charge, and Spielberg joined his team. It was a useful move. 'He had his own long-haired film society right in the heart of Universal Studios,' he says of Freedman. 'He employed a number of writers, directors, people dealing with esoterica, and he hired people from his college and people he knew from the East. I was just a young person, whom he liked at the time, and to whom he said, "Here, do two *Psychiatrists* for me."'

The Psychiatrist, written by Richard Levinson and William Link in the school of *Ben Casey*, *Doctor Kildare* and other successful doctor shows, featured Roy Thinnes as an idealistic LA shrink and Luther Adler as the obligatory older, more cynical colleague. Spielberg did *The Private World of Martin Dalton* (10 February 1971) and *Par for the Course* (10 March 1971). *Martin Dalton* was cribbed from a famous incident in Robert Lindner's collection of psychiatric case histories, *The Jet Propelled Couch*. A disturbed twelve-year-old (Stephen Hudis) invents a fantasy universe from TV and comic books, and begins to retreat into it. Responding to a subject close to home, Spielberg seized the chance to create a surrealist dream world and also to work with young actors, for which he already showed a flair.

It was *Par for the Course*, however, with golf pro Clu Gulager coming to terms with his imminent death from duodenal cancer, which attracted most attention, and which Spielberg regards as his best TV work. Always most comfortable illustrating an emotion than conveying it in dialogue, he wrote a scene in which two buddies bring Gulager in hospital a gift they know he will relish – the cup from the eighteenth hole at his course, which they've dug out of the centre of the green. Gulager breaks down and crushes the dirt and grass over his head.

Levinson and Link were so pleased with *Par for the Course* that they asked for Spielberg to direct *Murder by the Book*, the first regular episode, after two feature-length pilots, of the detective series *Columbo*. The role of the Los Angeles Police Department's scruffiest, least tidy but most perspicacious detective, who allowed himself in each episode to be patronised by his arrogant quarry before springing a brilliant deductive trap at the end, had been planned for Bing Crosby. He turned it down, however, when it looked as if the series' success might interfere with his golf. Peter Falk replaced him. The series' story editor, Stephen Bochco, later the force behind *Hill Street Blues* and *LA Law*, wrote *Murder by the*

Book, in which Columbo unmasks crime writer Jack Cassidy as the murderer of his collaborator Martin Milner. It aired on 15 September 1971 to excellent reviews, but allowed Spielberg little room for creativity. He did his best, opening the film not with the conventional theme but the sound of a typewriter, and setting up some sharp angles inside Milner's high-rise office to exploit its spectacular view of Los Angeles, but in most respects the film is routine.

Spielberg also made an episode of *Owen Marshall, Counselor at Law* called *Eulogy for a Wide Receiver*, about a football coach accused of feeding amphetamines to his players. However, any charm that series TV might have held for him was running out. In particular, its casts of B-movie players and studio trainees grated increasingly. 'At twenty-three, I was already saying, "Life's too short to worry about the size of someone's trailer. Or the fact that they don't like the hairdresser because the hairdresser has coffee breath." Little petty things used to make me crazy.'

If Spielberg needed a further caution that TV eroded talent, he could find it in the experience of Rod Serling, who as *Night Gallery* dragged into its second year with diminishing ratings, found most of his stories rejected. As the studio even barred him physically from story conferences and began buying scripts of its own, with the emphasis on action, it became clear to him that he'd been hired mainly as a master of ceremonies. 'I'll just be the front man, a short hunk of gristle,' he told a reporter. '[Night Gallery] is not mine at all. [It's] another species of formula series drama.'

After the autumn of 1971 Spielberg wasn't to escape such problems, but at least he encountered them on a higher plane, since Universal had by then grudgingly given him his first true feature and first international success. Much was to change for him, and for New Hollywood, with the making of *Duel*.

5

Duel

We're old now, but when we were the New Hollywood . . .

Steven Spielberg, 1994

THE YEAR 1971 carried a sense of threat for Americans. In February, an earthquake rocked the San Fernando Valley, shaking Universal's black tower to its foundations and toppling some of the ancient sets. Sixty-two people died when old apartment houses collapsed all over the city, as if they too had been built not to last but to act as movie backgrounds. In September, convicts rioted at Attica prison in upstate New York, took guards prisoner and plunged into a bloodbath. Servicemen were returning home from Vietnam at an increasing rate, but the war remained a running sore. Lieutenant William Calley was sentenced to life imprisonment in March for the My-Lai massacre, only to be released to house arrest by President Nixon pending his appeal.

The automobile, its pleasures and dangers, was, even more than usual, a national preoccupation. GM recalled 6.7 million Chevrolet cars and trucks and Ford 220,000 Pintos to correct design faults. Two Detroit car novels, Arthur Hailey's *Wheels* and Harold Robbins' *The Betsy*, were the year's big sellers. They were matched only by William Peter Blatty's *The Exorcist* and Tom Tryon's *The Other*, occult thrillers with suburban or rural settings that probed the unease about daily life bedded as deep in the mouth of America as an abscessed tooth.

Dennis Hoffman, the producer of *Amblin'*, kept asking what had happened to his film. Spielberg was directing and McMyler had a small role in *The Boston Strangler*. But he, the man who'd given them their chance, whose name was on *Amblin'*, who'd put up the money, had zilch. The Universal short subjects department finally offered $90,000 for the rights. 'But the sex and the joint have gotta go,' they said. 'This is a family company.' Indignantly, Hoffman refused, and Spielberg, while not making an issue of it, backed him up. *Amblin'* had served its purpose in getting him into the studio. What happened to it now didn't matter that much. Retrieving the film from Universal, Hoffman sold it to Paramount, which released it late in 1970 as the support film to what looked like a cheap youth picture. But *Love Story*, Arthur Hiller's adaptation of Erich Segal's best-seller, with its tearful celebration of young love on its deathbed, became the year's sleeper, making stars of Ryan O'Neal and Ali McGraw, and grossing more than $100 million. Everywhere, people stopped Spielberg and said, 'Say, I saw that movie of yours.' He wasn't any longer just some nephew or cousin of Sid Sheinberg's who had almost fucked up the Joan Crawford TV pilot. Something of his had made it to the Big Silver. He was a *movie* director.

All over Hollywood, young directors had become hot in the wake of Dennis Hopper and Peter Fonda's hymn to dope, rock and the road, *Easy Rider*. *Variety*'s 1970 Cannes Festival report acclaimed American cinema as 'the new *avant garde*', while 1971's *International Film Guide* rated it

> more innovative, more directly concerned with issues, and more deeply expressive of individual personal vision. Features like *Alice's Restaurant*, *The Strawberry Statement*, *Woodstock* . . . as well as hundreds of lesser known independent films, reject traditional romantic clichés and get very close to the bizarre configurations of contemporary American experience.

Old Hollywood didn't know what to make of this unexpected new direction in the industry. 'In those times,' says Michael Pye, 'there was just this moment when it was possible for a whole generation of young talent to come in and make very much the films they wanted, because no one was any longer very sure what sort of film a studio product would be.'

Overnight, directors fresh from film school had their fantasies funded by an industry hipped on being hip. 'Every studio in town was narcotised by *Easy Rider*'s grosses,' wrote the novelist Joan Didion, a devoted Holly-wood-watcher and occasional screenwriter, 'and all that was needed to get a picture off the ground was the suggestion of a $750,000 budget, a low-cost NABET or even a non-union crew, and this terrific twenty-two-year-old director.'

The 1970/71 releases included a score of first or early films by directors of Spielberg's generation: *Glenn and Randa* (Jim McBride), *Getting Straight* (Richard Rush), *Cover Me, Babe* (Noel Black), *Watermelon Man* (Melvin van Peebles), *Up in the Cellar* (Theodore J. Flicker). A few of the new-comers were his friends: John Korty (*Riverrun*) and Brian De Palma (*Hi, Mom!*).

At Universal, however, the revolution was a long time coming. Never one for quick decisions, Lew Wasserman rode out the first youth wave by ignoring it. As far as he was concerned, Universal was mainly in the TV business. In 1971, however, he appointed Ned Tanen, a producer from the music business with no particular qualifications except his relative youth, to acquire low-budget 'alternative' projects. By early 1972 Tanen had bought Monte Hellman's *Two Lane Blacktop*, Frank Perry's *Diary of a Mad Housewife* and John Cassavetes' *Minnie and Moskowitz*.

Everyone Spielberg knew seemed to have a feature deal. As he bounced around Hollywood, from the campus of USC for a screening of student films to a Preston Sturges retrospective in Santa Monica, over a roast beef sandwich at Musso and Frank's or at a party at Coppola's place, the stories kept coming. Phone calls from producers who'd unearthed some long-forgotten script and wanted to discuss it, offers from Metro or Fox to 'come in and talk a deal'.

Milius sent him his latest screenplay, *The Life and Times of Judge Roy Bean*, which he'd just sold to John Huston. It was an epic western – the sort of script that Howard Hawks or John Ford might have made. When *The Godfather* opened in March 1972, its baroque, Continental richness drowned him in darkness thick as chocolate sauce. That such films could be made in Hollywood was incredible!

Coppola, with William Friedkin and Peter Bogdanovich, had launched

The Directors' Company. It was a Renaissance gesture, an alliance of princes. They pledged to share in each other's profits and *never* to concede final cut to anyone. Old Hollywood smirked. They'd seen these groups before. They came and they went. Sooner or later they'd start bickering. One or another of them would do better than the rest. Someone would screw someone else's wife . . . It was an old story.

Spielberg watched these evolutions with alarm. Reputations were being made before his eyes. Fame was being conferred. People were becoming immortal. And *he* was directing *The Psychiatrist*! He would have jumped at anything Ned Tanen offered him, but there could be no *rapprochement* between the eager Spielberg and this moody executive with his permanent sneer, his dour pleasure in the deal, and his belief that Hollywood was characterised by 'negativity and illusion – especially negativity'. While Tanen was in charge, Spielberg didn't have a chance. It drove him crazy. 'The truth is,' said a friend, 'Steve would have made *anything* that got him into features.'

Spielberg says he first came across Richard Matheson's short story 'Duel' when his secretary Nora Tyson, with a blush about even *knowing* what was inside the world's most successful men's magazine, showed him the April 1971 *Playboy* containing the story, in which a lone motorist is pursued by a homicidal truck driver in a gas tanker. Matheson doesn't agree. He'd written the film script long before he and Spielberg met. He based it on an incident when a truck driver tried to bump him off the road near his San Fernando Valley home, a common enough event on an increasingly congested system of which the trucker, like the bikers of *Easy Rider*, regarded himself as a sort of cowboy hero, subject only to his own rules. Its hero, Dave Mann, an archetypal corporate cipher with a house in the suburbs, a wife and two children, sets out on a trip to save an important account. Cutting across country, he overtakes a fume-belching gas tanker, the driver of which regards this as an insult. With mounting violence, he pursues him across the Sierra until they crash together into a quarry. Only Dave, a better Mann for the experience, survives.

In a more probable, if less heart-warming, alternative version of the legend about how Spielberg encountered *Duel*, a pal in the mailroom, part of his carefully nurtured network, funnelled him an interesting screenplay already going the rounds of producers. However he came across it, Spielberg devoured *Duel* with the enthusiasm of a fan. Matheson had written a number of *Twilight Zone* episodes – and the original of *The Incredible Shrinking Man*.

The script also addressed some of the fears that were to motivate Spielberg for the rest of his career. A few years later, British critic Gavin Millar pressed him to identify the anxieties that drove *Duel*. Was it the technology of the truck that frightened him?

'No, not the truck,' Spielberg mused. 'Loss of control maybe.'

Since childhood, security for Spielberg had reposed in control, and in adulthood it remained a paramount concern. Control of his environment, his emotions, his work. Twenty-five years later, Oskar Schindler would expound to the Nazi camp commander Amon Goeth, 'Control is power.' Spielberg remembered puttering along the freeways in his uncle's Chrysler as trucks roared past, air horns blaring at this slow-coach. It wasn't the car he identified with in *Duel*; it was the *truck*; its omnipotence, its power.

The Vice President in charge of features programming at ABC TV in 1970 was Barry Diller, an ambitious executive in his early thirties, later to run 20th Century-Fox. Sensing the audience's greed for movies, he'd launched the ABC Movie of the Week, a Monday-night showcase for new features, and was hungry for product. Universal saw *Duel* as an ideal Movie of the Week. But Spielberg, itching to escape the TV ghetto, argued that it should be a full cinema feature. And if Sheinberg would OK it, that would bypass Ned Tanen.

'If you can find a star who'll do it,' Sid Sheinberg conceded cannily, 'we'll see.'

Spielberg sent the script to one of the few Universal regulars who could project the necessary combination of vulnerability and resolve in Dave Mann, but Gregory Peck, as Sheinberg anticipated, wasn't interested. The project reverted to Diller, who quickly approved both it and Spielberg.

'I saw an episode of *The Psychiatrist* which he'd done,' Diller recalls. 'I thought, "What good work."'

Staff producer George Eckstein was assigned to bring in the production at about $300,000. To star, a disappointed Spielberg was allocated Dennis Weaver. OK, so he'd been the stuttering motel 'night man' in Orson Welles's *Touch of Evil*, though most people remembered him as Chester B. Goode in the TV series *Gunsmoke*, limping after James Arness and calling, 'Mistuh . . . er . . . mistuh Dillon?' He'd found fame of sorts at Universal as a cowboy cop transplanted to the big city in *McCloud*, but a character actor was always a character actor.

From the moment he read the script, Weaver begged for more meat, with a scene or two where he confronts and defies the truck before the climax. 'I just don't want to be this guy the way he's written,' he complained.

But Spielberg, sensing Weaver's core of weakness, on which so many other directors had traded, insisted he play Mann as a pussy-whipped wage-slave who greets every problem with sweaty-palmed indecision.

Mann fails to rescue a broken-down school bus menaced by the truck. When his car impotently spins its wheels as he tries to start it, the children inside, his surrogate family, jeer. Mann cuts and runs, after which, in the ultimate indignity, the truck not only spares the bus but arrogantly helps it on its way. He's out-thought at every turn by the truck, which ambushes him at one point near a railway line, and tries to push his car into a freight train.

Too embarrassed to demand help in the lonely gas stations and greasy spoons, Mann finally waves down an old couple, who simply drive off. It's only when his self-esteem is completely eroded that he finds the grit to oppose and defeat his opponent. To drive home the point, Spielberg recorded Mann's self-pitying meditations on his life and nursed Weaver through his performance from the back seat, playing the recording of his internal monologue at the point where they would appear in the finished film. Cropped out for TV, but revealed when the film was shown on the big screen, Spielberg can be seen scrunched at the edge of the frame in a car interior.

Talk, often only half-heard, is the obbligato of *Duel*. For the first seven minutes – a sequence added for cinema release – the only sound-track is a radio programme, incorporating a conversation between a census helpline and a comedian who sounds like Shelley Berman (but who is actually credited under the improbable name 'Dick Whittington'). The census form is insufficiently exact, Whittington whines. 'Head of the house', for instance. Well, in theory, that's him, but it's his wife who really wears the pants. He moans on to the embarrassed, hapless operator.

Mann laughs, but he has the same problem, as we find during a chilly phone conversation with his wife, whom he failed to defend the previous night from the passes of a friend who 'practically tried to rape me in front of other people'.

'What did you want me to do?' Mann grumpily asks. '*Fight* him?'

This scene, written by Eckstein, and two or three others, including the opening drive out of Los Angeles, the attempt to push the car into the train, and Mann's encounter with the school bus, were done later to bring the film up to theatrical length at the request of Universal's European sales organisation, CIC. The additions caused many headaches, especially finding another truck sufficiently similar to the one that had gone over the cliff.

For his part, Spielberg repudiates almost all of the additions, despite the fact that, without exception, they amplify those themes in *Duel* which were to become typical of his work: paternal emasculation, the decline of the father's role in the family, and the importance of a man's reclaiming his woman and self-respect in combat with rivals. Also, years later, he would insert a similar scene to the encounter with the school bus into *Always*. A driver in that film has a heart attack but Brad Johnson resuscitates him, watched by admiring kids, an impressed Holly Hunter, and a ghostly, defeated Richard Dreyfuss. Looking good in front of the kids matters to Spielberg more than anything.

Duel is all about fathers failing, women taking control, men losing it. It's frankly Oedipal. With it, Spielberg struck out at Arnold's abandonment of his family and its resultant fragmentation. Though Spielberg always spoke warmly of his sisters – 'I come from a family of beautiful women,' he says, comparing Sue, the middle sister, to Sophia Loren – he was ambivalent about Sue's 1975 decision and that of the youngest, Nancy, to leave the US and work on a kibbutz in Israel. Leah's recent remarriage, to another computer engineer, Bernie Adler, also distressed him. Superficially his attitude to his stepfather was cordial, though he was not above jokes about his mother's 'taste for printed circuitry'.

A truer sense of his betrayal by both parents emerged in a tirade a few years later, where he excoriated David Mann as 'typical of that lower-middle-class American who's insulated by suburban modernisation':

It begins on Sunday; you take your car to be washed. You have to drive it but it's only a block away. And, as the car's being washed, you go next door with the kids and buy them ice cream at the Dairy Queen and then you have lunch at the plastic McDonald's with seven zillion hamburgers sold. And then you go off to the games room and you play the quarter games: Tank and the Pong and Flim-Flam. And by that time you go back and your car's all dry and ready to go and you get into the car and drive to the Magic Mountain plastic amuse-ment park and you spend the day there eating junk food.

Afterwards you drive home, stopping at all the red lights, and the wife is waiting with dinner on. And you have instant potatoes and eggs without cholesterol – because they're artificial – and you sit down and turn on the television set, which has become the reality as opposed to the fantasy this man has lived with that entire day. And you watch the prime time, which is pabulum and nothing more than watching a night light. And you see the news at the end of that, which you don't want to listen to because it doesn't conform to the reality you've just been through prime time with. And at the end of all that you go to sleep and you dream about making enough money to support weekend America. This is the kind of man portrayed in *Duel*.

This was an astonishing recital for someone who would say later, 'I never mock suburbia. My life comes from there,' who admired Norman

Rockwell and who would make his own tributes to Formica and frozen pizza in *E.T.* and *Poltergeist*. It is more explicable as an attack not on suburban values but on fathers who fail to abide by them.

Duel pioneered a new kind of TV feature by making virtues of its necessities. Second-rate actors? Who cares? Spielberg was, as he remained, indifferent to glamour in his performers, preferring anonymous suburban faces, rumpled clothes, unwashed hair, spotty skin. No sets? Cheap technicians? No matter; he would make the best of what he was given. His cameraman, Jack A. Marta, and composer Billy Goldenberg, a staff composer who'd scored his *Columbo* episode, were journeymen, a fact Spielberg exploited by taking over as much control as possible of camera and music. The emphatic comic-book framing and the homage to Bernard Herrmann's *Psycho* score in the *wheep-wheep*ing violins show his hand.

Fortunately one other technician on the Universal lot was the best in the business. Carey Loftin had begun stunt driving in 1935 as a motor cyclist on a fairground Wheel of Death. He graduated to car and bike stunts in serials, managed the crashes and chases for Abbott and Costello, doubling Abbott in the more hazardous scenes, a fact that delighted Spielberg, a fan of the two forties comics. Loftin also ramrodded the stunts on Stanley Kramer's *It's a Mad, Mad, Mad, Mad World*, another Spielberg favourite, and reached the peak of his career in 1968 with the vertiginous car chase around San Francisco for *Bullitt*.

Another veteran, Dale Van Sickel, drove the car in *Duel*. Loftin handled the truck himself. He arranged a parade of five gas tankers on the backlot for Spielberg. Four had modern flat-fronted GMC-Mack prime movers with wide windows that revealed the driver down to his knees. Spielberg chose the fifth, an ancient shit-brown Brand X eighteen-wheeler, mud-spattered, rusted and slovenly. Its old-fashioned divided windshield not only gave the vehicle a look of frowning malevolence but, if the glass was dirty, hid the driver completely. It looked as if the truck was driving itself. Sure, Loftin told him in his slow Tennessee drawl, he could rig that truck for anything the script demanded, even crashing the car at the climax and carrying it over a cliff.

Duel was shot on location around Lancaster and Palmdale, sixty or seventy miles outside Los Angeles, on the edge of the Mojave Desert. Between the desert and Los Angeles, Soledad Canyon, on the edge of the Pinnacles National Monument, offered miles of lonely blacktop, much of it twisting and mountainous.

Spielberg mapped out the entire film in storyboards, like a giant comic book, in this case forty yards long. Though they didn't invent them – Hitchcock, among others, used them all the time – storyboards became a major weapon of the Movie Brats. Men like Spielberg's regular artists Ed Verreaux and George Jensen were adept at generating hundreds of pages of graphic art, complete with framings and camera movements, from the director's stick-figure diagrams. Storyboards dictated a two-dimensional style, reducing narrative to a handful of poses. Following style, dialogue was scaled down to the two or three lines needed to fill a talk balloon. Teenagers raised on the same visual conventions loved the result but, applied to a serious subject, it imposed a *Classics Comics* glibness. Coppola, Scorsese and many others abandoned this crutch as they embraced the multivalent possibilities of film, but Lucas and Spielberg clung to it. Many would credit the failure of *Empire of the Sun* in part to storyboarding, and the success of *Schindler's List* to the fact that Spielberg abandoned it for that film.

Having worked out the action in advance, Spielberg walked the locations for days before shooting, banging stakes into the dirt where stunts would begin and end, and where his three cameras would be placed. Instead of resetting the camera for each new shot, he had the car and truck drive past each camera in turn, capturing three shots in the time it usually took to film one. The weather was perfect, blazingly sunny, the valley baking in the heat, the mountains a brown smudge on the horizon. One can almost smell the softening blacktop, the truck's oily fumes, the sizzling grease of the roadside café.

Shooting went two days over schedule, in part because Spielberg saw rushes only every three days, and had to drive miles to do so. The budget rose to $425,000, but Eckstein was delighted with the result. Scenes like the truck ploughing through a roadside snake farm to crush the booth where Weaver is making a phone call showed a glee in violence of which more disciplined directors were incapable. To Spielberg, the lessons of junk film and cartoon proved perfectly applicable to live action. 'The challenge was to turn a lorry into Godzilla,' he said. 'It was sort of Godzilla v. Bambi.'

Godzilla nearly won in real life. As a precaution against drivers going to sleep at the wheel, the truck had a 'Dead Man's Hand' which cut the engine if pressure was released. Since Loftin had to jump just before the collision, he tied down the control, but as he prepared to leap, leaving the truck to accelerate over the cliff, the cord slipped. He had no alternative but to ride the vehicle almost to the edge before jumping. 'My scissors cut at literally the instant Carey's butt left the cab,' said Spielberg. But the near-accident left a continuity error. The truck door is open – 'Leaving room for a sequel,' Spielberg joked.

With only three weeks between the end of shooting and the air date, Universal allocated four editors to cut the film. Spielberg rollerskated from one cutting room to another. But the effect is seamless. Among the first people to see it was Barry Diller. 'I saw a rough cut of *Duel*,' he said, 'and I remember thinking, "This guy is going to be out of television so fast because his work is so good."' In the event, however, *Duel* was sold to NBC, who scheduled it for their *World Premiere Movie* slot.

Before *Duel* was aired, Universal loaned Spielberg to CBS for another made-for-TV feature, this time a horror film called *Something Evil*. The producer was Alan Jay Factor, who'd been behind the innovative occult series *One Step Beyond*. Robert Clouse's script about a couple who move into a remote Bucks County farmhouse, to find it haunted by a spirit that menaces their son, skilfully conflated *The Exorcist*'s plot of a child's demonic possession and *The Other*'s rural setting. (The fact that films of both were in production but not yet released made it all the more attractive.) Sandy Dennis and Darren McGavin were reliable but undistinguished as the parents. The boy was Johnnie Whittaker, from the saccharine series *Family Affair*.

Spielberg, however, distilled a sense of uncategorisable menace from his simple materials. In particular, he drew on his delirious adolescent experiences with bright light in the temple and from the TV screen. Abandoning the blue acetate normally taped over windows to render them more natural, he overlit them. Figures moving against their glow were haloed and distorted. The 'God Light', a radiance pouring through clouds of smoke or dust, would appear in most of his films.

Duel aired on 13 November 1971. Its virtuosity impressed friends who had been underwhelmed by Spielberg's previous TV work. George Lucas recalls:

> Though I'd crossed paths with Steven at film festivals in the early sixties, it wasn't until some time in 1971 that I really took note of him. I was at a party at Francis Ford Coppola's house and *Duel* was on television. Since I'd met Steven I was curious about the movie and thought I'd sneak upstairs and catch ten or fifteen minutes. Once I started watching, I couldn't tear myself away . . . I thought, this guy is really sharp. I've got to get to know him better.

Deciding what, if anything, *Duel* was 'about' became an intellectual game. Most American critics saw the film as pop sociology, and ammunition in the fight against their particular *bêtes noires*: mechanisation, alienation, pollution.

Europeans detected less symbolism and more craft. 'With almost insolent ease,' said Tom Milne in the British cinema magazine *Sight and Sound*, '*Duel* displays the philosopher's stone which the Existentialists sought so persistently and often so portentously: the perfect *acte gratuite*, complete, unaccountable and self-sufficient.' Milne did, however, also note two themes which would later become Spielberg trademarks. One was the film's roots in medieval chivalry, a preoccupation that would surface again in *Indiana Jones and the Last Crusade*. With the truck's first swerve in front of Mann, 'the gauntlet is down', leading to 'a simple mortal combat between hunter and hunted [with] the huge lumbering lorry as the dragon, and the glitteringly fragile Plymouth sedan as the prancing, pitifully vulnerable knight in armour'. Spielberg later admitted he'd seen it as a man 'duelling with the knights of the highway'. Another theme was the opponents' solipsistic isolation from the world. Mann and the driver hardly exist outside their confrontation. Action is their character, as it would be for the shark-hunters of *Jaws*, Roy Neary in *Close Encounters of the Third Kind*, and Indiana Jones.

Duel boosted Spielberg's stock at Universal, especially among technicians, most of whom were on contract and depended on good word of mouth for their next job. They couldn't care less about what critics said, but the kid took care of his people and made them look good. Two weeks after *Duel* aired, renegade producer/director Tom Laughlin signed cameraman Jack Marta to shoot his highly successful *Billy Jack* films. Editor Frank Morriss found himself being offered more features. Jim Fargo, the assistant director, would be picked up by Clint Eastwood and direct features for him. Some went on with Spielberg. The composer Billy Goldenberg would work on *Amazing Stories* when Spielberg produced his TV series at Universal in 1985. Many of the people on *Something Evil* would also figure in Spielberg's later career, including cameraman Bill Butler and Carl Gottlieb, his old friend from Long Beach who has a small acting role in the film and would later appear in and co-write *Jaws*.

Universal received a dozen requests from other studios to borrow Spielberg for cinema features. To his frustration, they turned them down. Nor would they agree to let him do a feature for them. Instead, Levinson and Link snagged him for another pilot. Husband and wife Martin Landau and Barbara Bain were being relaunched after *Mission: Impossible* as investigating reporters Paul Savage and wife. No amount of protest would shift Sheinberg, and although Spielberg's old friend Barry Sullivan played the Supreme Court justice whose blackmailing the Savages probe, the experience was humiliating. After much tinkering and some changes in title, from *Watch Dog* to *The Savage Report*, the film aired in March 1972 as *Savage*, to generally indifferent reviews. It was, Spielberg said later, the only time he was ever forced to make a film. But even this wasn't enough for him to recant on his belief in consensus film-making.

*   *   *

After adding nine minutes to *Duel*, Universal sent it to Cannes in May, a curtain-raiser to its European cinema release. Spielberg went too, his first trip outside America. A friend snapped him on a rainy Paris afternoon scampering across the Place de l'Etoile, the Arc de Triomphe behind him, a lanky kid in flared jeans, square-toed boots, striped skinny-rib shirt and too-tight jacket. He stares around in awe. Paris! In July, in Rome, Spielberg asked the local Universal office to arrange lunch with Federico Fellini. Fellini agreed, and his publicist Mario Longardi went along to translate. To their astonishment, the American-style restaurant they chose in deference to his guest's palate refused to seat them because Fellini wasn't wearing a tie. The 'maestro' stormed out, shouting over his shoulder, 'Now we go to an *Italian* restaurant.' After lunch, Spielberg handed Longardi his camera and asked to be photographed with Fellini, demanding a number of re-takes, including one with his arm around the waist of a startled director. Spielberg later wrote saying that he had the pictures on display in his office, believing they brought him luck, but neither Fellini nor Longardi was convinced that this gauche kid would make it in the film industry.

The intellectual climate in Europe was just as uncongenial. In Rome, left-wing critics pressed Spielberg to endorse their reading of *Duel* as socialist parable: working-class truck v. bourgeois sedan. Four of them left noisily when he wouldn't agree. He was no more ready to enrol in the *avant garde*. As a consensus film-maker, he couldn't accept *Cahiers du Cinéma*'s *politique des auteurs*, which designated one single person on a film as its driving intellectual force. 'Those directors who believe in the *auteur* theory will have coronaries at an early age,' he told his Cannes press conference. 'You can't play all the instruments at once.'

Spielberg accepted all the compliments for *Duel*, even those absurdly at odds with his beliefs. Yes, it was an 'indictment of machines' – despite his passion for video games and electronic gadgets. And sure, Mann was a horrible example of how suburban life rots mind and soul – this from the archetypal enthusiast for suburban America. Talking to him after *Jaws*, Richard Natale would compare him to 'a computer, constantly clicking, reeling out facts and figures about the movie industry like a ticker tape. He is already adept at giving the quotable quotes, at circumventing the wrong questions.' He'd coax columnists, 'Let's call each other with gossip,' and tell San Francisco alternative journalist Mal Karman, 'If you need more stuff for your article, just make it up. I don't care.'

Duel opened in London in October 1972, though in a cinema outside the West End, and destined for a fortnight's run at most. But its reputation had been growing since Cannes. David Lean said, 'It was obvious that here was a very bright new director.' British critics, and in particular Dilys Powell, who described *Duel* in the *Sunday Times* as 'spun from the very stuff of cinema', reviewed it with such enthusiasm that Universal transferred it to the West End and printed a new poster plastered with their praise. It had a respectable, if not spectacular London season, but did better on the Continent. To François Truffaut, *Duel* exemplified all the qualities he and the other New Wave directors aimed for: 'grace, lightness, modesty, elegance, speed', without their shortcomings, 'frivolity, lack of conscience, naïveté'. The film finally cleared $6 million profit, but, more important, launched Spielberg's critical reputation, especially in London, a city that, despite his dislike of Europe, would increasingly become his second headquarters. In 1984 he told Iain Johnstone, Powell's successor at the *Sunday Times*, 'If it wasn't for your illustrious predecessor, I wouldn't be here.'

Back in Hollywood, events were conspiring to free Spielberg from the Universal TV treadmill. By the advent of what Joan Didion called 'the hangover summer of 1970', the dismal box-office receipts of youth films had been assessed, and their makers were out. 'Nobody could get past the gate without a commitment from Barbra Streisand,' she wrote. Casualties of the collapse littered Hollywood. 'All the terrific twenty-two-year-old directors went back to shooting television commercials, and all the twenty-four-year-old producers used up the leases on their office space at Warner Brothers by sitting out there in the dull Burbank sunlight smoking dope before lunch and running one another's unreleased pictures after lunch.'

Fortunately Spielberg wasn't seen as part of this group. The *Village*

Voice's film critic Tom Allen was already nominating him as chief of 'the post-Coppola generation' – those directors who, instead of fighting old Hollywood, elected to infiltrate and subvert it from within. It was a mantle he was more than proud to wear. Today, he still defines himself as 'an independent movie-maker working within the Hollywood establishment'.

Two unexpected losers in the change of direction were Richard Zanuck and David Brown. A Stanford Research Institute report in 1970 had convinced both men that movies were about to undergo a seismic readjustment. With TV flooding the market, it was futile for Hollywood to continue serving a 'movie habit' which no longer existed. Instead, Zanuck told the board, Fox 'must depend heavily on a very small proportion of highly successful films targeted for the youth market'. Those films, he went on, must offer something the audience couldn't get on TV. Zanuck gambled that the 'something' was sex. He commissioned film versions of two notoriously explicit novels and hired soft-porn impresario Russ Meyer to make a sequel to another.

It was these films, *Portnoy's Complaint*, *Myra Breckinridge* and *Beyond the Valley of the Dolls* which, Brown acknowledged, 'did us in at Fox'. Amid complaints about the raunchiness of the new slate and, worse, a pre-tax loss of $23 million, Darryl Zanuck arrived back from Europe in August 1970. Deadpan, he recited to the assembled board a digest of the verbal obscenities in *Portnoy's Complaint* ('"Beat my meat" – one. "Blow me" – two. "Boffed" – one. "Boner" – one. "Cock" – sixteen'), then announced that, 'As long as I am Chairman and Chief Executive of Twentieth Century-Fox, *Portnoy's Complaint* or any other film with the same degree of obscenity will not be produced.' The project was sold to Warner Brothers. After this vote of no confidence, Richard Zanuck and Brown couldn't last long. In January 1971 Darryl Zanuck reclaimed the studio he created. His axe-man Dennis Stanfill ensured that his son's dismissal took place with maximum humiliation. 'There's a ritual to severance,' he told an astonished Richard. When Louis B. Mayer had been ousted from MGM, his complimentary Chrysler was reclaimed even before he reached the parking lot. Now, in order to get into his car, Zanuck had to step over a painter effacing his name from the tarmac.

Zanuck and Brown went to Warners with a five-film contract as independent producers. The irony of their dismissal was that they had read the market correctly. Cinema *did* need to capitalise on its differences from TV rather than imitate the rival form. Films had to become national events, blanketing the media, dominating conversation, relegating TV to its domestic role. Assessing Richard Zanuck and David Brown's administration, Hollywood historian Stephen M. Silverman has described how Hollywood in the seventies followed their lead, 'marketing total escapist fare during the summer, and [developing] the "blockbuster or bust" mentality that quickly afflicted movie-making . . . If a picture did not pull in at least $100 million, it was considered a wasteful exercise.' The film-maker who would put Zanuck's and Brown's theories into practice and prove their validity was Steven Spielberg.

6

The Sugarland Express

I have more of a bubble-gum outlook on life than I think
Welles did when he made *Citizen Kane*.

Spielberg, of making his first feature

W ITH HIPPY Hollywood discredited, the yuppie producers who
were to dominate the 1970s found themselves suddenly in
favour. Michael and Julia Phillips, East Coast Jewish, with a background
in publishing rather than movies, exemplified them. From the moment
they arrived in 1971, Michael in his conservative New York tailoring,
the shapely Julia in hot pants, they were Hollywood's hippest couple.
Michael had read Law and worked on Wall Street as a securities analyst,
and Julia was a protégée of David Begelman, but they talked like liberals,
smoked dope, played touch football, liked surfing and lived at the beach.
They were cool. They didn't mind John Milius turning up at parties with
a .357 Magnum and firing it out to sea as the sun came up.

The timing of their arrival was impeccable. Journalists already talked
about the USC group as 'an invisible studio', but while it included plenty
of directors and writers, it had no producers. The Phillipses filled that
niche. Julia knew they could become the vital link between Old Hollywood and New. 'I think we perform the peculiar function of putting
together the Marty Scorseses and the Robert Redfords,' she drawled. 'We
are equally intimate with both these kinds of people and we can put the
old glove in touch with the new glove, you know?'

In his search for a feature, Spielberg saw less of the USC gang. On his
way back from Europe, he'd stopped over in New York, where he'd met

a man who was to become one of his closest friends. Burly, bearded, seven years older than Spielberg, Brian De Palma was the son of a Philadelphia surgeon. His childhood was tormented by rivalry with his brothers, an obsession with his mother and the infidelities of his father. At one point, he made midnight raids in black commando gear to sneak compromising photographs of him with his nurse. A science buff, early computer freak and maniac for Hitchcock, whose fascination with voyeurism and the erotic manipulation of women he shared, De Palma came to movies through underground theatre and film. His friends were actors like Robert de Niro, whose career he launched. In 1971 he'd just finished *Hi Mom!* with de Niro. When a friend of Spielberg's brought De Palma to his hotel, he brushed past Spielberg and walked around the room, examining the furniture. Spielberg was impressed. Here was someone who, unlike him, didn't give a flying fuck what people thought. When De Palma won a Warners contract and moved to Hollywood, they became friends, and remained close.

Another new friend was Sydney Pollack, who directed twenty *Ben Casey*, *Frontier Circus* and *Kraft Suspense Theater* episodes a year for Universal in the sixties before making highly-regarded features like *This Property is Condemned* and *They Shoot Horses, Don't They?* In 1972 he was just finishing *Jeremiah Johnson* with Robert Redford, from a script written in part by Milius.

Pollack, an ex-actor, grave and dignified, with something in common physically with Sid Sheinberg, increasingly occupied the role in Spielberg's life as older brother and counsellor. He and Freddie Fields introduced Spielberg to more influential people, including Guy McElwaine, an ICM agent, and Alan Ladd Jr, then production head of Twentieth Century-Fox. Spielberg knew Ladd through George Lucas, who liked Ladd's self-effacing style.

Two other members of the group, David Giler and Joey Walsh, were writers. Giler, later to contribute to the script of *Alien*, was developing a contemporary comedy based on *The Maltese Falcon*, *The Black Bird*. Walsh, an ex-child actor and recovering gambling addict who kept his hand in playing poker with Walter Matthau and Jack Lemmon, had collected some of his experiences into a screenplay called 'Slide', about

Charlie and Bill, two amateur gamblers with otherwise dead-end lives who become friends, get involved with a couple of call girls, share some laughs and a few losses.

Later, Julia Phillips would paint Spielberg as someone out of his depth in this society,

> hanging around with men who were too old for him. Who bet and drank and watched football games on Sunday. Who ran studios and agencies. The group centred around Guy [McElwaine] and Alan Ladd Jr, otherwise known as Laddy, and included such disparate types as Joey Walsh and David Giler, the former more for the betting than the football, the latter more for the drinking than the football.

Pollack too would incur her displeasure when he took over the Japanese gangster screenplay *The Yakuza*, written by Paul Schrader, one of the beach group, and had Robert Towne add an element of international romance. But few people shared her perceptions of Spielberg's new friends. Most admired Pollack as a director who expertly balanced box office and art. Ladd was also respected as the most thoughtful of studio bosses, the model of Hollywood's next wave of producers. The *New York Times*'s Aljean Harmetz, while conceding Ladd was 'taciturn and emotionally reserved', also rated him as 'perhaps more than any other current top executive in love with movies'.

All this time, Spielberg had hoped Universal would finance *The Sugarland Express*, but in the end they blew cool, deciding that, despite the success of *Duel*, the new film was too much like Fox's unsuccessful *Vanishing Point*. The script went into turnaround – for sale to anyone who would refund its development costs. Spielberg also negotiated for a while with agent Allan Carr, who planned a version of Bronte Woodard's novel *Meet Me at the Melba*, about life in the thirties South, but producer Joe Levine wouldn't OK him as director.

Grudgingly, Universal offered Spielberg a cinema feature from the studio's roster of stock projects, and for ten weeks in the spring of 1972 he worked unenthusiastically with writer William Norton on a Burt Reynolds vehicle. Norton was to make his name with a succession of violent rural thrillers, and *White Lightning* set the tone with its story of ex-con 'Gator' McClusky who returns to the swamps of the South to avenge his younger brother, slaughtered by crooked sheriff Ned Beatty. Spielberg was wary of Reynolds, as he was of all stars. The actor had just broken into the list of the top ten box-office earners at number three, beneath Clint Eastwood and Ryan O'Neal, and, like Eastwood, had firm ideas about what worked for him on screen. Most producers encouraged him to forget dialogue and even character, and to concentrate on sexual magnetism and good-ol'-boy humour. Also like Eastwood, Reynolds trailed a team of buddy/collaborators, notably his stunt coordinator Hal Needham, who enjoyed a degree of trust and control which any director would have to harness. Sensing he lacked the skill or the interest to deal with these problems, Spielberg, in *Variety*-speak, 'ankled'.

Of all the projects in play among his new friends, Spielberg preferred Joey Walsh's 'Slide'. He feared being pigeonholed as an action director and would often confide that he 'basically wanted to make romantic films', or 'women's films', or was 'really a director of comedies'. This last perception would survive until, during the making of *1941* in 1979, he confessed, 'Comedy is not my forte.' More important, however, was *Slide*'s buddy theme. Spielberg's fascination with the male friendship he'd never achieved in childhood and the way in which men supported one another and formed effective teams would dominate *Jaws*, the Indiana Jones films, *Always*, even *Schindler's List*.

He and Walsh worked on *Slide* throughout 1972. His method, the guided joint improvisation he'd used with Robbins and Barwood on *Sugarland*, was to become standard for him, the response of a natural film-maker to the hostile world of the written word. 'I don't know if Steven ever told me what to do – ever,' Walsh says, 'but when he didn't giggle like a little boy eating a cookie, saying "This is great," I knew something was wrong, and I always took that as a gauge and somehow I looked deeper into the scene.' Walsh wanted to produce the film, so as to prevent studio interference. Both Spielberg and McElwaine backed him up, and MGM seemed happy with the package. Spielberg, delighted, told journalists that 'Slide' would be his next film.

At Universal, business was picking up. The avatar of a new attitude to features was George Lucas's *American Graffiti*, which officially started production on 26 June 1972. Though he was technically working for Universal, Lucas shot most of the film well away from Hollywood, within driving distance of his Marin County home. Ned Tanen watched the daily budget, but otherwise left the thorny Lucas to himself. It was becoming clear to all the studios that these new film-makers, raised in a college environment and with little concept of normal employment practices, responded ill to being treated as employees. 'We are the pigs,' Lucas said of his generation of directors. 'We are the ones who sniff out the truffles. You can put us on a leash, keep us under control. But we are the guys who dig out the gold.' He compared a studio editor cutting his work, a practice taken for granted in Hollywood, to someone amputating his children's fingers. Old Hollywood was astonished and offended at the comparison, but soon John Milius would be able to say, 'Nobody in a studio challenges the final cut of a film now. I think they realise the film-makers are likely to be around a lot longer than the studio executives.'

The conflict between New and Old Hollywood came to a head for the first time when Lucas showed his final cut of *American Graffiti* to an audience that included Tanen and Francis Ford Coppola. Coppola was seen as the godfather of New Hollywood, able to deploy the same omnipotent octopoid power as Don Vito Corleone. When Tanen closed his deal with Lucas on *American Graffiti* he'd imposed two conditions. One was a reduction in the budget to $600,000. The other was that Coppola must act as the project's moral, if not financial, guarantor. Magisterially, Coppola agreed. Now, at the preview screening, he took it on himself to defend the film, and Lucas, when Tanen dared to criticise it. 'You should be getting down on your knees and thanking George for saving your job!' he blustered. Reaching for his chequebook, he offered to buy the film there and then from Universal. (Fortunately, Tanen didn't call his bluff; Coppola was, as usual, broke.) 'This film is going to be a *hit*!' he shouted – which it was, grossing $112 million. Though he didn't know it yet, Ned Tanen had already lost Lucas. Lucas had tried to interest him in a version of *Flash Gordon*, but been turned down. Even before *American Graffiti* finished shooting, Lucas smuggled a copy to Alan Ladd Jr, along with his script for another space opera. It convinced Ladd to back him in the new film, *Star Wars*, and so deprive Universal of $250 million.

If Old Hollywood thought it could depend on the loyalty of these newcomers, it was badly mistaken. They would be satisfied with nothing less than total independence. The Brats shared a conviction that their generation must remake Hollywood in its own image. Otherwise they risked the fate of their hero and archetypal Hollywood renegade, Orson Welles. The director of *Citizen Kane* had deteriorated into a bloated has-been living off TV commercials for Nashua photocopiers and Gallo wine. When Joe Dante, a Spielberg protégé, was in the early eighties asked to work on *National Lampoon* magazine's projected film parody of *Jaws*, called *Jaws 3 People 0*, his suggestion that Welles take a role horrified everyone. 'We'd have to put his name on the poster,' said one executive, aghast. The decline and fall of Welles was a lesson to New Hollywood of the dangers of fighting the system. So palpable was the curse which seemed to follow him that even Spielberg, given the opportunity to back the last film of Welles's life, *The Cradle will Rock*, would refuse to do so, despite Welles offering to cast Spielberg's then wife, Amy Irving.

It was one thing to vow that you wouldn't end up like Orson Welles, and quite another to see how you could win independence while continuing to live in a community where, for better or worse, art was organised on business lines. In her 1974 essay *On the Future of the Movies*, the *New Yorker*'s influential film critic Pauline Kael wrote of a 'natural war in Hollywood between the businessmen and the artists . . . based on drives that may go deeper than politics and religion; on the need for status, and warring dreams'.

Studios executives in the seventies were mostly ex-lawyers or agents, more comfortable in the gloom of the boardroom and the hush of the golf course. They seldom read a book or saw any movies but the latest productions. Martin Scorsese dismissed them generically as 'Youpeople', while Spielberg, like many of his friends, called them 'The Suits'.

None of the young directors had any quarrel with making money; it was the only way one measured success in a business where personal satisfaction with what appeared on the screen meant less and less. Nor were they entirely opposed to Old Hollywood, which had nurtured them and furnished the fantasies which drove them to make films. But all of them hated the compromises forced on them by the corporate caution of the agents and accountants. Spielberg lamented:

> The tragedy of Hollywood today [is that] great gamblers are dead . . .
> In the old days the Thalbergs and the Zanucks and the Mayers came out of nickelodeons, vaudeville, they came out of the Borscht Belt theatre, and they came with a great deal of showmanship and *esprit de corps* to a little citrus grove in California. They were brave. They were gamblers. They were high rollers. There is a paranoia today. People are afraid. People in high positions are unable to say 'OK' or 'not OK'. They're afraid to take the big gamble. And that's very very hard when you're making movies. All motion pictures are a gamble.

By the seventies, Hollywood had largely turned its back on the old virtues, as Spielberg saw them, of showmanship and mass appeal which had drawn audiences back to the cinema every Saturday night for the latest 'big picture'. Talky films with ageing actors had alienated teenage filmgoers, whose billions in disposable income were flowing into the pockets of record producers and clothing manufacturers.

Spielberg was one of the few newcomers to sense the path American movies must take in order to survive in the last quarter of the twentieth century. He knew instinctively that issues were Out and entertainment In. He became instrumental in transforming a cinema of stories and characters into one of sensation. *Jaws* would be one of the first films since *Gone With the Wind* to exploit a movie as a national event. 'Up until *The Godfather*,' says Julia Phillips, 'every time you had a picture you thought was going to have reviews and audience appeal, you let it out slowly in a handful of chichi theatres in the major cities, and let it build. Then you went in ever widening waves.' But Spielberg sensed that the twelve- to twenty-year-olds who, though they made up only 22 per cent of the population, represented 47 per cent of filmgoers, wanted the week's hot movie *now*. TV promotion and TV reviewers had made the measured opinions of *Time*, *Newsweek* and even the venerable *New York Times* redundant. Within a decade, studio bean-counters would be able judge whether a film was a hit or flop simply by the takings of the first weekend of its release. By the time the print-media critics caught up, their judgement was irrelevant.

Spielberg also saw that overseas markets would transform the selling of cinema. Action and special effects needed no translation, so his films were perfect for foreign audiences. Long before the American economist Theodore Levitt propounded the theory of 'globalisation' in 1983, Spielberg was making the kind of universally appealing product which Levitt foresaw would dominate world markets in the future. Coca-Cola, Volkswagen, McDonald's and rock stars like Madonna were sold in the same form and with the same trademark all over the world; so was *Raiders of the Lost Ark*, the emphatic comic-book logo of which, with its lettering of crimson and gold, would become as widely recognisable as the Coca-Cola wave. Increasingly throughout the seventies and eighties, Asia and Europe would almost equal Spielberg's domestic audience.

At Warners, Zanuck and Brown's five-film deal was winding down in mutual boredom. *Ace Eli*, from Spielberg's story, with Cliff Robertson as the pilot, still hadn't gone into production, and the administration was showing cold feet about most of the duo's projects. They had accepted only one 'youth' package, *Steelyard Blues*, assembled by Michael and Julia Phillips with actor-turned-producer Tony Bill. The script was by David S. Ward, and Alan Myerson would direct Jane Fonda and the then-hot Donald Sutherland.

In midsummer, word got around of an imminent move by the partners. Lew Wasserman had decided that he wanted Universal in the feature business. Rather than promote Sheinberg or Tanen, however, he offered Zanuck and Brown a bungalow on the lot and a role as, in effect, its feature division, developing projects with studio funding, and releasing only through Universal. They leapt at the opportunity. In July they left Warners to form Zanuck/Brown Productions, and six weeks later they announced the Universal deal. In the weeks before they left and in the month immediately following, agents were asked to come in and pitch. Fields and Spielberg joined the queue.

Anxious to be seen as creative film-makers rather than loose-cannon executives, Zanuck and Brown boxed the compass with their purchases: black exploitation and horror, comedies and thrillers, prestige pictures and women's stories. Some were trivial, but their choices showed they knew what the market wanted: not sex, but sensation and humour. Having succeeded with *Patton* at Fox by giving the story of an American military hero to a radical young screenwriter, Francis Coppola, they decided to have George C. Scott repeat the feat, this time playing Douglas MacArthur, and commissioned a screenplay from Barwood and Robbins. Would Spielberg be interested in directing? He said 'Probably,' though in truth he hated the idea of 'two years working in ten different countries and getting dysentery in each one of them'.

He remained keener on comedy, of which Zanuck and Brown had a number of films in development. From *American Graffiti*'s writers Willard Huyck and Gloria Katz, they'd bought *Lucky Lady*, a thirties farce about booze running. Paul Newman, another client of Freddie Fields, showed some interest in it, and in Spielberg, for First Artists, the consortium he'd just formed with Barbra Streisand, Steve McQueen and Sidney Poitier to take more control of their films.

Mike Medavoy, representing Michael and Julia Phillips, sold Zanuck and Brown a period script, *The Sting*, about a con trick perpetrated on a gangster in Depression Chicago. The brainchild of David S. Ward, it had attracted Tony Bill. Ward, however, wanted to direct it, and was leery of letting it be shown around as a script. Bill persuaded him to recount the plot into a tape recorder, and the Phillipses, impressed, financed the screenplay.

One casualty of Zanuck and Brown's move to Universal was *Ace Eli*. Lacking their protection, it was botched by Fox, who decided the ending, where Robertson commits suicide, was depressing. They reshot it, and producer, director and screenwriter all removed their names: Erman became 'Bill Sampson', Robert Fryer 'Boris Wilson' and writer Claudia Salter 'Chips Rosen'. Spielberg probably had some part in the choice of these *noms du cinema*, since 'Chips Rosen' resembles 'Josh Rogan', a pseudonym he assigned to Melissa Mathison when she wrote part of his *Twilight Zone: The Movie* episode in 1983. Spielberg himself, however, kept his screen credit for *Ace Eli*'s original story. Savagely reviewed in *Variety*, the film was dumped in sixteen cinemas, mostly in regional centres like Washington DC and Baltimore, earning a paltry $13,400 in its first week.

With no decision in sight from Newman on *Lucky Lady*, Zanuck and Brown put *The Sugarland Express* into their schedule, burying it under a black exploitation film, *Willy Dynamite*, Clint Eastwood's *The Eiger Sanction*, a reptilian horror film called *Sssssss*, and *The Sting*.

Wasserman wasn't fooled when Zanuck and Brown visited his home to outline their first year's production plans.

'We think Steve has a great future,' Wasserman told them, 'but I have to tell you we do not have faith in this project.'

They pressed, and the studio chief relented, though with ill grace. 'Make the film, fellows, but you may not be playing to full theatres.' Had Zanuck and Brown known Wasserman better, they would have realised that such predictions tended to become self-fulfilling.

Encouraged by the Phillipses, Schrader was writing *Taxi Driver* for Scorsese. Hoping to win over Spielberg permanently to their side, the Phillipses encouraged their conversations about a project on UFOs.

Spielberg grew up watching films about alien contact and invasion. Trying to get his vision on paper in 1970, he wrote a short story called 'Experiences', about UFOs over a midwestern town which are seen only by the kids parked in the local lovers' lane. It echoed his Boy Scout troop's experience in the Arizona desert and his own memories of the New Jersey hillside where hundreds of people watched a meteorite shower. The Phillipses could see the idea had promise, though they urged a stronger political message, suggesting that the failure to investigate might be a kind of Watergate cover-up.

Schrader, arguably the most original mind of New Hollywood, had never seen the films that influenced Spielberg. Raised by Calvinist fundamentalists, he skipped junk film entirely: his heroes were ascetics like Robert Bresson, Yasujiro Ozu and Carl Dreyer. However, once Spielberg began describing the international network of UFOlogists and their struggle to convince officialdom, Schrader's fascination with morally driven characters was engaged.

One of the leading investigators, J. Allen Hynek, had begun investigating UFOs for the US Air Force. After discounting 80 per cent of sightings, he was left with a residue of genuinely inexplicable phenomena. Inspired by Hynek, Schrader drafted a script, called variously 'Pilgrim' and 'Kingdom Come', about Paul VanOwen, a sceptical federal agent converted by what Hynek called a 'close encounter of the third kind' – physical contact with aliens, as opposed to lights in the sky or signs of a landing. He persuades the government to fund a fifteen-year investigation of the phenomenon, only to find, in Schrader's words, 'that the key to making contact isn't out there in the universe, but implanted inside him'.

After one Sunday at the Phillipses', Spielberg stopped his car in the middle of the night on Mulholland Drive, the road that weaves sinuously along the ridge between Los Angeles and the Valley. Climbing out, he flopped on his back across the bonnet to gape at the night sky. Tilting his head, he saw the Valley's net of light inverted, spread out above his head, as if the constellations had suddenly arranged themselves in orderly lines of red, green and diamond white. He was no longer looking down on a city but up at . . . something else: a space ship so huge that it filled the sky?

Now at least he knew what the UFO film would look like. He was less sure what it was about.

In October 1972, Goldie Hawn had signed a three-film deal with Universal. Her career, which soared after she left TV's comedy *Laugh In* to win a 1969 Best Supporting Actress Oscar for her first film, *Cactus Flower*, had slumped with a Warren Beatty thriller, enigmatically called $s, and the comedy *Butterflies are Free*. Zanuck suggested her as Lou Jean Poplin in *Sugarland Express*. Hawn wanted to ditch her ditzy image, and Spielberg was happy to agree. She signed in December.

Julia Phillips in her autobiography harps on Hawn's scruffy style and dirty hair, but to Spielberg these were her charm. She became the model for the tousled, untidy women of all his films: *Close Encounters*'s Melinda Dillon, sleepy in T-shirt and cut-offs; tomboyish Karen Allen and Kate Capshaw in two *Indiana Jones* films; Holly Hunter in *Always*; harassed mum Dee Wallace in *E.T.*; Laura Dern in *Jurassic Park*; Julia Roberts's Tinkerbell in *Hook*. All fit the 'younger sister/older brother' model with which Spielberg characterised his romantic relationships. Mostly sexless, these women in his films live for and through their children or boyish men. Femininity is a reward conferred by their lovers: in *Raiders of the Lost Ark*, *The Color Purple*, *Always* and *Hook*, women don 'girl clothes' as a sign of desirability. 'It's not the clothes,' sighs Holly Hunter deliriously in *Always* when Richard Dreyfuss presents her with a cocktail dress and high heels, 'it's the way you see me.'

For Spielberg, as for many directors, the erotic gratification of shooting films transcended sex. 'When I'm making a movie I become celibate,' he has said. 'I get into the routine of fucking my movie.' (He also avoided seeing other films at such times, fearful, he says, of his work being impregnated by the ideas of others.) He deprecated those film-makers preoccupied with 'sport fucking'. 'Location shooting is the Rites of Spring to most film crews,' he said. 'Holiday Inns across America are probably host to more sprung beds and screaming orgasms when a movie company comes to town than at any other time.'

Spielberg lost his virginity at seventeen in a Holiday Inn motel – 'With a creature,' he joked, in the wake of *E.T.*, 'that was anything but extraterrestrial.' During his days at Universal, he dated regularly, encouraged by the more aggressive De Palma, who made the pick-ups and set the pace. When Spielberg finagled one of the first portable phones out of the studio, he and De Palma enjoyed calling girls from their driveways to ask for a date, then ringing the doorbell half a minute later. De Palma, an enthusiast for voyeurism and porn, both of which are recurring themes in his films, shot all their excursions on the 16mm camera he always carried. Their conquests were mostly starlets as low in the pecking order as themselves. Spielberg briefly tangled with Sarah Miles, and with striking Hispanic Victoria Principal, but neither relationship was exactly serious. Miles was no stranger to romance, and the later star of *Dallas* was so nakedly ambitious that she founded her own talent agency and blitzed casting directors with head shots and resumés of its favourite client: herself. Spielberg later ruefully rated her 'a great mind trapped in a great body'.

'Spielberg has always surrounded himself with women,' Martin Amis observed. 'Surrogate aunts, mothers, kid sisters.' But he recoiled from relationships which might have forced him to assume responsibility for another's emotional well-being. Actresses never posed that problem. They were too self-absorbed for more than a passing involvement. But that cut both ways. An actress offered no reassurance or consolation when Hollywood turned and savaged you. 'You can't cry on a shoulder that's wearing a shoulder pad,' Spielberg told one friend revealingly.

On 14 December 1972, just a few days before Spielberg's twenty-fifth birthday, Universal printed out the red-covered Final Screenplay of *The Sugarland Express*. Shooting would begin on 8 January 1973 near San Antonio. Hal Barwood and Matthew Robbins took sole writing credit, from Spielberg's original story, but because of his intensive observation and discussion of the script during writing, Spielberg's signature was on almost every scene.

Scarfing up the remains of the youth boom, Warners and United Artists had also put films into pre-production about young outlaw lovers. *Badlands*, directed by another newcomer, Terrence Malick, a Rhodes Scholar and Harvard graduate with a convincing line of intellectual chat, was based on the 1958 plains states murders committed by Charlie Starkweather and his fourteen-year-old girlfriend, while Robert Altman's *Thieves Like Us* retold a Bonnie and Clyde story against a rural Depression background. Though both promised to be radically different in tone to *Sugarland*, Universal was nervous about so much competition. Spielberg didn't care. Scouting locations, he was already thinking about 'Watch the Skies', as the UFO film was now called. Visiting Texas with Mike Fenton and Shari Rhodes to cast small roles for *Sugarland*, he'd earmarked some isolated airfields for what he told columnist Archer Winsten would be 'an Air Force picture shrouded in science fiction'.

During this trip, Spielberg experienced a close encounter of his own that was to have far-reaching effects on his work. He found himself in a remote, old-fashioned hotel in Jefferson, Texas, with Diane Bucker, head of the Texas Film Commission, and Elliot Schick, the film's production manager (and later producer of *The Deer Hunter*). Around midnight, as he undressed, he kept glimpsing a figure from the corner of his eye, though it disappeared as he tried to focus on it. A moment later, the entire room went cold, especially around the four-poster bed. Panicked, Spielberg roused the others and, pausing only to snap some flash pictures, fled. Bucker's new Mercedes refused to start, so a mechanic was called. Once he had it going at 1.30 a.m., they drove sixty miles to the comforting anonymity of a Holiday Inn. Spielberg disavows any belief in the supernatural, putting such phenomena down to the power of suggestion. What the incident most resembles, in his retelling, is a movie, and in particular a favourite of his, Robert Wise's 1963 version of Shirley Jackson's *The Haunting of Hill House*, which he called *The Haunting*. True to form, Spielberg recycled the experience in *Poltergeist*, another demonstration that in his universe everything, even the incorporeal, aspires to the condition of film.

As shooting loomed on *Sugarland*, he began choosing his team. He persuaded Verna Fields to take leave from USC to edit. Carey Loftin again planned the stunts, using one of the Corvettes he and Max Balchowski rebuilt as camera cars for *Bullitt*. Finding a cameraman was harder. Since he'd be shooting in winter, and on the open road, often in bad light, Spielberg needed the best. 'Visually wooed,' he said, 'by the thought of all those cars,' he wanted, as on *Duel*, to put his audience into them, like kids on a fairground ride. To do that, a cameraman had to be intimate with Robert Gottschalk's spherical-lens Panavision cameras which, although they had only a shallow depth of field, allowed one to shoot on a wide-angle lens without distortion. In particular, he wanted to use the Panaflex, its lightweight and noiseless version, inside the cars.

He chose Vilmos Zsigmond, whom he'd met through McElwaine and Altman. A Hungarian with a massive ego, Zsigmond had bribed his way to the West with watches in 1956, bringing with him footage of the Soviet invasion. Within a decade he'd become one of Hollywood's best cinematographers, with a reputation, earned on films like John Boorman's *Deliverance* and Altman's chilly Western *McCabe and Mrs Miller*, which Spielberg admired, for shooting in bad light and worse weather.

A few weeks before he began shooting, Spielberg found himself judging a student film competition with Douglas Trumbull, largely responsible for the special effects on *2001: A Space Odyssey*, and composers Marvin Hamlisch and Jerry Goldsmith. The young director's name didn't register with Goldsmith, but Spielberg was so familiar with Goldsmith's themes for series like *Thriller* and *The Twilight Zone*, and for *Planet of the Apes* and *Patton*, that he could hum long stretches of the music. He flirted with asking him to write the score for *Sugarland*, but opted instead for John Williams, who, though less inventive than Goldsmith, could be relied on to turn in a score squarely in the Hollywood vernacular.

Williams's *Sugarland* music would indeed be consensus composing by a master *pasticheur*. 'I wanted John to do a real symphony for this film,' says Spielberg, 'but he said, "If you want me to do *The Red Pony* or *Appalachian Spring*, you're going to ruin your movie. It's a very simple story, and the music should be picking and soft, with just a few violins and a small orchestra; cradle-like."' He used Dutch harmonica virtuoso 'Toots' Thielmans to enliven fragmentary music of a folksy simplicity. Working with Goldsmith, however, became an ambition for Spielberg. 'I heard,' says Goldsmith, 'that Steve and Zanuck tossed a coin to decide between me and Williams to score *Jaws*.' Coincidentally, Goldsmith also did the music for *Ace Eli and Rodger of the Skies*, but still didn't associate its author with his fellow panellist.

*   *   *

From the start, the logistics of *Sugarland* promised the most problems. Universal's technical departments helped Spielberg visualise the action by building models of locations like the used-car lot so he could plan his shooting with military precision. An artist sketched every scene in storyboards which he took to Texas and taped around his motel room – 'so I could see exactly what the film would look like from a bird's eye view . . . I always had a visual overview in terms of day-to-day shooting.'

A hundred cars participated in the original chase. Universal's publicity claimed the film used 250, failing to mention that this included the crew's private cars and support vehicles. In fact only forty appeared on camera, and even that number threatened to be unwieldy. Richard Zanuck arrived on location the first day with trepidation.

I was thinking, well, let's take it easy. Let's get the kid acclimated to this big-time stuff. But when I got out there the first day he was about ready to get this first shot, and it was the most elaborate fucking thing I've ever seen in my life. I mean tricky; all-in-one shots, the camera going and stopping, people going in and out. But he had such confidence in the way he was handling it. Here he was, a young little punk kid, with a lot of seasoned crew around, a major actress on hand, and instead of starting with something easy, he picked a very complicated thing that required all sorts of intricate timing.

And it worked incredibly well – and not only from a technical standpoint, but the performances were very good. I knew right then and there, without any doubt, that this guy knew more at that age about the mechanics of working out a shot than anybody alive at that time, no matter how many pictures they'd made. He took to it like – you know, like he was born with a knowledge of cinema. And he never ceased to amaze me from that day on.

Zanuck was right about the shooting, but charitable about the performances. Then, as later, nobody got much direction from Spielberg, who simply outlined the action and let them provide the characterisation. 'The most I ever heard him say before a take,' recalls one actor in his later films, 'was, "Lots of energy" – which is what directors always say when they don't know what they want. And afterwards he said, "A nice sense of reality."'

Paul Freeman remarks diplomatically, 'Steven is one of those people who do their direction of actors in the casting. They trust the performer to know his or her business, and to get on with it. On *Raiders*, he knew Karen Allen and I were from the stage and were used to rehearsing, so he sent us off to improvise. When we came back and showed him, he said, "Fine." All that stuff in the tent between Karen and me was made up like that.'

Casting was, and is, agony for Spielberg. He often chooses actors from tests shot on his behalf, and almost never talks to the performers until they arrive on the set. 'Steven goes with his nose,' says Julian Glover, the villain of *Indiana Jones and the Last Crusade*. He looks for performers who physically resemble his conception of the character and who have enough experience not to need direction. Wayne Knight arrived in Hawaii to play the fat computer hacker and embryo thief Nedry in *Jurassic Park* without having met him.

> I got out of the van, walked up to him, and said, 'I hope I'm the guy you wanted.' He said, 'Yeah, you are.' . . . So I get in the Jeep, and Steven gets in the Jeep, and here we are, me and Steven Spielberg sitting in this Jeep. I had never had so much as a conversation with him, and it was like, 'So how about those Mets?' I had no idea what to say.

If Spielberg auditions someone in person, it is seldom with a scene from the film. Usually he asks for some trivial physical action. On *Raiders* he held casting sessions in the Lucasfilm kitchen, asking nonplussed actors to mix and bake cookies, in an attempt to throw them back on their natural reactions. Emily Richard, the hero's mother in *Empire of the Sun*, was requested simply to put her hair up for a moment. 'He actually blushed when he asked me,' says Richard, 'and I blushed when I did it.'

William Atherton's physical appearance rather than his acting recommended him for Clovis in *Sugarland*. 'He's a very soft-spoken individual with wild eyes,' Spielberg said. 'He could be so easily misunderstood by

somebody with a pair of binoculars. One look at Bill [in *Looking for Mr Goodbar*] and you think, "My God, he's going to kill Diane Keaton."'
Michael Sacks was chosen for 'Slide' because Spielberg wanted the cop and Clovis to look as much alike as possible. 'It's two men who really began in the same small town, and went in two different directions.'

Casting as he prefers, exactly to type, paid off best in his choice of John Ford veteran Ben Johnson as Chief Tanner. With an actor whose screen persona was so firmly established, direction was superfluous. As Sacks remarked admiringly, 'he has an extraordinary quality – he can say any cliché to you and make it seem profound.' So effective was Johnson, however, that Spielberg came to regret his subsidiary role, feeling he should have spent more time on Tanner, explaining the compassion both for his quarry and his men that leads him to chase the fugitives rather than force a shoot-out.

The Poplins' flight, trailed by scores of police cars, was again structured like a carnival ride, with incidents of random violence – an ambush by vigilante deputies, a chance pile-up at an intersection, the 'potty stop' scene, with Clovis flushing a gunman hiding in a Portaloo – breaking the exhilaration of sheer movement. Film historian Diane Jacobs rightly called Spielberg and his coevals 'excruciatingly conscious of their medium and its history'. Hollywood had nursed them through adolescence and handed them a means of expressing themselves. As a result, they revered its past to a degree that baffled the Suits. The studios' response to the credit squeeze of the sixties had been to sell backlots for office buildings and auction off their props. In June 1982, however, Spielberg would pay $60,500 at Sotheby-Parke Bernet for one of the surviving 'Rosebud' sleds from the last scene of *Citizen Kane* – a sequence which inspired the last shot of *Raiders*, where the Ark is sequestered in a giant warehouse choked with anonymous crates.

All Spielberg's films are 'about' cinema before they are about anything else. 'It's very clear his references are to film rather than literature,' says Tom Stoppard, who wrote the script for Spielberg's version of J.G. Ballard's *Empire of the Sun* and acted for more than a year as his informal *dramaturg.* 'If one was talking about *Captains Courageous*, one was talking about Spencer Tracy and the movie, rather than the book.' Julian Glover says:

> It's not that he ever said, 'This shot is a copy of one in *Stagecoach*; the remake, not the original,' or, 'Here's my *Lawrence of Arabia* shot. But you just had a sense . . . He asked me to do one shot [on *Indiana Jones and the Last Crusade*], and I said, 'Steven, I don't know why I'm making this move.' And he said, 'Well, in *Adam's Rib*, Spencer Tracy . . .' And I just held up my hands and said, 'That's fine.' Obviously he knew exactly what he was doing.

Kevork Malikyan, who played Kazim in *The Last Crusade*, had a similar experience. Spielberg spent hours staging his death. He was to collapse into Alison Doody's arms and slide down her body. After grabbing him, she pulls her hands back to find them covered in blood. The shot refused to gel, and Spielberg dropped it, never mentioning he'd been trying to recreate the death of a disguised Daniel Gelin in the arms of James Stewart in Hitchcock's remake of *The Man who Knew too Much*.

One can multiply such stories by the dozen. TV exposed the Brats to more movies than most Hollywood professionals saw in a lifetime. They wore their knowledge self-consciously, even arrogantly, and while Spielberg didn't carry it to the extremes of Schrader or De Palma, he prepared his first cinema feature with a sense that he was not so much creating something new as building on what had gone before. 'Once,' recalls John Milius, 'Steve and I were talking about how easily we could recreate the atmosphere of a Ford or Hitchcock film. He said, "But how is it we're able to do that?" and I said, "Simple. We *stole* it." '

Older heads despaired of the Brats' fascination with movie lore. The newcomers, too young to have worked on the films they admired, saw old films not, as their makers did, in terms of personal experience, but as collections of themes, catchphrases, stylistic tricks. Recycling a gibe of Oscar Wilde, British critic Philip French accused them of knowing 'the credits of everything but the value of nothing'. John Gregory Dunne agreed.

It always struck me that of all the people who were at the Phillipses that summer, there were very few who actually work . . . the social and cultural mines. [They were] basically gadgeteers. More interested in *things* . . . People graduate from Michigan State or wherever, take their book bags, come here to film school, and have no other basis in life except the movies they've seen. That's why they're making movies about Superman and poltergeists, and about psychic phenomena . . . Their problem is that they have never *done* anything.

'You get the feeling,' wrote Pauline Kael in an influential review that did much to put Spielberg on the map, 'that the director grew up with TV and wheels (*My Mother the Car*?), and that he has a new temperament. Maybe Spielberg loves action and comedy and speed so much that he doesn't really care if the movie has nothing else in it.'

The model for *The Sugarland Express* was, inevitably, another movie. In 1951, Austrian-born Billy Wilder paid an acid tribute to the affection of his adoptive country for bread and circuses with *Ace in the Hole*. A reporter named Chuck Tatum, played by Kirk Douglas at his most misanthropic, happens on the story of a lifetime, a man trapped in a mine under a New Mexico mountain. Rescuers expect to dig him out in a day or two, but Tatum, spinning out the story, persuades them to sink a shaft from the top. A ghoulish carnival gathers around the stricken man, with the reporter as its arrogant ringmaster. Tatum becomes famous, but the man dies.

To nobody's surprise, least of all Wilder's, *Ace in the Hole* flopped. 'Americans expected a cocktail,' he said, unperturbed, 'and felt I was giving them a shot of vinegar instead.' But Spielberg never concealed its affinities with *The Sugarland Express*: 'I loved the *Ace in the Hole* similarity. I liked the idea of people rallying behind a media event, not knowing who the characters are or what they're about, but just supporting them because they are on an errand of mercy to get their baby back – and that sparks a good deal of good old American sentimentality.' It was a theme he would return to in *1941*: the power of the media to convince people of almost anything, and the readiness of those people not only to believe what they hear but to act on it, often catastrophically. *Sight and Sound* saw the connection between Wilder and the anarchic hymns to road violence to which *The Sugarland Express* superficially belonged by summing it up as '*Ace in the Hole* meets *Vanishing Point*'. Few people grasped that Spielberg, as he been on the side of the truck rather than the car in *Duel*, wasn't deploring mob rule in *Sugarland Express* but relishing it.

Once he started shooting, Spielberg had his hands full controlling his first major feature crew, and in particular Zsigmond, who had ambitions to direct and wasn't backward in suggesting how he would have planned a scene. These problems were exacerbated when Spielberg insisted on operating the camera himself for many sequences. Lighting cameramen traditionally work with an operator who runs the camera while they concentrate on placing lights and mapping out movements. Spielberg, however, still had the amateur's love of shooting, and would continue to handle the camera on many scenes throughout his career, to the irritation of directors of photography.

'Vilmos is a very interesting man,' Spielberg said diplomatically, 'And when you employ his great camera eye, you also get *gratis* his thoughts. He would offer ideas beyond the definition of the American cinematographer.' Arguments were common, but Spielberg won most of them. 'When a cameraman [has] free rein,' he said, 'he becomes the director and the director becomes the apprentice.' And he felt he'd gone through his apprenticeship at Universal already. However it was Zsigmond who persuaded him that the camera, rather than occupying the position of a detached directorial Eye of God, should always represent the point of view of a character. Thereafter, Spielberg's films became more concerned with people and a little less like cartoons.

'Several crew members said they'd never been on a happier location,' Goldie Hawn remarked. 'Four of them ended up marrying local girls from San Antonio, which was our base of operations. One was a waitress, another took reservations at the Holiday Inn. Hollywood meets Texas. It was a happy company.' Spielberg was unaffected, even amused by the nocturnal sighs and moans, which, characteristically, he noted in relation to a movie. 'Walking along the hall at one in the morning at those Holiday Inns sometimes sounds like Gyorgy Ligeti's *Atmospheres* from *2001*.' Sex helped alleviate the tensions of working in a district fed up with film units. Sam Peckinpah was shooting *The Getaway* in the area, and his piratical crew had looted CB radios from their hired police cars. As a result, Zanuck/Brown had to buy twenty-five junked black-and-whites at auction. After the shoot, Spielberg bought the Poplins' car, with dozens of bullet holes still visible where the special effects technicians had drilled them, and drove it for years.

In February, he had cause to be glad he turned down *White Lightning*. Scandal erupted on location for Reynolds's *The Man who Loved Cat Dancing*, shooting in Gila Bend, Arizona, with his one-time playmate Sarah Miles. Miles's 'personal assistant' David Whiting was found dead after a Quaalude overdose, and evidence at the inquest suggested he and Reynolds had been sharing Miles's bed. In different circumstances, it might have been Spielberg, not *Vanishing Point's* Richard Sarafian, who had to handle this production and public-relations nightmare.

In May 1973, just as shooting on *Sugarland* ended, literary agent Roberta Pryor delivered to Zanuck in the California office and to Brown in New York typescripts of a new novel by an unknown writer. Both men read it overnight. Richer producers, once they got around to looking at it, were ready to buy the book, but by then Zanuck and Brown, often telephoning from public phones and restaurants to disguise their interest in the property, had snatched Peter Benchley's *Jaws* for $175,000, with a further $75,000 for writing the first-draft screenplay, plus 10 per cent of net profits.

A few days later, Spielberg spotted the manuscript on Zanuck's desk and took it home for the weekend. After reading until late, he tried to sleep, but woke from disturbed dreams. At 3 a.m. he picked up the book again, gripped by the story of a monster ravaging an East Coast resort until killed by a coalition of the local police chief, an Ivy League scientist and an old shark-hunter.

By Sunday night, he knew he had to film *Jaws*. All his life he'd feared the sea and its creatures. When he bought a house at Malibu in the eighties, he had nightmares of the waves undermining the foundations, and dreamed of piling up sandbags to protect it. He felt personally

attacked by the shark, and wanted to strike back. This was reflex thinking, punch/counterpunch, the sort that video games sharpened. On Monday he walked into Zanuck and Brown's office and said, 'Let me direct
this film.'

'We've got a director,' Brown told him.

He was Dick Richards, a competent technician but, more importantly,
a client of Mike Medavoy, who also represented Benchley and had
attached Richards to the project at its inception.

'Well, if anything falls out,' Spielberg told Brown, 'I love this project.'

He didn't have long to wait. Two days later, Zanuck and Brown
lunched with Richards, Benchley and Medavoy. To Benchley's mounting
irritation, Richards kept referring to 'the whale'. Finally Benchley blew
his top; nobody who was unable to tell a shark from a whale was going
to film his book. Richards said he'd rather make Raymond Chandler's
Farewell My Lovely anyway, and the fragile coalition collapsed.

Four days after Spielberg expressed interest, Zanuck and Brown
offered him the film – and found, to their dismay, that he'd changed his
mind.

'I don't know,' he told Zanuck. 'After all, it's only a shark story.'
Wouldn't it be perceived as another *Duel*: Everyman v. The Beast? At
other times he compared it to just an inflated episode of *Sea Hunt*, the
popular 1950s TV scuba series with Lloyd Bridges.

He was also finding the UFO project 'Watch the Skies' both more interesting and more challenging.

When pressed, Spielberg always professed scepticism about UFOs.
He never mentioned his teenage UFO feature *Firelight*, nor the phenomenon seen by other members of his Scout troop in the Arizona desert.
Later he would claim to have been converted by the US government's
objections to him making 'Watch the Skies'. 'I really found my faith,' he
said, 'when I heard that the government was opposed to the film. If
NASA took the time to write me a twenty-page letter, then I knew there
must be something happening.'

What he really believed is unimportant. Not for the first time, he was adopting the beliefs of his audience, sensing what polls later made clear: that many Americans, without having particularly strong convictions, felt there 'might be something to' flying saucers. For a consensus film-maker, that was enough. Five years before John Naisbitt's *Megatrends* became *the* fashionable read, Spielberg and *Close Encounters of the Third Kind*, as 'Watch the Skies' was renamed, exemplified its propositions: that the best way to beguile America's slow-reacting public is not to be original but to spot a trend and exploit it; that such trends seldom emerge in Washington or New York but are more apparent in a few heartland states, and in California; and that Americans had lost interest in travelling to outer space. What they now wanted was for outer space to come to *them*.

It was for the ability to chart the *zeitgeist*, to articulate the mood of the crowd before they knew it themselves, and then to exploit it, that Spielberg most admired Orson Welles, whose radio version of *War of the Worlds* in 1938 convinced thousands that Martians had landed at Grover's Mill, New Jersey. Welles, he said, 'was not so much writing a radio program about Martians invading New Jersey as about America's fear of invasion from Europe. War was just a few months away, but Welles's invasion was not the Stuka, it was the Martian; it preyed on the vulnerability of the time.' Spielberg, both in this film and in *Jaws*, would do the same. For the record he repudiated Welles's broadcast, but later he bought the original script for the programme and displayed it under glass at his home.

In Schrader's script for what would become *Close Encounters*, VanOwen bargains with the Air Force. He'll keep quiet, providing they give him the money to keep investigating. They agree, and he spends his life searching, a counterpart of the protagonists in films which Schrader later directed or wrote: Yukio Mishima, Hank Williams, Patty Hearst, John Latour of *Light Sleeper* and, archetypally, Jesus in *The Last Temptation of Christ*, visionaries drawn to self-destruction as their only means of redemption. At the end of his life VanOwen finds the aliens and, as Schrader put it, is 'taken off the planet, like Elijah. He had fought the good fight and he was transcended.'

But Spielberg wasn't happy with this approach.

'Steve took violent objection,' Schrader says. 'He wanted the lead character of this drama to be an ordinary guy, a Joe Blow.'

'I refuse,' Schrader said, 'to send off to another world, as the first example of earth's intelligence, a man who wants to go and set up a McDonald's franchise.'

Spielberg said, 'That's *exactly* the guy I want to send.'

After a series of increasingly recriminatory meetings, Schrader abandoned the project.

Throughout his discussions with Schrader, Spielberg had kept his options open on *Jaws*. He even came into the Zanuck/Brown office and handed out T-shirts printed with Doubleday's inspired cover design of a phallic shark rising from an inky ocean towards a swimming girl. But in the long nights, he fretted that the narrative expired after the first hundred pages, and didn't revive until the last hundred. Where was the drive for which he'd been praised in the reviews of *Duel*?

'I don't want to make a film,' he explained to his eventual star Richard Dreyfuss. 'I want to make a *movie*.'

Increasingly he visualised *Jaws* in far simpler terms than Benchley, as 'an experiment in terror . . . the behemoth against Everyman . . . There is nothing subtle about *Jaws*. There are underpinnings that are subtle, but what it's about is pretty slam-bang.' He told journalist Monte Stettin, '*Jaws* isn't a big movie. It's a very small picture. It deals with one social issue [i.e.] There is no place in the world to stay unprotected. Which is what this film is all about.'

Benchley's story had a journalistic simplicity. The town of Amity, an East Coast summer resort based on Martha's Vineyard, is terrorised by a rogue Great White Shark which snaps up unwary bathers. The police chief, Brody, a newcomer from New York, bows to pressure from local businessmen to hush up the deaths, but when the shark begins taking children from the shallows and wrecking the boats sent out to hunt it, he finds his courage again and hunts down the fish. He's helped by Hooper, a wealthy shark expert, and Quint, a local eccentric who shows them the brutal techniques necessary to kill the giant. In their final confrontation, Quint and Hooper are killed, but the shark spares Brody, sinking back into the depths with the body of Quint in its jaws.

Writing in the shadow of Watergate, Benchley drew the people of Amity as products of Nixonian moral blight. Quint is a ruthless environmental despoiler. (In case we miss this, he baits a hook with the body of an unborn baby dolphin.) The town's Chief Selectman has sold out to the Mafia in a land deal. Brody frets about losing his job, while his wife Ellen itches for sex and attention, which Hooper, the conceited Ivy League ichthyologist, provides. Spielberg disliked them all. 'The only likeable character was the shark,' he said, 'who was a garbage-eating machine and ate all the trashy characters.' In particular, the Spielberg of the broken home, the one man in the house of women, found Hooper distasteful. He saw him as emasculating and cuckolding the sheriff, and making the sheriff as vainglorious as he was. Benchley, already writing the screenplay, didn't agree.

Zanuck and Brown were so depressed by these conflicts that they contemplated ditching *Jaws* entirely. During a meeting with Peter Gimbel, the documentary producer whose *Blue Water, White Death* had shown in graphic detail the dangers of filming sharks, Gimbel offered to direct the film, and Zanuck and Brown, in a moment of frustration, invited him to buy them out. Fortunately for the team, Gimbel declined.

The partners finally convened a make-or-break conference with Spielberg, to which they pointedly wore their *Jaws* T-shirts, a reminder of his earlier commitment. Sidney Sheinberg also urged him to make the film and, with 'Watch the Skies' still lacking a script, Spielberg accepted at last. His deal gave him, on top of his salary, a meagre 2.5 per cent of net profits, against Zanuck/Brown's 40 per cent and Benchley's 10 per cent. Almost in passing, the trade papers of 21 June 1973 announced that *Jaws* had a director.

Spielberg was unaware that he had enlisted for the duration. The bane of Zanuck and Brown's days at Fox had been Darryl Zanuck's veto, exercised in its most extreme form when he fired them. Going into business on their own, they had agreed privately never to reverse a firm decision. As Bob Woodward put it, 'Loyalty was their vice.' They even refused to give interviews separately. If one spoke to the press, the other was always present, even if only on a telephone line. Like an old married couple, they often finished one another's sentences.

Meanwhile, the board of an ailing Columbia, Hollywood's most underfunded and troubled studio, had installed, at the urging of the town's most reclusive and Machiavellian power broker, Ray Stark, a new president, David Begelman. The ex-agent, one of Hollywood's great gamblers, took over in the summer of 1973. Within three years, he would have turned Columbia's loss into a huge profit. Begelman's first act was to sign a number of old friends and clients to lucrative production deals. Michael and Julia Phillips were given a contract for two pictures, both written by Schrader: Scorsese's *Taxi Driver* and 'Watch the Skies'. With *Jaws* still lacking a script, Spielberg signed that deal too.

All summer, editing on *Sugarland* had continued. Satisfied with finishing only five days over its fifty-five-day schedule and near enough to the $2.5 million budget, Spielberg initially spoke warmly of the film. 'I guess if I had *Sugarland* to do over again, I wouldn't change anything,' he said at the time. But within a few years he all but disowned it as mechanistic and heartless, unconcerned with its characters.

Universal had promised that, if he had a release print before 10 September, the film could open on the November Thanksgiving weekend. Spielberg delivered, but from the moment the studio viewed the rough cut, they decided they had a loser. Richard Zanuck drove down to Palm Springs and showed it to his parents. Darryl didn't think much of it either. Nor did Goldie Hawn, who found it 'too serious, too unrelenting and too uptight'.

It contrasted starkly with their period comedy thriller *The Sting*, which had worked out far better than Zanuck and Brown had dared hope. After ousting scriptwriter David Ward as director, they replaced him with the bankable George Roy Hill, who had a deal at Universal but also, more important, inspired confidence in Robert Redford and Paul Newman, who starred as the two swindlers of gang boss Robert Shaw. Hill realised the film brilliantly. With its Depression setting, lovingly recreated on the Universal backlot, its ragtime score skimmed from Scott Joplin and the inspired joint performance of Redford and Newman, it exuded the heady perfume of a hit.

Rather than damage *The Sting*'s Christmas release, Zanuck persuaded Spielberg to withhold *Sugarland Express* until the following April. As their Universal deal guaranteed control of advertising, he argued that this would give them time for some intelligent promotion. Spielberg reluctantly agreed.

'Our early ads were our own,' said Zanuck. 'Spielberg himself shot one of them.' They featured the image of a road leading to an empty horizon which he would use again for *Close Encounters*. In the middle distance was a police car. In the foreground, scattered over the centre line, were broken glass, handcuffs, a policeman's Stetson, a handgun, a rifle and a teddy bear. The advertising copy was ambivalent: '*It's Not Every Day You Take a Ride Like This!*'

These ads barely survived the press and trade screenings in the first weeks of March. 'Our campaigns didn't work,' Zanuck admitted. 'We learned that any ad with a gun is anathema to the East Side public on Third Avenue in New York City. On Broadway, however, show lots of guns. We learned a great deal.'

Zanuck and Brown took *Sugarland*, and Spielberg, to Cannes. Benchley was also in Europe to promote his novel, so the four men met in a cabana at the Hôtel Cap d'Antibes to chew over Benchley's screenplay, which Spielberg was due to start shooting almost immediately. After Benchley left, the film-makers gloomily contemplated the chasm between their perception of *Jaws* and that of the writer. Spielberg was still in their suite when Freddie Fields called from Hollywood. Zanuck handed him the phone.

The agent was bubbling. Paul Newman had decided to star in another of Zanuck and Brown's projects, the Willard Huyck/Gloria Katz rum-running comedy *Lucky Lady*, and, after seeing *Sugarland*, wanted Spielberg to direct.

To Fields's astonishment, however, Spielberg refused. Newman, he said, was wrong for a farce like *Lucky Lady*. (It would be filmed, unsuccessfully, with Burt Reynolds and Gene Hackman.) Zanuck was impressed. 'He was twenty-four years old, and he turned down Paul Newman like he swatted a fly.' But Spielberg was not as cool as he looked. He left before the Cannes prize-winners were announced, and heard via his walkie-talkie on location with *Jaws* just before filming started that, in the pork-barrel parcelling-out of awards among various national power blocs, friends of the jury and darlings of the festival director which characterised Cannes, Barwood and Robbins had been honoured for Best Screenplay. 'Wasn't there anything for the director?' he asked plaintively.

In America, Universal opened *Sugarland* in four hundred cinemas. The reviews were excellent. Most critics discussed it in the same column as *Badlands*, usually to Spielberg's advantage. Pauline Kael praised the film's brashness and speed. Spielberg, she decided, could be the new Howard Hawks. She liked *Badlands* too but, to her, Malick seemed too intellectual, too detached, like the American cousin of Jean-Luc Godard. *Time* also preferred *Sugarland* to *Badlands*, which it found cerebral and uninvolving. The *Time* reviewer threw in a mini-bio of Spielberg, praising his 'natural sense of style, a Pop artist's eye for the ugly-beautiful architecture of plastic America, and a boundless boyish enthusiasm'. In the ultimate accolade, Billy Wilder said, 'The director of that movie is the greatest young talent to come along in years.' Somewhat ruefully, he added, '*I* was Steven Spielberg – once.'

But nobody came to see it. Spielberg was in Martha's Vineyard, lining up his first shot on *Jaws*, when he received the news of Universal's decision to take *Sugarland* off after a few weeks. 'That's quite a bomb to be dropped on the morning of your next film.'

He blamed Universal for the failure, and in particular its weak, changeable promotion. 'People thought it was Goldie Hawn's film, and thought it was small – you know, a real "teddy bear". Also there was the title. Most people thought it was a kid's film. When it opened in New York, there were lines of kids waiting outside the theatre expecting to see *Willy Wonka and the Chocolate Factory*.' He told the *Los Angeles Times*, 'The failure of *Sugarland* . . . was not due to the presentation of Goldie as an anti-*Laugh In* character but to the promotional campaign, timing, release pattern and appreciation of the film by the studio.'

'We were aghast,' Zanuck said of Spielberg's complaints. 'Maybe [the ads] weren't the best in the world, but they were ours.' After some hurried conferences, Universal tried to resuscitate the film by pushing the screwball angle. New ads were designed with a grinning Goldie in *Laugh-In* mode clutching a teddy bear, and new copy ('*A Girl With a Great Following. Six Hundred State Troopers on Her Tail and the Rest of the Country Cheering Her On*'), but these simply made Spielberg more angry. He offered to reshoot the ending and have both the Poplins survive, but Zanuck and Brown vetoed the idea. Not only would it be expensive; it would probably make no difference. Spielberg was desolate. 'I would have given away all those reviews for a bigger audience,' he admitted.

Sugarland was to have as rough a ride in Europe as it had in the United States. In Britain, it opened for a week in its complete form, but after generally negative public reaction CIC withdrew it, cut a few scenes, then re-released it as a double bill with, in an unintended irony, Billy Wilder's *The Front Page*. The main loss was the scene Spielberg regarded as the film's core. Hiding out from the pursuers on a used-car lot, Clovis and Lou-Jean take over a mobile home and for a moment recapture their lost domesticity. Through the windows they can see, but not hear, the film at a nearby drive-in cinema. It's showing a Road-Runner cartoon, with the agile bird effortlessly outwitting the hapless coyote who pursues him. Clovis knows the cartoons so well that he fills in the soundtrack for Lou Jean. As the Coyote plunges over the cliff, Spielberg superimposes a reflection of the cartoon in the windscreen over Clovis's face, a pre-sentiment of disaster. 'That was the moment in the film when I wanted the audience to prepare themselves,' said Spielberg, 'but because they cut that out, the film goes along like *Cactus Flower* and in the last few minutes it's the ending of *Bonnie and Clyde*, and that was a shame.'

The success of *The Sting* lost Joey Walsh his MGM deal on 'Slide', his screenplay about the two gamblers. Suddenly Metro wanted the film set in Las Vegas, in their Grand Hotel and Circus, and the buddy theme ditched for a Mafia 'sting' sub-plot with Dean Martin. 'Well, of course it was just too funny,' Walsh says. 'This story has nothing to do with outside pressures, it's all about the pressure within [the gamblers] themselves. I wanted the film to be almost a celebration of gambling, the joy of it, going along with it, and then, at the end, you could see where the trap comes in.'

Spielberg too bailed out. Walsh is sure that, had he persevered, 'Slide' would have been as big a box-office success as *The Sting*. 'Steven would have built that last scene, that gambling scene, into one gigantic orgasm, climaxing the last forty pages of the script until you were on the edge of your seat.' In 1975 'Slide' was filmed, with Walsh as producer and Robert Altman directing, as *California Split*, starring Elliott Gould and George Segal. It grossed a respectable $5 million. Spielberg saw it, more than once, and acknowledged that Altman and Walsh had made a remarkable film. 'I really saw how grudgingly he wanted to get that out,' Walsh said. 'Remember this was going to be Spielberg's picture, *the* picture. This was when he wasn't making much in pictures. This is the one that really got to him. Steven said to me, "It is good, but I would have made twenty-five, fifty million dollars with this picture."' The remark betrayed Spielberg's sense of destiny. Altman remained a maverick, financing each film only after years of haggling that took their toll of his health and reputation. For Zanuck and Brown, however, the $100 million films were obviously just a matter of time.

An unexpected dilemma faced Spielberg after *Sugarland Express*. He wanted, as Scott Fitzgerald had said, to be famous and to be loved, but never imagined he might have to make a choice between them. He was driven to emulate the popular film-makers he admired, like Victor Fleming, the archetypal Hollywood professional who'd directed *Captains Courageous* and his favourite war film *A Guy Named Joe*. That route offered the mass audience, rapt, dazed and adoring. He might well have echoed the ruthlessly ambitious young actress in *All About Eve*: 'If there's nothing else, there's applause. Like waves of love coming at you over the footlights. Just to know every night that so many people love you.'

But he also aspired to compete with Stanley Kubrick and David Lean, whose films appealed to a smaller and more discriminating audience. The choice would continue to trouble him for a decade. As late as 1984, Harrison Ford would define Indiana's goals in *Indiana Jones and the Temple of Doom* as 'fortune and glory', but hesitate between his twin personae, scholar/surrogate father and grave-robber/seducer. In 1975, Spielberg chose applause, fortune, grave-robbing and Zanuck/Brown. 'I want people to love my movies,' he admitted, 'and I'll be a whore to get them into the theatres.'

7

Jaws

Jaws is a disaster movie only if it doesn't make money. *Then* it's a disaster.

Steven Spielberg in the *New York Post*, 28 June 1975

IN TIME, Spielberg would apologise for *Jaws*. He confessed to a London audience in 1978 that it now seemed to him 'violent, nasty, crude. There was nothing in the picture that was personal to me. It was a calculated movie. I made each cut with glee, knowing the effect that it would have on the audience. I don't ever want to be involved in another picture like that.'

Yet he was driven to make it. With flower-power films discredited, the industry was re-endorsing mass entertainment: popcorn movies. *The Godfather* and *Cabaret* would sweep the 1972 Oscar nominations: films with strong stories, high production values, hummable tunes. *Jaws* was *the* picture for the time, and for Spielberg's career as well, and such was his sensitivity to the market, and to the combined opinions of his colleagues and friends, that he could no more avoid making it than the shark in Benchley's story could ignore the pale legs of summertime tourists dangling so tantalisingly from the ceiling of his world.

Spielberg's instincts did not fail him. He finished *Sugarland Express* as simply another young director riding – late – the wave of enthusiasm for young directors. *Jaws* transformed him into an unignorable force, admired by some in the industry, suspected and resented by others. Hollywood embraces a *wunderkind* but never quite trusts him, and the greatest enthusiasts are the first to plot his downfall. *Jaws* won audiences, grossing $260 million from the US domestic box office alone, but the Academy of Motion Picture Arts and Sciences, through which his peers voted each year's Academy Awards, would withhold an Oscar from Spielberg personally for twenty years.

Even as he struggled during the first months of 1974 to find a film in the manuscript of *Jaws*, Spielberg refined 'Watch the Skies', now called, after Hynek's phrase, *Close Encounters of the Third Kind*. In October 1973, Universal had announced that he would direct for them another Barwood and Robbins script, 'Clearwater', but after *Jaws* there could be no film but *Close Encounters*. And since he'd decided that the film would be an anthology of his enthusiasms, an affirmation of the popular culture that had got him through adolescence, he would write the script himself.

Jaws's publication in February 1974 came almost as an anti-climax. A few thousand sales would push a book onto California's best-seller list, so Spielberg, Zanuck, Brown and friends bought a hundred copies of the novel each. Most of these were sent, with a personal note, to opinion-makers and members of the chattering class. Restaurateurs were prime targets; the team printed up a special poster for restaurants. By 7 p.m. on the first day, *Jaws* was the state's most successful book, though it needed no help nationwide. Within weeks, paperback rights went to Bantam for $575,000 and *Jaws* was climbing towards an eventual 9.5 million sales in the US alone.

The book's enormous success surprised the publishing world, as best-sellers usually do. Though the son of one novelist, Nathaniel Benchley, and the grandson of *New Yorker* humorist and occasional character actor Robert Benchley, Peter Benchley himself, who'd worked desultorily as a journalist, possessed the family talent in diluted form at best. Doubleday had optioned his four-page outline for $1000, part of a total advance of $7500, but his first drafts made them wonder if they'd wasted their money.

Benchley himself, unconvinced a shark hunt alone could carry the novel, piled on sub-plots. Spielberg complained that the book had a little *Peyton Place*, a little *Godfather*, a little *Enemy of the People*, and plenty of *Moby-Dick*. Amity's postmistress warns that the shark is a divine force, like Melville's white whale, and undestroyable, a view Benchley endorses when, after killing both Hooper and Quint and sinking their boat, the fish ignores Brody and retreats into the depths, 'an apparition evanescing into darkness'. Quint's corpse, like Ahab's, goes with it, arms wide, head back, 'mouth open in mute protest'. Later Spielberg would say, '[eventual scriptwriter] Carl Gottlieb and I have spent a lot of time taking out the similarities between Melville and Gottlieb, Melville and Benchley.'

Over the next few months, Benchley delivered three screenplays, none of which the producers or Spielberg liked, and, following his meeting with the trio at Cannes, left for Bermuda to write his new novel, *The Deep*. Spielberg fretted, confessing later that he tried to get off the film three times. Zanuck and Brown were equally restive. Not only did they lack both director and script, but, as the culmination of a long-running dispute with producers over TV income, the Screen Actors' Guild was threatening to strike from 28 June 1974. No studio was funding anything that ended after that date.

Even without a script, the production rolled on, a juggernaut that had acquired a life of its own. *Sugarland Express* grossed only $3 million on its first run, so Zanuck and Brown budgeted *Jaws* at $2.5 million – a spectacular miscalculation. The same year, Fox spent $2.8 million on Mel Brooks's *Young Frankenstein*, shot almost entirely on sets, without stars and in black and white. A more realistic comparison would have been *The Poseidon Adventure* ($5 million) or *Earthquake* ($7 million), but at first everyone envisaged a small film without more than basic mechanical or optical effects.

Spielberg hoped to keep as many as possible of his *Sugarland* family for *Jaws*. Designer Joe Alves, production manager Bill Gilmore and casting director Shari Rhodes all came on board the leaky ship. Zsigmond wasn't available, so Spielberg hired cameraman Bill Butler, from *Something Evil* and *Savage*. He also wanted the same editor, Verna Fields. Not only was she now Hollywood's hottest cutter; as an inner member of Ned Tanen's *kaffe klatsch*, she would be a useful buffer against his interference. She'd been set to edit Peter Bogdanovich's *At Long Last Love*, a grandiose attempt to revive the thirties musical. Rather than having his stars mime their songs to playback, Bogdanovich planned to record them live and on location, an interesting challenge for an editor. He still didn't have a cast, however, and, with the strike looming, Fields chose *Jaws*, bringing her son Ric with her as Spielberg's gofer and trainee. Bogdanovich was so furious that he burst into tears, but she chose wisely; *At Long Last Love* bombed comprehensively.

But *Jaws*'s most pressing need remained a script. One of Zanuck's unfulfilled projects at Fox had been Howard Sackler's play *The Great White Hope*, about black boxer Jack Johnson. Sackler, he remembered, was a keen scuba diver, and happened to be in town, kicking his heels while Peter Bogdanovich made up his mind about a screenplay he'd commissioned. Sackler agreed to spend four weeks in the Bel Air Hotel rewriting *Jaws*. Spielberg, who looked over his shoulder and made suggestions, credits the playwright, who worked on the understanding that he would remain anonymous, with most of the episodes that differ from the book.

Joe Alves, after cruising the east coast for locations, chose Edgartown on Martha's Vineyard. Not only was the island community unspoiled compared to Cape Cod and Hyannisport; with only a three-foot tide, but plenty of deep water just offshore, the unit could shoot at all times of day. From the start, Spielberg was adamant that nothing would be shot in the studio tank. This mustn't look like Irwin Allen's 1960s TV series *Voyage to the Bottom of the Sea*, all crystal water and pretty ripple patterns. But how to corral the shark, if not in a tank? Though everyone agreed that the Great White wasn't tameable, and none had lived in captivity more than a few hours, they hypothesised that a specimen might conceivably be trapped and brought into American waters . . .

'Sure, yeah,' Spielberg laughed as he recalled this proposal. 'They'd train a Great White, put it in front of the camera, with me in a cage.'

Australian documentary film-maker Ron Taylor and his wife and partner Valerie, who knew *Carcharodon Carcharias* intimately, became celebrities after their close encounters with these monsters were featured in Peter Gimbel's 1971 documentary about the Great White, *Blue Water, White Death*. Gilmore hired them to shoot shark footage off the Great Barrier Reef. But they were adamant about not promising a twenty-five-foot specimen. Despite anecdotal evidence of Whites almost twice that long, none had ever been filmed.

Reluctantly, Zanuck and Spielberg accepted the idea of a mechanical shark. But what about the moment when Hooper is attacked while dangling below the boat in a steel cage? Surely that demanded the real thing.

Zanuck came up with the solution. 'Why don't we make a miniature cage and put a midget in it?'

Spielberg was impressed. 'From a *producer*, that's a wonderful idea.'

Two small cages were made, one for the stunt man and the other for the camera. The narrower gauge of the bars, however, meant that full-strength steel couldn't be used.

'I had a casting session for short people,' says Spielberg. 'I saw about ten, but they were mostly dwarves calling themselves midgets. I'd just about decided to forget the idea when there was a knock on my door, and in walks a short person covered in blood. He's bleeding from his ear. A cut on his forehead. His nose is bleeding. His shirt is all stained and he's dripping on the carpet.

'And he says, "I had a wreck just outside the gate. The police are towing my car away right now, but I didn't want to miss our appointment."'

The man was Carl Rizzo. At four foot nine he was the perfect size and, he swore, an expert scuba diver who 'had spent his life in the water with sharks'. Spielberg was impressed. 'Anyone who would come into my office in that condition, wanting the job that badly, he could go into the water with the Great White Shark. The man was fearless!'

Rizzo and second-unit director Rodney Fox arrived on the Great Barrier Reef to work with the Taylors. They carried storyboards and sketches – and, just in case, a dummy of Richard Dreyfuss in a wetsuit.

The Taylors, towing a skiff with the steel cages, sailed out to Dangerous Reef, dangled some well-rotted horse shanks overboard and began cruising, with Fox filming on 16mm and Rizzo in his wetsuit sitting on the transom with a cup of coffee, awaiting his big moment.

It came, unexpectedly, when a Great White surfaced near the skiff, grabbed one of the cages in its jaws and dragged it into the water. Rizzo immediately got up, went into the cabin of the boat and locked himself in the lavatory. When Fox tried to trip the door catch with a butter knife, Rizzo held it shut. Valerie Taylor finally persuaded him to come out with promises that the camera cage would stay close enough for them to fend off the shark if it came too near, but as Rizzo climbed into the cage he confessed to Fox, 'I lied to Mr Spielberg. I've never worn scuba gear in my life.'

Shooting was scrubbed for that day, and for the rest of the week the few sharks that approached refused to attack the cage. One did show signs of returning each day for a free meal, but local abalone fishermen decided the Taylors' lavish 'chumming' was making the area too dangerous, and the shark turned up dead one morning, tied to their boat. Fox shot some scenes with the dummy standing in for Dreyfuss (and Rizzo), and came home.

Joe Alves completed his sketches for an artificial shark and started looking for someone to build it. At Spielberg's suggestion he hired Bob Mattey, who engineered the giant squid that attacked the *Nautilus* in Disney's 1954 *20,000 Leagues Under the Sea*. Mattey came out of retirement to meet this unique personal challenge. *Jaws*'s budget inched up to $3.1 million. Spielberg tried to reassure Zanuck. The film, he said, would make ten times that.

'Steve,' Zanuck told him morosely, 'if that happens, it will be a real disappointment. The expectation is so high, people have been waiting for this movie since the book. They're anticipating it to be even better than they expected. If it's no better than they expected and the film only makes $31 million, there's going to be a cry of disappointment from the financial people.'

The crew desperately needed a list of sequences to start planning shooting, but Sackler's script remained only halfway satisfactory. In March, Spielberg also sent the script to Carl Gottlieb, whom he wanted to play Meadows, editor of the Amity *Leader*. The chubby writer, then script editor of ABC-TV's *The Odd Couple*, accepted. Figuring he had nothing to lose, since he'd been hired to act, not write, Gottlieb, with six screenplays – unproduced – under his belt, returned the script with three pages of comments.

Spielberg still hated casting, but his choices on *Jaws* were shrewd.

The producers wanted Charlton Heston as Brody, but couldn't afford him. In any event, Chuck was just finishing *Earthquake* and getting ready to play *Macbeth* on stage in Los Angeles opposite Vanessa Redgrave. Even if he had been free, Spielberg would have resisted. He had scant respect for stars; their inflated salaries offended his prudent nature. Actors in general, Spielberg feels, enjoy an exaggerated importance. 'I like people who bring very little baggage,' he said of his casting philosophy in the seventies. 'It's very hard when you have an icon playing an ordinary person. My main drive since I began was not to use people who were on the cover of *Rolling Stone*.' While he lavished millions on Douglas Trumbull's special effects for *Close Encounters*, he resisted giving more than union scale to performers. For the next twenty years, actors would complain that Spielberg paid as little as the law and the unions permitted. 'No one crafts better deals for himself than Spielberg,' the *Los Angeles Times* quoted a prominent agent as saying, 'often at the expense of the talent he hires.'

The first role cast was Brody. Spielberg initially favoured Robert Duvall for the police chief, but decided on Roy Scheider. He'd attracted attention with his mask-like face and trademark broken nose as a tough cop in *The French Connection* and *The Seven Ups*, but even after that, offers had been so thin he'd made two films in France. Spielberg played against his tough-guy image, which Scheider, who prided himself on his 'legit' New York credentials in Shakespeare for Joseph Papp, was pleased to abandon. They refined his transplanted New York cop into the most Fordian of the film's characters, a man who keeps quiet and hides his anger until it serves some purpose to unleash it.

Hooper was harder to cast. Timothy Bottoms or Jeff Bridges, both hot after Peter Bogdanovich's *The Last Picture Show*, were pencilled in. Diminutive *Cabaret* singer/dancer Joel Grey put in his bid too. But after briefly favouring Jon Voight, Spielberg urged Zanuck and Brown to troll the shoals of hungry wannabees, has-beens and never-was's whose agents were burning up the phones.

Of these, Richard Dreyfuss was typical. Notoriously hard to handle, he'd ducked the draft in 1972, pleading grounds of conscience, and instead worked as an orderly in the LA County Hospital, which he left with a ferocious amphetamine habit. Since *American Graffiti*, his career hadn't ignited, though he'd just made *The Apprenticeship of Duddy Kravitz* in Canada, playing a young man on the make, and had hopes that this would be his breakthrough.

Spielberg offered him Hooper. Dreyfuss said he was too busy; in fact he found the role 'meaningless'. Spielberg insisted. What had he to lose? *Jaws* would take only two months to shoot.

'More like six,' snapped Dreyfuss. 'The shark won't work, and you'll have nothing but grief.'

Dreyfuss left for the Montreal opening of *Duddy Kravitz* – and was horrified by his performance. 'I thought I was awful and that I would never work again.' When Spielberg offered him *Jaws* once more, Dreyfuss asked for some character changes. 'Sure,' Spielberg said. So Dreyfuss signed, 'out of desperation', he said, and for much less than the $200,000 that would have been paid even a minor Hollywood name. His casting was announced on 30 April. Ironically, *Duddy Kravitz* opened shortly after and was an instant success, which did nothing to improve Dreyfuss's temper as he faced weeks of work in the icy waters off Cape Cod.

Dreyfuss would be pivotal to the success of *Jaws*. For all his tearaway private life, he embodied the integrity Spielberg admired in Hollywood's old-time stars, in particular Spencer Tracy. Perhaps because Tracy too had been an addictive personality. Spielberg found that Dreyfuss fitted those clothes. 'He's as close an actor to Tracy as exists today,' he says. 'Most of us are like Richard Dreyfuss . . . My central protagonist has always been – and probably always will be – Mr Everyday Regular Fella.'

Increasingly he was visualising *Jaws* as a Spencer Tracy film for our time. His nearest parallel was *Captains Courageous*. Spielberg also confided to Dreyfuss his ambition to remake Tracy's 1943 fantasy, also directed by Victor Fleming, *A Guy Named Joe*. Dreyfuss told him, 'If you cast anyone else in the part of Pete, I'll kill you.' Spielberg relieved him of the necessity for homicide by giving him the role when he made *Always* in 1989. Benchley had written Hooper as self-assured, seductive, professional, the hired gun who ambles into town and takes on the menace, only to be destroyed himself. Dreyfuss makes him an extension of the intellectual Curt in *American Graffiti*, untidy, clumsy, shorter than

Spielberg directing Joan Crawford in the *Eyes* episode of *Night Gallery*.

Universal Studios and the black tower about the time Spielberg first came to work there in 1967.

Below left: Verna Fields, the editor credited with either saving or stealing *Jaws* (1975).

Right: Producers David Brown and Richard Zanuck at the time of *Jaws.*

Below: The giant white shark claims another victim.

Left: Spielberg, Roy Scheider, Richard Zanuck and David Brown contemplate imminent disaster on location for *Jaws.*

Right: Spielberg with the tiger shark flown in from Florida to give colour to the film.

Dr J. Allen Hynek, UFOlogist and inspiration for *Close Encounters of the Third Kind* (1977).

Spielberg adopts Indiana Jones mode for the shooting of *Close Encounters*.

Producer Julia Phillips at the time of *Close Encounters*.

Bombay, February 1977. Trying to get thousands of extras to point into the air at the same moment and chant the song of the alien ships resulted in a nightmare shoot on *Close Encounters of the Third Kind*.

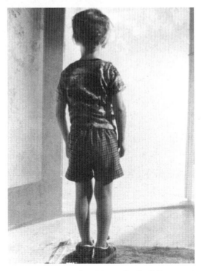

Young Barry Guiler (Cary Guffey) faces the 'God Light' of the aliens.

Spielberg and François Truffaut, who played Claude Lacombe, compete to direct *Close Encounters*.

John Belushi as Wild Bill Kelso in *1941* (1979).

Below: No amount of extravagant advertising could make *1941* a hit.

Director Steven Spielberg... he thrilled you with "JAWS"... he astounded you in "CLOSE ENCOUNTERS OF THE THIRD KIND"... and now he does it again...

IT'S MAD, MAD, MAD!

COLUMBIA PICTURES and UNIVERSAL PICTURES Present An A-Team Production of A STEVEN SPIELBERG FILM

Starring DAN AYKROYD NED BEATTY JOHN BELUSHI LORRAINE GARY MURRAY HAMILTON CHRISTOPHER LEE TIM MATHESON TOSHIRO MIFUNE WARREN OATES
ROBERT STACK TREAT WILLIAMS Director of Photography WILLIAM A. FRAKER A.S.C. Screenplay by ROBERT ZEMECKIS & BOB GALE Story by ROBERT ZEMECKIS & BOB GALE AND JOHN MILI
Music by JOHN WILLIAMS Produced by BUZZ FEITSHANS Executive Producer JOHN MILIUS Directed by STEVEN SPIELBERG

almost everyone else, but a winner just the same; another clone of Spielberg's idealised high-school self.

Also unlike Benchley's Hooper, Dreyfuss is Jewish, and 'immensely proud of being [so]', says the actor. 'I was raised in Bayside, which is 90 per cent Jewish. I went every week to Temple Emanuel from the time I was nine until I was sixteen . . . In a sense, everything I do has to do with my being Jewish.' Spielberg didn't overtly play the ethnic card in *Jaws* or in *Close Encounters*, but in both films it was his ace in the hole, a covert suggestion that the characters don't belong, but a promise too that they may, like Spielberg, prove canny and resourceful when the chips are down.

As usual, smaller roles became playthings of the producers. Having used Richard Zanuck and Linda Harrison's son Harrison as the child in *Sugarland Express*, Spielberg wasn't surprised when Zanuck requested the role of Ellen Brody for Linda.

'Sorry, Dick,' Spielberg said, 'you're a little late. I already had to give the part to Lorraine Gary.'

Casting Gary, Sid Sheinberg's wife, cemented that useful corporate relationship. But, blonde and rangy, with long experience in TV movies, Gary was also a better choice than the glamorous Harrison would have been. She would project Spielberg's preferred image of Ellen as loyal and quietly supportive. In fact, he wanted everyone in the film to be likeable, even Quint.

In the case of the eccentric, ill-tempered shark-hunter who shows Brody and Hooper how to kill the monster and is himself killed by it, this was a tall order. Howard Sackler had, however, made an important contribution towards it. In Florida, he'd heard stories about the torpedoing of the USS *Indianapolis* as it returned from delivering to the USAF on the island of Tinian the atomic bomb that would be dropped on Hiroshima. The ship sank in twelve minutes, and 1100 men went into the water, but, because of secrecy, nobody reached the survivors for days, by which time sharks had devoured many of them.

The incident fired Spielberg's imagination. He went over to John

Milius's house and told him about it. Immersed in *Dillinger*, his first film as director, Milius had been too busy to script *Jaws*, but the *Indianapolis* story was the sort of giant myth he thrived on. Milius skimmed the research material and, in fifteen minutes, wrote a nine-minute monologue in which Quint recalls the sinking and the sharks.

Milius, Spielberg sensed, really wanted to play Quint himself. Instead they offered the role to Sterling Hayden. Sailing round the world had weathered the star of Huston's *The Asphalt Jungle* and Kubrick's *The Killing*, while years of exile because of tax problems and his decision to inform on old friends to the House un-American Activities Committee had ground in the necessary cynicism. Hayden lived in Paris on a barge, writing and occasionally acting. Zanuck and Brown negotiated with him for months, but tax liens against him ensured the IRS would seize anything he earned in the US.

In April, *The Sting* won Oscars for Best Picture and Best Director. Robert Shaw's performance as the gangster Lonigan had done much to make the film a hit. David Brown suggested offering him Quint, and a copy of the novel was sent to him at the Volnay in New York where he was living while he played in Strindberg's *The Dance of Death*.

Even for Quint, the hard-drinking, argumentative Irishman was coarse-grained. As Dirk Bogarde sneered, Shaw 'only does two things really well . . . shout above rain and wind and stand with his legs apart'. Spielberg agreed, until he saw him in William Friedkin's film of Harold Pinter's *The Birthday Party*. Under control, that intensity made a powerful impression.

Shaw, a novelist himself, decided that *Jaws* was 'a story written by a committee . . . a piece of shit'. Still, his wife Mary Ure urged him to take the part, so he told Zanuck and Brown he'd read the script when it was finished, then left for Ireland. He'd been offered Trevor Howard's role in the remake of *Brief Encounter* opposite Sophia Loren – a romantic lead, after playing scores of henchmen and heavies. But producer Lew Grade offered only $50,000. They were still haggling in early May when the *Jaws* script arrived with an offer of $100,000 for four weeks' work.

By now, the story had been radically restructured. Gone were the Mafia and the Hooper/Ellen affair. Instead of a cuckold seething with resentment, Brody was a man of principle who, after bowing to political pressure and playing down the first shark death, digs in his heels and is vindicated. Hooper became a beady-eyed obsessive, too interested in sharks to bother with sex. If there was an affair, it was between him and Brody, who found friendship as they spent Act Two chasing red herrings and zeroing in on the shark. Even Quint became a gruff good guy, his vendetta against sharks justified in a soliloquy about surviving the sinking of the *Indianapolis*. With Spielberg's approval, Shaw would condense Milius's nine pages into a moving confession of hatred and guilt. The three men bond into a team by getting drunk and harmonising in a song – potent emblems of union in John Ford's films. And in the final, most audacious alteration, Brody kills the shark, exploding an air tank in its jaws.

A veteran of all-star casts, Shaw assessed the competition and decided he could steal the film from Dreyfuss and Scheider. He accepted, provided he could be done before *Brief Encounter*'s 8 July start. He still had fifty-five working days in the US before exceeding the crucial 183 days, after which his worldwide income for the year would be subject to US tax. Zanuck and Brown assured him they'd begin on 28 May and finish no later than 25 June, with a Christmas 1974 release. Fortunately for those who admired the Noël Coward/David Lean original, he never played in *Brief Encounter*. Richard Burton got that thankless job, while Shaw worked on *Jaws* for 16½ weeks.

Shaw's window of opportunity wasn't the only pressure on Zanuck and Brown. *Jaws* cried out to be shot in August, at the height of the holiday season. Instead, because of the threatened Screen Actors' strike, it would have to be finished while the water was still cold and the weather variable.

While Edgartown rubbed its hands at the thought of a film unit in residence, Spielberg sequestered himself in a house overlooking the ocean, which he papered with thousands of storyboard drawings; four hundred for the final sequence alone. For company he had Ric Fields, his spaniels Elmer and Zalman, a local cook/housekeeper, and Carl Gottlieb, who metamorphosed into *Jaws*'s third and final screenwriter.

Arriving to play Meadows, Gottlieb was astonished to be asked by Spielberg to rewrite the script. A week's dialogue polish stretched into seven weeks' work. Strategically, using Gottlieb was shrewd. Benchley, Sackler or any other writer would be looking out for themselves or for Zanuck and Brown. Gottlieb, however, Spielberg could trust and influence: he was a patriot for *him*.

Six days a week, Spielberg was up at 6 a.m. with a cup of tea, memorising the day's pages – he never, on this or any later film, took a script onto the set, though he was seldom far from his storyboards – before setting out in the shivering dawn to chivvy four hundred extras into pretending it was July. Days were spent bobbing on the SS *Scup Bucket* or the SS *Garage Sale*, ungainly floats which acted as camera platforms and support vessels for the *Orca*, Quint's forty-two-foot boat, and its fibreglass replica, *Orca II*, which the shark would sink at the climax. To the unpaid technical advisers who lounged around Edgartown dock, *Orca*, built on the hull of a scallop boat, looked top-heavy. There was too much glass. It would never survive a storm. Crews gritted their teeth at their remarks and worked on.

After dinner each night, Spielberg, Gottlieb, Verna Fields and the stars rewrote the script over the dirty plates, improvising dialogue into a tape recorder. The actors left early, and by 10 p.m. Spielberg too was nodding. Gottlieb typed up the next day's lines until midnight, to be printed and distributed by morning. Locals got used to a harassed writer sticking a tousled head out the door and yelling at a passer-by, 'What sort of fish would kids catch around here?' Throughout the day, as Fields edited the film in her improvised cutting room, she stayed in touch with Spielberg via walkie-talkie, pedalling down to the dock on her bike if he had specific queries.

Spielberg's later remark that *Jaws* was made up as they went along overstates the case, but it is true that hurried fixes characterised the writing. Hal Barwood and Matthew Robbins made uncredited improvements. Briefly worried that the film lacked humour, Spielberg cast around for someone to write a few comedy scenes. John Landis, who'd won brief fame by directing and starring in *Schlock*, a $60,000 send-up of horror films, was surprised and delighted to be summoned to Martha's Vineyard.

He flew in, only to leave a few hours later. Though he and Spielberg shared obsessions, Landis's ambition was too naked, his personal style too hectic. Judith Belushi said he reminded her of a cartoon character who never spoke without an exclamation mark at the end of every sentence. Spielberg decided that making *Jaws* was hard enough without such a loose cannon on the team.

Roy Scheider's role expanded as Spielberg, not for the last time on his films, enlarged the character most resembling his father. For the second shark attack of the film, in which a dog and a boy on a rubber float are taken, he underlined the sheriff's shock by imitating a famous shot from Hitchcock's *Vertigo*, tracking back quickly from Scheider's face but zooming in at the same time, from 250mm to 30mm, so that the framing doesn't change but the face stretches and flattens in an almost physical assault. He also wrote in a new scene where Brody, agonising at the dinner table, smiles wearily as he sees his young son imitating every worried gesture.

In this process, Lorraine Gary's character shrank, to her irritation. She all but disappeared from the completed film. Even Gottlieb's role was pared. 'I had the schizophrenic sensation,' he said, 'of having to write myself out of a scene.'

Benchley too was less in evidence as the film progressed. While he and Gottlieb shared script credit, they never physically worked together. Convinced his book had been traduced by the replacement of its sex and corruption sub-plots with, as he saw it, formula situations and action, Benchley complained to the *Los Angeles Times*:

Spielberg needs to work on character. He knows, flatly, zero. Consider. He is a twenty-six-year-old who grew up with movies. He has no knowledge of reality but the movies. He is B-movie literate. When he must make decisions about the small ways people behave, he reaches for movie clichés of the forties and fifties . . . One day, Spielberg will be known as the greatest second-unit director in America.

Benchley did, however, agree to play a cameo as a TV reporter stepping gingerly over sunbathers as he covers Amity's ill-fated 4 July. For his part, Spielberg put an arrogant 'Major Benchley' into *Close Encounters* as the Air Force's mouthpiece who tries to bluff UFO believers into recanting.

The budget hit $3.5 million and kept climbing. Zanuck and Brown fumed at the cost, much of which was avoidable. On *Sugarland Express*, they had been able to negotiate with the Chicago office of various unions to waive their strict staff requirements, but the New York and Boston locals of the technicians' union, IATSE, were less helpful. There were seldom less than a hundred crew-members on the beach locations, only half of them needed. Paul F. Connors, IATSE's Boston business agent (who happened to be seeking re-election), raided the location and found twenty-three non-union locals working on the production. He demanded union replacements.

The union also dictated a sit-down hot lunch for everyone, while the Teamsters insisted every performer and crew-member check in at Transportation and be bussed to work, even when they lived five minutes from the location. 'If I see you getting into someone's car,' one driver growled at an actor, 'I'll close down this production.' Spielberg still had his bullet-riddled Texas Highway Patrol black-and-white, but for 5½ months he, like the rest of the cast and crew, walked, biked or was driven.

Union feather-bedding wasn't the only added expense. Film was flown to California for processing, so Spielberg didn't see his rushes for forty-eight hours. Nor were the locals grateful for the influx of money. Hotel rooms soared from $14 a night to $45. It was $60 cheaper to fly wetsuits from Los Angeles than to buy them locally. The production spent $30,000 a day on the island, but still the authorities demanded $100,000 bonds to restore sites, with a $1000 penalty for every day a new building like Quint's barn-like boathouse remained standing. Such greed would rebound later in the decade when a swelling number of big productions, including most of Spielberg's, based themselves in London.

Shooting should have finished by 1 July, leaving clear the 4 July weekend, traditionally the moment when the Gulf Stream changes course, bringing warm water to Cape Cod and with it the rich annual tourist harvest. By 6 June, however, work was at a crawl and the schedule fourteen days behind. The crew were uniformly hostile, but forced to stay by Universal's seniority system, under which they risked heavy penalties if they walked off a project. 'If they could have quit,' said Spielberg, 'I'd have lost forty of them the first week.'

While Spielberg was preparing *Jaws*, veteran director Henry Hathaway had told him, 'I'll give you some advice, kid. Make sure the crew and the cast believe in what you're doing, even if you don't *know* what you're doing.' It became harder and harder to keep up an appearance of Olympian confidence. One local glimpsed Spielberg scampering by in the dawn, muttering hysterically, 'The director doesn't know what he's *do*-ing!' The problem was not the actors but the shark. *Jaws* was Spielberg's introduction to a problem faced by all directors of special-effects movies. Shooting *Gremlins* in 1984, Joe Dante contrasted it with his 1980 film *The Howling*, which took twenty-eight days to shoot: *Gremlins* took twenty-six weeks.

We shot the material with the actors, then had a little break, then tooled up to do the Gremlin effects. Weeks and *weeks* of Gremlin effects. Some of it was torture. You have to fool around with camera speeds; fool around with angles. You shoot reams of footage. And after you've watched the eightieth take of this Gremlin smiling and moving his eyes, you can't tell any more. This is better? This is worse?

Increasingly, producers would separate live action from effects, sending the actors home after the former. On *Jaws*, however, it had been assumed – wrongly – that everything could be done at once.

While the crew bobbed offshore, wrestling with the shark, Shaw ducked into Canada or Bermuda to cut down his time in the US, offering everyone a welcome relief from his ill-temper and interference. Murray Hamilton, who played the Chief Selectman, fretted about the roles he was losing, and Lorraine Gary sulked over her vanishing lines. Roy Scheider threw tantrums.

Nobody had taken into consideration that Martha's Vineyard is the home of every big yacht and sailboat on the eastern seaboard. So on the horizon line, the regattas were going constantly. In the climactic scene . . . we're supposed to be in a boat at sea miles offshore and totally alone. And there are all these damn boats all over the place. First, we tried to shoot in between the sailboats. That didn't work. Then we tried getting up at 5 a.m. to get out there before the yachts did. That didn't work either. Finally, we decided we'd simply have to reshoot when the regatta season was over.

Richard Dreyfuss, convinced his one chance at major stardom was leaking away as he wasted time on a guaranteed loser, consoled himself with serial partying. From time to time, he paused to criticise Spielberg and the production in the media. 'What comes out of Steven unconsciously,' said the actor, 'is that he's a big kid who at twelve years old decided to make movies, and he's still twelve years old – he's focused every one of his powers and capabilities on making movies and blocked everything else in the world out of his personality.'

Spielberg put the best face on it, remarking, 'We all complained on location . . . I took it out on everyone involved with the filming, while Dreyfuss had access to the media.' Ironically his star's speed-freak vitality proved crucial to the morale of the unit. Using a metaphor he once applied to his mother, Spielberg called him 'a major energy input. Everyone plugs into Dreyfuss to wake up in the morning. We stretch our umbilicals over to him and join navels. I guess you would call the phenomenon Rickymania . . . he's like a hydroelectric plant.'

Spielberg felt able to confide in Dreyfuss to an extent he couldn't with other people in the crew. One night towards the end of shooting he kept the actor up until dawn outlining, scene by scene, other ways in which he might have shot *Jaws*. He could have done it as a Hitchcock pastiche, like Brian De Palma, or as a dynastic saga, like Coppola, or as a Bergmanesque morality tale where the shark represented God. Dreyfuss was stunned. Invention on this protean level seemed less a gift than a burden.

*　　*　　*

Mattey's polyurethane shark, nicknamed 'Bruce', was built on a steel armature, which perched on a twelve-foot steel tower that rested in turn on an underwater sled. Three copies were made. Each weighed 1.5 tonnes and cost $150,000 to build, and at least an equal sum to operate. A crew of thirteen was needed to control it. When the sled was towed, the shark moved realistically along the surface. Or should have. In practice, the eyes crossed and the jaws, which gushed blood as they bit, wouldn't close. Meticulously, Mattey refined the mechanism, but he wasn't a man to be hurried. 'Ask him what time it is,' Spielberg sighed, 'and he'll tell you how to build a watch.'

Tides and currents tore the creature apart if you fought them. Because of dents, scrapes, barnacles and the corrosive effects of salt water, 'Bruce' had to be scrubbed down, repaired, dried with hair dryers and repainted each night. Tanks sprang leaks, motors burned out, tools and equipment were stolen. After a storm stopped shooting for days, Gilmore contemplated moving to a cheaper and safer location – the Caribbean perhaps; even Indonesia.

By 17 July, only ninety-six shots had been filmed. The old budget and schedule were memories. *Jaws* now looked like taking four times as long as planned and costing three times as much. Gilmore and Spielberg often weren't speaking. The culminating disaster came on 30 July, with scenes of the *Orca* sinking. The boat had been built with large eye-bolts at each corner, allowing it to be anchored in any position or dragged by underwater cables to simulate the power of the shark. However, while Spielberg was filming a shot of Scheider inside the cabin, a chunk of planking as big as a table-top ripped loose. Two Arriflex cameras went over the side, a minor loss compared with that of the film, which was salvaged. Ric Fields caught the next New York shuttle, hand-carrying the precious thousand-foot magazines of exposed film in a bucket of fresh water. Eastman's labs saved everything.

Celebrity tourists, the kind who couldn't simply be turned away, were a constant irritant. TV newsman Walter Cronkite, a keen yachtsman, cast an eye over the production. So did actress Ruth Gordon, as well as

novelist Thornton Wilder and veteran *New York Times* reporter Scotty
Reston, both of whom had houses on the island. John Milius dropped
by. Spielberg left him playing with 'Bruce's' biting mechanism while he
got on with shooting. Michael and Julia Phillips made three or four visits,
each time pressing Spielberg on *Close Encounters*. He told them he still
wasn't happy with the script. He also worried about the obvious and
growing rift between the couple. If they split, which one would inherit
the project?

Zanuck and Brown were likewise in a state of nerves, exacerbated by
the open secret that *Jaws* was in trouble. 'Everywhere we went,' said
Brown, 'people treated us with sympathy, like we had some kind of
illness.' They flinched from gibes that their shark looked more and more
like a turkey.

Late in July, Sid Sheinberg called Zanuck, Brown and Spielberg to
Hollywood for a disaster meeting. According to legend, he kept them
waiting two hours before demanding, 'Why shouldn't I close down the
picture?' The trio convinced him a corner had been turned. For one
thing, the Actors' Guild strike was off. Thereafter, however, Zanuck and
Brown spent far more time in Martha's Vineyard. Would they have fired
Spielberg? Brown insists it never crossed their minds. 'We believed we
had a hit. [He] was working hard and diligently, and it was our judgement
– not an easy one to arrive at, mind you, but we had worked with Steven
before – that we would not change course.' But nobody forgot that
Zanuck had thrown Akira Kurosawa off *Tora! Tora! Tora!* A few years
later, he would also replace John Hancock with Jeannot Szwarc as director of *Jaws* 2.

Whether from accumulated tension or its removal, the cast took the
opportunity of one Zanuck/Brown visit to stage a food fight in the staid
Harbor View Hotel. Scheider was the catalyst. 'I realised we were all
going bananas with weather and technical delays,' he said, 'so I dumped
the fruit salad on Spielberg's head.' Spielberg poured red wine over
Scheider. 'Richard Dreyfuss looked like a mountain of ravioli,' said
Scheider. 'I can't believe it but Zanuck just sat there calmly and never
got so much as a spot of gravy on him.'

As they left (after picking up the tab), Zanuck and Brown reiterated the importance of keeping 'Bruce' under wraps. Throughout the production, they had gone on the national chat-show circuit with Benchley, the writer burying his enmity in deference to a deal with Bantam to promote book and film at the same time. Everywhere, they found enormous interest in how the shark would be reproduced on screen. It was essential to maintain that mystery and sense of menace. 'If anybody in the audience laughs at the shark,' Verna Fields had said, 'we're sunk.'

Each night, the fish and its shed were shrouded with tarpaulins. A couple of locals tried to get pictures, and failed. The Directors' Guild magazine *Action* printed a tongue-in-cheek report that they were using a real shark, raised in captivity, given a transplanted chimpanzee's brain and trained to deliver lines by the voice teacher from Mike Nichols's film *Day of the Dolphin*. From Scotty Reston, news of the film's troubles reached the *New York Times*. The writer L.M. Kit Carson, then a critic for the French magazine *Oui*, spent a day nosing around in search of a story, and on returning to his hotel room found the door locked and his luggage in the hall. On the drive to the airport, however, a garrulous Teamster confided that the shark didn't work. Carson published this revelation, along with the driver's opinion that 'all the people who make movies are crazier'n a sackfulla assholes.' Finally a *Christian Science Monitor* reporter sneaked some shots of the shark.

This guerrilla war with the press embarrassed and angered the *Jaws* unit, used to thoroughly tamed Hollywood reporters who knew better than to bite the hand that fed them. 'It's amazing how many people came up to Martha's Vineyard and gave us a line about being really interested in the production,' grated Roy Scheider, 'when they really just wanted to expose the fact that we were having difficulties with the mechanical shark. And what really hurt was that these people were taken in and made comfortable and taken into our confidence, and then we were terribly betrayed.' After *Jaws*, Spielberg would become fanatical about security. His next film became the best-guarded of all time.

Location shooting finally lurched to a halt on 15 September. It had lasted 155 days. For weeks, 'Bruce' had looked less and less like a force of nature and more and more like a piece of plastic. Spielberg said his whole attitude at that point was 'Aw, fuck it!' Hearing that the crew proposed to toss him overboard once the last shot was finished, Spielberg, who now hated water even more than before *Jaws*, escaped in a small boat with Dreyfuss, leaving the first assistant to finish the film. As he sailed away, he stood up in the boat and, in a parody of General Mac-Arthur, announced, 'I shall *not* return!' He and Dreyfuss drove to Boston, booked into a hotel and, sitting in the bar, exulted that it was all over at last. Still the fact hadn't sunk in. For months afterwards, Spielberg woke, nerves arcing as if he'd just had an electric shock, from nightmares of SS *Scup Bucket*. Years later, he could still imitate with eerie accuracy the suck-sob sound of compressed air operating the internal mechanism of 'Bruce', a noise with which he'd lived daily for months. To friends, he swore he would never do another film on location.

While Spielberg took three weeks' holiday, 'Bruce' was shipped across country and installed in the very MGM 'Esther Williams' tank which Spielberg had struggled to avoid using for the main shooting. Happy now, however, to be working with controllable light, he shot the discovery of the half-sunken boat. With this and other tricky moments in the can, he and Verna Fields started fine editing.

John Williams began the music. Spielberg at first thought of cooling his violent scenes with an emollient soundtrack – maybe even a delicate piano theme for the shark, something like Williams's score for Altman's *Images*. 'No,' the composer said after he saw the rough cut. 'What you've got here is a pirate movie with a touch of *Fantasia*.' His *Jaws* music, by turns eerie in the style of Bernard Herrmann, then crudely manipulative, especially in its chugging Shark Theme, which owed almost everything to the use by Disney in *Fantasia* of Stravinsky's *Rite of Spring* for the dinosaur sequences, was one of the most striking of all film scores.

Meanwhile Zanuck and Brown were toughing out the last weeks in limbo between the end of shooting and the first previews. This was when nerve cracked and desperate deals were made. Robert Shaw, smelling a hit, offered to swap his salary, which had ballooned to $322,000, for 1 per cent of the profits. Zanuck and Brown were tempted, but turned him down – shrewdly, since within ten days of its opening, *Jaws* would gross $22 million.

They finally knew that all their effort and anxiety had paid off when they showed the first fine cut to Sid Sheinberg. At the end of the screening, the executive turned to them and, with the unabashed enthusiasm of the most devoted punter, said plaintively, 'Isn't there any more?'

Everyone was sucked into the publicity machine. Even Verna Fields, whom some insiders had credited with 'saving' the film with her editing, went on the promotion trail. In March, *Jaws* had two sneak previews. One in Dallas simply reproduced the cover logo of the book on its marquee, but the graphic was so familiar that three thousand people queued for three hours in a hailstorm to get in, and were happy to sit through the night's regular film, *The Towering Inferno*, for a first look at *Jaws*. So many were turned away that Universal hurriedly scheduled a second screening at 11 p.m. Afterwards, Spielberg decided the film needed a big shock in the second act. He rewrote the discovery of the half-sunk fishing boat so that, as Dreyfuss swims up to a hole in its hull, the head of the dead owner pokes out. Diplomatically, Shaw had agreed to a mere $5000 for another day's shooting of cutaways, so Spielberg found the producers inflexible when he went to them for $100,000 to film these additional shots.

'If you want them,' said Zanuck, '*you* pay for them.'

Spielberg did so, though, since Dreyfuss refused to go anywhere near a boat, they filmed in Verna Fields's chilly swimming pool. The actor got pneumonia.

The next preview, at the Lakewood Shopping Center in Long Beach, was attended by Sheinberg and Wasserman. Henry 'Hi' Martin, Universal's chief of distribution, taped the audience reaction. At two shock points, the appearance of the dead man's head and Scheider's first glimpse of the shark's giant maw, excited murmuring continued for a minute. The final applause was thunderous, the comment cards a distributor's dream. Delighted executives piled into the men's room to replan their release strategy. Obviously this film was going to make everyone a great deal of money. The first impulse was to forget the traditional graduated release starting in 125 to 150 key theatres, and instead to flood the country, opening at eight hundred cinemas simultaneously. After seeing it again, however, wiser heads prevailed. With exhibitors clamouring, they could afford to give *Jaws* to only the hottest houses, and still make them pay for the privilege. Trade screenings across the country fanned the already fevered word-of-mouth. Exhibitors howled, however, at Universal's terms. Almost all the seat price went to the studio – which, even though most cinemas made the bulk of their income on popcorn and Coca-Cola, was unprecedented. So was the studio's requirement that cinemas advertise the film on local TV at their own expense. Disgruntled exhibitors appealed to the Department of Justice, which ruled Universal must offer the film more widely, though the other restrictions remained.

To exploit *Jaws* to the limit, the film needed a lenient censorship rating. Spielberg himself admitted it deserved an 'R' rating, which would have barred anyone under eighteen, denying it to its largest audience, the teenagers. Scenes were cut, including the horrific climax of the first daytime beach attack, when the shark was shown colliding with a screaming child with a man's head in its mouth. He consoled himself for the loss of three days' shooting with the knowledge that, by delaying the first full shot of the shark until Act Three, he was maximising the effect of the moment which had already electrified preview audiences. The result was a 'PG' certificate, astonishingly mild, given that the science fictional *Rollerball* was rated 'R' for some bloody sports scenes that hardly compared with *Jaws*. To mollify the censors, Universal added notes to its advertising, warning that the film might be 'too intense' for pre-teens. In the week before release it also, in supposed deference to public interest, published full-page 'educational' ads listing grim statistics about sharks.

Jaws opened on 20 June 1975 in 407 US cinemas and fifty-five in Canada. For three days before, Universal swamped the media, neutralising the more patronising reviews, like that in the *New York Times* which dismissed it as 'nothing more than a creaky, old-fashioned monster picture reminiscent of *The Creature from the Black Lagoon*'. Diane Jacobs, like many, would see the film as commercial surrender after the relative purity of *Duel* and *The Sugarland Express* – 'as if after painting *Guernica* Picasso got it into his head to make an Excedrin commercial'. But Pauline Kael wrote that 'parts of *Jaws* suggest what Eisenstein might have done if he hadn't intellectualised himself out of reach'. As for what the public

thought, one only had to look at the queues winding round the block
at every cinema showing the movie. No reaction, however, pleased Spielberg more than the gibe from Cuban president Fidel Castro, that *Jaws*
showed how far American capitalists would go to protect an investment.
Here was convincing proof that *Jaws* was more than a hit. It was news.

8

Close Encounters of the Third Kind

We must all start with the believable. That is the essence of our craft.

Chuck Jones

S PIELBERG'S TRIUMPH with *Jaws* was comprehensive. Among critics, it established him as an artist, with the public as a showman, but last, and most important for his career, it convinced the industry he was a money-maker. They could whip the rug away if his next film didn't click – Dennis Hopper, no less hot following *Easy Rider*, became a leper almost overnight after his self-indulgent *The Last Movie* – but for the moment his credit was almost limitless.

Some people, however, would always see him as an upstart. *Maître d's* assessed his K-Mart clothes and the leased brown Mercedes that replaced the clunker from *Sugarland Express*, and gave him the table by the toilets. At LA's then-trendy restaurant L'Ermitage, his long hair won a 'Madam' from a short-sighted greeter. Spielberg shrugged it off. He was more deeply hurt when he slipped into the sound stage where Hitchcock was shooting *Family Plot* in 1975. The master of suspense had his back to him, but after a few moments he raised a hand and an assistant hurried to his side. The director said a few words, then got up and waddled away, after which the assistant came over to Spielberg and said, 'Mr Hitchcock feels it disturbs him if you watch him work. Would you please leave the set?' It was a grotesque replay of his ejection from *Torn Curtain*, and a reminder, not that one was needed, of how Old Hollywood regarded even the most successful of its newcomers.

Corporate Universal was more grateful. If, as Dennis Stanfill had said when he executed Darryl Zanuck's orders to fire his son, there was 'a ritual to severance', acceptance had its ritual too. One's office and the way it was furnished radiated significance. When Richard Zanuck returned to Fox in 1979, part of the deal was a room of the same dimensions, to the square inch, as the one from which he'd been evicted, and his old desk, which had also been his father's. Stanfill, by then chairman, knew better than most that 'what goes around comes around'. He'd preserved the desk, and personally supervised its re-installation.

As his reward for *Jaws*, Spielberg got the bungalow he'd coveted – or at least half a bungalow, since he had to share with John Milius. He compensated with a lavish desk boasting a cassette deck, clock, AM/FM stereo, calculator, night light, paper shredder, pencil sharpener, computer phone, and colour TV that also showed who was at both front and back doors. It was sophisticated enough, he joked, to take itself to the bathroom twice a day.

Through Milius, who taught scriptwriting at USC while trying to set up new directing projects like *The Wind and the Lion* and his surfing epic *Big Wednesday*, Spielberg met Robert Zemeckis and Bob Gale, two bright students whom Milius encouraged to collaborate. They shared a flair for intricate plots and outrageous but winning comedy characters, especially villains. On a visit to Universal, Zemeckis took the opportunity of being in Spielberg's bungalow to screen his student film, *Field of Honor*. 'My God, it was spectacular for a film student in his early twenties to have made such a picture with no money, ' Spielberg said. 'With police cars, a riot and lots of crazy characters – very well done and dubbed to Elmer Bernstein's score of *The Great Escape*. I said: this man is worth watching.' Spielberg put Zemeckis to work doing odd jobs on *Jaws*, including monitoring screenings around Los Angeles. Eager to please, he tried to boost audience reaction by applauding at impressive moments, in particular that where Quint is taken by the shark. The first time he did this, however, he went into Spielberg's office the next day to find him aghast. Word had got around that some ghoul had applauded at Quint's death.

Having intrigued Milius with a script called *Tank*, Zemeckis and Gale hit him with an unnamed scenario about the wave of panic that swept over a trigger-happy California a week after Pearl Harbor at rumours of a Japanese invasion. Even the war-loving Milius enjoyed its parody of gung-ho heroics. He supplied a working title, 'The Night the Japs Attacked', and offered not only to help prepare it for production but to produce it himself. He took it to Herb Jaffe at MGM, who disliked its theme – 'I was practically accused of being a war criminal,' Milius recalls – but suggested he might be interested with the right director in charge. Spielberg, for example.

After *Jaws*, Milius, feeling Spielberg needed to mellow back, had introduced him to skeet shooting, and they often met to shoot and talk at the Oak Tree Gun Club. (Spielberg, like Luis Buñuel, developed the ear complaint tinnitus from firearms, which would permanently impair his hearing.) Once he had a finished script of 'The Night the Japs Attacked', Milius invited Spielberg for an afternoon's shooting, and arranged for Zemeckis and Gale to drop by with a copy.

Zemeckis and Gale pitched 'The Night the Japs Attacked' to Spielberg. Perhaps the obbligato of gunfire stimulated his imagination. Perhaps, as he claimed later, 'They caught me in a weak moment.' Maybe, as Milius has intimated, he was once again attracted to a project someone else had already got up and running. He almost certainly enjoyed the resonances with Orson Welles's *War of the Worlds*. Whatever the reason, Spielberg agreed to support the film, with the proviso that Milius drop MGM and take it to Universal.

Universal meanwhile had quietly renegotiated Spielberg's contract, on which four films remained. He still owed them, but had forty years in which to deliver. Meanwhile, he was free to work for other studios. He promptly allied himself with John Milius's company, A-Team Productions.

There was no shortage of offers. His first impulse had been to do a period adventure in the style of Errol Flynn. While he was still shooting *Jaws*, Fox announced he would direct such an unnamed swashbuckler by Jeffrey Alan Fiskin, later screenwriter *of Cutter's Way* and *The Pursuit of D.B. Cooper*, about two brothers, an aristocrat and a peasant, fighting for the same woman. But before he could even get on a sound stage, he complained, the market was swamped by remakes of *The Prince and the Pauper* and *The Three Musketeers*.

He turned down Universal immediately on *Jaws 2*. 'Making a sequel to anything is just a cheap carny trick,' he told the audience at the San Francisco Film Festival in October 1975. 'I didn't even answer them [when they asked me]. I didn't call or write or anything. I understand that they plan to star the "sons" of Robert Shaw and Roy Scheider as two kids hunting a new shark.'

Motown records had recently hired Rob Cohen, late of Fox, to head its film division. His first production was to be Barwood and Robbins's script of William Brashler's novel *The Bingo Long Travelling All Stars and Motor Kings*, about a 1930s black baseball team. While *Jaws* was in production, Universal offered Motown $3 million for the distribution rights to *Bingo Long*, and suggested Spielberg to direct, which the record company accepted. 'The trouble was,' Cohen recalled, 'that as *Jaws*'s opening got nearer and nearer, Steve became less and less available. We were set to begin shooting within about a month of that, and there were a million things to be done. We couldn't postpone production because we had a pay-or-play deal with James Earl Jones, so we simply had to go ahead with [John Badham].'

Spielberg's unavailability was calculated. Friends had urged him to drag his feet until the Academy Awards. If, as expected, *Jaws* swept the board, his budgets and choice of projects would increase tenfold. The competition for Oscars was strong: Kubrick's *Barry Lyndon*, Milos Forman's *One Flew Over the Cuckoo's Nest*, Altman's *Nashville*. All these films, not to mention a strong foreign presence, with Isabelle Adjani in Truffaut's *The Story Of Adèle H* and Glenda Jackson in *Hedda Gabler*, had powerful credentials. But *Jaws* was such a phenomenon that, most people reasoned, it would surely be nominated for Best Film and Spielberg for Best Director, with other nominations for screenplay, music, editing and special effects. Sid Sheinberg was utterly confident. 'I want to be the first to predict,' he announced, 'that Steve will win the Best Director Oscar this year.'

So foregone was the conclusion that a TV crew filmed Spielberg at home when nominations were announced in February 1975. As expected, *Jaws* was shortlisted for Best Film. Traditionally, directors of Best Film were also nominated as Best Director. But Spielberg's face showed his disappointment as the Academy named Kubrick, Forman, Altman, Sidney Lumet for *Dog Day Afternoon* and, incredibly, Federico Fellini for his autobiographical *Amarcord*. 'I can't believe it!' he moaned, with understandable anguish. 'They went for Fellini instead of me!'

Nominations for John Williams, Verna Fields and the film's sound team, all of whom won Oscars, only rubbed in salt. 'It hurts,' Spielberg acknowledged later, 'because I feel it was a director's movie.' He attributed the rejection to 'a *Jaws* backlash. The same people who had raved about it began to doubt its artistic value as soon as it began to bring in so much money.' But box-office success is never a drawback at the Oscars. Spielberg was simply the first of New Hollywood's directors to submit to the Academy's ordeal and, in a snub calculated to show that the Movie Brats remained outsiders, Old Hollywood nominated a foreigner. They would do the same for *Star Wars* two years later, fobbing it off with minor awards. There were many in New Hollywood too who would withhold their nomination. 'You would be surprised,' Spielberg said later, 'at the number of friends who turn away when you achieve success. Some acquaintances who I thought were my friends turned into snipers when *Jaws* hit the top.'

He resented as well those whom he felt profited unfairly from the success of *Jaws*. 'The shameless credit-grabbing . . . would rock you back,' he complained. 'There are several individuals whose careers have taken off as a result of their avowed contribution . . . when the sad fact is that these people did the least work of all.'

At best, the comment seems unkind. Peter Benchley spent decades deep-sea fishing, fruitlessly, for another best-seller. Carl Gottlieb's later credits consisted mostly of two *Jaws* sequels and trivia like *Doctor Detroit*. Nor, despite filming *Jaws 2* and Benchley's *The Island*, did Zanuck and Brown ever have such a hit again. The actors were no luckier. Dreyfuss is still best remembered for his Spielberg films, while the character of Brody exploited Roy Scheider's vulnerability so effectively that he was stuck playing men of action haunted by the past: the agent guilty about his dead wife in *Last Embrace*, the compromised spy in *Marathon Man*, a psychiatrist in love with an apparent murderess in *Still of the Night*. Lorraine Gary clung to her fragile celebrity until the fourth outing, *Jaws: The Revenge*, in 1987, by which time she was the only remaining member of the original cast.

Spielberg probably meant his gibe for only one person – Verna Fields, whose reputation had soared. In an orgy of gratitude, Universal made her a vice president in charge of new talent, and it was rumoured that she would be associate producer of *Close Encounters*. According to Julia Phillips, Spielberg 'resent[ed] all the credit she was giving herself for its success and asked me to kill her off'. He had Phillips remove Fields's name from an Eastman Kodak ad in the trade press in which, as Hollywood's hottest, indeed only, female line producer, Phillips lauded fellow women professionals in the film business like Fields; Marcia Lucas was substituted. Paul Schrader confirms: '[Steve] was furious with Verna, Zanuck and Peter Benchley. He felt they had all conspired to take away his credit.'

Towards the end of 1975, Zanuck and Brown drew Spielberg into their efforts to build up overseas momentum for *Jaws*. In November he was summoned, along with Shaw, Dreyfuss and their wives, to a charity weekend in Acapulco organised by Zanuck's sister Darrylin, whose ailing Mexican garment business needed an injection of show-business pizzaz. At one of her cocktail parties, Spielberg sipped ginger ale by a swimming pool choked with rubber sharks, pondering the nature of celebrity and the fact that the *Jaws* image, which he had urged Zanuck in vain to merchandise, was making millions for everyone except the film-makers. *Sugarland Express* had taught Spielberg that selling a film was as important as making it. He learned even more from the junkets and promotional meetings with foreign distributors of *Jaws*. In later years, nobody would be more skilful at squeezing the last drop of profit from a film in the furthest corners of the world.

On the way back from Mexico, he stopped off with Peter Benchley in the Bahamas, where the writer was finishing *The Deep*, another underwater story, this time about sunken Caribbean treasure. Spielberg made interested noises, but when the book landed on Hollywood desks in

October 1976, with a price tag, unnegotiable, of $1 million, plus another $250,000 for Benchley's services as screenwriter, Zanuck and Brown, given first refusal, passed. Spielberg benefited indirectly, however, since Peter Guber, an independent producer working with Columbia, persuaded the studio to buy it. Though no *Jaws*, *The Deep* did inject vital cash into the studio just when it needed it to finance the ballooning *Close Encounters*.

Even as he planned *Close Encounters*, Spielberg was thinking of the film that would follow it. Universal were ready to back 'Clearwater', now renamed 'Growing Up', an intimate picture about his adolescence in Arizona, but his instincts warned him not to be diverted from blockbusters.

Above all, he was tantalised by comedy, as were most of the USC crowd, in the main because they were a desperately humourless group. Introspection in childhood, alienation in adolescence and marginalisation in young adulthood doesn't encourage a jocular view of the world. Amusing an audience, like amusing women, is a function of confidence, a commodity the Movie Brats conspicuously lacked. Nor had film comedy offered them as lonely teenagers the same degree of escape from reality as the heroics of genre melodrama. What little of it they liked was farce, heartless and unsparing, and the yammering, violent comedy of cartoons. Almost without exception, the films Spielberg backed as a producer were comedies, as if, having realised he could never be funny himself, he left that aspect of his creative activities to surrogates. First, however, he had to try for himself.

In the autumn of 1975, ABC TV's comedy show *Saturday Night Live* broadcast a sketch called 'Victims of Sharkbite'. Jane Curtin interviewed alleged survivors of shark attacks, including manic comic John Belushi, whose supposedly missing limbs keep falling into view. Spielberg made a note to meet the programme's team. A few weeks later he flew to New York, where Scorsese was making *Taxi Driver*, and sat in with him and Marcia Lucas at the Astoria Studios on Long Island during the editing of the final shootout. Of all the USC group, Scorsese remained the one for whom Spielberg still felt some awe. 'Both of us make movies that provoke strong reactions,' he wrote. 'The difference is that Marty does all this on his own terms. He doesn't fret about what's going to "work" or not "work" for an audience.'

On the same trip he went to dinner with the *Saturday Night Live* team at One Fifth Avenue, where the staff watched without surprise as Belushi gobbled food with his hands and ad-libbed comic schticks. Spielberg, however, was astonished. Nobody in Los Angeles behaved like this. He mentioned 'The Night the Japs Attacked', which, after complaints from Asian-Americans about the word 'Japs', had been retitled in turn 'The Great Los Angeles Air Raid', 'Hollywood '41' and 'The Rising Sun'. Belushi, one of whose specialities was samurai warriors – his samurai baker who hacks his cakes with a sword was famous – yelled: 'You want to see my Japanese submarine skipper?' Grabbing a coat rack, he inverted it over his head as an imitation periscope, with the hooks as handles.

'Gveet Yaaaankeee shipping!' he said in mock-Toshiro Mifune broken English, and stayed in character all night.

The two men felt an immediate affinity. Both had been bullied at school for ineptitude at sports. Both desperately needed large, appreciative audiences. With his usual enthusiasm for clowns and cut-ups, Spielberg became convinced that Belushi could be the greatest screen comic since Lou Costello – and, if he lost a little weight, a romantic lead as well. Leaving the restaurant, he assured him solemnly, 'If I ever make this movie, you're it.' Such formal public promises were to become characteristic of Spielberg. Often he emphasised his seriousness by placing a finger on the person's forehead, as if anointing them. 'You,' he would say, 'are going to work for me again.' Eventually he gave the gesture to E.T, investing the alien's magic finger with a glowing, almost divine power.

In New York, working alone in a suite at the Sherry Netherland, he finished rewriting *Close Encounters*. On the armature of Schrader's moral fable he wound skeins of dream. He included overt references to *Pinocchio* and its theme tune, 'When You Wish Upon a Star', with which he originally intended to end the film, and covert stylistic ones to *Bambi*, *Frankenstein*, DeMille's *The Ten Commandments* and Chuck Jones. Barry's mechanical monkey is meant to recall James Dean playing with such a toy at the opening of *Rebel Without a Cause* (and not, as some people believed, the prologue of *2001: A Space Odyssey*). François Truffaut would be struck by the film's similarity to Hitchcock's *The Birds*, but there are resonances as well with *North by Northwest* in the clambering over the rocks of Devil's Tower, William Cameron Menzies' *Invaders from Mars* and Don Siegel's *Invasion of the Body Snatchers* in the rural setting, and Jack Arnold's *It Came from Outer Space* in the confrontation with the visitors.

The main character, Roy Neary, an electrical linesman in Muncie, Indiana, is a downmarket Arnold Spielberg, an amateur visionary raised on Disney but becalmed now in suburbia. With Jilian Guiler, a mother who's lost her child to aliens, and Claude Lacombe, a Frenchman who's been investigating UFOs for years, Neary is drawn by an implanted compulsion to Wyoming, where the first formal meeting between earth-men and aliens is to take place. Lacombe has been communicating with the aliens via a five-note tune based on a music teaching method developed by Zoltan Kodály and a colour code invented by Scriabin, but it is Neary, notwithstanding his lack of education or training, who wins a place on man's first stellar voyage. Belief is enough. When you wish upon a star, makes no difference who you are.

One leftover from Schrader's concept was the age of Neary, who was fortyish. Spielberg, however, had shown an early draft to Dreyfus, who said he was sorry Neary wasn't ten years younger, so he could play him. As a result, Spielberg rewrote the part to fit Dreyfus. Once the script was done, Spielberg read it through and sensed a lack of humanity and humour, especially in the character of Neary. He rang Jerry Belson and asked him to come to New York and work with him. Belson arrived the next day, and spent five days taking the chill off the story and glossing over the inconsistencies rooted in undigested lumps of Schrader's original drafts. According to Schrader, every writer Spielberg knew was called in at some point to paper over inconsistencies, including Milius, David Giler and Walter Hill. Barwood and Robbins worked for four days on the kidnapping of Barry, and were rewarded with cameos at the end as airmen returned by the aliens. Richard Dreyfuss acknowledged,

'[Spielberg's] not the best screenwriter there is, obviously, but somehow he got it all together there.'

Spielberg's personal life was also transformed in 1976, when he met and fell in love with Amy Irving.

'Fixing up' Steven was a hobby among his friends. It was Brian De Palma who thought of Amy. Six years Spielberg's junior, she was the archetypal Jewish princess, a green-eyed lookalike for the young Lauren Bacall, with a mass of wavy chestnut hair. Her mother was the actress Priscilla Pointer, her father Jules Irving, who had directed the LA Actors' Workshop and the Lincoln Center Repertory Theatre in New York. She'd been through the Professional Children's School in New York, graduated from the London Academy of Music and Dramatic Arts, and was playing in *Romeo and Juliet* on stage in Los Angeles when her agent sent her to George Lucas's auditions for the role of Princess Leia in *Star Wars*. She made the shortlist, but meanwhile De Palma, who was sitting in on the tests in search of people for *Carrie*, grabbed her to play the homecoming queen. He also suggested her for the role of Neary's wife in *Close Encounters*. Spielberg saw her, but immediately rejected her as too young, and apparently forgot about her.

De Palma hosted a charity premiere of *Carrie*, to which he invited both Amy and Spielberg. At dinner afterwards, they met. The effect was electric, all the more so since Amy, overwhelmed by the company, got drunk. Next day Spielberg confessed to Julia Phillips, 'I met a heartbreaker last night.' It was like being struck by lightning, he told her. Phillips urged him to call her, but it took him a month to do so. Almost immediately they started an affair.

Amy seemed an odd match for the casual workaholic Spielberg. She skied, flew a sailplane, meditated and, despite her Jewish birth, had been raised as a Christian Scientist. Acerbic and highly strung, she resented emotional commitment even as she courted it. She was ambitious and independent, and by far the more experienced of the pair. In liberated San Francisco, and later New York, she had embraced the sexual revolution. 'I remember it all very clearly,' she said, 'living in New York as a single

woman, standing on the salad bar line, going home with the wrong guys
for the wrong reasons.'

Her effect on Spielberg was immediate and obvious. He became more
genial, more social, spent less time hunched over video games, playing
his collection of more than seven hundred movie soundtracks or
noodling their themes two-fingered on the electric piano that was his
latest plaything. He began to replace the movie posters on his walls with
original art, though, predictably, his purchases were rare Disney cels and
paintings by Norman Rockwell.

Amy also badgered him to improve his appearance. 'I helped Steven
make a big metamorphosis in his wardrobe,' she said later. 'Now he's a
real fine dresser.' A beard that had been an occasional feature of his
twenties also reappeared, though it would alternate for a while with a
diffident-looking moustache, immortalised in his cameo appearance as
the clerk at the end of John Landis's *The Blues Brothers*. The beard
disguised his unappealing mouth, though Martin Amis spoke for many
when he described it as 'look[ing] like a stick-on afterthought, a bid for
adulthood and anonymity'. Later in the year, at Julia Phillips's urging,
he bought a house on Coldwater Canyon, which he asked Joe Alves, his
designer from *Jaws*, to decorate. Spielberg and Amy talked about living
there together, but neither quite wanted to make the move, and his
crowded schedule made it easy to put off a decision.

Close Encounters was now scheduled to start shooting in the summer of
1976. Anyone trying to get a straight answer out of Spielberg about the
new film's plot faced an uphill struggle. Early in the year, he conceded
cagily to a journalist:

All I can tell you is it's a science fiction picture, totally wrapped up
in a lot of political controversy. It's a very interesting and topical
story, something that I believe in. We'll be shooting in six states,
Brazil, and there are five pages with capital letters that say 'Where
Do You Plan To Spend The Winter?' And yet with all that it will be

an incredibly inexpensive movie. We'll make the whole movie for about a million-five.

In a year of development, however, that estimate had been left far behind. After *Jaws*, Spielberg loathed the idea of locations so much that he rethought the film as totally studio-shot. This increased the cost to $4.1 million. Columbia agreed, only to see him change his mind again and reinstate scenes on the remote Texas airfields he'd spotted in the location scout for *Sugarland*. He also insisted on releasing in 70mm, using the 65mm ToddAO process which reserved 5mm of the film for a wider magnetic soundtrack. With Lucas, who developed his own THX sound system for his films and installed high-tech recording studios at the Skywalker Ranch, Spielberg had become convinced that the impact of sound was almost as important as that of image. As the summer warmed up, costs hovered around $12 million.

Much had changed too among the film's makers. The Phillipses were estranged. Julia wanted to produce; Michael, who'd grown a beard, proposed to visit India and Discover Himself. Though they're credited jointly on the film, he wasn't involved in the main preparation or shooting, only in preliminary negotiations and those on release and publicity. Spielberg was upset. He'd felt comfortable with a married couple as producers. It was more 'family'. When he had his own company, it would be run first by Kathy Kennedy and Frank Marshall, who became a couple and eventually married, and, when they left, by Walter Parkes and Laurie MacDonald, also husband and wife.

Other producers were auditioned for *Close Encounters*, including William Sackheim, who had recut *Eyes* on *Night Gallery*, but Julia persuaded Columbia she could manage it. In the power vacuum, however, more control than ever passed to David Begelman. Hiring the elegant and charming Begelman had been a gamble for Columbia because he himself was a legendary gambler, with a prodigal lifestyle driven by an innate urge to self-destruction. 'There is something in me that can't stand success,' he once told executive Peter Bart. 'If everything is going really great, I will find a way to mess things up. It's a compulsion.'

Begelman opened negotiations on *Close Encounters* with all the cunning he applied to the big Friday-night high-stake poker games to which he was addicted, and at which he routinely dropped vast sums. Spielberg didn't protest. Begelman was a brilliant manipulator who could find the money he needed. If everyone else on the film was short-changed, that was the fate of all creative people in Hollywood. In time Spielberg would have the power to negotiate total control, but for the moment he was content to let Begelman work on his behalf, and take his unequal share.

Begelman's ace in the hole was the British electronics company EMI, rich on sales of TVs, body scanners and other high-tech electronics. It had recently bought Columbia's music division and, as part of the deal, undertaken to finance three films. Time Inc., the publishers, were also attracted to putting some money into film. Begelman scared up more capital in Europe. The US would outlaw film production as a tax shelter in December 1976, but in West Germany the loophole remained open. Between them, these companies put $7 million into *Close Encounters*, with EMI sharing production credit on screen, a significant concession.

Begelman's power typified the prevailing flow of power towards agents, most of whom now regarded a studio spot as the next step after a successful few years in personal management. Every month or two, a top representative from ICM or William Morris moved to studio production. In 1975, in a development which would seem, in retrospect, historic, Mike Ovitz and four other young and ambitious agents were fired by William Morris for protesting at what they saw as the company's lack of enterprise. They set up shop as Creative Artists Agency, soon to be the most powerful agency in the world.

Anxious to head off any possible conflict over who had written *Close Encounters*, Julia Phillips asked Paul Schrader to notify the Screenwriters' Guild Arbitration Board that he expected no screen credit. No trace of his work remained in the script, she assured him. 'We were all gentlemen,' said Schrader, 'and if [Spielberg and the Phillipses] told me that such a thing was true, it was.' When he read the final script, however, he saw the character of VanOwen in Lacombe, and much else besides.

'I recognised the infusion of heavily spiritual elements that had not been there when Steven first approached me with the project – particularly the ending and the notion of the five tones, the five colours that I had designed. The idea of flying saucers as a religious experience. This is not in Steven's nature. It is in my nature.' He remains bitter about what he sees as Spielberg's duplicity. For his part, Spielberg says, 'It surprises me that Schrader would slink after someone else's success by vividly inflating his imagined contributions.'

Another person who bridled at the new film was J. Allen Hynek. He wrote an acerbic letter to the producers, pointing out that they were using his terminology and ideas without credit or payment. They hurriedly recruited him as Technical Consultant, and he too has a final cameo among the crowd welcoming the aliens.

Other rivalries were also crystallised by Close Encounters. Rather as they assembled twenty or more French directors under Godard, Truffaut and Chabrol as the New Wave, journalists lumped Spielberg with Lucas, William Friedkin, Scorsese, Bogdanovich, Milius, Schrader and a dozen more film-makers in their twenties under the broad leadership of Coppola. It was an understandable error, but a grievous one. As with the nouvelle vague, the generalisation presupposed a level of friendship and a shared commitment which didn't exist. If it was hard to discern any similarity between the right-wing Catholic upper-middle-class Eric Rohmer and the ex-juvenile delinquent Truffaut, the gap between, for example, Peter Bogdanovich and Martin Scorsese was even wider.

People were already separating into Lucas, Spielberg or Coppola camps, a division that became increasingly clear after the Lucas/Coppola friendship cooled over Apocalypse Now, which Lucas co-wrote and expected to direct. In addition, Spielberg, Lucas and Coppola had visibly drawn away from Milius, De Palma and Scorsese. As Michael Pye says, 'people like Lucas and Spielberg were building empires rather than making films.' From now on, the Three, but especially Spielberg, would become patrons and power-brokers. The rest, however readily the others returned their calls and looked at their rough cuts, were reduced to clients, acolytes, supplicants. The irascible loner Scorsese regarded the change with indifference, the self-absorbed Milius with humour, De

Palma, who remained Spielberg's closest personal friend of the group, with truculence. 'They're running a business,' De Palma said of the Three, 'and I don't want to run a business. I want to make movies.'

Among the Three themselves, and especially between Spielberg and the other two, there were equally fundamental variations. Both Coppola, with his property deals and ducal *gravitas*, and Lucas, with his preoccupation with history, the quasi-Zen mysticism of The Force, and the relocation of human conflicts 'a long, long time ago in a galaxy far, far away', were drifting from Spielberg's essentially earthly, contemporary and American concerns.

Attitudes to money dramatised the growing divisions. Lucas distributed bonuses to everyone who worked on his films, down to the janitors, gave percentage 'points' to actors he admired, like Sir Alec Guinness, and swapped them with friends, usually to his cost. He shrugged off his exchange of a point in *Star Wars* for one in John Milius's flop *Big Wednesday*: 'It proved I was a good friend but a bad investor.' In this area, Spielberg was almost a mirror image of Lucas. He offered no such lavish gifts, nor did he expect any. Lucas's generosity surprised him, while the profligacy of Coppola's operation earned his disapproval.

With *Close Encounters*, Spielberg staked out his territory and began to assemble the support group which evolved into his company Amblin Entertainment. Most of the faces on the film were familiar. Joe Alves was again production designer and Vilmos Zsigmond on camera. Still ambitious to direct, the photographer saw that the film would increase his prestige. Soon he demanded that his name be included in all advertising, no matter how trivial, for any production he lit. Eleven different directors of photography eventually worked on the film, including Douglas Slocombe (the India sequences), William Fraker (the desert opening), and John Alonzo and Laszlo Kovacs (retakes on the kidnapping of Cary Guffey and the Ohio tollgate sequences, plus Dreyfuss's entry into the mother ship for the alternative 'Special Edition' ending). Allen Daviau also shot new material, the first time for years that Spielberg had worked with his *Amblin'* cameraman, who'd muddled along doing documentaries and commercials, though after *Close Encounters* he used him increasingly. Some people suggest that Spielberg, confident now of his technique, no longer needed the best lighting cameramen. Others, more credibly, feel that he wanted as many loyal foot-soldiers as he could find for the Amblin family.

Dreyfuss reluctantly took the role of Neary. Even after Spielberg's rewrites, the actor was doubtful. He'd been offered $500,000 and a share of the profits to play the magician Harry Houdini in a new film, and hoped for a similar deal on Close Encounters. Julia Phillips out-manoeuvred him by sending the script to Hollywood's best middle-aged actors, Gene Hackman, Jack Nicholson and Al Pacino. Nicholson was interested, but asked Spielberg to wait until he finished his first film as a director, Goin' South. This news nudged Dreyfuss into accepting the part for $300,000.

Spielberg, as usual, didn't want stars. The little-known Melinda Dillon was Jilian Guiler and Teri Garr Neary's wife. Dreyfuss's nephew played her son. Cary Guffey, the kidnapped Barry, was a four-year-old Spielberg spotted in Atlanta and manipulated into a winning performance by subterfuges like presenting him with gifts to produce a smile, and having a man in a rabbit suit pop out to evoke wonder at the first sight of the aliens.

Schrader's supporters feel Spielberg's decision to cast a Frenchman as the investigator Lacombe was calculated to distance the character from the original vision of a scholarly, middle-aged VanOwen, but Spielberg was more influenced by polls suggesting that most Americans thought UFOs an exclusively American phenomenon. Showing that there were researchers elsewhere, like Aimé Michel and Jacques Vallée in France, made UFOs seem less an exclusively American obsession and more an international phenomenon. His first choice for Lacombe, Lino Ventura, the blocky specialist in crime thrillers, spoke no English. Yves Montand declined. So did Jean-Louis Trintignant, France's best-known actor in America since he starred as the racing driver romancing Anouk Aimée in Claude Lelouch's 1966 A Man and a Woman. Spielberg considered Philippe Noiret, then remembered François Truffaut, who had played a director in his own movie about film-making, La Nuit Americaine. Since Warners financed it, and most of the cast, including Truffaut, spoke

English, the film had wide play in the US as *Day for Night*. Spielberg had also admired Truffaut in *L'Enfant Sauvage*, his film of 1970 where the director played a nineteenth-century doctor who tries to educate and civilise an abandoned 'wolf boy'. *Close Encounters* was about communication too. Impulsively, he offered him the role.

As Truffaut himself found when they met, Spielberg, like most American film-makers, knew few foreign films. His favourite French directors, Spielberg confided, were Lelouch, whose sentimentality and flashy technique Truffaut detested, and Robert Enrico, who'd directed two popular vehicles with Ventura. It also emerged, not to his credit as far as Truffaut was concerned, that Spielberg had written to Philippe de Broca saying he'd watched his action comedy *That Man from Rio*, with Jean-Paul Belmondo, nine times and that he'd never seen anything like it before or after. (Spielberg's enthusiasm isn't surprising. De Broca planned the film 'to contain everything that I'd wanted to see when I was twelve'.)

Though he'd praised *Duel*, Truffaut was almost as ignorant of Spielberg's work as Spielberg was of his, but the idea of working on a Hollywood film intrigued him. He'd been thinking of writing a book about screen acting, and here was a chance to observe it from the inside. 'I was there a lot,' he said, 'but, like Greta Garbo, I can only say I had the feeling of waiting.' All the actors contracted for twenty weeks, and were warned they might be working in Wyoming, Alaska, India, Alabama and Outer Mongolia.

Truffaut too finally signed in March, with the proviso that he must be finished by August, when he hoped to shoot *The Man who Loved Women*. Since his English was poorer than it had seemed in *Day for Night*, a translator was written into the film. Bob Balaban took the role, despite being refused a script. '*Nobody* gets to read the script,' casting director Juliet Taylor said severely. Later, when the plot demanded a map-reader, Balaban metamorphosed into a cartographer, a change typical of the film's disordered but somehow convincing narrative. As the critic James Monaco says, *Close Encounters* is 'shot through with false leads, gaping holes, and circuitous side trails . . . But it doesn't seem to matter.'

For special effects, Spielberg retained Douglas Trumbull, though not without misgivings. Trumbull had ambitions as a director, and had already made the highly regarded *Silent Running* in 1971. However, he'd worked on *2001: A Space Odyssey*, which made him indispensable for a film that was to exist in the shadow of Kubrick's masterpiece. Spielberg ran it repeatedly before and during shooting, and the whole *Close Encounters* team strove for the same, in Trumbull's phrase, 'awesome simplicity'.

For his aliens, Spielberg wanted to be just as circumspect as Kubrick had been. His wide-eyed, hairless creatures, who would eventually be played, except in close-up, by masked pre-teen girls on rollerskates, owe much to the space child which appears at the end of Kubrick's film, but it took months of experimenting with stop-motion dolls and mechanised puppets before Italian Carlo Rambaldi came up with the spindly humanoids who emerge from the mother ship. Rubbery, big-eyed, hairless, without visible noses or ears, they resemble the photographs of alien corpses supposedly found in a flying saucer that crashed at Roswell, New Mexico in 1947, and may have been inspired by some shaky footage of their dissection which circulated on the UFO underground, reputedly part of fourteen cans of 16mm shot by the US military. Shown worldwide on TV in 1995, the film was widely dismissed as a fake, but in the seventies it enjoyed a near-holy status among believers.

For the site of first contact, Spielberg visualised something as remote and simple as Kubrick's monolith. To avoid odious comparisons, he settled on a mountain. 'You want to find the most unique mountain,' De Palma advised. 'You don't want [the 'invited' humans] to think it's ten mountains in ten parts of the country.' After discarding Ship Rock in Oregon and rejecting Monument Valley as too obvious, Joe Alves found Devil's Tower National Monument, an 865-foot-high volcanic monolith in Wyoming.

Hollywood had no stages even half the size demanded by the arrival of the alien mother ship. Some of the biggest enclosed spaces in the country were hangars left over from the military's flirtation with dirigibles. The largest, in Tillamook, Oregon, was too remote for a film crew, but Alves found three more, conveniently remote, on the flat, muggy Gulf coast near Mobile, Alabama. The largest of them, 450 feet long, 250 feet broad and ninety feet high, more than accommodated Alves's sets for the stretch of hillside highway called 'Crescendo Summit' where Dreyfuss, Dillon and a group of hard-core believers first see the space-ships, and the landing area in a box canyon behind Devil's Tower, christened 'The Dark Side of the Moon'.

For a film that was to carry an overwhelming impression of visual artistry, *Close Encounters* was shot with little apparent attention to style. Above all, Spielberg feared comparisons with *Star Wars*. 'Mine is a film that's rooted on earth,' he said, 'not in stellar space. It's about extraordi-nary encounters in middle-class suburbia. It's not a movie that keeps attacking the senses with visual assaults.' (He would make a similar disclaimer for *Jurassic Park*, saying it was 'not science fiction but science actuality'.)

The mother ship is all the more impressive for its appearance in the night skies over present-day Indiana rather than in outer space. The film's major advertising graphic, a stretch of road leading over a hill from behind which an unearthly glow fills the night sky, could also hardly be more prosaic, nor could the advertising line, 'We Are Not Alone'. The most effective moments of both *Close Encounters* and *2001* spring not from special effects but from imaginative shooting of the real and normal. Kubrick gave his ships the Pan Am logo and set them waltzing to Johann Strauss. Spielberg compared his to ice-cream cones, nicknamed one 'The Quarter Pounder' after a McDonald's hamburger, and turned them into practical jokers who delight in turning lights on and off, trashing houses, raiding refrigerators. They even cruise the roads like joyriding teenagers, inviting the police to chase them. Nor had Trumbull forgotten the techni-cal lessons of Kubrick's film. Bowman's exercise jog round the outer walls of the zero-gravity ship is echoed by Spielberg's similar use of a revolving drum to show Neary's cab going crazy as the alien ship passes above. By tilting both cab and camera 90 degrees anti-clockwise, he makes the glovebox appear to erupt junk, an effect he would use again in *Poltergeist*.

When the production moved to Mobile in March, Spielberg put into practice some of the lessons learned on *Jaws*. Special-effects sequences were left until last. And the press was rigorously excluded. *Close Encounters* would be Hollywood's best-kept secret.

Mobile became the most hermetic of closed sets. Cast and crew worked, ate, sometimes even slept inside the stifling hangar, which 150 tons of air-conditioning equipment, enough for thirty large houses, did little to make habitable. Occasionally they emerged to cruise pretty but provincial Mobile. 'I'm not saying it isn't a nice town,' said one crew-member plaintively. 'I just wish there was more of it.' Nobody entered without a name badge. Even Spielberg himself, who lived in a Winnebago parked outside, was briefly barred when he forgot his. Scripts were numbered, and distributed only on a need-to-know basis. Most actors got only their own lines. Since everything above the heads of the actors was masked out with black velvet, leaving room for the wonders to be added by special effects, many secondary performers had no idea what the film was about, so nosy reporters often got grossly misleading accounts of the plot, some of which found their way into print.

Bored, Truffaut asked for an office within the complex. There, for six hours a day, he pecked out the screenplay of his new film, *The Man who Loved Women*, and even part of the one that followed, *The Green Room*. He also rewrote his own dialogue when Spielberg's proved undeliverable, and wrote long letters to friends in Paris. To them he confided that he found Spielberg unpretentious, good-humoured and patient, with an enthusiasm that was infectious. 'This film of flying saucers means a great deal to him,' he told Serge Rousseau. 'It's a childhood dream come true.'

On the other hand, he sensed little intellectual conviction under the film's elaborate technique, a fact he couldn't resist mentioning to Spielberg. 'In order to be a story-teller,' he told him, 'you have to live a life. If your stories are not about life, you're just a very good craftsman.' It would take him years, Spielberg conceded much later, to realise that Truffaut was right. Watching him work with Cary Guffey, Truffaut made another important suggestion. 'You should have a film about kids,' he said, 'because you are a kid yourself.' This remark became the germ of *E.T.* Moved by Truffaut's counsel, Spielberg probably wasn't aware that the Frenchman gave it to many others. Bob Balaban recalls: 'I spent nine months standing next to Truffaut. He told me that, as a director, it's better to focus on the things that really interest you, because each [film]

takes a chunk of your life, and life is basically short. He said all that
mattered to him was the relationship between men and women and
children.'

Aside from members of the Columbia board, who made repeated
nervous trips to Mobile to stare at the sets and convince themselves their
money wasn't being wasted, the only regular visitors were Amy Irving,
and Robert Zemeckis and Bob Gale, who arrived periodically with the
latest drafts of 'The Rising Sun', now called 1941. For eight weeks Spielberg directed all day, but at night found himself 'dragged helplessly
through the streets by this crazo script'. To feed their imagination, the
three screened lots of World War II propaganda movies, a technique
George Lucas used on Star Wars, the space dogfights of which copied
camera movements from wartime flying films. Some, though perhaps
not enough, of the stereotypical characters in these films found their way
into 1941. The closest parallels, however, were to Stanley Kramer's 1963
It's a Mad, Mad, Mad, Mad World, of which 1941 became a virtual remake.

Julia Phillips, progressively more ill-tempered and paranoid with
stress and cocaine, dismissed Zemeckis as 'a pest' – not her last failure
to understand that Spielberg was quietly building his own circle of
trustworthy collaborators, in which she and other producers would have
no place. Truffaut too aroused her anger. She was convinced his deafness
was feigned, and that he thought her a Hollywood whore. Nor was she
any happier with Irving, increasingly a fixture in Spielberg's life. No
slouch at emotional manipulation herself, she assessed her as calculating
and devious. 'Every time Amy is afraid she's losing Steven,' she said, 'she
opts for a tearful confession.'

Spielberg, in his offhand way, was using Phillips, as he would other
women throughout his career, as a buffer. He even, Phillips says, coaxed
her to derail Irving's suggestions that they live together once the film
was finished. From her evolved the team of women who became the
Spielberg inner circle. It was a model he knew from adolescence: someone like his mother and sisters, loyal to him alone, and dedicated to
protecting him from the world. Her influence, as woman and producer,
was fundamental. It was she who persuaded him to invest some of his
money in a new house. They also enjoyed what she insists was an

innocent flirtation enlivened with a few dark-car gropes and kisses. For his part, Spielberg tried to limit her increasingly self-destructive drug use.

More crucial was what she taught him about producing. If Spielberg pioneered Film as Event, Phillips championed Film as Commodity. With the exception of Disney, Hollywood studios usually begged businesses to exploit a title or logo because it promoted the film. *Jaws* triggered a frenzy of spin-off T-shirts, magazines and books, few of which paid anything back to the production.

Phillips, however, signed lucrative licensing agreements for *Close Encounters* merchandise. After *Close Encounters* Spielberg formed Entertainment Merchandising Inc. with LA businessman Sam Grossman to market spin-offs from *1941* and other films, and Amblin's marketing division was to become one of its most profitable. Within a few years, such deals, which gave the film-maker between 6 and 10 per cent of the wholesale price of every baseball cap, beach towel, plastic toy, board game, hamburger, soft drink and candy bar which used the film's name, would be ticketed in the tens of millions. Even Phillips was astonished by the scale of spin-offs. 'I sometimes think,' she complained in 1991, 'that movies are almost an afterthought for the tie-ins, the ads and special offers at McDonald's. The ancillaries throw off more money than the movie.' Fifty items were licensed for sale with the *E.T.* logo. By *Jurassic Park*, the total topped a thousand.

Lucas was toughing out the last weeks before *Star Wars*' 25 May release. He showed successive rough cuts to friends. 'They all thought it was a disaster,' he said, though in Spielberg's memory it was Lucas who had the most doubts. 'When I sat with George a few weeks before the film opened, he was predicting $15 million in domestic rentals. 'Cause he thought he'd made a Walt Disney film that wouldn't have much appeal beyond very young pre-teens.' Spielberg was more supportive than De Palma, who was convinced it would flop. At one memorable dinner, Spielberg and *Time*'s Jay Cocks sat on one side of the table, loyally lauding the film, while De Palma demolished it. Lucas, unperturbed, kept eating, and, in Spielberg's recollection, changed nothing. Fully expecting it to fail, however, he'd booked a holiday for himself and Marcia in Hawaii to coincide with the first week of release.

In August 1976 everyone was sent home from Mobile while Trumbull's Future General started adding space ships and bizarre cloud formations to the top half of the images shot in Alabama. Instead of the razor-sharp craft of Lucas's film, Spielberg remembered his 1972 TV film *Something Evil*, where he'd overlit windows to turn bodies into blurred, undefined outlines. The blaze from the mother ship became so blinding that the aliens who emerged were barely visible. The same light appeared during Barry's kidnap, which Spielberg reshot to make it more terrifying, with heating vents unscrewing themselves and mysterious beings plunging down the chimney. The logic is obscure, the effect mesmerising.

Columbia was panicking. The budget had soared to $19 million, and John Milius joked lugubriously, 'It will either be the best Columbia film or it will be the last Columbia film.' The studio needed $50 million profit before the film went into the black: $133 million in gross receipts. They hoped to recoup $24 million even before the film opened in exhibitors' guarantees. New York cinemas were asked to pledge a minimum $150,000 income from seat sales, and a twelve-week run. In New Jersey the figure dropped to $50,000, but with no promise of exclusivity. Each cinema was levied $2000 for promotion. Nervous about a December release, many exhibitors pressed Columbia to bring the film forward to mid-November, giving a chance for word-of-mouth to build before the Christmas season. The studio agreed, over protests from Spielberg, who would always argue that he'd never been given time to finish the film as he wanted.

After watching a rough cut, Daniel Melnick, who'd become head of production, pointed out to Spielberg that *The Exorcist* had gained a box-office boost from an eerie pre-credit sequence, added much later, of Max von Sydow encountering the devil in the deserts of Iraq. *Close Encounters* might do the same. Melnick personally went before the board to extract the $4 million needed for such an opening scene, and for more exotic locations.

In February 1977, while he thought about a possible new introductory sequence, Spielberg went to Bombay to shoot scenes of locals re-enacting their own close encounter. It was a nightmare, with extras unable to remember the film's five-note musical motif, nor co-ordinate their single gesture, pointing in unison at the sky when the investigators asked where the sound had come from. Evenings were spent in mutual complaint sessions with Douglas Slocombe and his crew, the basis of an enduring friendship between the two men. The visit also produced a useful addition to the film. Passing an oil refinery festooned with lights, Spielberg fused the image with the inverted lights of the San Fernando Valley to create a new vision of the alien mother ship.

Julia Phillips's drug problem was now common knowledge, exacerbated by some incautious TV interviews given when she was obviously spaced out. On the way back from India, Spielberg had to stand over her while she flushed her precious supplies of the potent local hash down the toilet; he couldn't afford to have her arrested as she arrived back in the US. When Jeff Walker, then West Coast editor of the alternative magazine *Crawdaddy*, interviewed him towards the end of the shoot, a casual question about Carlos Castaneda triggered a detailed rejection of hallucinogens. 'He absolutely wanted it to be known that no, *he* never took LSD, *he* never took drugs, that it was not a factor in his film-making or his artistic consciousness.'

For the new opening, Spielberg had written scenes of Amazon Indians encountering World War II aircraft in the jungle, but, flinching from yet more inoculations, he reset them in Sonora, Mexico. In May, Truffaut and Balaban were recalled to Lake Mirage in the Mojave Desert where Lacombe discovers a squadron of World War II planes, still miraculously preserved in the same condition as when they flew into the Bermuda Triangle thirty years before.

John Williams's music had maximised the momentum of *Jaws*, but Spielberg wanted less from him now. Unlike *Star Wars*, the raw narrative of which Williams chromed in Straussian brass and clashing cymbals, *Close Encounters*' music is mostly questioning horns and *misterioso* strings in the style of Bernard Herrmann, rising occasionally in a crescendo that ceases abruptly, with a bump, as if of astonishment. The most distinctive motif is the aliens' five-note call, which Spielberg chose from hundreds picked out by Williams on the piano in an all-day session. He didn't want it to sound like door chimes, but this was often how it was to be used. Roger Moore punches it out on a keypad in *Moonraker*, and Vilmos Zsigmond had his chimes altered to play the five-note theme.

During this period, Spielberg added another anecdote to his growing legend. Noticing a gawky thirteen-year-old boy wandering round the set, he offered him a Coke, and found that he was Patrick Read Johnson from Wadsworth, Illinois. His mother, desperate at his obsession with film and persistent production of 8mm movies, had written to Herb Lightman, editor of *American Cinematographer* magazine, begging him to show the boy round Hollywood. Lightman took Patrick with him on a set visit to *Close Encounters*, and Spielberg, impressed, invited him to a preview of *Star Wars*. (Johnson later became a special-effects technician. In 1980 Spielberg persuaded Disney to release his first feature, *Spaced Invaders*.)

Spielberg was glad that *Close Encounters* bore little resemblance to *Star Wars*. The differences encouraged him to make his film even more prosaic. Long domestic arguments between Neary and his wife were left in, and he also retained a visit by Neary to the power station where he works and a sequence where, gripped by the implanted vision of Devil's Tower, he loots his own yard and that of neighbours to build a huge model in his living room.

In May, the Lucases fled to Maui to escape the expected bloodbath of *Star Wars*' opening. When it became clear that the film was a hit, Spielberg himself, with Amy, took a week's break from the treadmill of supervising special effects. It was there, on the beach at Mauna Kea, that he and Lucas discussed *Raiders of the Lost Ark* and planned their radical business strategy. Afterwards, Spielberg returned to LA and the last and most nerve-racking part of the production process, the fine tuning of the film and the preparation of publicity and promotion. But nobody who had seen *Close Encounters* doubted that it would be a masterpiece. On his last day, Dreyfuss went up to Spielberg. 'This has been the most horrible experience of my life,' he told him, 'and thank you so much.'

9

1941

I'm not a funny guy.

Steven Spielberg

IN AUGUST 1977, Cliff Robertson, who had never ceased to resent David Begelman's treachery over *I Shot Down the Red Baron, I Think*, discovered that the same man, now head of Columbia, had forged his endorsement on a $10,000 cheque and used the money to buy travellers' cheques for a holiday trip. Robertson promptly reported the forgery, and, in one of the most astonishing of all Hollywood scandals, brought to light misappropriations totalling $61,000. The industry was astounded, less at the act of stealing than at the relatively picayune sums involved; Begelman earned $300,000 a year and lived rent-free in a $5000-a-month mansion. Other falsifications, even more brazen, soon came to light. These included a statement by Yale, from whose Law School Begelman always claimed to have graduated, that it had no record of him ever attending the university.

Such was Begelman's popularity in the industry, however, that most people gave him the benefit of the doubt, assuming a financial crisis brought on by his gambling or, more likely, a mental breakdown driven by the urge to destruction that he acknowledged as a fundamental flaw in his character. He continued to manage Columbia even as his arraignment approached, though increasingly Dan Melnick assumed the day-to-day running of the studio. If anyone deserved censure, the industry perversely decreed, it was Robertson, for his disloyalty to the system in going public. After his conviction and a period of therapy, Begelman resumed a seat of power; Robertson was almost universally excoriated for having failed to be a good sport.

Spielberg sided with Begelman. Like everyone else in Hollywood, he accepted corporate larceny as a fact of life. 'Here the studios have all kinds of ways to prove that they have actually made no profit,' he shrugged, 'so why should we be cut in on anything?' If there was a lesson, it was this: be quicker than the other man, better counselled, better prepared.

Julia Phillips was also punished for getting on the wrong side of the establishment. For months she battled Columbia for control of promotion and release on the film she'd done so much to realise, until, exasperated by her complaints and increasing reliance on freebase cocaine, Begelman in late summer barred her from the lot. Her husband Michael reappeared from his voyage of self-discovery to take over the reins. Now it was Julia's turn to go to Hawaii and sit on Sunset Beach, blearily watching John Milius riding waves to try and forget about the massive public rejection of *Big Wednesday*.

Spielberg's agreement with Dennis Hoffman to direct a feature within ten years of their 1968 *Amblin'* contract also returned to haunt him. According to depositions sworn by Hoffman in 1995, Spielberg responded by revealing his true age, and assuring Hoffman that he had been a minor when he made the deal, which was therefore invalid. Hoffman agreed to accept $30,000, he said, and the contract was torn up. Later, Spielberg agreed to buy 20 per cent of Hoffman's Designer Donuts company.

Begelman, Melnick and their lieutenants didn't know what to expect of *Close Encounters*, since Spielberg edited not at Columbia but secretly and under guard, in a rented apartment in Marina del Rey close to Doug Trumbull's headquarters. After the first screening of the rough cut, however, they were elated. Bob Cort, the young vice president in charge of advertising, 'leaped in the air like a giddy child,' wrote Peter McClintic, 'whooping and giggling and pounding Spielberg and Trumbull like players who had just won the seventh game of the World Series'.

Alan Hirschfield, chairman of the Columbia board, was particularly moved by the use of 'When You Wish Upon a Star' in the finale. Spielberg wasn't so sure about it. Preparing the film for the first sneak previews, on 19 and 20 October, at the Medallion in Dallas, he vacillated between three possible musical endings: Cliff Edwards's original from *Pinocchio*, an orchestral version of the song, or an optimistic coda by Williams. Hirschfield insisted he use Edwards for at least the preview, and it was this that closed the Dallas screenings. But some of the 1400 audience sniggered at Edwards's reedy tenor, so Williams's piece replaced it. Responding to criticisms of the film's length, Spielberg also cut seven minutes after the previews, though it still ran over two hours, an irritant to exhibitors, who could squeeze in five shows a day only by starting the last at 10 p.m.

His editing delayed the release by some weeks, which dislocated Columbia's elaborate promotion plans. Journalist Bill Warren recalls:

> I was invited down to this colossal press event at the Bonaventure – twice . . . It was a particularly plush function. Not just loads of food, but free pocket tape recorders to interview everyone in sight . . . All the press materials, including the tape recorders, had been prepared for the cancelled press conference the month before . . . so most of the batteries were dead.

The majority of preview-goers loved the film, but a disappointed Hirschfield told friends that it was 'no *Jaws* or *Star Wars*'. Journalist William Flanagan, who wrote on personal finance for *New York* magazine, agreed. On Monday 31 October he told readers, 'In my humble opinion, the picture will be a colossal flop. It lacks the dazzle, charm, wit, imagination and broad audience appeal of *Star Wars* – the film Wall Street insists it measure up to.' These attacks, resonating with the Begelman scandal, dismayed investors. Columbia shares, which had soared from $7 to $18 in expectation of a hit, slumped to $15, and by Tuesday the flood of 'Sell' orders forced the New York Exchange to suspend trading in the stock. On Wednesday, in some desperate damage control, *Time*, a loyal investor, published a rave by its film critic Frank Rich, who'd bluffed his way into the Dallas screening by convincing a ticket-holder that *Close*

Encounters was a Disney wildlife documentary. The rot in Columbia shares stopped at $16 while the market waited for the 15 November opening.

But the gala preview at the Ziegfeld on 44th Street for the Cancer Research Institute was a spectacular success. Reviews were no less rhapsodic, and within hours, though snow fell that day in New York, people were queuing round the block to see the film. Its folksy sentiments, suburban setting, crystal-chandelier spaceship, even its feelgood aliens beguiled the most cynical audience. Spielberg's genius, not only as a cinema poet but as a technician, a marshal of cinematic forces, a market strategist, a cultural historian, was spectacularly on show.

And yet, if *Jaws* established Spielberg as a force in the industry, *Close Encounters* marked the beginning of his decline as an artist, and, some argue, of American cinema.

With this film, Spielberg had his own close encounter with photographic special effects. They kidnapped him, carrying him off to a distant galaxy where he was subjected to mind-altering experiments. He returned to earth with the conviction that anything was possible on film. Under his influence, chance began to disappear from Hollywood movies. For *Barry Lyndon*, Kubrick worked for months with cameraman John Alcott, developing a method of shooting by candlelight to reproduce the mood of eighteenth-century drawing rooms. Soon, however, film-makers found it easier to tweak the image optically to achieve such effects. The serendipity Truffaut celebrated in *Day for Night*, where a hotel vase could be substituted for a prop one or, in an extreme case, a script reconstructed when one of the stars died, also ceased to be matters of account for Hollywood. By 1994, when, in a similar case to *Day for Night*'s fiction, Brandon Lee died in an accident on the futuristic kung fu thriller *The Crow* when a prop pistol malfunctioned, director Alex Proyas could continue shooting with doubles and Lee's image with a new face 'morphed' in. Not only did nobody notice, but the film was a hit. Michael Crichton had already foreshadowed the possible wholesale replacement of performers with video simulations or computer animation. Spielberg, impatient with actors and devoted to the total control offered by animation, became the pioneer in putting Crichton's forecast into effect. Under his influence, all Hollywood film began to aspire to the condition of cartoon. It's no coincidence that its most skilful combinations of computer-generated images and live action, *Who Framed Roger Rabbit*, *Death Becomes Her* and *Forrest Gump*, should have been made by Robert Zemeckis, his most faithful protégé.

In 1979, *New Yorker* television critic Michael J. Arlen became one of the first writers to articulate the growing disquiet with this trend. He spoke of 'the tyranny of the visual' – the growing preference, especially on TV, for graphic over verbal story-telling, the tendency to avoid difficult subjects, or, having reluctantly addressed them, to glamorise even the most squalid historical eras with a Hallmark Greeting Card/Classics Comics approach, shooting hovels in soft-focus and giving rags a touch of *haute couture* style. (It was a trend of which, ironically, even Spielberg would be a victim when the Academy gave its 1982 Costumes Oscar to the dhotis and loincloths of *Gandhi*.)

Spielberg instigated this change in Hollywood, but he had plenty of equivalents in other arts, particularly musical superstars like Michael Jackson, Barbra Streisand and Andrew Lloyd Webber, with all of whom, significantly, he would pursue his ambition to make a giant musical. Spielberg had much in common, artistically, with these stars. An evaluation of Streisand by jazz critic Whitney Balliett could apply equally to Spielberg: 'The songs she sings are of small matter now . . . They are all part of a steadily unfurling carpet of sound . . . What she does so ingeniously is *Streisand* each song . . . She smoothes the melodic hills, raises the valleys, equalises the emotions, and encases the lyrics in a kind of silken sheen.' It insults Spielberg's intelligence to believe he didn't recognise this tendency in himself, nor the criticism it attracted. Yet he acquiesced. Only someone with Martin Scorsese's rigorous self-doubt would not have, which was why Spielberg respected him so much. Even as he admired *Raging Bull*, however, Spielberg knew he didn't dare make such a film at that time. But he believed that he was capable of doing so, and retained enough perspective to see that, eventually, he must try, if he was to live with himself.

* * *

For many directors even younger than himself, Spielberg was now a touchstone and role model. They were eager to work with – or for – him. So confident were Universal of his judgement that they offered to fund any project he recommended, no matter how untried the talent. Even *Variety*, not easily startled, couldn't keep the surprise out of its report on Universal's proposal. 'It may be the newest kind of completion bond,' it wrote on 30 November 1977. 'And it's more bankable than an insurance policy from Lloyd's of London.'

The first beneficiaries were Zemeckis and Gale. Their script 'Beatlemania' followed a group of New Jersey teenagers desperate to see their idols on Ed Sullivan's New York TV show in February 1964. Milius's executive producers on *Big Wednesday*, Tamara Assayev and Alexandra Rose, had taken it to Warners, who were interested, if only for the potential soundtrack album which might rival *American Graffiti*'s best-selling compilation of fifties rock. There was no enthusiasm, however, for Zemeckis as a director.

Spielberg recommended the project to Verna Fields at Universal. She passed it to Ned Tanen, who invested $2.6 million in the retitled *I Wanna Hold Your Hand*, 'on the assurance,' reported an awed *Variety*, 'that Zemeckis could handle the project, that Spielberg would serve as executive producer on the project and that if his judgement proved wrong he'd step in and direct the film himself.' In the event, Spielberg did little on the film. He said later that his only advice to Zemeckis was, 'Wear comfortable shoes.'

With some modifications, the Universal deal would be that with which Spielberg would metamorphose from director to producer, and on which he would base the success of Amblin Entertainment. Charitable commentators put his generosity down to memories of the years he'd spent trying to find someone to back his first feature. Undoubtedly this came into it. But there were more potent forces at work, in particular his fear of losing control of his world. Spielberg had begun to turn into what he'd always wished to become, a one-man studio.

Working with a cast of unknowns, except for De Palma's wife and star Nancy Allen, Zemeckis finished *I Wanna Hold Your Hand* without incident and under budget early in 1978. Spielberg brought in his *Duel* editor Frank Morriss to cut it. It opened in April to mostly kind reviews, but the under-eighteens, in their cradles when The Beatles were at their peak, didn't come to see it. It lost more money than any Universal film in the previous three years, a failure which should have warned Spielberg that teenagers preferred stories set in contemporary America or the mythic past and future.

In February 1978, in Copenhagen as part of a European trip to promote *Close Encounters*, Spielberg, asked about his plans, announced he would make the low-budget 'Growing Up' for Universal, scripted by Zemeckis and Gale from his own story, with shooting beginning in Arizona in March. The modest film would, he said, deal mainly with the things that absorbed modern kids, in particular TV. He wanted to show them acting out the plots of popular series like *Charlie's Angels*, as he had acted out Hollywood movies of the fifties. But 'Growing Up' would never be made. Instead he became sidetracked by the project originally due to follow it, the big-budget comedy *1941*, to be produced jointly by Columbia and Universal. Twenty people, he told the Danish press, were already creating the storyboards.

The coalition between studios was a new idea born of soaring budgets. In 1974, Warners and Universal, both having bought novels about a skyscraper fire, sensibly pooled their resources and made just one film, *The Towering Inferno*. Universal were nervous about backing *1941*, the budget of which was already topping $9 million, but nobody wanted to cut loose their single most profitable film-maker. Milius took the film to Columbia, which had similar reservations. A compromise was reached. Columbia would release it in the US and Universal throughout the rest of the world. Alan Hirschfield announced *1941* to the Columbia board as 'a broad farce, special-effects comedy in the genre of *Mad, Mad World*, and [it] could be an enormous picture'. John Milius would both write and produce, he said.

To bolster their resolve, Spielberg reassured the board, with a *chutzpah* even David Begelman might have envied, 'I will not make this film if it goes over $10 million.' His statement carried conviction. *Close Encounters* was bulldozing box-office records around the world. In three weeks in the US alone, it grossed $72 million. In London, it was chosen as the Royal Command Performance film. Spielberg and Amy, flanked by the security guards that were now a fixture of their life, came to London with the Hirschfields, Dreyfuss, Trumbull, Williams, Truffaut and Cary Guffey to shake hands with the Queen. Julia Phillips cancelled at the last minute. David Begelman also dropped out when the Palace discreetly removed him from the list.

A few days later, Spielberg stepped on stage at London's National Film Theatre to inaugurate a season of his films. On the drive there, he confided to NFT programmer Adrian Turner that he'd spent the day with Stanley Kubrick, who was preparing *The Shining* at Elstree. 'It's the main reason I came,' he said. At the NFT, he was greeted with an enthusiasm bordering on adulation. When he said he wouldn't discuss *Close Encounters* because it wasn't in the season, Turner asked who had already seen it in the cinema. Almost the entire audience raised its hands.

Back in LA, Spielberg, took over his new fourteen-room raw wood and fieldstone house at the top of Coldwater Canyon, with Amy as live-in companion. *Newsweek* patronisingly dismissed the house as 'a combination home and penny arcade that's filled with pool tables, pinball machines, computer games and other devices to delight the heart of a gadget freak'. He also rented a beach house at Malibu for weekends, installing a cutting room with a Steenbeck editing table. He and Irving were one of Hollywood's most visible and apparently contented couples. Instead of De Palma and Milius dropping in to talk movies, the guest list expanded to include people with a New York background and a wider cultural interest, among them Rob Reiner, Lisa Eichorn, Penny Marshall and Tim Mathison, though they also invited potential collaborators like John Landis to dinner, a sign that he'd been accepted into the inner circle.

While Spielberg worked on *Close Encounters*, Amy made *Fury* for De Palma, playing a psychic with latent powers to destroy, the sort of role for which her quickfire temper made her a natural. Spielberg himself had yet another brush with the supernatural when his grandmother died in a Phoenix nursing home. Spielberg's mother received the news at 2 a.m. At 5 a.m. the phone rang again, and Leah heard her mother's voice calling, 'Help me! He's coming to get me. He'll be here any minute. I'm terrified.' The next day, Leah's brother, the family tearaway who had joined the circus when Leah was still a girl, arrived at Leah's house in Los Angeles. Confusingly, LA psychic Thelma Moss connected the dead woman's son, whom she supposedly feared, with the spectral call. Generally open to the idea of psychic phenomena, Spielberg could make little sense of this and other phantom intimations of life on The Other Side. His confusion would drive him to make *Poltergeist* in 1981.

The Oscars presented on 29 March 1978 acknowledged both *Star Wars* and *Close Encounters* with faint praise. *Star Wars* was nominated for Best Picture and Lucas for Best Director and Best Original Screenplay, Alec Guinness for Best Supporting Actor. It also earned nominations for Best Art Direction, Sound, Editing, Music, Costume Design and Visual Effects. Spielberg was nominated as Best Director for *Close Encounters*, Melinda Dillon for Best Supporting Actress, with nominations too for Best Cinematography, Art Direction, Sound, Music, Editing and Visual Effects. Richard Dreyfuss was nominated as Best Actor – not for *Close Encounters*, however, but for *The Goodbye Girl*, the Neil Simon comedy he'd done with Herbert Ross while Spielberg was busy shooting the special effects of 'CE3K', as the fans were beginning to call it.

For political reasons, Spielberg escorted Julia to the Oscar ceremony, but his thoughts were elsewhere – as was Amy, who had elected to play a deaf-mute dancer in the low-budget *Voices* for Robert Markowitz, and was on location. Their relationship, after having taken a long time to warm up – 'Amy and I must have been together for a year and a half before we got to be friends,' Spielberg said – was now cooling. To her friends, Amy talked about having children, but Spielberg recoiled from such a commitment. She also disliked having her career options curtailed. 'People who know you,' she said, meaning Spielberg's film-making colleagues, 'don't think about you as being anybody else.' It was a common

problem with directors' wives. Friends assumed the wife was the husband's professional property, and were nervous about auditioning her.
If they didn't hire her, the director might be upset. Of perhaps he'd be
more irritated if they did.

When Amy decided to do *Voices*, she made a point of letting people
know she hadn't asked Spielberg's advice before she accepted. It was the
kind of comment that had Hollywood exchanging glances and raising
eyebrows. With it, she presented him with another catch-22. If the film
was a hit, it would prove she knew better than he, and could therefore
do without him. If it flopped, she would look foolish and, inevitably,
would blame Spielberg. Irving learned sign language for *Voices*, and
taught Spielberg a few words, including 'I love you, Amy.' During his
ritual close-up as the Best Director award was announced, he had agreed
to sign this message to her, but lost his nerve and instead mouthed the
words silently into the lens.

If Spielberg hoped that *Close Encounters* would earn him his due from
Old Hollywood, the voting proved otherwise. Zsigmond was honoured
for his photography, but in every other category where *Close Encounters*
competed with *Star Wars*, Lucas won. Lucas's victory was hollow, however, since the key awards all went to Woody Allen for *Annie Hall* or to
Fred Zinnemann's *Julia*. Dreyfuss at twenty-nine became the youngest
actor to take the Best Actor statuette. Allen, pointedly contemptuous of
the Oscars and Hollywood, played clarinet that night at Michael's Pub
in New York, then went home to bed without, he said, knowing or caring
that he'd won Best Picture, Best Film and shared the Best Screenplay
Oscar as well.

The question asked more than any other while Spielberg toured the
world promoting *Close Encounters* was, 'Will there be a sequel?' At the
earliest press conferences, he admitted that a script was in preparation
for Columbia. The fact didn't delight him. It was Michael and Julia
Phillips, not his own instinct, that had taken him to Columbia, and now
it was he, not they, who was stuck there by the studio's option to
make a sequel. Melnick could simply, if he wished, commission *Close*

Encounters 2 and assign it to whomsoever he wanted, as Universal had done with *Jaws*. To head them off, Spielberg wrote a brief treatment called 'Night Skies' that might serve as the basis of the new film.

During the research for *Close Encounters*, Allen Hynek had described an incident in 1955 when a Kentucky family claimed to have been terrorised by a dozen aliens surrounding their farm. Unlike the playful visitors of *Close Encounters*, these interlopers were mischievous and occasionally violent. Spielberg imagined the family cowering in their farmhouse as the aliens, unsure of which was the intelligent species, tried to communicate with chickens, rode on cows and, in a reference to a rash of cattle mutilations often credited to aliens, dissected an animal before resolving to cut up a human as well. Eventually a child makes the vital contact that saves the family.

In March 1978 NASA announced that Spielberg had paid $500 to reserve space in the cargo bay of the first Space Shuttle flight, scheduled for 1980. He wanted, they said, to film the earth and moon from orbit for use in the sequel to *Close Encounters*. Even if he had acquired such footage, however, he would have used it sparingly. 'Night Skies' was intended to be intimate, rural. His model was *The Twilight Zone*, an exemplar he would try repeatedly to replicate in *Poltergeist*, *The Twilight Zone: The Movie*, his *Amazing Stories* series, and in *E.T.*; creeping out to look for the alien at night in their yard, the teenagers of that movie even imitate the *Twilight Zone* theme.

Columbia continued to rock with aftershocks of the Begelman scandal. Arguments about whether he should be jettisoned deepened the rift between Ray Stark loyalists and those who backed the board and Hirschfield. In Hollywood, most people felt he must be dismissed, if not as a simple matter of justice, then to reduce the public-relations disaster of his continuing presence inside the company. The accountants in New York, however, argued to keep someone who had proved himself a money-maker. The balance of power shifted significantly when Dan Melnick, now in effective charge of the studio, hired someone to take the job his promotion had left vacant. He chose Frank Price, head of

Universal's TV division, whose prospects there were blocked by Shein-berg and Wasserman. A twenty-year veteran of the corporate wars, Price allied himself with Stark, who would back him on films like *The China Syndrome* and *Kramer versus Kramer* that built on the success of *Close Encounters*. In return, Price approved a treasured Stark project, a film of the musical *Annie*. The change undermined Hirschfield's anti-Begelman position, and he was fired in July 1978.

Spielberg, who was essentially pro-Begelman, loathed the new Col-umbia administration, particularly Price, who'd imported his Universal team and looked set to steer Columbia towards a corporate style geared entirely to maximum marketing, especially on TV. Both Alan Ladd Jr at Fox and Warner Brothers' production head Terry Semel looked more cordial, more *family*, and more attuned to his kind of film-making. In particular, Spielberg was impressed with Steve Ross, whose Kinney Services had acquired Warners in 1969. Ross, tall, soft-spoken, silver-haired and diabolically skilful at personal manipulation, was to insinuate himself into Spielberg's life and career like a suave and tailored forties Hollywood Mephistopheles, changing them forever.

The clamour for a sequel to *Close Encounters* had modified into a call mainly to know what Neary saw inside the mother ship. If that was all they wanted, Spielberg decided, he could satisfy them and Columbia, and at the same time fine-tune the film, correcting the imbalances imposed by deadlines, second-guessing, bad advice and the hasty post-production caused by the studio's decision to bring forward the release date. Instead of a new film, he proposed a revised version of the original. At the same time he would continue to work on 'Night Skies', to be produced by him but written and directed by some talented newcomers he would choose. Columbia were delighted with the compromise. Billed as the 'Special Edition', the new version could be premiered at Cannes in May, giving *Close Encounters*, in effect, an entire second incarnation for the summer of 1980 without the cost of a new film. They agreed to fund seven weeks of additional shooting, providing the new version included the scene everyone clamoured for: a view inside the mother ship.

While a mother ship interior was built and shot, Spielberg took up the scissors with relish. Out went the Phillipses' Watergate sub-plot of the

USAF hushing up encounters of the first and second kind. In particular he dropped a scene where USAF Major Benchley tries to explain away UFOs to a group of believers. The meeting ends in confusion as a patriarchal Roberts Blossom starts lecturing them on his sighting of Bigfoot.

Dreyfuss's performance suffered most, since Spielberg knew he'd over-played the suburban reality of Neary's life. He cut his visit to the electrical substation during the blackout, as well as a scene that survived from Schrader's drafts, showing how, looting chickenwire from a neighbour's yard, Neary builds a huge model of Devil's Tower, turning his living room, in Schrader's words, 'into a kind of Zen garden'. He also restored most of the seven minutes cut after the preview, including the discovery of a cargo ship high and dry in the Gobi Desert. The new film was three minutes shorter, but not, in the estimate of most people, much better. In particular, many felt the spaceship interior resembled the atrium of a particularly gaudy shopping mall.

Norman Levy, Frank Price's head of marketing, announced that the old version would be 'retired', and eight hundred existing prints destroyed, with only the negative and a few archival copies retained. Seething, Spielberg insisted that Levy was misinformed – *Variety* headlined its report with a hand-rubbing 'Col "Encounters" Plans News to Steven Spielberg' – and that both versions would continue to circulate, but Columbia had their way, and soon the Special Edition was the only version generally available. Adding insult to injury, Price drained another $2 million from the project for the studio's notional contribution. As Julia Phillips commented acidly, this meant that the most successful film in screen history remained, two years after its first release, and with grosses of $77 million in the US alone, technically in the red. Columbia was thus relieved of the necessity to pay the Phillipses their portion of the profit.

A number of events influenced Spielberg's decision to make *1941* – which, as late as the last day of shooting on *Close Encounters*, he was still calling 'The Rising Sun'. One was *Annie Hall*'s success, which he took as a personal challenge. Early in 1976 he'd told British journalist Barbara Paskin:

I've always been a frustrated comedian, a frustrated director of comedy. I've wanted to do what Woody Allen's been doing for a long time now. People laugh when I tell them that. But I really started my career making short joke movies. Movies that were a play on words, that contained visual gags, films that were slightly reminiscent of your *Goon Shows* and the *Monty Python* skits. I was very caught up in that and I'd like very much to return and get back into comedy.

Another factor was his growing admiration for John Belushi, whom he adopted as a sort of feckless but good-hearted younger brother. 'John was to me the opposite of his film image,' he decided. 'He was a very tender man looking for love and looking for people to like him and people he could like back . . . I think John sort of was the messy side of all of us. John represented messy bedrooms all over America.' He'd enjoyed Belushi's first film, *National Lampoon's Animal House*, directed by John Landis, which came out during the making of *Close Encounters*. As Bluto, the fraternity's ultimate party animal, Belushi was Harpo Marx's Mr Hyde, a goggling, inarticulate Lord of Misrule, addicted to food fights and voyeurism.

Many felt later that the frantic physical comedy of *1941* was Spielberg's attempt to duplicate *Animal House* on a grand scale. Surely, he reasoned, the teenage audience he and Belushi shared was ripe for another farce. There was also an element of competition with Landis, whose stock was rising in Hollywood. The two men were natural antagonists, a rivalry that would crystallise a few years later in another disaster, *The Twilight Zone: The Movie*.

Not long after meeting Belushi in Los Angeles, Spielberg went to New York to discuss his role. The actor took him to his hideaway, a soundproofed vault on Morton Street with a massive sound system. Food scraps and candy-bar wrappers littered the floor. As Spielberg sat down gingerly, Belushi put on a blues album at deafening volume and began haranguing him about his love of rhythm and blues. Spielberg tried to turn the conversation to *1941*. He no longer wanted Belushi in the small role as the Japanese sub captain, he said. Instead of an imitation Toshiro Mifune, he could – and did – hire Mifune himself, as well as veteran horror-film actor (and German-speaker) Christopher Lee as a Nazi officer. Belushi was now pencilled in for the more important central role of off-the-wall pilot 'Wild Bill' Kelso, who rampages across the west after phantom squadrons of Zeros before crashing spectacularly on Hollywood Boulevard, the set for which was even then being built at Burbank.

Spielberg later slighted the screenplay of 1941 as about as tasteful as Mad magazine, but initially he loved its yammering energy. Though they had already written their script for the more focused Back to the Future, Zemeckis and Gale at the time were preoccupied with mechanistic stories involving a multitude of characters and coincidences, all building towards a vigorous action climax. 1941 was characteristic. Set on 13 December 1941, it covers Kelso's wild flight, his night-time landing in the camp of Colonel 'Mad Man' Maddox (Warren Oates), and his eventual crash. The sole voice of reason, Californian coastal defence commander General Stilwell (Robert Stack, in a role originally offered to John Wayne, who patriotically refused when he heard that two American aircraft crashed in the film), minimises the Japanese threat while trying to relax watching Dumbo in a Hollywood Boulevard cinema.

Meanwhile, in parallel stories, a riot is building between enlisted men led by Sitarski (Treat Williams) and zoot-suited locals at a nearby dance, USAF Captain Birkhead (Tim Mathison) is trying to seduce Stillwell's secretary Donna (Nancy Allen), who is sexually aroused by aircraft, a Japanese submarine with a Nazi officer on board is cruising off Santa Monica, and the house-proud Douglases (Ned Beatty and Lorraine Gary) are appalled when artillery is sited in their Santa Monica garden. The stories coalesce in a violent final two reels which combine a jitterbug contest and riot, and the destruction of the Douglas house and the nearby amusement park, at the conclusion of which a ferris wheel rolls down the pier and into the Pacific.

Belushi was delighted with the story, but wouldn't be rushed on his performance.

'We'll work it out on the set,' he assured Spielberg. 'I'm best there. I'm fast. I like to improvise. I won't let you down.'

When Spielberg, his ears ringing, left Morton Street, Belushi thanked him for offering the part. Unaccustomed to gratitude from actors,

Spielberg was further disarmed. The actor's enthusiasm helped soften the blow when Belushi's agent, Bernie Brillstein, told him his price had risen to $350,000. This was more than Dreyfuss had got for *Close Encounters*, but Spielberg swallowed and paid it.

At their next meeting in Hollywood, Belushi offhandedly introduced Dan Aykroyd to Spielberg as Sergeant Tree, the gung-ho tank commander who spouts patriotic speeches straight out of John Wayne movies and installs an artillery piece on a Pacific headland to blast the passing Japanese sub and Ned Beatty's house as well. Aykroyd, a better actor than Belushi and, above all, more controlled, slipped into character and reeled off reams of statistics about tanks and artillery. Spielberg promptly cast him. Not only was he a natural for movies; he would also keep Belushi under control and, hopefully, away from drugs.

In hiring ex-*Saturday Night Live* comics like Aykroyd and Mathison, Spielberg also believed he was buying insurance. Even if the film wasn't funny, the performers were sure to be. Brillstein wasn't so sure. He'd read the script and found it flat. He also worried about letting his client loose in Los Angeles, a supermarket of narcotics which the insecure and self-destroying Belushi would be unable to resist. But the actor ignored Brillstein's warnings about the writing and the director's lack of comedy experience. Belushi had been dazzled by *Close Encounters*, whose ideas he embraced with almost religious fervour. There was also a growing perception that the director had the Midas touch. Being cast in *1941* affirmed Belushi's stardom. 'I can't turn down *Spielberg*,' he told Brillstein.

While *1941* lurched towards its troubled birth, Spielberg dealt with other unfinished business. MGM finally sold him the rights to *A Guy Named Joe*. A succession of screenwriters started work on adapting it. Still feeling Dreyfuss was too young for the self-sacrificing pilot, Spielberg raised the project with Robert Redford and Paul Newman. Both were interested, but both wanted to play Joe. Nor did any leading lady come to mind. Later, he confessed his real reason for shelving the project: 'I wasn't mature enough emotionally then.'

In July, Dennis Stanfill fired Alan Ladd Jr from Fox. Ladd and his
team set about forming a new group, The Ladd Company, but for the
moment a potential haven was closed to Spielberg. Coppola had meanwhile conceived another off-the-wall money-making scheme, this time
to buy up strip clubs and topless bars in San Francisco's sleazy Broadway
district and turn them into smart nightclubs and theatres. Spielberg
agreed to be one of the backers, along with rock impresario Bill Graham.

With Lucas, Spielberg also hammered out details of their joint production of *Raiders of the Lost Ark*. Both were tentative about complicating
an eleven-year friendship with a business relationship, especially one as
volatile as that between producer and director, though Spielberg more
so. People were watching, and quite a few of them, including some
friends, wouldn't be sorry to see them fall out. 'This movie,' acknowledged Spielberg, 'is the proving ground of whether we – not just George
and me, but all our friends – can continue to make movies together
without feeling envious or competitive or resentful.'

To make sure, right from the start, that nobody muddied the water,
they jettisoned middlemen. Without agents, they wrote out their deal
on the lined paper of a school exercise book. Late in October, Lucas's
long-time lawyer Tom Pollock, who shared their no-suit-no-tie style,
handed it to every studio simultaneously. It was a technique he'd pioneered in the early seventies, when, representing Barwood and Robbins,
he submitted scripts like *The Bingo Long Travelling All Stars and Motor
Kings* to a dozen companies at once.

Details of the proposal leaked almost immediately to columnist Liz
Smith. 'Hollywood will practically explode,' she wrote, 'and every executive suite in the cinema world may have to be redecorated after the
screaming, scratching, clawing tantrums and furniture-throwing that will
accompany [its] exposure.'

As foretold, the Suits took as a gigantic insult the suggestion that they
pay $20 million to make the film, including $1.5 million to Spielberg
and $4 million to Lucas, as well as bearing almost all the costs of distri-
bution and agreeing to pay Lucas's and Spielberg's share out of the first
dollar earned. Some said $20 million was too little to make the film: the
opening scene alone, of Indy invading a booby-trapped Inca temple,

spluttered one, would cost at least $50 million. Nobody believed the film would be finished in eighty-five days, as promised. Spielberg had gone over time and budget on *Jaws*; what guarantee that he wouldn't do so again?

Nor were they enthusiastic about homages to serials, pulps and comics. TV's *Batman* had run from 1966 to 1968, but features based on the *Doc Savage* stories and *Flash Gordon* had flopped. Lucas explained that these knowing parodies were played for 'camp'. 'The secret [of *Raiders'* success] is, of course,' wrote British critic John Brosnan, 'that Spielberg and Lucas have an unashamedly personal involvement in the material, and their obvious enjoyment of putting it on the screen is communicated to the audience.'

The furore was nowhere greater than at Universal, where Wasserman and Sheinberg had a series of anguished meetings to consider the project. 'Lew and Sid,' said one insider, 'it drove them crazy. As far as they were concerned, that deal was asking for unheard-of pieces of profit, and ownership. And they passed on it, because it was something that went beyond their definition of how things should be.' Indignation blinded them to a deal which one of the wiser executives called 'almost as innovative and implicit with change as the advent of sound'. Even Disney rejected the project out of hand.

The reaction dramatised the contrasting management philosophies of Old Hollywood and New. 'The most important thing to remember about a deal, and about negotiation,' wrote producer Dawn Steel, articulating the studio line, 'is that it is all about appetite. It's not the details or the complications of a deal that matter, it's how much you want it, and how much you're willing to spend for it . . . Deal-making is . . . about putting a price on your appetite and then sticking to it.' But Spielberg and Lucas were ascetics. They had no appetites as the lawyers and accountants understood them. The Lear Jet, the yacht, the Bel Air mansion and the recognition of every head waiter in town meant nothing to them. Julia Phillips complained testily of Spielberg, 'I taught the little prick he deserved limos before he even knew what it was like to travel in a first-class seat on a plane.'

If one pressed Lucas, Milius and Spielberg to define their needs, almost all would reply that they wanted to keep enjoying the things that got them through adolescence: comic books, TV, movies and their gang. Adolescents at heart, they craved games to play, candy and hamburgers to eat, old cars to ride around in, friends with whom to hang out and a place to do it. Big agents and studio heads ate at Ma Maison, George Lucas at Hamburger Hamlet. Most of all, as Scott Fitzgerald had said of all men, they wanted to be famous and to be loved.

Only Michael Eisner, quietly-spoken, dark-suited head of production at Paramount (and later of Disney), saw that the *Raiders* deal, once one got over the shock of its unconventional terms, was a worthwhile risk. Even if it needed to gross $60 million before the studio saw a profit, the track records of Lucas and Spielberg almost guaranteed that any such profit would be enormous. 'We're supposed to be creative people,' Eisner told Pollock. 'So let's make a creative deal.'

Eisner left the details to his head of business affairs, Dick Zimbert, a bean-counter whose ability to put more beans in Paramount's basket than those of its clients was legendary. Zimbert invented the 'rolling break'. Directors, writers and stars only began earning money on their 'points' when the film broke even, but under Zimbert's formulae, this horizon, delayed, sometimes indefinitely, by bank interest and the costs of marketing, distribution and new prints, receded as fast as the film approached it. Zimbert's expertise dazzled almost everyone. 'Most of the people who were negotiating rolling break-even,' wrote Dawn Steel, then a junior producer at Paramount, 'had no idea what it meant.'

With Zimbert's guidance, Eisner coaxed Lucas and Spielberg into shouldering some market costs, part of the loan interest, and paying the studio a small fee for distributing the film. He also improved Paramount's share of the rental income, from 40 to 50 per cent. Nor was the deal without guarantees. 'We built in some serious penalties if they went over,' says Eisner, 'and they agreed without hesitation. I figured either they don't care or they've got this thing figured out.' Assuming the latter, Eisner also wrote in provision for a minimum of four sequels.

Just to check his reasoning, Eisner ran the deal past his CEO, Charles Weber, who in turn asked the opinion of his friend, the entrepreneur Robert Stigwood, who had backed the hits *Grease* and *Saturday Night*

Fever. Stigwood urged him to go for it – and, backing his judgement, negotiated a private deal with Lucasfilm for future projects.

In December 1978, Eisner signed, and *Raiders of the Lost Ark*, for better or worse, was set as Spielberg's next film after *1941*. New Hollywood had supplanted the old with scarcely a murmur. The sandcastle meeting assumed superstitious significance for Spielberg. It became his practice to leave the US on the eve of opening a new film and spend the week of its release in Hawaii.

In retrospect, 1978 was not the year for *1941*. Vietnam had become the national embarrassment, and the public, after refusing for a decade to look at any film on the subject except John Wayne's *The Green Berets*, was embracing it with masochistic fervour – just as Wayne, coincidentally, had open-heart surgery. In the Philippines, Coppola was winding up an epic shoot on *Apocalypse Now*. Already on screen, Jane Fonda in *Coming Home* was having sex with paraplegic veteran Jon Voight. *The Deer Hunter*, the *Schindler's List* of its day, 182 minutes of relentless delving into the moral morass of Vietnam, with a *leitmotif* of Russian roulette that paralleled this most agonising of self-inflicted national wounds, was a hit. Grown men broke down during screenings, gloated director Michael Cimino, and retreated, sobbing, to the toilets, leaning on their buddies' arms. An urge for films about abasement and humiliation swept Hollywood. In *Midnight Express*, Brad Davis, a nice American boy arrested for drug smuggling, was brutalised in a Turkish prison. Woody Allen decided he was ready to go *mano a mano* against Ingmar Bergman and made *Interiors*, his first drama – and first flop. Sackcloth and ashes were *à la mode*. Crow was served at all the best restaurants, with humble pie to follow.

Against this current of angst, Spielberg swam stubbornly towards farce. As if in reaction, he oversold *1941*, pushing its multiple stars, the variety of incident, the wealth of influences. In August 1978 he'd assured *Variety*, somewhat incoherently, that he was making an 'action misadventure . . . with a chock full of nuts'. Chuck Jones was retained as visual consultant, and Spielberg told a London audience that he hoped *1941* would resemble a Road Runner cartoon. He suggested similarities to Norman Jewison's *The Russians are Coming, The Russians are Coming*, a low-budget 1966 comedy about a Soviet submarine stranded off the eastern United States. It would also have the feeling of Laurel and Hardy, he said. And *Hellzapoppin*. And Mack Sennett, *and* the Three Stooges.

The film even opened with a quotation, this time from Spielberg himself. Susan Backlinie, the nude bather devoured at the opening of *Jaws*, was called back for another swim, interrupted this time by Mifune's surfacing submarine. But it was the parallels with childhood favourites that Spielberg relished. The film has homages to *Doctor Strangelove*, and to *The Quiet Man*: its brawl takes place to Victor Young's sprightly reel that accompanies the battle between Wayne and Victor McLaglen in John Ford's classic. But it was the parallels with Stanley Kramer's 1963 *It's a Mad, Mad, Mad, Mad World* he pursued most energetically. There were multiple similarities, not only in the pie- and cake-fights, brawls, buildings being blown up, planes and cars crashing and human victims caught in elaborate traps, like a collapsing fire escape, but in its characters. Kramer had cast his old friend Spencer Tracy as C.G. Culpepper, the only man to keep his head in the frantic pursuit of the fortune hidden by dying criminal Jimmy Durante. Robert Stack has a similar role in *1941*. Spielberg's aircraft scenes with Tim Mathison and Nancy Allen recall Buddy Hackett and Mickey Rooney trying to fly a plane in Kramer's film, and being talked down by Paul Ford, while Ned Beatty and Lorraine Gary are the Milton Berle and Ethel Merman of *Mad World* writ small. Kramer had wanted to make 'the comedy to end all comedies'. Instead *Mad World* showed that enormous resources were less important than a sense of humour – a lesson Spielberg was now to learn.

Spielberg approached the film with his customary innovative flair. He told William Fraker, who lit *1941*, that he wanted a less gaudy, over-illuminated look than the typical Hollywood farce, so the cameraman shot almost everything, including Greg Jein's miniatures of Santa Monica's Ocean Park amusement park and pier, in smoke or through fog filters. In a reverse of Spielberg's usual method, the miniatures and effects work were shot first, and the actors integrated later. It was an early and ominous indication that people mattered less than the gags.

During his European promotion tours of 1978 Spielberg discovered the new Louma crane system, which put a lightweight camera at the end of an extendable fifteen-foot boom and allowed it to glide across a set without the use of a massive dolly. It became the film's primary camera, perfectly suited to shoot the brawl between Army boys and zoot-suiters, for which he hired the Burbank Studios, with the largest stages in Hollywood. Scenes with the eighty-foot submarine would be filmed in MGM'S giant tank, where he'd shot parts of *Jaws*.

Belushi arrived in Los Angeles in October 1978, and Spielberg took him to the hangar where Hollywood Boulevard had been recreated. The comedian was awed. This was nothing like the poky sets of *Saturday Night Live*.

'Gee, you're making a real Hollywood movie,' he said.

'Yeah,' Spielberg said proudly. 'We build it up, then we destroy it.'

Shooting went on through November in the same miasma of self-congratulation. The stages, unlike those in Mobile, were cool and comfortable. Everyone enjoyed the jokes: the mood on the set was of genuine hilarity. Inspired, Spielberg increasingly abandoned his storyboards and improvised new gags. The finale in particular developed into an intricate interlocking set of actions, each triggering the next, like one of the Rube Goldberg contraptions which Spielberg admired and wrote into films like 1985's *The Goonies*.

Kramer had filled *Mad World* with cameos for famous comedians like Buster Keaton and the Three Stooges. *1941* might have benefited from the same idea, but the distinguished bit-players with whom Spielberg scattered the film were, with the exception of Slim Pickens, mostly dramatic actors, like Lionel Stander and Elisha Cook Jr. John Landis appears. So, though he was more a hero for Milius than Spielberg, does veteran director Sam Fuller. He also found a role for Eddie Deezen, a long-faced, big-eared actor with a voice like fingernails on a blackboard whom he'd noticed in *I Wanna Hold Your Hand* and recognised as a lookalike of his adolescent self. Deezen has the thankless role, shared with a dummy, of the coastwatcher perched on the ferris wheel which ends up in the Pacific.

Belushi was difficult. The actor came on the set with only a notional grasp of his lines, and worked his way into the part. Even the simplest scene demanded six or seven takes. At Spielberg's request, Aykroyd nursemaided him off the set, hiding, out of loyalty, the real reason for his erratic behaviour: the hourly snort of cocaine, without which Belushi's attention and energy wavered. At night, Belushi partied with other cokeheads among the cast and crew; one member of the unit counted twenty-five regular users. Treat Williams, who played Sitarski, accompanied Belushi on his nocturnal excursions from bar to club to 'connection', watching in awe as the comic snorted $500 of coke in a single line, then jammed on guitar until dawn. The pace soon began to tell. On 4 December, Belushi arrived late to work, a cardinal sin for Spielberg, who worked at lightning speed and counted every minute. The next day, he still hadn't arrived an hour after his call. Thirty minutes later, model and actress Lauren Hutton drove onto the lot and delivered a Belushi so stoned he half fell out of her car.

Among the new staff taken onto the payroll for 1941 was Kathleen Kennedy, a thirty-one-year-old producer from San Diego daytime TV who'd accepted a job indexing special-effects shots in order to break into features. She found Spielberg's office a rat's nest. 'I got there and he had written stuff on napkins, on the backs of envelopes, on any piece of scrap paper he could find in the house. I spent that first day and night sorting his ideas out.' A brilliant organiser and fanatically loyal, Kennedy soon made herself indispensable and was bumped up to Milius's assistant.

Kennedy accompanied the furious Spielberg to Belushi's trailer, and found Hutton trying to din the day's dialogue into his fuddled brain. Seeing Spielberg's fury, Hutton hurriedly left, and Spielberg raged at Belushi. He was being paid what was, for the director, an enormous sum, and giving nothing for it. Spielberg assigned associate producer Janet Healy to stay with him every minute, making sure he arrived on time and knew his lines.

Spielberg plunged deeper and deeper into a film which, his instinct warned him, wasn't working. 'If you're having this much fun making a movie,' he told himself, 'something must be wrong.' To cover himself, he reshot repeatedly, hoping for better effects. The skidding crash of Belushi's P-40 along Hollywood Boulevard was done three times, at

$1 million a time. He also repeated the elaborate sequence where the ferris wheel rolls down the pier into the Pacific. A joker on the unit printed up T-shirts which reproduced his incautious promise, 'I will not make this film if it goes over $10 million.' Each week, a new shirt made its appearance with the old figure crossed out and a higher one substituted. It's an index to Spielberg's good humour that the crew wore these openly, and he never complained.

Piling on detail merely made the film more unwieldy. Spielberg had missed the lesson of *Animal House*, which, for all its food-fights and sight gags, hinged on slapstick, not hardware. *1941* also lacked a pretext for its action, Hitchcock's 'MacGuffin', which, be it ever so trivial, the characters were looking for, and which focused the narrative. Spielberg ended shooting with the ominous conviction that he'd made a dud. At the wrap party, everyone got a facsimile combat ribbon – 'The point of which,' said Jeff Walker, who later marketed the ribbon and a *1941* baseball cap to a largely indifferent market, 'was, "I survived *1941*."' On 9 December, Spielberg told the *New York Times*, 'I'll spend the rest of my life disowning this movie.' The man who'd so skilfully estimated the taste of his audience on other occasions would turn out to be right again.

10

Raiders of the Lost Ark

Those Good Old Saturday-Matinee Serials Inspire This Year's
Perfect Summer Movie.

Sub-head in *Time* magazine, 15 June 1981

AFTER *1941*, Belushi and Aykroyd went on to co-star in John Landis's
big-screen celebration of Jake and Elwood Blues, the blues-singing
brothers from Chicago in black suits, hats and shades (but white socks)
who had been their most popular creation for *Saturday Night Live*. Backed
by Universal, *The Blues Brothers* began modestly, but news of Spielberg's
spending on *1941* drove Landis to paroxysms of competitiveness. A
modest story of two guys trying to raise $5000 to save their old orphanage
evolved into a car-chase comedy, the multi-vehicle pile-ups of which
dwarfed both *Sugarland Express* and *It's a Mad, Mad, Mad, Mad World*.
Blues Brothers eventually cost $33 million – more than *1941*. (Estimates
of *1941*'s cost varied. Spielberg set it at $26.5 million before re-editing
and redubbing, but some guesses at the total expenditure went as high
as $40 million.) Landis persuaded Spielberg to play a cameo – not
inappropriately, he's the clerk in the Cook County Tax Assessor's office
who accepts the brothers' payment.

On 14 April 1979, Francis Coppola threw a combined fortieth birthday
and Zoetrope tenth anniversary party at his Napa estate. As bands played,
cheerleaders chanted 'Francis has the power,' and Coppola led his guests,
who included Robert de Niro, Dennis Hopper, Wim Wenders and George
Lucas, in shouting, 'We will rule Hollywood! We will rule Hollywood!'
As his own modest first step towards this goal, Spielberg moved into

Lucasfilms, a shabby converted warehouse of green-painted cinderblock across the road from Universal's black glass tower.

Still convinced Belushi had a place in the hearts of American filmgoers, Spielberg, while editing *1941*, sent him a script by Lawrence Kasdan. Born in Miami, the son of two failed writers, raised in West Virginia and Wisconsin, educated in Michigan, Kasdan was, like Spielberg and Lucas, more a citizen of the movies than of any actual city. A prolific and facile writer, he spent seven years as a prize-winning advertising copywriter in Los Angeles before deciding to break into movies with a calling-card script which, according to legend, he wrote during lunch hours on the lawn in front of the Los Angeles Museum of Modern Art. Kasdan saw 'The Bodyguard', about the romance between a rock star and the tough guy sent to guard her from a deranged fan, as a Steve McQueen film. However, McQueen and sixty-six other producers turned it down, mostly because its rock concert and Bel Air mansion settings made it too expensive. Kasdan responded with another script which even the most penny-pinching producer would find attractive. A romantic comedy strongly influenced by Howard Hawks, its main characters were a misanthropic Chicago journalist and an attractive ornithologist who fall in love while sharing a Wyoming cabin from which she's observing a pair of eagles. Kasdan called it *Continental Divide*. Spielberg liked the script so much he sent it to Lucas at the end of 1977. Lucas promptly hired Kasdan to take over from an ailing Leigh Brackett on the second *Star Wars* film, *The Empire Strikes Back*.

In *Continental Divide*, Spielberg found the abrasive charm of his favourite Tracy/Hepburn films. If Belushi lost weight and kicked drugs, he could be excellent as the journalist. Bernie Brillstein agreed. Rumours of their interest sparked a bidding war, and Universal paid a delighted Kasdan $150,000, with a further $100,000 if the script was filmed.

Spielberg called a meeting at Coldwater Canyon with Kasdan, Hal Barwood and Matthew Robbins. In 1979 Barwood and Robbins had launched a production company, Plotto, with *Corvette Summer*. Robbins directed, Barwood produced and both wrote this comedy about Mark Hamill searching LA for his stolen vintage Corvette, but the public saw it as a pale imitation of *American Graffiti*. Ned Tanen, however, would, if Belushi agreed, accept the pair as producer and director of *Continental Divide* at Universal under the same terms as *I Wanna Hold Your Hand* and Zemeckis and Gale's second, more successful film, *Used Cars*; Spielberg must act as executive producer and promise to step in and direct if necessary.

Everyone in the house that night sensed that *Continental Divide* was the last chance for Barwood and Robbins, a team who, like Lucas's writers on *American Graffiti*, Willard Huyck and Gloria Katz, and his USC director friend John Korty, seemed irredeemably consigned to New Hollywood's also-rans.

Belushi arrived, drunk, with his wife Judy, and became drunker. He loved *Continental Divide*, he said. He recognised the main character, Ernie Souchak, as a version of columnist Mike Royko, whom he'd met and admired while living in Chicago and working with the Second City comedy troupe.

Then he turned to Robbins. What else had he directed? The atmosphere chilled as Robbins explained about *Corvette Summer*. The news that he'd made only one other film, and that a flop, infuriated Belushi. He began rambling about how he'd been bullied and patronised on *Goin' South* by another inexperienced director, Jack Nicholson.

'Jack treated me like shit,' he snarled. 'I hate him. If I see him, I'll punch him.'

Spielberg was silent. Robbins looked in vain for a romantic lead in the stumpy, bloated actor. What actress would want to play opposite him? Had Spielberg's instinct failed him, as it was rumoured to have done on *1941*? After two hours, the Belushis disappeared into the night. The others sat around, disconsolate, while Spielberg apologised, and reassured them. Somehow, the film would be made, without Belushi if necessary.

In the wake of *Close Encounters*, Spielberg had been confident he could raise money on any project. Ironically, however, his very success proved a liability, as he found when he went round the studios with *Continental Divide* and his after-school film.

I said, 'I can make this movie for $2.5 million. There's three people in the entire cast. It's a wonderful story.' And they said, 'We don't want you for this kind of movie. There are a lot of directors who can do this as well as anybody . . . We want you to do a movie about the size of the World Trade Center. Utilise all the tricks, utilise all the effects, utilise all the sound stages, and here's the money.' And, on cue, a door opens and wheelbarrows come in with ten-thousand-dollar bills.

Spielberg and Lucas asked Kasdan to write *Raiders*. The story had changed radically since the partners' sandcastle conference. Among other things, they'd ordered up Universal's 1941 *Don Winslow of the Navy*, watched all twelve episodes – and been bored out of their minds. The direction of serial veterans Ford Beebe and Ray Taylor was flat, the characters cardboard. There was a striking contrast between the dismal acting scenes and the car chases and fights, artificially pepped up by shooting at eighteen frames a second and projecting the film at twenty-four: the famous 'Western Eighteen'. It also became clear why serial heroes wore large fedoras pulled down over their eyes: it disguised the fact that doubles replaced them for most of the action. 'These things sure don't hold up after twenty-five years,' Lucas said.

Privately, both Spielberg and Kasdan were pleased, since they loathed serials. When Spielberg quoted from a film, it was more likely to be an A-movie, like a Spencer Tracy/Katharine Hepburn romance, of which there would be more than an echo in the love scenes of *Raiders*. Some scenes in the film would be based on serials, but many more would derive from fifties adventures like *Journey to the Centre of the Earth*, which prompted the rolling rock of the opening and the gimmick of a beam of sunlight revealing the position of the Well of Souls, and *King Solomon's Mines*, the main character of which, white hunter Allan Quartermain, played by Stewart Granger, Indiana finally resembled. What *Raiders* and the later Indiana Jones movies most starkly recalled, however, is James Bond films, as if Spielberg, having failed to achieve his ambition one way, acccomplished it in another. Action never played as important a part in serials, which betray their genesis in radio by being prodigiously talky and humourless. But Harrison Ford's lechery and ironic off-handedness under pressure, the sense of 'making it up as he goes along', are palpably derived from Sean Connery's characterisation of Bond.

Lucas and his first collaborator, Philip Kaufman, had plotted the film in sixty two-page scenes, each building to a climax. Since neither Spielberg nor Lucas could write screenplays, however, Kasdan, accustomed to working alone and at white heat, spent a frustrating two weeks with the two of them and a tape recorder, fleshing out this skeleton, acting out scenes and wrangling over the character of Indiana. Lucas saw Indiana as a charming but untrustworthy womaniser: Cary Grant turned action hero. Spielberg imagined him more like Fred C. Dobbs, Humphrey Bogart's seedy, unshaven and venal drifter from *The Treasure of the Sierra Madre*. Both character and story shifted towards adventure, and the twin aspects of Jones fused into the forties Bond clone of Indy.

From a hundred-page transcript of their conversations, Kasdan fashioned his script, which became one of Hollywood's best-guarded secrets. With memories of the union and security problems on *Jaws* and *Close Encounters*, Spielberg agreed with Lucas that the film must be shot in Britain. By October, even before *1941* was previewed, their Welsh production designer Norman Reynolds was scouting locations. At La Pallice, just outside La Rochelle on France's Atlantic coast, he found some submarine pens built by the German navy in 1942 to shelter the U-boats that harried Allied shipping. The concrete bunkers were larger than the biggest film studio in existence. The French navy, which now operated La Pallice as a coastguard base, rented them out for a long sequence, eventually only partly filmed, of a hidden Nazi base hollowed out of an island within which Indy, arriving on a submarine, finds jet planes and super weapons, creations of some Nazi genius. A freighter was brought from Ireland for the *Bantu Wind* in which the Ark is carried by the villain Belloq and the Nazis to a Greek island for the final apocalyptic opening of the Ark, and a full-size mock-up of a German submarine rented from the company making Wolfgang Petersen's *Das Boot*. Reynolds also booked most of La Rochelle's hotel space for a shoot that must, he stressed to Lucas, end before the town's tourist high season in August.

In Tunisia, the sliver of Mediterranean Africa wedged between Algeria and Libya, similar arrangements were being made near Nefta, Lucas's production headquarters for *Star Wars*. Abandoned trucks and the giant polystyrene skeleton of a *bantha*, one of the film's monsters, still rotted in the desert, reminders of a catastrophic location shoot which, though plagued by sandstorms, icy winds, unseasonable rains and dysentery, had provided Lucas's film with some of its most spectacular scenes. Despite his permanent sunburn damage, Lucas counselled Spielberg to shoot closer to the summer than he had, and to have all food flown in. In the end, neither provision would stave off disaster.

Over the months of *1941*'s editing and the preparation for *Raiders*, Spielberg persisted with attempts to cast *Continental Divide*. Richard Dreyfuss refused the Belushi role. So did Peter Falk, Dustin Hoffman, Robert de Niro and George Segal. From Segal the script went to his *California Split* co-star Elliott Gould, who showed it to his ex-wife, Barbra Streisand. She toyed with turning the story on its head and playing the journalist – possibly with Robert Redford as the ornithologist.

Wearily, Barwood and Robbins dropped out. But Spielberg persisted. Why? A clue may lie in the story itself. The eagle expert is the classic New Age woman, independent, environmentally conscious, preoccupied with her work, and more in love with it than she ever could be with any man. The journalist is the reverse: urban, unattractive, antisocial. Though they have an affair, the two agree at the end to live apart, visiting one another as the mood takes them. It was a plot that reflected his relationship with Amy, whom he may have hoped would take the ornithologist's role.

Voices had failed conspicuously, and their relationship took another step towards dissolution. His silent endearments at the Oscars had charmed her – 'but he hasn't done anything like that since,' she complained petulantly to a journalist. 'I guess he figures that should last a long time.' She was thinking, she said, of working in Europe, perhaps with Richard Gere and Mick Jagger in *Suffer or Die*, a film to be directed by Michelangelo Antonioni (but which was never made). Would she ever let Spielberg direct her? 'I know he's an incredible movie-maker,' she purred, green eyes gleaming, 'but the kind of films he makes aren't necessarily the kind I want to be in.'

1941's first preview was set for Denver in October. John Williams's martial score, reminiscent of one of Spielberg's favourites, Elmer Bernstein's music for John Sturges's 1963 wartime prison-camp adventure *The Great Escape*, included a *Star Wars*-type march theme as brassy as the music for *Close Encounters* had been spare. 'Too *loud*!' complained the preview cards, as uniformly negative as those for *Jaws* had been the reverse. After another bad preview at the Medallion Theater in Dallas in late October, a location which had been lucky for *Jaws* and *Close Encounters*, Spielberg realised the 'loudness' had less to do with noise levels than the film's barrage of action. It was too *visually* loud, too loud in character, in incident, especially in the opening forty-five minutes which set up its seven plots. As Joe Dante, Spielberg's protégé and the director of *Gremlins*, would say concisely of films which relied too much on action and effects at the expense of character, 'There was just too much *stuff*.' And stuff, everyone realised with a sinking feeling, wasn't something you could eradicate from *1941*. It was stuffed with stuff. Take it out, and you had a pillow without the feathers.

Gala openings at eight locations across the country on 18 November were cancelled while Spielberg cut some of the *longueurs* and toned down the soundtrack, but still people complained. A charity premiere was set for 14 December at LA's Cinerama Dome. The reaction was worse than anyone had feared. Marvin Goldman, influential chairman of the National Association of Theater Owners, dismissed the film as 'overdone, overproduced, over-everything. It was like building a $1 million mousetrap to catch one mouse in the kitchen.'

On top of this, the seizure and imprisonment of American hostages in Teheran by the Khomeini regime had created a national sense of rage and humiliation. Nobody wanted a film that mocked American arms. Both studios tried frantically to bail out by accusing Spielberg of bad management and overspending. Asked by *Variety* if making *1941* taught him anything, he replied, 'I learned not to invite Universal and Columbia executives and sales people to previews any more. Let them stay at home and watch *Laverne and Shirley* on TV. I'll preview my pictures and make the changes.'

Though he claimed not to have read a single review of *1941*, Spielberg also waded into the press, which nominated him as a scapegoat for other high-budget flops like Michael Cimino's $36 million western *Heaven's Gate*, about to bankrupt United Artists. He told the *Saturday Review*:

The press loves to design its own failures. Although nobody liked *The Blues Brothers*, nobody wants to admit that it's going to do almost $60 million worth of business around the world. As for *1941*, we need $60 million to get into the black and we're about $11 million short. But based on TV, cassette, cable, and reissue money, Universal is confident that the film will make that $11 million. Still, the critics bury their heads in the sand and say, 'How could this film do $50–$60 million when I gave it the worst review I've ever written?' Believe me, Hollywood is not being crippled by $30 million movies.

He also insisted, controversially, that major directors had 'earned the right to spend someone else's money', providing they used it to make a popular film. This was to become a refrain in Spielberg's relations with the press, to which he was constantly required to justify the high cost of his films. As late as 1995, fielding questions from the public on CNN's *Larry King Live*, he insisted that 'What did it cost?' was the wrong question. Rather, one should ask, 'Is it worth $7?' – the price of a cinema seat.

In his darker moments, however, Spielberg was furious about the failure of *1941*, blaming it on friends and collaborators who'd failed to warn him he was going off the track – though, on past evidence, he wouldn't have heeded them. John Williams, he said, had 'overwritt[en] over my overdirection over Zemeckis and Gale's overwritten script.' It would be years before he acknowledged his responsibility for *1941*. 'Until then,' he said in 1982 of the disaster, 'I thought I was immune to failure. But I couldn't come down from the power-high of making big films on

large canvases. I threw everything in and it killed the soup. *1941* was
my encounter with economic reality.'

Emotional reality too was about to descend on Spielberg. In July *Variety*
had announced that Amy would play Ophelia opposite Richard Chamberlain's Hamlet at LA's Ahmanson Theater between 12 October and 24
November, after which she and Spielberg would marry. In the meantime
she took a role in Jerry Schatzberg's *Honeysuckle Rose* shooting in Texas.
Country singer Willie Nelson played, in effect, himself, an ageing
musician falling in love with a beautiful young guitar player (Amy) and
abandoning his wife. Not for the first time in the movies, life imitated
art, and Amy began an affair with the grizzled, ponytailed but seductive
Nelson.

Unaware of what was happening in Texas, Spielberg planned his usual
week's holiday in Hawaii, this time with Amy, to coincide with the release
of *1941*. He'd intended to return a week later to direct an episode of
ABC's TV sitcom *Laverne and Shirley*, produced by his friend Penny
Marshall. Ratings for the show were falling off and the producers had
decided to move the setting from Milwaukee to California in a bid for a
bigger market.

The rejection of *1941* was so extreme that Spielberg suggested to Amy
they take a three-week holiday in Japan and get married there. She told
friends before they left, 'I'll be pregnant by April. We can't wait to start
a family.' But it was on the flight that their relationship ended explosively
– whether over her infidelities, her resistance to the idea of marriage or
his to having children nobody can, or will, say, though years later Amy
said she'd decided to wait until her thirties before settling down. 'I
thought I would be missing out on something.'

A distraught Spielberg returned to Los Angeles alone, with both his
professional and private life in ruins. 'The wonder child of Hollywood,'
gloated journalist Ben Stein, 'was now spoken of in sneering tones at
studio commissaries as a wastrel, a man who had seen his best days
before he was thirty, [someone who] could not be trusted to bring in a
picture at anywhere close to the promised budget.' Even Arnold

Spielberg, who was still working in electronics around San Francisco and with whom he remained regularly in touch, had no comfort. 'I hated 1941,' Arnold told him. It was the last straw. 'Don't talk to me, Dad,' Spielberg said wearily.

Far worse, however, was Amy's rejection. It had hurt him, he told friends, more than anything since the divorce of his parents. 'Life has caught up with me,' he sighed to Leo Janos in *Cosmopolitan*. 'I've spent so many years hiding from pain and fear behind a camera. I avoided all the growing-up pains by being too busy making movies. I lost myself in the world of film. So right now, in my early thirties, I'm experiencing delayed adolescence. I suffer like I'm sixteen. It's a miracle I haven't sprouted acne again.'

He responded to his rejection, as to all things he disliked, by decreeing that it didn't exist. *Continental Divide* was abruptly dropped. He sold his rights to Tanen, who was still eager to do the film with Belushi, but not with Matthew Robbins. 'When all of us were off doing other things, and our backs were turned,' Spielberg said, '[Tanen] immediately put Michael Apted into the picture ... I was contractually bound to be executive producer if I wasn't the director, so the name went along with the movie.' British director Apted started shooting on the $11.5 million production in October 1980, just as Spielberg did the last pick-ups on *Raiders*. Belushi starred opposite Blair Brown, but made no great impression as a leading man.

In adolescence, film-making had dissolved loneliness and despair for Spielberg, and it would do the same now. One's emotional life was eaten away too by the pressures of film-making, but that was a small price to pay. Later, he would try to pass off the crash of his first major relationship as a trifling incident in a life devoted to work.

I didn't stop to notice if women were interested in me, or if there was a party that I might have been invited to. I didn't ever take the time to revel in the glory of a successful or money-making film. I didn't stop to enjoy. By the time *Jaws* was in theatres, I was already deeply into production on *Close Encounters*, and by the time *Close Encounters* was released I was deeply into production on *1941*, and before 1941 was over I was severely into pre-production on *Raiders of the Lost Ark*. So I never had the chance to sit down and pat myself on the back or spend my money or date or go on vacation in Europe. I just haven't done that . . . because I put my movie-making ahead of some of the results. I thought if I stopped, I would never get started again, that I would lose the momentum . . . of being interested in working. I was afraid that if I stopped I would be punished for enjoying my success by losing my interest in working.

Those who knew Spielberg recognised the evasions in this statement. He had his share of sexual relationships, albeit transitory ones. And he could, and did, exult in his success. Among his friends, Spielberg's interest in the box office of his films was notorious. 'Steven was the one who ran out to buy the trades,' John Milius said. 'He was always talking about grosses.' Julia Phillips writes of driving him around the cinemas of Westwood after *Close Encounters* to see the crowds, and videotaping the long lines of patient punters.

Columbia were pressing for 'Night Skies', the promised low-budget sequel to *Close Encounters*, so Spielberg, still in shock, started auditioning screenwriters. Kasdan would have been the logical choice, but Lucas had hired him to write the second *Star Wars* film, *The Empire Strikes Back*. Instead Spielberg gave the project to John Sayles, a lanky New York psychology graduate who was earning a reputation for imaginative low-budget scripts. Spielberg had liked *Piranha*, which Sayles wrote for the King of the Z Movies, Roger Corman, in which killer fish ravage Texas. After Joe Dante filmed it, Universal wanted to sue, but Spielberg, who rated the film the best rip-off of *Jaws* to reach the screen, persuaded them not to bother. He also kept an eye on Dante, whose career was to flourish with his help.

To direct, he proposed a couple of maverick newcomers. One was Tobe Hooper, a young Texas film school graduate who'd made a name with a blood-boltered low-budget piece of rural Jacobean horror, *The Texas Chainsaw Massacre*. Christened 'The *Citizen Kane* of Meat Movies', it catapulted him into a Hollywood career and lifestyle.

Another was Ron Cobb. Born in Burbank, Cobb had become popular with anti-establishment cartoons for the *Los Angeles Free Press* before drifting towards fantasy art. After drawing for *The Magazine of Fantasy and Science Fiction* and *Famous Monsters of Filmland*, he fought in Vietnam, and returned to become friendly with film people like John Milius and screenwriter Dan O'Bannon. Though a brilliant visualist, Cobb shared the eccentric lifestyle, though not the right-wing politics, of Milius, who nevertheless called him, approvingly, 'a pipe-bomber'. There was no denying Cobb's design skill, however. He worked on John Carpenter's *Dark Star* and spent two and a half years in London on the version of *Alien* to have been directed by Alex Jodorowsky. Many of his designs were used in Ridley Scott's eventual film. His intricately realised creatures and space ships also impressed George Lucas, who used some of them in the Tatooine cantina sequence that became one of *Star Wars*' most popular moments.

Mavericks like Hooper and Cobb hardly fitted into Spielberg's universe, but as he would acknowledge later, his personal problems had grievously skewed his judgement. In the same confused state of mind he hired Rick Baker, one of John Landis's oldest friends, to design a group of aliens which worked better than Carlo Rambaldi's puppets in the original film.

Baker had raised the ape suit to the level of high art in the 1976 *King Kong*. Dino de Laurentiis originally commissioned a thirty-foot robot, but the mechanical monster never worked, and appeared only in one brief long shot. For the rest of the film, Baker's expressive anthropoid did the acting. Busy preparing John Landis's *An American Werewolf in London*, Baker set up a 'Night Skies' unit in the same building. Imagining from Spielberg's description that he wanted something grim and violent, he visualised an sf version of Sam Peckinpah's bloody symphony of rape and rural slaughter, *Straw Dogs*. His aliens were appropriately scary and, while costing a lot to engineer, would, he was certain, shock the audience at least as much as Bruce the shark had.

In April 1980, *Variety* published details of Columbia's slate for the next year. The tone in which it publicised the still-unnamed 'Night Skies' might have been chosen to infuriate Spielberg. He would be expected to 'confer' with the studio, said production head John Veitch, adding,

'Steven is not a one-man show.' The report went on, '[Frank] Price noted he was not overly concerned with working arrangements with Spielberg in light of recent experiences on Col-U co-production 1941. "Frankly, 1941 was good experience for Steven," Price said. "I think it will be a while before he tackles another broad comedy, but his record in suspense, which this film is, is hard to equal."'

During 1980, Kathleen Carey, a slight thirty-two-year-old divorced magazine editor with curly blonde hair, became Spielberg's full-time companion. As calm as Amy was mercurial, she encouraged Spielberg to read more, and to take time off to enjoy his success. 'She has taught me that there is life after movies,' he said. With memories of his awkward cohabitation with Amy, Spielberg and Kathleen lived apart, but on weekends they settled into domesticity, Kathleen keeping him supplied with pizza and Haagen-Dazs ice cream, and sitting through film screenings and schmoozing sessions with old pals. Friends believed that, in the long term, Kathleen represented the greatest hope for Spielberg's teenage persona to develop into adulthood. By the summer, however, though he and Kathleen remained a couple, he was seeing actresses again, among them Valerie Bertinelli, eighteen-year-old brunette star of the TV series One Day at a Time, the more experienced Barbara Hershey, and Debra Winger, who was to become a long-term friend. Despite gossip, Spielberg shrugged off the relationships as 'brother and sister' associations that 'never got past the hand-shaking stage'.

Amy, changeable as ever, was less happy with independence. Her first film after the break-up was Joel Oubianski's The Competition, in which she played a piano virtuoso opposite Richard Dreyfuss, who had a chance to exorcise his long-time crush on her. At the end of 1980, rather than going into a new film, she opened on Broadway as Mozart's skittish young wife Constanze in Peter Shaffer's Amadeus. Next door, the Royal Shakespeare Company was playing David Edgar's adaptation of Dickens's Nicholas Nickleby. One of its leads, Emily Richard, had joined the New York cast in part to recover from the trauma of a stillborn baby. She recollects:

The two theatres shared a corridor, so I would bump into Amy from time to time. We didn't get to know one another until we were both at some sort of reception backstage. We started to chat, and I told her about losing the baby. Then I started to cry. Amy began to cry too. She said, 'I'm not going to let anything stand in the way of having a family.' So there we both were, in a corner, crying into our drinks.

Despite *1941*, Spielberg was now perceived as one of the few directors of New Hollywood fit to wear the mantle of a studio head. He was flattered, but not surprised, to be approached to take over various studios, among them Disney. For years he'd watched the machinations inside Disney as the founder's nephew Roy Disney, the group's largest single stockholder, and Walt's son-in-law Ron Miller, who ran the lucrative theme parks and kept the company churning out cheap children's movies while it coasted on revenues from selective re-releases of classics like *Snow White* and *Fantasia*, vied for control.

In 1979, weary of the animation department's domination by the so-called 'Nine Old Men' who had degraded the studio's traditional excellence with xeroxing and other cost-cutting techniques, its best young director, a mild-mannered but perfectionist ex-Mormon missionary named Don Bluth, had walked out with sixteen colleagues to launch his own studio. Spielberg admired Bluth's stand, not to mention the quality of his work, and would later become his financial backer.

Desperate to recapture the youth market Disney had lost to *Jaws* and *Star Wars*, Miller, who'd become president and chief operating officer in February 1980, approached Spielberg to take over as head of production, releasing exclusively through their Buena Vista network. Spielberg was interested and opened negotiations but, as he might have guessed from the reaction to Bluth's departure, Miller would brook no independence; nor would he agree to share profits with Spielberg. He also feared that Spielberg might have designs on the studio's traditional characters. It was an item of faith within Disney that Mickey Mouse and Donald Duck were inalienable, unchangeable, eternal. All incoming executives were warned, 'Don't fuck with the mouse!'

In this air of mutual suspicion, discussions didn't last long. Instead of installing a *wunderkind*, Disney decided to make its own run at the youth market, producing the video-game sf story *Tron*, which made extensive use of computer animation. It also funded Ray Bradbury's *Something Wicked this Way Comes*, which Spielberg had been interested in directing. Both flopped, exacerbating still further the crisis in the Magic Kingdom.

Spielberg was evolving his own vision of a film studio, one which had little in common with the oligarchy of Disney. He admired the atmosphere of Lucasfilm. 'George has a fully staffed company of great people,' he told *Rolling Stone*, 'the kind of people you'd like to take home to dinner and be friends with for the rest of your life.' But Lucas's management style was resolutely hands-off. Except for broad policy, he took little interest in business. Spielberg was different. Disappointments with delegation had convinced him he needed day-to-day control. 'Steven is an expert in micro-management,' says David Puttnam, who had a chance to watch him at work when he was briefly head of Columbia. 'He needs to know what's going on at every moment on every project in which he's involved. That, and some very good advisers, is the basis of his success.'

In Spielberg's ideal company, the rigour of this structure would be disguised in an atmosphere of familial congeniality. His team would protect him from unpleasant decisions as his mother and sisters had done, and allow him to pursue his fantasies in tranquillity. For a while, he'd found this calm in the Malibu home of the Phillipses, but they had abandoned him. Their replacements would need above all to be loyal to him personally, irrespective of what studio paid the bills.

With *Raiders*, Spielberg found his ideal lieutenant in one of Lucas's foot-soldiers who became its line producer. Personable and outgoing, a college athlete and skilled amateur magician, Frank Marshall was as much a contrast to Spielberg as Brown was to Zanuck. He also bridged Old and New Hollywood. His father was a composer and arranger for, among others, John Ford, but Marshall had entered movies with New Hollywood director Peter Bogdanovich on *Targets*.

'We had practically no money,' Marshall reminisced of those days, 'so we had to do everything. And it was non-union, so not only did I act in [*Targets*], but I helped build sets, I did a little shooting, I ran around, I drove cars. I got to know every facet of how a movie gets made.' Old Hollywood disliked such disregard for demarcation and the pecking order, but New Hollywood demanded it. By the time of *Nickelodeon* in 1976, Marshall was credited as associate producer. When Bogdanovich decided to take time off after that disaster, Marshall worked with Martin Scorsese on his The Band concert documentary *The Last Waltz* and for Walter Hill before joining Lucasfilm.

The other component of the future management team came from *1941*. Kathleen Kennedy, the production secretary who had proved her loyalty in battle with Belushi, transferred to *Raiders* as Spielberg's personal assistant. She became the linchpin of Amblin, a synthesis of secretary, lieutenant and young sister, with a legendary ability to charm people without compromising Spielberg's tough business methods. In time, Marshall and Kennedy became lovers, then husband and wife.

Lucas's decision to shoot *Raiders of the Lost Ark* in Britain cut costs by half. Elstree studios on the fringes of London suburbia had been an ideal headquarters for *Star Wars*, and by the spring of 1980 all its seven stages and most of its twenty-seven acres were occupied by *Raiders*. These were historic premises. Here Alfred Hitchcock shot *Blackmail*, the first British talkie, in 1929, and *Stage Fright* in 1950. David Lean, Michael Powell, even Ronald Reagan had passed through – Reagan to make *The Hasty Heart* in 1948. On the backlot rotted a mountain of grey-white vinyl, all that remained of Moby-Dick from John Huston's disastrous 1956 version of Melville.

Elstree had been bankrupt when Lucas rescued it with *Star Wars*. Now it was seldom idle. As *Raiders* geared up, Stanley Kubrick, who'd bought a mansion in nearby Borehamwood, was winding down his protracted production of Stephen King's *The Shining*. There was a near-disaster when one of its stages, among the loftiest in Europe, and used for the main lobby of the Outlook Hotel, burned in the last few days of Kubrick's tenancy, but Lucas rushed through repairs and even raised the ceiling to accommodate the Well of Souls where Indy and Marion discover the lost Ark guarded by four giant black statues of jackal-headed Anubis and thousands of snakes.

Elstree's large stages weren't the only attraction of a British location. Another strike by the American Screen Actors' Guild had just begun, bringing most production in Hollywood to a halt. UK actors and technicians also worked for less, and British unions, unlike the American IATSE and Teamsters, would rather make life more comfortable for their members than shake down a production for every penny. The British government also offered tax incentives to visiting producers, even when, as with all the Indiana Jones films, Spielberg and Lucas edited and shot their special effects in the US, and imported most key personnel. An exception to this rule was *Raiders'* director of photography, Douglas Slocombe, who'd shot everything from Ealing's comedy classics *The Lavender Hill Mob* and *Kind Hearts and Coronets* to films for Joseph Losey, Roman Polanski and Fred Zinnemann. *Raiders* would cement Slocombe's special relationship with Spielberg, forged during the Indian sequences on *Close Encounters*.

The combined imaginations of Kasdan, Lucas and Spielberg had pushed the story of *Raiders* well beyond its initial inspiration in the Saturday-afternoon serials. Indiana now had a lover, Marion Ravenswood, the feisty, resentful daughter of an old colleague and competitor. First seen managing a drinking den well above the snowline in Nepal, she's less than pleased to see her old flame when he comes looking for a clue to the location of the Ark, an amulet that was part of her father's collection. Also on its track are some Nazi agents, including Toht, a giggling looka-like for Peter Lorre, and Belloq, an urbane Frenchman who is Jones's equal, indeed master, in tracking down rare artefacts. Indy, however, has his helpers too: a scholarly colleague, Marcus Brody, from the college where he teaches archaeology, and Sallah, 'the best digger in Egypt' as well as a vital guide once they locate the city of Tanis, where the Ark lies buried under centuries of sand.

Almost every broad-shouldered actor in Hollywood had been tested for Indiana, including John Beck, Tom Selleck and Harrison Ford. Selleck emerged as the front runner. Indy had to be a 'jock jester', a fighter who could be funny at the same time. Selleck's rugged build, thick black moustache and wide grin, not to mention a modest price-tag, made him ideal. Ford had none of Selleck's self-confidence. After *Star Wars*, he'd played second leads in films like *Heroes*, *Force Ten From Navarone* and the comedy western *The Frisco Kid*. His only starring role was as last-minute replacement for Kris Kristofferson in a wartime London romance, *Hanover Street*, and that flopped. Reluctantly he'd agreed to play Han Solo again in *The Empire Strikes Back*, but only if his character could be made 'more dashing'.

The fact that Spielberg and Lucas called him back for more tests convinced Ford he had the role. In fact, both of them were unsure. Kasdan's wry script made the part a long reach for Ford, and they opted finally for Selleck. But news of the decision leaked before Spielberg could break it to Ford or close the deal with CBS, who had Selleck under option while they waited for reaction to the pilot of *Magnum P.I.*, its new Hawaiian detective series. Ford read first in *Variety* that he hadn't been chosen after all, and was furious. When *Magnum*, which premiered in December 1980, proved an immediate hit, CBS locked Selleck up tight. Lucas and Spielberg were forced back to Ford, who was unforgiving.

Spielberg, by previewing his visual conception of the character, based on some drawings of Ford as Han Solo by comic-book artist Jim Steranko, convinced him that *Raiders* promised leading-man status. Even so, the actor insisted on rewriting his part. In addition, he exacted a hefty 7 per cent of *Raiders*' net takings as his fee. (Ironically, Spielberg could have used Selleck after all: the actors' strike held up shooting on the first episodes of *Magnum*.)

Spielberg always imagined Amy as Marion Ravenswood. He offered the part to Debra Winger, who turned him down. After that, having overpaid for Harrison Ford, he started looking for bargains. Publicist Jeff Walker remembers being in Spielberg's office while he shuffled through a folder filled with pictures of models clipped from magazines, telling an assistant, 'Call her in . . . Her too . . .'

However Amy's late and, for Spielberg, unfortunate replacement, at least in terms of good relations on the set, was Karen Allen, whom he'd noticed playing a small role in *Animal House*. Though freckled, red-headed, green-eyed and gentile, Allen had much in common with Amy: New York background, ambitions for the stage rather than film, and a short temper. Spielberg did his best to transform her into Amy, blotting out the freckles and darkening her reddish hair, but the temper remained.

For the rest of the cast, he shopped in Europe. After flirting with making Sallah an agile little Arab, and interviewing actors like Kavork Malikyan for the role, he decided instead on someone larger than life and chose John Rhys-Davies, a burly Welshman with a booming voice. Ronald Lacey became Toht, and Denholm Elliott Marcus Brody.

Truffaut's success in *Close Encounters* tempted Spielberg to consider another Frenchman for Belloq. Initially he wanted Jacques Dutronc, the singer/songwriter who'd appeared in some films by Claude Lelouch. But Dutronc, rangy and laconic, a drinking and fornicating pal of self-destructive rock star/actor Serge Gainsbourg, couldn't be pinned down, so he turned to Italian Giancarlo Giannini, who was close to being signed when Spielberg saw the BBC's TV film *Death of a Princess*, about the execution of a Saudi princess for an illicit affair, and was impressed by the performance of British actor Paul Freeman. Freeman, passing through Hollywood on his way back from Belize, where he'd been playing in the film of Frederick Forsyth's novel about mercenaries, *The Dogs of War*, dropped in to Lucasfilm to meet Spielberg and Lucas, and was cast on the spot.

Three months later, Freeman was on his barge, taking a romantic holiday on the Home County canals with a new girlfriend when he glided past a lock cottage and saw a chalked notice leaning against the wall. 'Will Paul Daneman on the *Ripple Vale* Ring Your Agent.' Even allowing for the confusion of his name with that of another actor, he knew that Spielberg had reached out for him.

Freeman arrived next day at Elstree. An arcade-size Asteroids video game had been installed in the office of co-executive producer Howard

Kazanjian, earmarked for Spielberg. He was playing it when Freeman entered. Throughout the early spring of 1980, Spielberg spent any spare time at Elstree riveted to the Asteroids screen. There was a special rightness to his choice of what novelist Martin Amis, to whose 1982 book about video games *Invasion of the Space Invaders* Spielberg wrote an introduction, classed as 'one of the most mystical of the video games'. 'On the charcoal grey screen,' Amis explained, 'spectral boulders roll and tumble. You are the tiny triangle in the middle, firing bombs or "photons" in repeated salvos of four. When you hit a boulder, it breaks in two. When you hit half a boulder, it breaks in two too.'

Asteroids might have been a metaphor for Spielberg's problems with his career and his life. As he cracked each obstruction, more appeared. Emotionally bruised by the break-up with Amy, he brooded. His deficiencies in caring and sharing nagged at him. When Jim Steranko praised him as someone with 'the sensibilities of an action director', he cavilled. 'Essentially I'm a love story director, but nobody's aware of that except me. In several years, when I start making very small pictures, people will say, "Yeah, but didn't he also make an action picture called *Raiders of the Lost Ark*?"'

Freeman knew none of this, though he sensed that Spielberg was distracted. He'd had to wait for his Hollywood interview too, while Lucas and Spielberg lay on the floor, playing with that year's hottest audio toy, Sony's portable Walkman, and Kathleen Kennedy fed them cassettes.

Raiders was only Freeman's third film, but he knew that an emergency summons usually meant second thoughts. Perhaps he'd been replaced, as he himself had replaced others. 'It didn't really matter to me one way or the other,' Freeman recalls. '*1941* had just flopped, and people were wondering if Spielberg was really so great.' But when they went into his office it wasn't exactly the role Spielberg discussed.

'I just wanted to know what you planned to do about this French accent,' he said.

Relieved, Freeman slipped into Standard Broken English. 'I zort I would do zumzing like zis.'

Spielberg smiled, and said, 'Great. Well, that's fine then.' He had no more questions.

Despite motor-mouthed technicians and inquisitive tabloids, nobody at Elstree knew much about Lost Ark Productions or its movie. Lucas had imported his own management team, some of whom, like Kazanjian, had graduated with him from USC. British left hands had no idea what Hollywood's right hands were up to. Why, demanded actors forced to change in the toilets, had all the dressing rooms been fitted with industrial-strength padlocks and large bathtubs, but without plumbing? Nobody on the Elstree staff had the slightest idea.

Freeman, since he would appear in the first scenes shot, knew the plot, though most didn't, not even Karen Allen. Auditioning actors only saw their own pages. Bill Hootkins, a heavily-built London-based Texas actor with a megaphone voice, hadn't been shown more than his own lines either, but since he played Major Eaton of US Military Intelligence, who briefs Indiana and Brody in the second reel, they contained the entire story. On the night of his casting, he rang a friend.

'I'm in the new Spielberg film,' he announced conspiratorially.

'What's it about?'

'It's the Bible,' Hootkins replied slowly, as if realising its improbability for the first time, 'with Nazis!'

Harrison Ford meanwhile fretted about the script. Such anxiety was to become more pronounced as his stardom increased. A later director, Philip Noyce, called him an 'anal [actor], incredibly intelligent and detail-oriented, [who] worries tremendously about every scene and situation'. For all his physical magnetism, Ford had a limited range. Attempts to broaden his appeal beyond action/adventure exposed his threadbare technique, dismissed by one critic as a 'small but familiar repertoire of apologetic shrugs, hesitations and lopsided smiles'.

Ford had joined Spielberg on the flight from Los Angeles to London early in June, and they went through Indy's part line by line, refining and simplifying. Anything smacking of doubt or intellect was replaced by wisecracks and sight gags. When Marion ruefully notes, as she undresses Indy to treat his wounds, 'You're not the man I knew ten years ago,' his response, 'It's not the years, honey, it's the mileage,' was a Ford contribution. So was his response when Sallah enquires about his plans as the Ark is whisked away from under their noses en route to Cairo in a Nazi truck: 'Don't ask *me*. I'm making this up as I go along.'

Like the shark in *Jaws*, and Spielberg himself, Indy only functions when he's in motion towards a well-defined goal. This momentum, maintained inexorably by Spielberg, kept everyone from questioning a script that, even more than *Close Encounters*, made little sense. The opening sequence, in which Indy penetrates an ancient but efficiently booby-trapped Peruvian temple to snatch a tiny gold idol, is a *tour de force* of technique, but a moment's thought must suggest that the traps would only work with a system of hydraulics and photo-electric cells, beyond even the most inspired Inca engineers. The clue to the position of the Ark in buried Tanis is contained in an amulet which must be placed on top of a rod of specific height and erected in a scale model of the city within Tanis itself. Only then, and only as the sun shines through the gem in the amulet, will the position of the Well of Souls be revealed. But why should the inhabitants of Tanis need a scale model of their own city in order to locate the Ark?

As the story rolls on, such inconsistencies accumulate. When, in the endless switching of the Ark from hand to hand, Belloq snatches it from the *Bantu Wind*, in which Indy is trying to carry it away from Egypt, and transfers it to a submarine, Jones throws himself into the sea, clings to the sub deck, and is next seen on the other side of the Mediterranean, climbing ashore, damp but unharmed, after presumably having been hauled hundreds of miles, much of it underwater. (Spielberg shot, but didn't use, a scene of crowning improbability in which Indy lashes himself to the periscope with his whip.)

No matter. The Indiana Jones films offer a child's vision of a world where narrative logic surrenders to the vision of the moment. And Indy himself, especially after Ford and Spielberg finished defining him, was the perfect inhabitant of that world, an invulnerable Peter Pan, half god, half child. The adult of *Raiders* is Belloq. It's he who understands the importance of the Ark ('It's a radio for talking to God!'), and who articulates the philosophy of archaeology to an indifferent Indy. Marion to Indy is less a lover than a tomboy playmate. Only Belloq responds to her femininity, offering her (in yet another improbability, though a charming one), in the middle of the Egyptian desert, a smart dress, high heels and serious attempts at seduction.

The ten-hour airborne conference would be all the direction Ford received, or needed, on *Raiders*. Thereafter, he directed himself.

'Steven would say, "What are you going to do this time, Harrison?"' recalled Bill Hootkins. 'Steve would watch the camera rehearsal, say "Fine," and Ford would do it.'

Hootkins had worked with Ford before, on *Hanover Street*. Playing opposite him in a moment of high pathos, he conceived an admiration for his pragmatism. '*Hanover Street* was only his second main lead, and this was one of his biggest scenes. I asked, "You want me to back up a bit on this, or pump it up a little to get you into it?" And Ford is the only actor who ever had the guts to say to me on a major scene like this, "Don't worry. It's only make-believe."'

The sets were quickly completed, and Elstree staff found out what the baths were for when two thousand snakes arrived from South America. Spielberg flew to La Rochelle to shoot the sub pens and on to Tunisia for the desert excavations, both of which had to be done before high summer. Paramount's penalties meant that even a day over schedule could be disastrous. Urgency was added by the fact that delays on the second *Star Wars* adventure, *The Empire Strikes Back*, being directed by Irvin Kershner, had severely overstretched Lucasfilm. Lucas's deal with Twentieth Century-Fox on *Star Wars* guaranteed him 77.5 per cent of the film's income after the studio had covered its costs, but while he would eventually be $100 million richer from the two films, at the moment he had an acute cash-flow problem.

On paper, *Raiders* needed eighty-five shooting days, but Lucas asked Spielberg to do it in seventy-three. They axed much of the action and dialogue, and scaled down many sets. The Nazi super-weapons which Indy was supposed to find in the submarine pens at La Pallice disappeared, and the experimental Flying Wing aircraft in which the Ark was to have been flown from Tunisia to Berlin (before Indy blows it up) shrank from four engines to two. Ron Cobb had enjoyed elaborating Toht, giving him a Strangelove-like mechanical arm with a machine gun firing through his forefinger, but this too was ditched, the only reminder a running gag in which Toht, having rashly snatched up the crucial amulet in an early scene without realising it was red hot, carried its impression in scar tissue on his palm – an image that made more sense when the hand was plastic. In consolation, Spielberg gave Toht a gadget invented for Christopher Lee's Nazi submarine officer in 1941. An object of chains and steel rods that looks like a torture instrument but is actually a collapsible hanger for his leather coat, it got no reaction for the humourless Lee, but Ronald Lacey's snigger as he whips it out won him one of *Raiders'* best laughs.

Four artists storyboarded the new slimline script. 'I just got it right down to the bones,' Spielberg said, 'right down to what I absolutely needed to tell the story I wanted to tell. On *Raiders* I learned to like instead of love. If I liked a scene after I shot it, I printed it. I didn't shoot it again seventeen times until I got one I loved.' When he displayed any doubts, Lucas told him quietly, '*Raiders of the Lost Ark* will be the summer's biggest film.' How did he know? Lucas just said, 'Trust me.'

Paul Freeman arrived in La Rochelle on a Sunday morning, and was delighted to find himself in a good hotel with a four-star restaurant. He was told to relax; Spielberg would see him later in the day. Noting that the restaurant offered a fourteen-course seafood lunch, Freeman settled down to a treat. 'None of the Americans were eating,' he says, 'but after a while one came in and said, "Steven will see you now." I said, "I'm still on course number three." From time to time, they'd come back, but we didn't get together until later in the afternoon.'

It was his last chance for a peaceful meal. On Monday, the film began to roll. 'I've never seen a camera crew so flat out,' Freeman said. 'You'd see them asleep with their faces in their lunch. [Spielberg] was running between shots, and shooting it like a TV film – thirty set-ups a day sometimes. The camera crew couldn't keep up. They were exhausted.' Rather than lose time by cutting during a complex take, Spielberg would sometimes just yell directions. 'I had to get used to people talking during a shot,' says Freeman. 'In the middle of the action, Spielberg would call, "Paul, look over here!" It wasn't what one was used to.'

The pace told once they moved to Kairouan in Tunisia. Spielberg heeded Lucas's warnings about local food, for which he had no taste anyway, and ate almost entirely out of tins, in particular Harrods' canned spaghetti. But avoiding the local tap-water was almost impossible in such heat. Most of the crew and cast caught amoebic dysentery; second-unit director Michael Moore dangerously so. He was shipped back to the States, and Lucas took over his job.

Then Ford succumbed, a fact which, fortuitously, gave the film one of its biggest laughs. Confronted by scimitar-wielding giant Terry Richards in the casbah, Ford was supposed to fight him, sword against bullwhip, but when it came to film the sequence, he was too sick to even stand upright. Instead he just looks at Richards in exasperation, pulls a revolver and shoots him dead.

Lucas was around for three weeks of the nine-week London shoot, two weeks of the five in Tunisia, and throughout the shooting at La Rochelle and in Hawaii. Many assumed he was simply keeping an eye on his investment, but some detected a more complex role, as a lightning-rod to deflect resentment from Spielberg, especially in Tunisia's 130-degree heat. When a group of young German tourists gave effective improvised performances as Nazi soldiers, Lucas turned up with pages of dialogue for a new scene to involve them, and spent a day shooting it. Paul Freeman says, 'I suspect he was giving we performers a message: "Look, acting's not so hard. Anyone can do it."'

Freeman came to know Spielberg well during the Tunisian locations. 'Steven and I used to have lunch together – because sometimes I was the only person on the set who was talking to him. Harrison often got pissed off, mainly because of the speed he was working.' They went for strolls in the desert, during which Spielberg reminisced about Arizona, excursions with his father and hunts for scorpions.

Ford, estranged from his wife Mary, was involved with screenwriter Melissa Mathison. A close friend of Kathleen Kennedy, Mathison came from London, where she'd been working, to join him in Tunisia. Kathleen

Carey also briefly visited Spielberg. Mathison, not very happily, had worked for Coppola on the scripts *The Black Stallion* and *The Escape Artist*, both stories with boys as main characters, and Spielberg, feeling lonely, told her about 'Night Skies' and the long-delayed 'Clearwater/ Growing Up/After School' project, which he was now calling 'A Boy's Life'. In his mind, the two had been growing together into a story of a friendship between a lonely suburban kid, as he had been, and a lost alien who became the sort of uncritical companion he'd searched for in vain through his childhood.

'I kept thinking about . . . where the story was going,' Spielberg said, 'and I asked Melissa if she would care to sit with me and let me test this out on her. So we sat down, and I told her the story, and she wept.'

Afterwards Mathison grabbed his arm and shook it. 'You *have* to make this film,' she told him urgently.

Her suggestions about the script, informed with feminine compassion, impressed Spielberg, and he asked her to try her hand at the screenplay that would become *E.T.* To his surprise, she refused. Writing for the changeable Coppola had been a torment, and she was thinking of giving up screenwriting altogether. But during a car ride from Nefta to the location at Sousse, Ford and Spielberg pressed her. Weakened by dysentery, she couldn't refuse. Throughout the shooting, she and Spielberg spent every spare moment discussing the story. She started work on the script in October 1980; *E.T.* would go before the cameras almost a year later to the day, and be released nationally the following June, a tribute to the white heat at which Spielberg could work.

From Tunisia, the unit flew to Hawaii for the eleven-minute opening 'teaser' which Hollywood execs had been convinced would cost too much to film. 'It's not part of *Raiders* at all,' Spielberg admitted. 'It belongs to the film that comes before it – *Raiders of the Lost Fertility Idol*, if you like.' But the sequence respected the spirit of the serials, which always began with a brisk reprise of the previous week's cliffhanger. It also established Indy's grave-robbing skill and his rivalry with Belloq. And its gadgetry set the tone of the film with comic-book energy. British actor Alfred

Molina found himself thrust into an unlikely characterisation as Satipo, Indy's Peruvian guide. New to film, he was almost scared off for life when, for the first shot of his career, the spider wrangler furnished his back and shoulders with hairy tarantulas the size of saucers.

By mid-July, the crew was back at Elstree and gearing up to shoot the Well of Souls. Reptile wrangler Michael Culling had accumulated a few boas and cobras for featured roles, but most of the snakes were harmless striped grass snakes imported from South America, augmented with two thousand rubber fakes. Only Ford and Karen Allen, or their doubles, would need to confront the cobras, and then only through glass. Still, the actors viewed their squirming co-stars nervously, particularly after Spielberg, seeing the scene for the first time through the lens, decided there weren't enough snakes, and had 4500 more imported from Denmark.

Production manager Robert Watts beefed up safety precautions. Bill Hootkins says:

> You've never seen anything like it. The doors of the stage were open permanently, and an ambulance was backed inside, with the doors open. Standing on either side were two enormous men in white coats, with a syringe of anti-venin in each hand. This stuff had been flown in from India, and turned out to be ancient. It would have been like injecting us with water.

Stanley Kubrick had moved his production office and cutting rooms to his nearby mansion, but a few people remained at Elstree, including his daughter Vivian, who was cutting her documentary about the making of *The Shining*. Helping her was one of Kubrick's editors, Gordon Stainforth.

Stainforth remembers the mood at Elstree as initially congenial. Spielberg was driven out from the Athenaeum Hotel on Piccadilly every morning, early enough to drop in at the commissary for coffee and a word with the remnants of the *Shining* crew or the advance guard of Warren Beatty's forthcoming Russian Revolution saga *Reds*. The day's storyboards were on display. Performers were flattered to know

Spielberg's plans, though it also got any questions out of the way before expensive shooting time. For the same reason, he always filmed the first rehearsal of a scene, just in case spontaneity produced a unique performance. Once a week, he hosted a cast and crew party, for which the local MGM, Universal or Warner Brothers distributor contributed a print of some classic, often starring Spencer Tracy or other Spielberg favourites.

The *gemütlich* atmosphere evaporated once shooting started on the Well of Souls. 'Vivian came into the cutting room one day crying,' recalls Stainforth. 'She's a great animal lover, and she was very upset about the way the snakes were being treated. So I was dragged along to this stage to see what was going on.'

A floor of planks had been laid seven feet above the actual floor of the stage, and strewn with sand. This in turn was covered by a writhing reptilian carpet. Some snakes had fallen through onto the concrete floor below. Vivian was certain many more were being crushed by the feet of actors, stunt men or technicians. Stainforth thought most of the motion-less reptiles were plastic, but acknowledges, 'There were some dead snakes around; no doubt about that.'

'Spielberg was up on some scaffolding actually lining up a shot,' he recalls. 'Vivian climbed up and said, "Steven, this is so cruel."

'Spielberg was looking terribly embarrassed by the whole situation. "Vivian, they're being looked after fine," he said. "If there's a problem, we'll look into it. We're too busy to do it now."

'He was quite pleasant about it, but this was not nearly good enough for her. We went back to the cutting room, and Vivian picked up the phone and rang the RSPCA to complain about the way the snakes were being treated.

'The whole film ground to a halt. It was closed down for a whole day. The guy in charge of the snakes was so angry, if Vivian had been a bloke, she'd have been killed. But the fact that she was a girl, and Kubrick's daughter . . .

'A couple of days later, I had the chance to go back, and the transforma-tion was fantastic. They'd gone completely over the top. There was this row of plastic dustbins almost as far as the eye could see around the stage, and in the bottom of each one there was a little bit of straw and a leaf of lettuce, and each one had about three garter snakes. There were vast glass cases for the dangerous snakes, and about three doctors on hand in white coats.'

Kubrick himself came hot-foot to watch the fun. 'When there's a scandal like this,' says Stainforth, 'Stanley revels in it. He was positively buoyant. Of course he took Vivian's side, and then there was a definite clash between Spielberg and Kubrick. And I remember Stanley puffing on his cigar, and saying with a grin, "Steve's a jerk."'

Karen Allen apparently agreed with Kubrick. Throughout the filming, her irritation with Spielberg had grown visibly. It wasn't simply that, with her black hair and heavy make-up, she'd been turned into a surrogate Amy Irving, though this was frustrating enough. They also differed fundamentally in their attitude to screen acting.

When they met, Allen told Spielberg, 'I'm from the Al Pacino school of acting.' She had played Pacino's girlfriend in the ambiguous study of sado-masochism, *Cruising*, and been angered, as had the cerebral Pacino, by director William Friedkin's slashing of her role.

'You're going to get introduced to the Sam Peckinpah school of acting,' Spielberg replied.

After this exchange, their relationship deteriorated. 'Karen wasn't particularly happy with the way Spielberg was working,' Paul Freeman admits, 'because she wanted to rehearse. She found it frustrating that she wasn't able to explore her character and make it more immediate. During the movie she was always talking about how she was going to use the money to go back and set up a theatre company.'

Her anger increased during the Well of Souls sequence. Though stunt artists replaced her when Marion hangs over the pit and the statues collapse on her, there were more than enough anxious moments as she faced the snakes. 'The pythons were really vicious,' she complained. 'They aren't poisonous, but they bite and hold on. I always kept a close watch on them and if any of them got near my bare feet, I just turned around and walked straight off the set.'

Spielberg didn't welcome such independence. Nor did he feel she was looking sufficiently agitated. 'I threw snakes at Karen's head,' he admitted, 'because I didn't think she was screaming for real. I set her on fire. I tossed a tarantula on her leg. But I always kissed her, gently, after every take.' It's hard to know whether the vermin or the kiss aggravated her more.

Marion spends two of her biggest scenes, first in Belloq's tent and, later, the final confrontation with the force of the Ark, bound to a post – in the first, gagged as well. 'I know she very much didn't like being tied up,' acknowledges Paul Freeman. 'In that thing at the end, when she was tied up for a long time, it freaked her out quite a bit. She didn't like that. They had to make arrangements to stop and let her out, then shoot it again.' In a business where rhapsodic tributes to directors are the norm, Allen has been acid in later comments about Spielberg. 'Steve and I were not the best of friends,' she said. 'He looks at actors as part of the scenery. But I think he'll grow out of that.'

Bringing in *Raiders* a week under its published schedule and well within budget was a prodigious feat of cinematic technique and a tribute to the power of pure will. And though Spielberg didn't lack competent, indeed inspired collaborators, the creative achievement is almost entirely his. His casting worked superbly, and his subordinates, while seldom understanding exactly what he had in mind, delivered the effects he visualised.

When they didn't, he could be coldly dismissive. The cast, who, unusually on a Hollywood film, were admitted to rushes, watched this happening. 'Everyone on every film tells you that the rushes are great,' says Paul Freeman. 'Spielberg was the only director I ever heard say, "That's no good. We'll have to do it again." Of course, it was almost always about something someone else had shot. But he was inevitably right.'

Every technical department of *Raiders* acknowledged that Spielberg's vision never wavered. He was like a man mentally humming a piece of music he'd heard a thousand times before. His first cut was three hours long, but he quickly refined that to less than two hours. Once post-production started late in the autumn, it was John Williams who again provided the actual music, another march, heavy on the brass, that would be among the most imitated scores of all time. The advertising logo, with cartoon letters tapering from crimson at the top to cooler yellow, also became one of the most readily identifiable of all film emblems. The film in which Spielberg invested least of himself became his greatest hit.

11

Poltergeist and *E.T.:*
The Extraterrestrial

HORROR VS. HOPE

Headline to *New York Times* report on the release of *Poltergeist*
and *E.T.*, 30 May 1982

MICHAEL EISNER and Jeffrey Katzenberg at Paramount gave *Raiders* red-carpet treatment. They considered a gala premiere in the art deco Avalon Ballroom on Catalina Island, thirty-one miles offshore from Los Angeles, but a few sneak previews in other cinemas, from the first of which Spielberg fled in panic after twenty minutes, made it clear the film needed no such kitsch promotion. (He didn't see *Raiders* with an audience until forty-four weeks into its release, when he slipped into Hollywood's Cinerama Dome, famous for its good projection and sound equipment.)

Paramount entered the film in the Cannes Festival and scheduled a US opening on 11 June 1981, plum date of the summer season. So positive was the word-of-mouth that, in the four days beforehand, shares of Gulf and Western, Paramount's parent company, rose 2½ points. *Raiders* also meant prosperity for Lucasfilm, which later produced two sequels, creamed millions in marketing and launched a Prague-based TV series, *Young Indiana Jones*.

Even more than *Jaws*, *Raiders* became a media event that spilled beyond the world of film. In April, NASA, alert to the importance of mythology in the space effort, invited Spielberg and Lucas to watch the Space Shuttle lift-off at Cape Canaveral. Links to other sf films and TV shows, in particular *Star Trek*, would follow. Not blind to the magnitude

Amy Irving, Spielberg's intermittent companion and wife from 1976 to 1989.

'Karen didn't like being tied up.' Karen Allen protests about her bonds to Spielberg and Ford during the climactic sequence of the first of the Indiana Jones films, *Raiders of the Lost Ark* (1981).

Right: George Lucas and Spielberg on location in Hawaii for *Raiders.*

Left: Harrison Ford in uniform for *Raiders.*

Carlo Rambaldi with his designs for Puck in *E.T.: The Extraterrestrial* (1982).

Puck duplicates Spielberg's gesture of laying a finger on the forehead to indicate approval.

Above: Spielberg directs Tobe Hooper directing Craig T. Nelson and James Karen in *Poltergeist* (1982).

Right and below: Hooper and Spielberg collaborate to recreate Spielberg's childhood nightmare as a sentient tree tries to devour Oliver Robbins in *Poltergeist*.

The Spielberg collaborators: *(above)* composer John Williams; *(left)* John Milius (directing *Red Dawn*, 1983); *(below)* Matthew Robbins, co-writer of *The Sugarland Express* and uncredited script adviser on most Spielberg screenplays; *(opposite above)* Paul Schrader, an uncomfortable partner on *Close Encounters of the Third Kind*; *(centre)* long-time producer and studio manager Frank Marshall, on the left, during *Poltergeist*; *(below)* editor Michael Kahn, on the right.

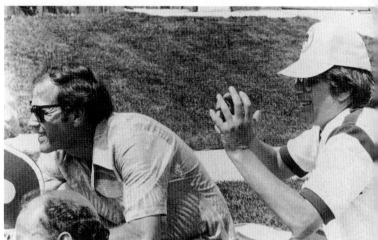

Above: Pensive on the set of *Temple of Doom*, Spielberg's mood is lightened by a visit from star and girlfriend Kate Capshaw.

United at last. Spielberg and wife-to-be Capshaw in 1988.

of the compliment, Spielberg treasured the NASA cap with which he was presented, and wore it often over the next few years for photo shoots.

In March, Spielberg was embarrassed by the revelation in the *Los Angeles Times* of his true age. A journalist sifting through the records of Cal State Long Beach noted that they referred to Spielberg as having been born in 1946. Spielberg's press agent refused to respond, saying he would answer questions only about *Raiders*.

Imitating *Raiders* would become a cinema industry of its own. In 1983, Brian G. Hutton's indifferent *High Road to China* cast Tom Selleck in a role not unlike the one he'd lost to Ford. Richard Chamberlain played Allan Quartermain in a 1985 remake of *King Solomon's Mines* that owed much to *Raiders*, including the casting of John Rhys-Davies, who played Sallah in Spielberg's film, and followed up in 1986 with *Allan Quartermain and the Lost City of Gold*, an even more obvious pastiche. The 1985 Australian *Sky Pirates* and countless other films thrust action stars into fedoras and bomber jackets and despatched them in search of lost cities, temples, tribes and treasures. Indy even became an icon of one man battling and beating the forces of evil when he was adopted as a mascot by Phil Berman and Tim Gregory, two biochemists fighting to find a cure for AIDS. Almost in passing, *Raiders* also flooded the Ark market. When Richard Gere danced before the Ark of the Covenant in Bruce Beresford's 1985 Biblical film *King David*, teenage audiences jeered, 'That's old stuff!', convinced he'd stolen a concept invented by Spielberg.

So complete was the triumph of *Raiders* that Spielberg didn't go on a national promotional tour. He used the time to catch up with Hollywood, the landscape of which, in two years, had changed dramatically. Disney was even closer to bankruptcy, financial and artistic, but Columbia, under Frank Price, looked healthy for the first time in years, and had begun to attract takeover bids from corporations looking to enter show business, in particular its eventual buyer Coca-Cola. Sleepy no longer, Universal seemed more and more an extension of its studio tour, now one of Los Angeles's major tourist attractions. Instead of selling off his lot, Wasserman had extended the Universal theme park over almost every square foot of the 450 acres between the black tower and the Hollywood Hills.

In one of the most surprising developments, MGM was enjoying new vitality under an improbable president, David Begelman. After paying his debt to society at a substantial discount with a $5000 fine and the production of the documentary *Angel Death*, a tract against the drug PCP – 'Angel Dust' – he had the last two of his three years' probation revoked and the remaining charges against him dismissed. Told by an accommodating judge, 'You can go forward without the stigma of probation,' he went into partnership with Freddie Fields as a producer, then, in December 1979, took over as president of MGM, with Fields also on the team.

With the skeleton of what would become Amblin Entertainment in place, Spielberg was anxious to wet his feet as a producer, and was searching for projects which, unlike the Zemeckis and Gale films, offered hands-on experience. With George Lucas and Kirk Douglas, he invested in *Home Movies*, a low-budget non-union film made by Brian De Palma with some of his students at Sarah Lawrence. United Artists grudgingly bought it, then put it out with the minimum of advertising. 'They're scared of little pictures,' De Palma complained. 'The bottom line is that they'd rather have a film that cost $5 million than a $300,000 picture, because anything that's cheap takes on an onerous cast.' It was a valuable lesson to Spielberg that a film needed all the resources of a major studio behind it in order to succeed in an increasingly competitive market.

Francis Coppola was making his Las Vegas musical romance *One from the Heart* in Los Angeles, and in February Spielberg went to watch him work. Abetted by his director of photography, Vittorio Storaro, who had designed an elaborate lighting system to 'wash' the set with colour at the touch of a button on a computerised console, Coppola had surrendered to the dizzy promise of the latest high technology, often directing from a video screen, and occasionally from his stainless steel caravan which the crew christened 'The Silver Fish'. Spielberg acknowledged the promise of video, and agreed that one day all film-making might be digital, but it didn't blind him to the emptiness of Coppola's method and of the film itself, doomed to failure. (In August 1981, Paramount showed it to potential exhibitors, all of whom scorned it.)

Spielberg went on to San Francisco to meet with Lucas, who was about to start the new *Star Wars* film, *Return of the Jedi*, and wanted to get the second Indy adventure moving before he did so. Having agreed a budget of $28 million, Paramount were already counting their profits. Although he was not entirely enthusiastic about repeating himself, Spielberg had agreed to direct it. He didn't want someone else messing up the sequel, as had happened on *Jaws*.

He also felt a debt to Lucas, who had invested heavily – financially and emotionally – in the film. His divorce from Marcia had not only forced the wholesale division of his assets but left him depressed, and questioning his future. Living and working by the principles of the sixties, respectful of collaborators and benign towards the environment, had left him a virtual recluse struggling to make ends meet.

Since Lawrence Kasdan was making his first film as director, the erotic thriller *Body Heat*, which Lucas had privately helped finance (while insisting his name not appear anywhere on it), Lucas's old friends from *American Graffiti*, Willard Huyck and Gloria Katz, were hurriedly called in to write what became *Indiana Jones and the Temple of Doom*. Lucas's first impulse had been to make a film as innovative as *Raiders*. Negotiations had been opened with the Chinese government to film scenes like a motorcycle chase along the Great Wall and the discovery of dinosaurs in a lost valley. However the Chinese refused permission to film on the wall, and inflated the prices for everything else needed to make the film. The Sri Lankan government was more amenable, so the location was moved there, with further scenes to be shot in India.

Much of the material in the story given to Huyck and Katz was left over from *Raiders*. Lucas restored a number of stunts dropped from the first film, including one in which Indy escapes from a pilotless plane by pressing a rubber boat into service as an improvised parachute. There are some self-homages too, in one of which Jones, faced by twins of the masked swordsman from the first film, goes for his gun, only to find the holster empty. John Williams would also re-use much of the original *Raiders* music.

Consistent with Lucas's mood, however, the new film has a darker and more strident tone. Set in 1935, earlier in Indy's career than *Raiders*, it begins, as usual, in the middle of another adventure, with Indy in a Shanghai nightspot, christened 'Club Obi Wan', after Alec Guinness's character in *Star Wars*, negotiating with gangster Lao Che and his two sons to exchange a gigantic diamond for the ashes of a long-dead emperor. In the ensuing double-cross and brawl, Indy and his sidekick, a ten-year-old Chinese street kid, nicknamed Short Round, find themselves on the run with Willie Scott, a nightclub singer who was favouring the audience with 'Anything Goes' in Mandarin when the fight broke out. Escaping from the pilotless plane and sliding to safety in India, they are pressed, in another airing of Spielberg's *Peter Pan* fascination, into rescuing village children stolen by a death-worshipping cult to work in its mines and provide victims for human sacrifice. Indy, Short Round and Willie penetrate the boy maharajah's palace and free the children after a chase through the tunnels on ore carts.

Wanting truly evil villains for this film, not simply the well-mannered Nazis and suave Belloq of *Raiders*, Lucas took a leaf from a favourite film of Spielberg's, George Stevens's 1939 version of the Rudyard Kipling poem 'Gunga Din', and resurrected its villains, the Thugs. A sub-group among devotees of the goddess Kali, the Thugs practised ritual strangling – Thugee – as a form of worship. Silent and anonymous, travelling the roads of India, murdering travellers and burying them with their ritual pickaxes, the Thugs kept their sect and practices secret for centuries. Renaming them 'Thugees' (or, in some versions, 'Thuggies'), *Temple of Doom* transformed them into repositories of noisome rites from a number of belief systems: Aztec cardiectomy, Hawaiian volcano sacrifice, European devil worship. Critics would complain that the film seemed set in a sort of Third World theme park, with a new race, creed and colour around every corner.

Huyck and Katz would need to write three major drafts to incorporate the hefty list of requirements imposed by producer, director, stars, the studio, exhibitors and censors. As his price for participating, Harrison Ford demanded better billing, more money and fewer distractions from his character than in *Raiders*. His eventual credit, 'Harrison Ford starring in . . .' made his the first name on the film. He also wanted to do more of his own stunts, a decision that had disastrous results. To reduce competition for the limelight even more, the omnicompetent Sallah and Brody were dropped for the admiring Short Round, named for the Korean kid in Sam Fuller's 1951 *The Steel Helmet*.

Spielberg too demanded alterations. Turned off independent women by his clashes with Karen Allen, he wanted Indy's companion to be a blonde bubblehead who spends most of her time squealing and complaining; the very mirror image of the feisty Marion Ravenswood. Her model was the shrill blonde Betty Hutton, who starred in the first film he ever saw, Cecil B. DeMille's *The Greatest Show on Earth*. To underline his contempt for the character, he took a leaf from Lucas's christening of Indiana Jones for his wife's dog and called the character 'Willie', after one of his own spaniels.

The most pressing piece of unfinished business in Spielberg's life was the *Close Encounters* sequel 'Night Skies', which had now become an embarrassment. John Sayles, reflecting Spielberg's gloom when he commissioned the screenplay, had created a script close to John Ford's *Drums Along the Mohawk*, where settlers in the War of Independence battle the British and their bloodthirsty Indian mercenaries. The chief of the alien group was named 'Scar', after the Indian who kidnaps John Wayne's niece in *The Searchers*. Rick Baker had followed the same brief, producing aliens which, as promised, were more cunningly engineered than those of *Close Encounters*, but also more frightening.

Recovered now from Amy's departure and the failure of *1941*, Spielberg found it hard to imagine he ever wanted to make so bleak a film. 'I think I must have taken leave of my senses,' he admitted. He turned down both the script and the designs. Sayles accepted philosophically, but Baker was furious, particularly after Spielberg questioned his $700,000 costs and suggested he'd spent too much time working for John Landis on *An American Werewolf in London*, and not enough on his project. When Spielberg described the new alien he now had in mind, a genial character he'd christened 'Puck' who resembled the figures who emerge from the mother ship at the end of *Close Encounters*, Baker reportedly stormed out, telling him, 'Call Rambaldi!' He later found himself locked out of his make-up lab, which contained, as well as his 'Night Skies' materials, all those for *American Werewolf*. Spielberg did contact Rambaldi, but the Italian requested nine months to design Puck. Spielberg gave him six, and when he delivered Baker charged that the result incorporated some of his ideas.

Yet another strike, this time of the Directors' Guild, threatened Hollywood in 1982, and studios were stockpiling films. Universal reminded Spielberg of the four still outstanding on his old contract, and offered him Ray Bradbury's *Something Wicked this Way Comes*, about the threatened invasion of a small town by a sinister circus and its ringmaster, which is foiled by two boys and the father of one of them. Peter Vincent Douglas, one of many small independent producers with a Universal 'first look' deal, had developed the novel for his father Kirk to play the ringmaster. Spielberg liked Bradbury's book but, given his dislike of working with stars, it's unlikely he ever seriously considered making a film with the egotistical Douglas. Ultimately he turned it down, after – according to the irritated star – keeping him waiting for a year, but Bradbury's folksy small-town vision and the idealised father hero stayed with him.

Surgeon/novelist/director Michael Crichton was making a reputation with high-concept science fiction thrillers, a few of which, in particular *The Andromeda Strain*, had succeeded as films. Jerry Goldsmith, who scored the adaptations of *Coma* and *The Great Train Robbery*, believed that Crichton and Spielberg, whom he'd come to know as a friend, were natural collaborators. 'I tried for years to get them together,' says Goldsmith, 'then finally they met without any help from me. And then I never heard from either of them again.'

Their introduction was engineered by Brian De Palma, who was interested in Crichton's new book, *Congo*, an African adventure about the rediscovery of King Solomon's legendary diamond mines, guarded by a tribe of feral gorillas. Frank Yablans had bought the novel for Fox, and for three months Spielberg and De Palma dickered with Fox and Universal about a version to be produced by Spielberg and directed by De Palma, before giving up in frustration. Spielberg angrily blamed Hollywood. 'A deal is a work of science fiction,' he told *Time* magazine. 'I wasted three months learning how not to make one. Eventually, Brian and I walked away. The whole "movie game" is just one more useless experience.' He also tried to set up a film of William Goldman's creepy novel *Magic*, about a ventriloquist haunted by his own dummy, but Richard Attenborough beat him to it.

Spielberg found consolation and a welcome at MGM. David Begelman's apparent revival of its fortunes would turn out to be illusory. His production slate (*Buddy, Buddy, All the Marbles, Pennies from Heaven, Whose Life is it Anyway?, Yes, Giorgio, Cannery Row*) was a catalogue of flops that prefaced the studio's sale to Kirk Kerkorian, leading to its amalgamation with UA and eventual extinction, but for the moment he exuded his usual urbane confidence. 'The sense of poised dynamism he wore like his cashmere sports coats,' said UA executive Steven Bach, 'was so persuasive it seemed to dispel a near decade of doldrums. Culver City became Deal City almost overnight.' Begelman told Spielberg that, notwithstanding any existing relationships with Columbia, Paramount or Universal, he would be welcome at Metro as an independent producer. They signed a deal – with one non-negotiable requirement. Spielberg demanded – and got – the office once occupied by Louis B. Mayer's 'genius boy' producer Irving Thalberg.

Ever since her discussions with Spielberg in Tunisia the year before, Melissa Mathison had been at work on the new script of the lost-alien-on-earth story, bringing her drafts to the Marina del Rey apartment where he was editing *Raiders*. She and Spielberg spent hours discussing revisions next to an open tape recorder. Three rewrites transformed 'A Boy's Life' into *E.T. and Me*, and then *E.T: The Extraterrestrial*.

The plot of *E.T.* is so transparently simple, even naive, that one can hardly credit the years of thought that went into it. In fact, it's the distillation of Spielberg's decade of loneliness in adolescence. Ten-year-old Elliott, living with his divorced mother, older brother and younger sister in an upstate Californian town, reflects the teenage Spielberg in Scottsdale. When an alien botanist, part of a long-lived space-faring race

– he's supposedly nine hundred years old – is left behind by a spaceship fleeing nosy locals, Elliott lures him to the house with candy and hides him among his stuffed toys, turning him into a companion who won't patronise him as do his brother's friends.

Elliott becomes the beneficiary and victim of Puck's most distinctive characteristic, an ability to empathise. The alien's chest literally lights up at moments of high emotion, revealing his pulsing heart, and he can transfer power through the touch of one glowing finger. Soon they are sharing feelings. When Puck samples beer for the first time, both feel drunk, even though Puck is at home and Elliott is studying biology at school. Asked to kill and dissect a frog with the rest of his biology class – as Spielberg had himself been – Elliott is reminded so much of his new friend by the trapped creatures that he releases them, and, reeling with compassion, plants a kiss on the lips of his favourite little girl in the class. In an excruciating evocation of adolescent sexuality's mingled lust and embarrassment, Spielberg cuts to the girl's feet in strapped shoes twisting, perhaps in delight but more likely in revulsion, among the squirming frogs.

But Puck's empathetic ability is also his weakness; separated from his own kind, he languishes and almost dies. Inspired by a comic strip, he persuades Elliott and his brother to help him build a transmitter so he can 'call home'. They cobble one together from junk but, in the process, alert the leader of those hunting him. Captured by this man, known only as 'Keys' because of the bunch that jangles at his belt, Puck appears to die, but is resurrected, apparently by Elliott's love. In a sustained final sequence containing some of Spielberg's most memorable images, the kids carry Puck to his forest rendezvous with the returning spaceship, eluding Keys by sailing over his head on their bikes, borne by Puck's telekinetic power.

Almost as soon as he finished *Raiders*, Spielberg explained to Columbia's Frank Price that he'd changed his mind about 'Night Skies'. He described *E.T.*, expecting him to accept it in exchange. Not surprisingly, however, Price turned it down. In the conventional wisdom, children's films – and this was surely one – were notoriously risky. Other studios were no more enthusiastic about this suburban fantasy, but in January 1981 Universal accepted it, mostly to preserve their relationship with Spielberg, which they valued at more than the $10 million the film would cost. Price's refusal so angered Spielberg that he decreed the executive should 'cease to exist'. Given the motility of studio heads, there was always the chance Price might transfer into a position of influence over some future project, so Spielberg specified in every contract that he would never have to work under him again. He was to be glad of this when, in the game of musical chairs that is Hollywood's management structure, Price became president of Universal.

Spielberg offered 'Night Skies' to Begelman at MGM under the same terms as he'd proposed to Columbia. He would produce the film but not direct it, leaving that to a talented newcomer. To avoid compromising E.T., he changed the story radically, transforming the malign presences which besiege the family from aliens to ghosts. 'Night Skies' was dropped as a title; the film would eventually be called Poltergeist.

That Spielberg should create the blackest of all his films at the same time as his sunniest indicates his divided state of mind at this period. Stung by gibes that, while others in the Brats group, especially Scorsese, were making more profound films while he stuck with comedy and adventure, he insisted that he wasn't out of touch with the spirit of left-handed endeavour the Star Wars films called 'the dark side of The Force'. 'I'm working on my dark side,' he told journalist Dale Pollock defensively, 'really I am. I'm working on it every day.' Each day of facing his demons made him, however, feel older, wearier, more desperate. This period of his life, he said later, was so tormented that his pubic hairs turned grey.

Throughout Poltergeist's tangled making and acrimonious aftermath, Spielberg insisted the film was his idea, based on experiences like the ghostly phone call to Leah from his dead grandmother and the terrified fantasies of his time in Cincinnati. Thelma Moss, the psychic researcher who inspired the character of the compassionate investigator Dr Lesh, played by Beatrice Straight in the film, loyally but improbably insisted that 'as far back as 1976, his research folks were meeting with me.' Tobe

Hooper, the credited director of *Poltergeist*, has a different story, and one which rings truer to Spielberg's habit of acquiring projects already launched by other directors.

After Spielberg pulled out of 'Night Skies', Hooper moved to Universal to direct *The Funhouse*. To his delight, he was assigned the old office of Robert Wise, who made *The Haunting*. In Wise's desk was a book about the malicious spirits called poltergeists which manifest themselves in showers of stones or frogs, noises, flying objects and general mischief. Hooper took it for an omen. He insists that he proposed a psychic thriller about poltergeists to Spielberg and that they collaborated by mail on a treatment while Spielberg was in London on *Raiders*.

Apparently without Hooper's knowledge, however, Spielberg also approached America's most successful horror writer, Stephen King, to script the film. They had an amiable lunch, after which King departed for England, leaving his publisher to negotiate a deal on his behalf. Doubleday, King says, 'asked this incredible amount of money to do the screenplay. This is for somebody who had never done a screenplay that had been produced.' MGM – and Spielberg – refused to pay it. 'I got a letter from Spielberg saying he was really unhappy that it turned out this way.' On reflection, King wasn't sorry – and the later history of *Poltergeist* probably made him even less so. 'Spielberg is somebody who likes to have things his way,' he told the sf and fantasy film journal *Cinefantastique*. 'Really, as far as writing, it would have been the experience of working with him and watching him work – I could've used that. But in the end, I would've been hired help.' Spielberg and King flirted with working together on a film for the next decade, but never found the right subject. Universal bought the novel *The Talisman*, co-written by King and Peter Straub, on the understanding that Spielberg would direct it, then cooled their heels waiting for him to commit. In 1994, King proposed a ghost story of his own and he, Spielberg and writer/director Mick Garris met at Spielberg's East Hampton house for a week-long conference, but again they couldn't agree, though in 1996 Garris would land the plum project of remaking King's *The Shining*.

*   *   *

At MGM, which had put *Poltergeist* on the 1981 summer schedule at a modest $9.5 million, Spielberg, Frank Marshall and Kathleen Kennedy dug in with their team, now expanded to include Marvin Levy, who, after working on publicity and advertising for *Used Cars* and *1941*, had left Columbia to join Spielberg. Unsure as yet in the role of producer, Spielberg wasn't ready to gamble with either his reputation or his bank balance, so a new company, Extra Terrrestrial Productions Inc., was formed to make the film. If it flopped, ETP Inc., its liability limited, could fold, writing off its deficit. Any time total independence looked momentarily attractive, he needed only to recall the mess into which Coppola had fallen in trying to go it alone.

Even in these early days of Spielberg's emergence as a producer, however, the secrecy that was to mark Amblin Entertainment already operated. The press complained that both cast and crew had been sworn to silence, that office phones were unlisted, and that MGM staff had been instructed to deny that Spielberg was even making a movie there. Behind the scenes, however, deals were already being made in the company's name. James Kahn's novelisation of the *Poltergeist* script, published by Warner Books in May 1982, would be among the first of many products to bear a credit to Amblin' Enterprises. (The apostrophe was dropped the next year.)

Spielberg's office furnishings at MGM included three arcade-sized video games, a gift from Steve Ross of Warners, which also owned the video-game manufacturer Atari. Spielberg had met the silver-haired and cultured Warners CEO through his long-time friend Terry Semel, Warners' production head, and had immediately fallen under the spell of this consummate manipulator.

Ross belonged in the movies. Born of a poor Jewish family in Brooklyn, he used his charm, cunning and mathematical skill to insinuate himself into the mortuary business of Eddie Rosenthal, whose daughter he married. Noting that the firm's limousines were idle at night, he began hiring them out. This pushed the company into parking lots and car rental, areas controlled by organised crime. Ross, however, made his accommodation with the Mob, with whom he was to be on cordial terms until his death in 1992, and built on his power to move into show business, buying

Warner Brothers in 1969. The smell of his early associations clung, however. 'Steve is Mafia,' snapped a former president of Time Inc. after Ross merged the prestigious publishing firm with Warners in 1988 to create the world's largest entertainment conglomerate.

Ross was an anthology of opposites. Always a high-stakes gambler, and fascinated by the secret of 'counting cards' at blackjack, he affected at the same time an aristo's ease with culture, buying expensive art deco antiques in Paris and making friends of local artists, including Willem de Kooning and his wife Elaine, who lived near his house on Long Island.

Yet he found show business and its people fascinating, filling his parties with celebrities and competing with the eagerness of a fan for the most reclusive of them. Most of them reciprocated, in particular Spielberg. 'Steven was a young man, in his early thirties,' Terry Semel reminisced, 'with no business sophistication. He found Steve, who was so much older, so fascinating. Steve Ross was into things we knew only a little about – art, planes, homes.' Their relationship was cemented when Ross revealed that *It's a Wonderful Life* was his favourite film.

Ross resolved to lure Spielberg from Universal/MCA. He was helped by Spielberg's hostility towards both Ned Tanen and the man who succeeded him as president, Frank Price. Late in 1981, when Semel became president of the movie production division of Ross's corporation, he offered his friend almost *carte blanche* to make a Warners film. He and Semel reviewed the roster of projects. They never got past a feature version of *The Twilight Zone*, the rights to which Ted Ashley, former head of the studio and once Rod Serling's agent, had bought from the writer's widow Carol. Spielberg was instantly enthusiastic. He saw it, however, not as a single story but as a film of episodes – and, what's more, remakes of episodes from the original series. Semel agreed. Who argued with the director of *Jaws* and *Raiders of the Lost Ark*? To the well-concealed chagrin of Sid Sheinberg, Spielberg signed a contract to divide his future productions between Warners and Universal. In the corridors of the black tower, serious thought was given to finding an incentive that would keep the company's hottest director from slipping through their fingers completely.

*   *   *

After marathon auditions for *E.T.*, Spielberg ditched his original choice for Elliott when editor Ed Warschilka Jr sent him a reel of a film he was cutting, *Raggedy Man*, about a boy growing up with an absent father. A ten-year-old San Antonio boy named Henry Thomas played Sissy Spacek's son, and Spielberg decided his tentative spunkiness exactly fitted his vision of Elliott. As the boy's young mother, he'd wanted Shelley Long, later the mainstay of the TV series *Cheers*, but Long, with conspicuously poor judgement, preferred to do *Caveman* with Ringo Starr. Dee Wallace, the heroine of the Joe Dante/John Sayles werewolf drama *The Howling*, replaced her. Peter Coyote would be the enigmatic Keys, and Drew Barrymore, daughter of John Drew Barrymore, the youngest member of the theatrical dynasty haunted by alcohol and drugs, Elliott's little sister Gertie.

The six-year-old Barrymore auditioned by telling Spielberg about the punk band in which she played. She gave him the name of the band, its drummer, its bass player. Afterwards, Spielberg asked her mother, Ildiko Jaid, herself an actress, 'Has she toured with this punk group?' 'She has no punk group,' Jaid explained wearily, already sensing the self-destructive temperament that, within a decade, would turn Drew from moppet to drug-addicted raver.

While he cast *E.T.*, Spielberg was also at work, though less publicly, on *Poltergeist*. On paper, the Hooper/Spielberg treatment for *Poltergeist* seemed bland. Out of the blue, the white-bread suburban family of ace real-estate salesman Steve Freeling is assaulted by ghosts. At first playful, then malicious, they invade the house which, it emerges, a penny-pinching developer (and Steve's employer) has built on an old graveyard, without first removing the corpses. Finally the most militant of the unquiet spirits abducts five-year-old Carol Anne via a TV screen and holds her in some fifth-dimensional maze, the gateway to which is her bedroom closet. When psychic investigators fail to retrieve her, the family calls in Tangina, a plump, diminutive, self-important but effective medium who recovers the little girl by sending her mother into the maze to retrieve her.

Though set in Southern California's imaginary Cuesta Verde, not far from Richard Nixon's home town of San Clemente, the story, with its tract houses puddled in a green valley, its run-of-the-mill parents, including a tousled wife in shorts who smokes a clandestine joint upstairs while her husband snores in front of the hissing TV, a copy of Ronald Reagan's memoirs in his hand, their jumpy son, half-grown, frightened of everything from the clown doll lurking under his bed to the tree outside the window, has Cincinnati and Spielberg's childhood all over it. The film rounds up his fascination with TV, as well as all his fears of the toys in his own bedroom, and the terrors he visited on the hapless Anne, Sue and Nancy when he locked them in closets.

With Stephen King out of the picture, Spielberg assigned the screenplay to Michael Grais and Mark Victor, two young screenwriters who attracted his attention with an unproduced script, 'Turn Left or Die', about air-traffic controllers. He should, as with *E.T.*, have hashed over the story with them in front of a tape recorder until everyone shared the same vision. But that would have put his signature all over it, something which, in his new role as producer, he was anxious to avoid.

Inevitably, however, the Grais/Victor script didn't satisfy him, and, in a frenzy of what he (though probably not James Joyce) thought of as 'stream of consciousness', he rewrote it, scribbling a hundred pages over five white nights. 'I couldn't write alone,' he said, so Kennedy and Marshall moved into his house with him. Each morning, he read them his night's work, and they threw in their ideas or urged him on. Then he showed what he'd written to Hooper, 'who hung round with me while I was writing that draft'. This comment set the tone for Hooper's role. In this, as in most choices about cast and crew, Hooper was firmly sidelined. He nominated special-effects technician Craig Reardon to build the monster which emerges from the closet to repel the investigators, but Spielberg rethought the concept and, rejecting Hooper's approved model, chose instead an early sketch which Reardon felt was less effective. Industrial Light and Magic built the gaping creature, christened 'The Esophagus'.

Spielberg chose the cast and crew, and, in a further display of territoriality, also wrote the shooting script and started Ed Verreaux on the storyboards. Though he's the credited director, and 'A Tobe Hooper

Film' receives a full panel, it became increasingly hard for anyone, even Hooper himself, to believe he controlled *Poltergeist*.

When the storm broke over the film, many wondered why Spielberg hadn't simply fired Hooper and taken over the direction himself. But there were persuasive legal arguments against this. The Directors' Guild barred any producer, except under the most extreme circumstances, from taking director credit on a film prepared by someone else; too many unscrupulous money men were ready to step in and claim a film as their own. Nor could a director shoot two films at the same time; some directors would over-commit themselves simply for the money. Had he worked on *Poltergeist* and *E.T.* concurrently, Spielberg would have transgressed both rules.

In his insistence that the original treatment was all his own work, Spielberg may have been influenced by the growing flood of claims, all disproved, from religious visionaries and unsuccessful screenwriters that *Raiders* plagiarised ideas submitted to ICM or Paramount years before. His well-publicised assistance to young directors and writers attracted hundreds of projects a week, though an increasingly defensive Spielberg would soon follow larger companies in refusing all unsolicited material. After that, wannabees took to lurking by the gates of his home and flinging scripts into his car. Even so, *Poltergeist*, on the hallowed principle of 'Where there's a hit, there's a writ', attracted a $37 million suit from actor Paul Clemens and writer Bennett Michael Yelin claiming Spielberg cribbed it from their 1980 screenplay. Director/writer Frank DeFelitta also detected resemblances to *The Entity*, then in production (and starring Spielberg's sometime companion Barbara Hershey).

To confer a distinct identity on *Poltergeist*, Spielberg chose new collaborators. None of the cast, including Craig T. Nelson and JoBeth Williams as the parents, Oliver Robins as their son Robbie and Heather O'Rourke as Carol Anne, had worked with him before, though Dominique Dunne, who played the eldest girl Dana, was the daughter of John Gregory Dunne's brother Dominick. Michael Kahn would as usual cut the film, but cameraman Matthew Leonetti, who'd worked on productions as disparate as *Breaking Away*, *Raise the Titanic* and *Fast Times at Ridgemont High*, was new, as was production designer James H. Spencer from

Sylvester Stallone's hit boxing drama *Rocky*, whose work was integral to recreating Spielberg's idealised suburbia. Spencer was to enjoy a long association with Spielberg productions via *Twilight Zone: The Movie* and *Gremlins*. Instead of John Williams, Spielberg asked Jerry Goldsmith to write the music. The two men had become friends. At a dinner in December 1981 where the Composers' and Lyricists' Guild presented Spielberg with an award for advancing film music, he said that had he not directed films, he would have studied music and composed for them.

It will probably never be known with absolute certainty who really directed *Poltergeist*. It has joined a small group of films, including the 1942 *Journey into Fear* and the 1951 *The Thing*, which, though signed by one director, bear the indelible stylistic trademarks of another. Orson Welles had intended to direct *Journey into Fear*, and even took a small role in it, but bequeathed the project to Norman Foster while he went to Brazil to make *It's All True*. Yet, in defiance of all evidence to the contrary, the film looks and sounds like Welles's work. *The Thing* is also palpably a film by Howard Hawks, with all his trademark male bonding and overlapping dialogue. Nevertheless, Hawks insists that it was directed by his editor Christian Nyby, who desperately wanted a screen credit, and it's Nyby's name that appears on the screen.

Of the shooting of *Poltergeist*, Craig Reardon was quoted in *Cinefantastique* as saying, 'Tobe Hooper was always there, but the film was essentially guided by Steven's strong hand. As he said in an interview, Steven wants to do everybody's job as well as they do, but concedes that he needs help.' Many of the actors, however, insisted that Hooper was in charge. In writing the music, Goldsmith recalled, 'I worked only with Steven. One day Hooper came into a screening and sat down. Steve just ignored him, and after five minutes he got up and left.' His estimate of the shooting: 'Hooper said "Action" and that's the last thing he did.' But, in fairness to Hooper, Goldsmith was never on the set. Frank Marshall articulated the official Amblin version. 'The creative force on the movie was Steven. Tobe was the director and was on the set every day. But Steven did the design for every storyboard and was on the set every day except for three days when he was in Hawaii with [George] Lucas.'

To assume that *Poltergeist*, with its many stylistic similarities to Spielberg's other work and references to themes that had preoccupied him and would continue to do so, was entirely someone else's work would be to credit Hooper with an inspired act of pastiche, and one he never repeated in his subsequent erratic career. The most credible theory holds that Hooper directed the performances, Spielberg the action, and that they collaborated, often to the frustration of Hooper, on complex sequences which combined acting and special effects.

The tendency has been to divide the film into 'Hooper scenes' and 'Spielberg scenes' on the basis of their degree of violence. The sunny domestic moments must be Spielberg's, of course, while Hooper is plainly responsible for the steak that, slug-like, inches moistly along the kitchen counter, or the psychic investigator's hallucination when, as he washes his face, the flesh sloughs away like clay into the basin. However, the evidence doesn't support this. Spielberg conceived the film's most terrifying sequences, the attack of the animated tree and the emergence of the monster from the bedroom closet, both of which spring directly from well-documented childhood memories. He also bears some responsibility for what look like typical 'Hooper' images. As Craig Reardon was preparing the gelatine face to be shredded, Spielberg said, 'Hey, I want to do that!' and it's his hands, not Reardon's, that rip the flesh down to the skull. Saint Steven has his devils too.

Poltergeist, Spielberg had promised, would be his 'revenge on TV'. The omnipresent tube is the first thing one sees in the film. When Carol Ann toddles down the cranked metal staircase that will become a route for the ghosts and stares into the fizzing grain of the screen, her calm conversation with 'the TV people' and her triumphant 'They're here!' resonate with the feelings of every child who ever imagined another world at a tangent to his or her own.

The rest of the film is a canter through his enthusiasms. Bits of *Something Wicked this Way Comes* join leftovers from 'Something Evil', 'After School' and 'Growing Up'. The film also owes something to a 1962 *Twilight Zone* based on Richard Matheson's short story 'Little Girl Lost', where a child rolls under her bed and into another dimension. There are hints of *The Wizard Of Oz*, and Vincente Minnelli's Halloween sequence in *Meet Me in St Louis* where tiny Margaret O'Brien fights her dread to throw flour in the face of the neighbourhood ogre, a scene Spielberg paid tribute to in *E.T.*, just as he would allow Joe Dante a few years later to make a revisionist gloss on *It's a Wonderful Life* with *Gremlins*. He may also have already read Chris Columbus's script for this film. A violent comic fantasy about furry pets metamorphosing into gibbering imps which overrun a Capra-esque country town, it has many affinities with *Poltergeist*.

The storm over *Poltergeist* was not long in breaking. First, in May, the MPAA's Classification and Ratings Board gave it an 'R' certificate, barring children. Spielberg had already removed some of the script's worst moments, including a spider attack on the psychic investigators. (He also cut a final image where, after Steve Freeling shoves the TV out of the motel room where the family has taken shelter, the set rolls off down the balcony of its own volition. Even without this hint that Tangina's exorcism hasn't been entirely successful, and the ghost remains lurking in the machine, MGM still produced two sequels.) He strenuously defended the rest, however, flying to New York with MGM chairman Frank Rosenfelt to demand a Parental Guidance certificate for the film rather than the Restricted that would have barred it to everyone under eighteen. In the face of such heavy pressure, the Board acquiesced. 'I don't make "R" movies,' Spielberg muttered afterwards.

It soon became clear, however, that he must accept that his films had become darker, more violent and less suitable for sub-teen audiences. After shooting finished on *Jedi*, Lucas took a Hawaiian break, and Spielberg took a few days off from shooting *Poltergeist* to join him and build their ritual sandcastle. Lucas showed him the final script of *Temple of Doom*. The last third, which would take place in the sect's subterranean temple and in the mine, was obviously going to be controversial. After setting up his idealised family of Indy, Willie and Short Round, the film shows it all but destroyed when Indy, fed a narcotic by the priests of Kali, turns into a monster who assists in the near-sacrifice of Willie.

When she's suspended over a pit of molten flame, it's Short Round, the surrogate Steven, who drags his 'father' back to sanity.

By pushing film closer to the violence of comic strips, Lucas had put himself and Spielberg on a collision course with the censors. The fact made Spielberg nervous. He valued his squeaky-clean image, and while acknowledging that the Kali sacrifice scenes reflected his own vision of the family, he agreed that he wouldn't want any ten-year-old to see them. Lucas argued that their audience had become more hip since *Raiders*, accustomed to horror, eager for sensation, and Spielberg was persuaded. For added evidence, there was the enthusiastic early reaction to *Poltergeist*, which Begelman believed, rightly, would be one of the big hits of the 1982 summer season. (In fact, it was the only profitable film made at MGM during his tenure.)

Spielberg agreed with Lucas to start shooting *Temple of Doom* in April 1983, and Robert Watts, elevated to producer, with Kathleen Kennedy as associate, was sent on an Asian tour looking for locations.

Spielberg returned to the set of *Poltergeist*, and a mounting furore over its authorship. By now, rumours of battles on the film had become public. Hooper himself avoided interviews, then issued conciliatory statements that Spielberg's interventions delighted him. The truce ended when Hooper saw the final prints. The credits allocated Spielberg joint producer credit with Frank Marshall, sole authorship of the original story and equal screenwriting credit with Grais and Victor. MGM issued trailers in which Spielberg's name as producer appeared in type double the size of Hooper's. It also widely released promotional footage showing Spielberg directing scenes, and publicity photographs of Spielberg outlining his vision with authoritative gestures to an apparently dutiful Hooper.

Confronted with Hooper's complaints, Spielberg was unrepentant. 'Tobe isn't what you'd call a take-charge sort of guy,' he said. 'He's just not a strong presence on a movie set. If a question was asked and an answer wasn't immediately forthcoming, I'd jump up and say what we could do. Tobe would nod agreement, and that became the process of collaboration.' Hooper responded angrily that he'd done 'fully half' of the storyboards, and exercised effective control on the set. The Directors' Guild intervened on his behalf, demanding $200,000 in damages and withdrawal of the offending trailers. This was bargained down to a $15,000 fine and pulling the trailers in the LA and New York areas only. The DGA also mentioned 'broader issues of dispute . . . between the producer/writer and the director', without being more specific. In June 1982, as part of the settlement, Spielberg published a full-page open letter to Hooper in *Variety* praising his 'openness in allowing me, as producer and writer, a wide berth for creative involvement, just as I know you were happy with the freedom you had to direct *Poltergeist* so wonderfully'. The device fooled nobody, but Hooper, powerless in the face of Spielberg's influence, was forced to eat crow. His career never recovered.

While *Poltergeist* was still being mixed and the music recorded during October 1981, Spielberg was at work on *E.T.*, scheduled for June 1982 release. It was a visibly more personal film. John Williams was back in charge of the music, and Allen Daviau had been astonished to receive a call from Spielberg for the first time since *Close Encounters*. Spielberg praised his camerawork on William Graham's comedy western *Harry Tracy, Desperado*. He sensed in the film the playful mysticism he wanted for *E.T.*, and asked Daviau to shoot it, making good at last on his promise before he shot *Amblin'*.

Not that Daviau was given much rope. Spielberg encouraged him to study Derek Van Lint's work on Ridley Scott's *Blade Runner*, and films like *Apocalypse Now* and *Last Tango in Paris*, lit by Vittorio Storaro, whom Spielberg rated the most gifted lighting cameraman in the world, despite his cranky theories. Storaro had been Spielberg's first choice to shoot *E.T.*, but the Italian, bitter about his experience on *One from the Heart*, for which American union regulations forbade him taking full screen credit, was returning to Italy to work with Bernardo Bertolucci again. Daviau and Spielberg also studied Edouard Manet, and the gaudy illustrations of Maxfield Parrish. Not noted for a strong personal style, Daviau dutifully absorbed all these influences, or tried to, confident that, in the end, Spielberg would operate the camera and set the tone.

Most of the film was made on interiors in the old David Selznick Studios, but Spielberg also took the unit to a Culver City high school, to the satellite towns of Northridge and Tujunga, and for six days further north, to Crescent City, for the forest scenes. Worried as ever that his story would be leaked and its impact diluted, Spielberg insisted, 'E.T. does *not* stand for Extraterrestrial.' Already at work on the marketing, he chose the alien's long, wrinkled finger as the film's most potent emblem, and commissioned Intralink Film Graphics to design the film poster. They were required to do so, however, without seeing any film. 'Steven would look at what we were doing,' said Intralink president Anthony Goldschmidt, 'and say, "No, the fingers would be longer, and the skin would be a different colour."'

Directing a cast of children brought Spielberg close to being a father, and left him eager for the first time to have a family of his own. However, he was guarded in speaking about his relationship with Henry Thomas and Drew Barrymore. He'd been stung over accusations after *Close Encounters* that he had taken insufficient interest in the progress of little Cary Guffey after the film. He later admitted, 'E.T. made me yearn to be a father. I was a surrogate parent for ten weeks, and it was a great experience, like being with my old Scout troop.' As Joe Dante, also unmarried and childless, said of his own work on the 1985 space adventure *Explorers* with an all-teen cast, 'You see the kids more often than anyone else does, even their families. And they confide in you. It was really fascinating to see that all the pressures and fears that I had as a kid haven't changed at all.'

Melissa Mathison had begun by visualising Puck as a creature so gentle that he's closer to plants than to man. Early in her version, he takes counsel from tomatoes and artichokes in Elliott's garden about whether or not to make contact with the humans and, when he does so, it's by rolling back to Elliott's feet not a baseball, as in the final version, but an orange. Spielberg wanted nothing so mimsy. As signposts, he had Mathison screen some movies that, to him, embodied the vision of childhood he wanted for E.T. They included *Bambi*, Charles Laughton's film of

Davis Grubb's novel *The Night of the Hunter*, the psychopathic preacher of which mercilessly pursues two children after murdering their mother, *The Blue Bird*, Walter Lang's version of Maurice Maeterlinck's play, with Shirley Temple as the daughter of a poor woodcutter searching without hope for happiness in a dreamlike blue gloom, and Jack Clayton's 1967 *Our Mother's House*, from Julian Gloag's novel about children who hide the death of their mother and set up their own loveless menage.

Aware that children are most impressed by what happens to children on screen, Spielberg concentrated on them to the virtual exclusion of adults, who are shot almost entirely from a child's eye view. If he'd chosen to take François Truffaut's advice about putting his own experience into his films, he could hardly have done so more effectively than with *E.T.* He was working with children, and dealing with subjects close to his heart: parenthood and family responsibility. He roughed out Puck's features for Carlo Rambaldi by creating a collage which, to him, conveyed both the wisdom of age and the innocence of childhood. Learning a lesson from Walt Disney's animators, who'd discovered that the most loveable faces were those closest to a baby's, with wide eyes and a high forehead, he pasted onto the photograph of a baby's unjudgemental face the eyes of poet Carl Sandburg clipped from another photo, and the forehead and nose of Ernest Hemingway and Albert Einstein. The result was a one-size-fits-all father figure without the censoriousness that comes with age. For Puck's snuffling sounds, Spielberg used the calls of otters and other wild animals, though any intelligible words were recorded by actors, including, anonymously, Debra Winger, still one of Spielberg's closest friends, who croaked his plaintive 'E.T. call home.' Spielberg also shot a five-minute cameo of Harrison Ford as the headmaster of Elliott's school, but dropped it in editing.

E.T. shares with all Spielberg's films from *Something Evil* onwards the theme of parental mortality, and an Oedipal disquiet at the absent father and sexually desirable mother. Elliott's father is almost more present than the mother who remained at home. Young and pretty, she's been robbed of maternity by her divorce. It's the father to whom the children relate. They know, as she doesn't, that he's in Mexico with his new girlfriend, whom they familiarly refer to as 'Sally', and when they try to help Puck by building him a transmitter, both agree, 'Dad would know what to do.' Forced to compete for their affection, the mother has elected to be their pal. As a result they ignore her authority, sending out for pizza without permission, and cursing – Elliott's insult 'Penis breath!' always drew a delighted gasp from teen audiences – while one of her eldest son's friends playfully gooses her as she wanders around the kitchen in her robe while they play poker.

No serious science fiction writer would have given house-room to the tale Spielberg told in *E.T.* Even by the standards of the animal films like *Lassie Come Home* which it resembles, the story is sentimental and trite. Yet Josef von Sternberg was right to say that 'the best source for a film is an anecdote', and with *E.T.* Spielberg showed that he shared with John Ford the ability to invest sentiment and cheap humour with the dignity of a universal pronouncement. Suffused with Gothic melancholy and a poignant Freudian sense of loss, *E.T.* would send audiences weeping from the cinema. Even as hard a case as the novelist Martin Amis was moved. He wrote:

> Towards the end of *E.T.*, barely able to support my own grief and bewilderment, I turned and looked down the aisle at my fellow sufferers; executive, black dude, Japanese businessman, punk, hippie, mother, teenager, child. Each face was a mask of tears . . . And we weren't crying for the little extraterrestrial, nor for little Elliott, nor for little Gertie. We were crying for our lost selves. This is the primal genius of Spielberg.

At his Cannes press conference, Spielberg traded on the almost reverent atmosphere of the moment to reassure journalists that the film wouldn't be mass-marketed. He almost sounded like a solicitous father when he told them, 'It will go into six or seven hundred [cinemas] and then will roll out into more theatres as the summer progresses. It will be handled very carefully.' (In fact this was almost the same release pattern as *Jaws* and *Raiders*.) He sounded less like the maker of *E.T.* than its custodian. 'I made *E.T.* for *us*,' he went on – meaning, most listeners believed, themselves, i.e. all right-thinking people. 'I never thought of how it would be accepted, or how it would be in the theatres. I am the last person to predict any outcome for any movie that I've ever made.'

Others were not so diffident in their forecasts. *Time* described one 'professional cynic' emerging moist-eyed from an early screening to predict '$350 million'. He wasn't far wrong. By the time it opened on 11 June 1982, following 450 special previews across America in the two preceding weeks, half the world wanted to see *E.T.* Puck, rueful, big-eyed, hammer-headed, wrinkled as an old boot, became an improbable icon. In a phenomenon other film-makers had experienced, notably Federico Fellini with his 1954 *La Strada*, where Giulietta Masina's self-sacrificing and affectionate waif Gelsomina became the object of a national cult in Italy, the creature assumed near-mystical significance to millions. A book of *Letters to E.T.* would be published. The film had something for everyone. Environmentalists, to the anger of loggers in the area where Spielberg shot the film, took it as a plea for the preservation of the redwoods. Reading it as a parable of redemption and even resurrection by the power of love, one American preacher detected thirty-three parallels between Puck's story and that of Christ, including one that compared his magic finger to that of God enlivening Adam in Michelangelo's Sistine Chapel frescoes.

Everyone wanted a seat on this bandwagon. Instead of the usual hack-for-hire, well-regarded novelist William Kotzwinkle agreed to write the tie-in novelisation and picture book. Neil Diamond recorded a ballad tribute to Puck, 'Turn on Your Heart Light'. Michael Jackson narrated an album called *The E.T. Storybook* which included another *E.T.*-inspired song, 'Someone in the Dark', by Alan and Marilyn Bergman, Oscar-winning composers of 'The Way We Were'. The singer, who had his own print of the film, which he claimed to have seen fifty times, weeping on each occasion, asked to meet Puck, so a photo session was arranged with one of Rambaldi's dummies.

'He grabbed me, he put his arms around me,' Jackson said ecstatically. 'He was so real that I was talking to him. I kissed him before I left. The next day, I missed him.'

The little visitor also waddled onstage at the Hollywood Bowl in June 1982 to shake hands with John Williams after a concert that included the E.T. theme; Spielberg said it was like watching your own kid at his first recital. This appearance of a non-robot E.T. confirmed rumours of human operators. Small people Pat Bilon and Tamara de Treaux, and legless Matthew de Merritt, did some of the scenes in Puck costumes.

The sentiment surrounding E.T. blinded nobody, least of all Spielberg, to its power as a money-maker. Kathleen Kennedy received 6 per cent of the film's net profits, a tribute to her management of what British TV commentator Marshall Lee summed up as a film designed 'to pluck your heartstrings and pick your pocket at the same time'. Amblin was criticised in some quarters for exploiting their loveable little earner. Early forecasts predicted at least $1 billion from the film, and Amblin licensed thirty-three E.T. products, though Spielberg complained that 150 were marketed, mostly by pirates. He even attributes the film's lack of success in the Oscars to this flood of tie-ins. People thought Amblin was over-exploiting what seemed to many a devotional film.

Companies which didn't grasp the merchandising value of E.T. would regret it – as would some who overestimated that appeal. Because of secrecy about his appearance, dolls of Puck took months to get into the stores, by which time the fad had peaked. Originally Elliott was to have lured Puck to the house with denture-testing caramels called Milk Duds, but candy-coated chocolate M&Ms were substituted after Milk Duds's manufacturer decreed that Puck's appearance was 'unappetising'. When M&M/Mars refused to co-operate in a massive pre-release sales drive of M&Ms for the film, Kennedy switched again, to Hershey's little-known but almost identical Reese's Pieces, which became Puck's preferred candy, and that of E.T.'s audiences. It was Charlton Heston, president of the Screen Actors' Guild, who foresaw where E.T.'s long-term profits lay when he commented, 'Video cassettes may turn out to be the biggest prize package opened in Hollywood since sound came in.' The worldwide sale of thirteen million copies of E.T. on video when Universal released it in October 1988 would be one of the studio's – and Spielberg's – greatest sources of profit. In 1989, *Business Week* estimated that Spielberg's personal take from E.T. video cassettes alone exceeded $40 million.

*   *   *

After *E.T.* Steve Ross coveted Spielberg even more. As Terry Semel continued to negotiate on *Twilight Zone*, Universal, sensing Warners moving in on their turf, wooed the director too, shrewdly offering his girlfriend a job on their Backstreet record label.

'They've hired Kathleen Carey,' said Ross, slamming down the phone when he heard the news. 'I don't believe it. Now, what can *we* do?'

His answer was to seduce Spielberg with glamour. In the summer of 1982, Ross and his new wife Courtney entertained Spielberg, Semel and their companions over a four-day weekend at their Villa Eden near Acapulco. Spielberg was stupefied by the house, Ross's collection of modern art, but above all by his movie-star style. 'Steve to me was a blast from the past. He had silver-screen charisma, much like an older Cary Grant, or a Walter Pidgeon. He had flash. He was a magnetic host – eventually that became his calling card. And at Acapulco, he *was* the weekend.'

Charles 'Skip' Paul, head of Atari's coin-operated-games division and later MCA's general counsel, had already offered Universal $1 million as an advance on 7 per cent royalties for an *E.T.* video game, and been turned down. He was dumbfounded when, following the Acapulco weekend, Ross told him he'd done a private deal with Spielberg that guaranteed Universal $23 million in royalties. Nobody believed such a contract could yield a profit for Atari, and as its engineers struggled to digitalise *E.T.*, this became evident. 'It wasn't a game,' complained Paul, 'it was a *thing* waddling around on the screen.' Stores returned a record 3.5 million of the four million modules shipped. Another Atari game based on *Raiders* did no better. But Paul would later date Spielberg's gradual defection from Universal to Warners from Ross's apparently profligate deal on *E.T.* 'Steve's viewpoint was, so what if I overpay by $22 million? How can you compare that to the value of a relationship with Spielberg? And I think he was dead right.'

12

The Twilight Zone: The Movie

You're moving into a land of both shadow and substance . . .

Rod Serling's introduction to the original *Twilight Zone* series

O N 5 MARCH 1982, John Belushi died in Bungalow Three in the grounds of the Château Marmont hotel in Los Angeles, his constitution of what Dan Aykroyd called 'Albanian Oak' toppled by an injection of cocaine and heroin. Inevitably *1941* and its problems were raked up by the press. Spielberg made no public comment and, while John Landis and his wife went to the funeral, he was absent – probably at the urging of Kathleen Kennedy and Frank Marshall who, since *E.T.*, were conscious of his image and the need to distance him from anything likely to mar it.

Damage had already been done, however, by his disputes with Hooper on *Poltergeist*. Rumours also circulated of arguments with Dee Wallace over her credit on *E.T.* Wallace complained about the secrecy on the set, which 'almost got to the point of ridiculousness', and it was suggested that Spielberg blacklisted her. Wallace neither confirmed nor denied the story, remarking only, 'It would be sad if someone of such creativity and power could be so small. It doesn't make sense to me – but then, stranger things have happened in Hollywood.'

The Oscars on 29 March offered Spielberg the usual disappointments. *Raiders* was nominated for Best Picture, Photography, Art Direction, Sound, Original Score, Editing and Visual Effects. Spielberg received a Best Director nomination too, but the film won only Art Direction, Sound and Editing, the key awards going to the British *Chariots of Fire*.

Belushi was to have presented the award for Best Special Effects. Aykroyd stepped in, having promised the show's producer Howard W.

Koch not to mention his friend, but Spielberg felt the knife was being twisted in his wound when, before giving the statuette to *Raiders*, Aykroyd commented, 'My partner would have loved presenting this award with me. He was something of a special effect himself.'

Koch winced. He'd particularly wished to avoid reminders of Belushi's death on worldwide TV. The previous year's ceremony had been delayed for twenty-four hours when President Reagan was shot on Awards day by John Hinckley, a besotted fan of Jodie Foster. Since then, the public had increasingly perceived Hollywood as a community of the obsessed and the addictive. Cocaine had ended the careers of directors like Hal Ashby (*Harold and Maude*, *Being There*), and Julia Phillips had blown her *Close Encounters* profits on the drug. Rumours also spoke of its widespread use on the set of *Poltergeist*. Coke and booze made the careers of actors like Richard Dreyfuss increasingly erratic. He'd already abandoned the role of the promiscuous, drug-using choreographer in Bob Fosse's autobiographical *All that Jazz*, where Roy Scheider replaced him. In October 1982 Dreyfuss would wrap his Mercedes around a tree and be committed to a detox centre.

Even more damage had been done to Hollywood's image by the Begelman affair, as widely publicised in *Indecent Exposure*, a best-selling blow-by-blow account by David McClintick, the *Wall Street Journal* reporter who broke the story. Traditionally, the film industry investigated its own crimes, held its own trials, buried its own dead. The trade press knew better than to dig too deeply into a scandal, or to publicise any that did come to light. However, after the Begelman case, which one writer compared to a Hollywood Watergate in its seismic effects on the film business, the chances of hiding anything from the press or public were severely reduced.

Of all people in Hollywood, Spielberg seemed the least likely to become embroiled in scandal. He no longer even drank coffee, let alone smoked pot, carrying bags of Roastaroma herbal tea everywhere. The roots of his strictness were evident at The Milky Way, the milk bar which his mother, with his help, had opened at 326½ Beverly Drive in early 1981. Kosher was so strictly kept that diners were forbidden to bring food of any kind, for fear of compromising dietary rules.

Spielberg's private life was cosily domestic. In August he told *People* magazine, 'I think Kathleen and I will have kids. We've just been so busy with our careers that we haven't dealt with each other on a marital basis. But now we're thinking about it.' His sole indulgence was to pay $60,500 at Sotheby-Parke Bernet in June for one of the three surviving prop sleds from *Citizen Kane*, a trophy of Old Hollywood which he proudly hung in his office.

In March 1982, Zoetrope had declared bankruptcy. Sombrely, Coppola remarked, 'I probably have genius, but no talent.' He asked friends to bail him out with personal loans of more than $1 million. Their understandable refusal left him so strapped that his home phone was cut off for more than a year. Coppola's friendship with Lucas and Spielberg was hardening into rivalry. In public, however, Spielberg defended Coppola's entrepreneurial flair, though often in ambiguous terms. Grandiose even in defeat, Coppola proposed, after watching the British director Jack Clayton film his script of *The Great Gatsby* at Pinewood studios outside London, that a consortium of himself, Lucas, Spielberg, Scorsese, De Palma and Michael Powell, Zoetrope's 'director in residence', should buy this flagship of J. Arthur Rank's empire. Sited in a mansion just outside London in grounds that provided backgrounds for scores of movies, including many of the Bond films, Pinewood boasted the '007 Stage', the world's largest. Spielberg put his name on the bid, which escalated from $3 million to $20 million but lapsed when Rank wouldn't contemplate anything less than $30 million.

To Hollywood, Zoetrope's collapse and the success of *E.T.* were twin indications of the tilt away from the personal films and maverick directors Coppola favoured and towards the consensus film-making of Spielberg. In a hurried effort to make up for having turned down *E.T.*, other studios rushed out their own versions. Big-eyed, loveable aliens, and even robots, proliferated as the perception of science fiction film slid towards the juvenile. British director Brian Gibson, who'd been working at Zoetrope, saw the shift from up close when Coppola's bankruptcy threw his project 'The Tourist' back on the market. One moment, he was sharing space at Zoetrope with David Lynch and Jean-Luc Godard; the next he was on the street. Clair Noto's sensual script involving shape-changing aliens who, exiled to earth as to some intergalactic Siberia, gravitate towards the porn cinemas and S&M clubs of San Francisco, found a new home at Universal, with H.R. Giger, *Alien*'s designer, doing the decor and Hanna Schygulla set to star. But the day after *E.T.* was released, two men with cardboard cartons knocked on Gibson's office door. They were the incoming occupants. 'The Tourist' was never made.

Asked about his plans, Spielberg confirmed that he'd be directing *Indiana Jones and the Temple of Doom* in Sri Lanka and at Elstree, but not until April 1983. Before then, he had plenty of potential proposals, both as director and producer. They included a 'secret project' called 'Worlds After', which was being developed first as a novel, 'Reel to Reel', a backstage Hollywood musical written by Gary David Goldberg, and *Always*, for which Jerry Belson, author of the ironic satire on beauty contests, *Smile*, was updating Dalton Trumbo's *A Guy Named Joe* screenplay into a film which, Spielberg said optimistically at the time, would be 'my *Annie Hall*'. For TV, he was developing the eccentric domestic comedy *Twister* (not to be confused with Michael Crichton's novel of the same name about tornadoes, which he bought in 1994), and, for Warners, a story called 'Starfire', plus three adventures from the *Blackhawk* comic book series. Brian De Palma also expected him to produce his next film, 'Carpool', which would explore his voyeuristic fascination with the rear-vision mirrors of automobiles.

Twister did become a *succès d'estime* for director Michael Almereyda in 1989, but except for *Temple of Doom*, Spielberg made none of these films. The fact suggests Spielberg's lack of direction at this time, and his need for the focus and system that would be offered by the formation of Amblin. His immediate project remained *The Twilight Zone*. Initially he approached it with anticipation. As he accumulated power, Spielberg was driven more and more to recycle and, in the process, retrospectively rehabilitate the films and series he'd enjoyed as a child. His parents had been wrong: all that time staring at the TV hadn't been wasted. He'd inserted clips of the Road Runner and Wile E. Coyote into *Sugarland Express* and of DeMille's *The Ten Commandments* into *Close Encounters*, as well as tributes to Disney in both that film and 1941. And if his signature is on *Poltergeist*, it's in the glimpse of *A Guy Named Joe* running on the TV. Collaborators were often nonplussed by this rooting in the past. 'A few years after *Empire of the Sun*,' recalls J.G. Ballard, author of the original novel, 'he rang me out of the blue and asked if I'd be interested in adapting a film called *House on Haunted Hill*.' Ballard had never seen William Castle's cheesy 1958 horror flick, with a trademark Castle gimmick, in this case 'Emergo', a plastic skeleton that popped out above the screen on a wire and gibbered over the heads of the audience. He declined the offer, but not all writers could afford such luxury. Most learned the Spielberg recipe. Wesley Strick, commissioned by Amblin to rewrite one of Spielberg's favourite thrillers, J. Lee Thompson's 1962 *Cape Fear*, admitted he 'consciously styled it a bit for Steven Spielberg's sensibilities. There were a lot of "movie movie" moments, and some cute touches of Americana . . . It was a bit antiseptic.' When Martin Scorsese inherited the project, he ruthlessly weeded out all such references, in particular those in which the family of Nick Nolte's rural judge, about to be terrorised by a man he's railroaded into jail, join in a sing-song round the piano.

Warners' first impulse after it put *The Twilight Zone* into production had been to cash in on the success of *Alien*, *Close Encounters* and *Star Trek: The Motion Picture* by using a single story to carry the entire film. Staff producer Mark Rosenberg was assigned to find one strong enough to compete with these powerful fantasies but which, at the same time, remained true to Serling's ironic and intellectual tone. The closest he came was Steve DeJarnatt's *Miracle Mile*, in which a man in a diner on Wilshire Boulevard, in the middle of Beverly Hills' art deco Miracle Mile business district, intercepts a panic telephone call revealing that a nuclear holocaust is imminent, and spends the film trying, unsuccessfully, to convince others. (It was filmed with moderate success in 1989, DeJarnatt directing.)

With Spielberg's arrival, the idea of a single story was discarded. He preferred to recreate episodes from the TV series itself, updated and improved. Spielberg would direct one sequence himself, and co-produce the film as a whole. Terry Semel, delighted by his enthusiasm, even suggested it be called *Steven Spielberg Presents The Twilight Zone*, but Spielberg declined this honour.

John Landis was an obvious choice to collaborate, since both he and Spielberg loved the series and had spent evenings reminiscing about favourite programmes – occasions Landis would celebrate in the film's prologue, where Dan Aykroyd and Albert Brooks do the same. Spielberg now felt he had more in common with the neurasthenic, bearded Landis than when he rejected him to write *Jaws*. In the furore over *1941*, he'd nominated him as a film-maker on the same epic scale as himself and Coppola. 'If we don't take chances, who will?' he argued when journalists accused him of splurging other people's money. 'If Francis doesn't take his Machiavellian risks, and John Landis doesn't exploit the success of *Animal House* with *The Blues Brothers*, and if I can't try to make the noisiest movie of all time – without some degree of failure, you can't move forward.'

An American Werewolf in London had restored Landis's reputation, tarnished by *The Blues Brothers*. In its wake, CBS paid him $4.5 million to make a thirteen-minute video for the title track of Michael Jackson's new album *Thriller*. Landis responded with a tribute to horror films, narrated by Vincent Price, that contributed substantially to the album's worldwide success. (The clip for Jackson's second hit, *Bad*, would be directed by Scorsese.)

Feeling himself on a roll, Landis was at pains to emphasise that he was his own man. Offered collaboration on *Twilight Zone*, he demanded total control of his own segments, which included the framing sequences linking each episode. Though technically working under executive producer Frank Marshall, he insisted on joint producer credit. His regular partner George Folsey Jr produced his contributions, which were shot by his preferred cameraman, Stevan Larner. Communications between the Landis and Spielberg offices were kept tenuous, a error that finally proved fatal.

Superficially, Joe Dante, whom Spielberg selected to make one of the episodes, was more tractable. The son of a New Jersey golf pro, he grew up in the same cultural isolation as Spielberg, losing himself in horror and science fiction films. In the seventies he and Allan Arkush had been the Corman studio's entire promotional department. Corman gave Dante and Arkush a chance to direct *Hollywood Boulevard* and, in 1978, backed Dante in *Piranha*. His 1980 *The Howling* established his reputation and made a fortune, but like many other young directors, Dante found himself, in the midst of critical acclaim, down to his last $100 and forced to borrow from friends. He was so depressed that when a package arrived in the mail from Spielberg, he was convinced it had come to the wrong address. It contained the script of *Gremlins*, which he directed a year later.

The third director came from Australia. Film-struck Melbourne doctor George Miller had worked weekends in an emergency medical service, with his producer Byron Kennedy driving the ambulance, to finance his 1980 *Mad Max*, a low-budget fantasy of an anarchic future Australia where the roads are ruled by biker gangs and the only law is cops like Max Rockansky, a calm avenger in black leather, played by the young Mel Gibson. Warners financed Miller's 1981 sequel *Mad Max II: The Road Warrior*, an even bigger hit.

Spielberg already admired the *Mad Max* films and, when he met Miller and Kennedy in 1981, liked their creators. Miller, bearded, soft-spoken and reclusive as George Lucas, left executive decisions to the brash, technocratic Kennedy, who had visited Hollywood in the seventies and returned a convert to the new American cinema, its mythomania and wealthy teenage audience. In particular Miller shared Lucas's fascination with anthropologist Joseph Campbell, author of the classic study of narrative, *The Hero with a Thousand Faces*. Both *Mad Max* films fed on Campbell's theory that all heroes had their roots in the tribal shaman. The idea to offer Miller an episode of *Twilight Zone* came on the spur of the moment – 'Hey, George Miller's in town. Let's get him to do one,' as one observer put it – but it was to generate the film's most effective segment.

Scripting *Twilight Zone* proved harder than directing it. Serling had written eighty-nine of the 150 TV shows. The rest were adapted from their own stories by writers like Charles Beaumont, Richard Matheson or George Clayton Johnson. Beaumont was dead, and as Johnson was a wild-eyed, white-haired, famous eccentric on the science fiction scene, Spielberg turned to Matheson to update three episodes, widening their scope and beefing up those horror elements which the teenage audience enjoyed best. As a sweetener, his old collaborator on *Duel* received a share of the profits.

Matheson's *Nightmare at 20,000 Feet* had been one of the series' best episodes. Few viewers forgot recovering mental patient William Shatner being driven comprehensively crazy by a maniacal gremlin eviscerating the engine of the plane in which he was flying home. Dante was given *It's a Good Life*, Jerome Bixby's much-anthologised story of a boy super-mind who kidnaps travellers to populate his infantile paradise. Any who try to escape or protest at the unrelieved diet of hamburgers and candy, or the endless cartoons on TV, are wished away to a worse hell, turned inside out, or forced to stare eternally at a raving TV set, robbed of a mouth with which to scream.

For his own contribution, Spielberg chose *The Monsters are Due on Maple Street*, a Serling original in which formerly good neighbours are turned against one another by a series of inexplicable power failures. Rumours, fanned by the local teenage sf fan, that aliens have landed, lead to riots and anarchy. At the end, two extra-terrestrials watching from a nearby hill congratulate one another on the ease with which humans can be manipulated, and summon an invasion force. Spielberg may have meant the troubled story as an attack on those adults in his adolescence who mocked his obsessions. If so, he was to be disappointed; *The Monsters are Due on Maple Street*, which was to have ended the film, would never be made.

Early in June 1982, Landis delivered the untitled script of his episode, which he had adapted from an old short film screenplay of his called 'Real Scary', to both Amblin and Warners. The following Saturday, 12 June, Terry Semel called a hurried meeting at his home. Spielberg wasn't available, *E.T.* having opened the day before, but both Semel and script supervisor Lucy Fisher articulated their strenuous objections. Landis, unsentimental at the best of times, had poured all his misanthropy into his story. His main character, Bill Connor, who loathes Jews, blacks and Asians, leaves a bar after a near-brawl with some blacks to find himself transported to Nazi Germany as a Jew, then to America's deep South as a victim of the Ku Klux Klan, and finally into a Vietnam firefight as an Asian. The script ended with Connor hauled away in a Nazi cattle-car to the gas chambers, his cries unheeded.

Landis insisted, rightly, that he'd respected Serling's format and style. Not only was the racial theme a Serling favourite: a number of episodes had shown villains given their comeuppance in alternative worlds. There were even parallels with an episode called A Quality of Mercy, in which an American soldier about to wipe out a Japanese platoon is forced to relent when he and its commander briefly swap personalities. Ironically, however, Landis's astringent contribution now contrasted starkly with the affectionate pastiche of the rest. Semel and the others persuaded him to give Connor some 'humanity' by adding a scene to the Vietnam sequence in which he rescues two children from a helicopter attack. In return, Landis was promised a budget large enough to let him blow up an entire Vietnamese village, the kind of violent set-piece he relished.

Throughout June, persistent rumours had again linked Spielberg with the ailing Disney studios. Its film revenues were plunging, from $34.6 million in 1981 to $19.6 million in 1982, and heading for a $33.3 million loss in 1983. The animation department had never recovered from Don Bluth's walkout with its best young artists in September 1979. Tron, Disney's computerised animation/live action sf story, had been so bad that, after a preview, Ted James, analyst for Montgomery Securities, urged his clients to sell their Disney stock immediately.

Initially the studio had been interested mainly in using Spielberg's and George Lucas's films as the basis for new Disneyland and Disney World rides. When both directors said they'd had better offers from Universal, Disney upped the ante. On 28 June, the New York Daily News announced that Spielberg had been offered the job of head of production, and that he was inclined to accept, claiming he was tired of Universal executives reminding him about *1941*. At Disney, said columnist Marilyn Beck, 'he would have almost complete autonomy and the run of the lot'.

Disney sang to Spielberg like a siren. *Pinocchio*, *Dumbo* and *Bambi* had formed his character. They were integral to his mental landscape. In business terms, the studio was just as seductive. Even in decline, the Disney name carried enormous prestige, and its market of middle-class sub-teens was exactly the same as his own. Disney also owned half a dozen projects that interested Spielberg, among them *Peter Pan*, and had picked up Kirk Douglas's project to film Ray Bradbury's *Something Wicked this Way Comes*.

The studio desperately needed someone like Spielberg. But both Card Walker, the president, and Ron Miller, the head of production, were leery of ceding Walt's Magic Kingdom to an outsider. Nor was Walker convinced that Spielberg had the 'Disney spirit'. He conceded the merit of *E.T.*, but cavilled that, had it been a Disney film, profanities like 'penis breath' would never have been permitted.

Even while he negotiated with Spielberg, Miller cast around for someone else. One of his first choices was Michael Eisner, the innovative head of Paramount who had been the only executive with vision enough to take on *Raiders*. Eisner was interested. He was close to the end of his effective life at Paramount. His subordinates, especially Jeffrey Katzenberg, his head of production, and Dawn Steel, were showing their teeth and demanding more power. Both were beginning to make their own alliances, in particular with record producer David Geffen, who was systematically building his Hollywood power-base before launching into movies. But Eisner had no intention to going to Disney with his hands tied. He asked Miller if he could run the theme parks too. Miller shook his head: divide and rule had been the foundation of Disney management for decades, and to try and change it would split the company. When Eisner temporised, Miller broke off negotiations and hired Dennis Stanfill, head of Fox when *Star Wars* was made. Confident that the dour Stanfill, who proudly rated himself a businessman, not an artist, would be ineffective, Eisner and Spielberg watched Disney's fortunes slide, and waited for their moment.

*   *   *

With directors in place for *Twilight Zone*, attention turned to the format. Most people found it hard to visualise the series without Serling's black-suited presence. The vaults contained some Serling introductions that had never been aired, and for a while Spielberg toyed with using special effects and overdubbing to have Serling introduce the movie, a device he would employ by proxy when Tom Hanks shook hands with John F. Kennedy in Robert Zemeckis's 1995 *Forrest Gump*. Burgess Meredith, a regular in the series, was finally hired to speak some Serling-like voice-overs. To jog the memories of those who didn't know the series, a Landis prologue was added, with Dan Aykroyd and Albert Brooks whiling away a night drive across the desert recalling old TV shows. The shock ending has Aykroyd transformed into a fright-wigged monster. Aykroyd also returns at the end of *Nightmare at 20,000 Feet*, where he's the ambulance driver taking a raving John Lithgow to hospital.

Sensing that his audience wouldn't be interested in the ironies and subtleties of the Serling versions, Spielberg wound up the pace and temperature of the film. Matheson inflated *It's a Good Life* to accommodate Dante's Expressionist interior for the supermind's house and some shrieking animated monsters that erupt from a TV set. He also wrote in roles for Kevin McCarthy, a regular in the series, and Billy Mumy, the boy in the original episode. Despite these gestures, Carol Serling didn't care for the treatment of her husband's work:

> Rod's stories were about people. They weren't about space-ships and green-eyed monsters . . . The movie, on the other hand, placed an emphasis on special effects. How could it be otherwise with Spielberg? That was antithetical to Rod's original intentions. Take the Joe Dante episode. [It] has these wonderful special effects. But I don't know that they improve the story.

At Indian Hills, outside LA, Landis and George Folsey built a Vietnamese village on an artificial lake. Peopling it proved more difficult. Vic Morrow, waning star of the successful World War II war-drama TV series *Combat*, was eager to play Connor, but the children posed a problem. Californian Labor Commission rules demanded a welfare officer on the set at all

times if children were used, and forbade working after 8 p.m. Even if
the Commission approved, the Screen Extras' Guild, through which all
non-speaking artists had to be hired, would never agree to placing children in a simulated firefight. Folsey and Landis decided to go illegal.
Six-year-old Renee Shinn Chen and seven-year-old Myca Dinh Le were
hired for $500 each, payable in cash, and the shooting scheduled for
late July.

Spielberg left day-to-day management of Twilight Zone to Frank Marshall. It was Marshall who signed the $2000 cheque for petty cash
presented to him on 20 July by George Folsey. Warners' production
manager for the project, James Henderling, referred it to Ed Morey, head
of production. Many suspected the money was to pay non-union child
actors, but Bonne Radford, then Amblin's accountant, later its head of
animation, insisted no children were to be used in the scene. In the face
of this denial, Henderling co-signed Marshall's cheque.

Spielberg always insisted he knew nothing of these arrangements, and
nobody could ever place him at Indian Hills on the night of 22/23 July
when Landis shot his firefight. The one witness who claimed to have
seen him there later agreed that he could have confused him with Marshall, who was present, along with Carol Serling, when the Bell UN-1B
helicopter, flown by Dorcey Wingo and with stunt men Gary McLarty
and Kenny Endoso firing machine guns from the open doors, descended
on the village.

As they flew over the huts, special-effects technician James Camomile
ran a nail along the line of electrical contacts that connected a 49.5 volt
battery to explosives all over the village. Half a dozen reasons were offered
to explain what followed. Some charges were accidentally triggered in
reverse order. It was suspected that the huts had been excessively spiked
with gasoline. Wingo's inexperience as a movie pilot was mentioned. He
lost control as he flew into a mushrooming ball of flame. As Vic Morrow
and the two children floundered into the shallow lake, the helicopter
crashed on top of them. One skid crushed Renee Chen to death, and as
the craft sagged, its rotor decapitated Morrow and Myca Le.

*   *   *

Old Hollywood had long experience of dealing with such disasters. Little had changed since 1935, when the Warners special-effects department built models of a stretch of the Pacific Coast Highway and a car wheel that helped lawyer Jerry Geisler persuade a jury that director Busby Berkeley hadn't been drunk when he crashed his car and killed three people, but was rather the victim of a rare technical fault – an argument eerily echoed at the Twilight Zone trial.

While George Folsey assembled a legal team in expectation of criminal charges, Frank Marshall and Kathleen Kennedy hurriedly left Los Angeles for their holiday home in rural Idaho. Marshall returned two weeks later, and even played a cameo in Nightmare, as the ground engineer who discovers the damage done by the gremlin. After that, he disappeared for Europe, allegedly to scout locations for Temple of Doom. He didn't return for months.

Before he left, he emphasised to Warners' publicity vice president Robert Friedman that, if only for the sake of the studio's investment in future productions, Spielberg's name must be kept free of scandal. This stance, tailored to Spielberg's preference for denial, became both Warner and Amblin policy. Phone queries were blocked. Magazines like Cinefantastique which published pictures of the fatal shoot were purged from Amblin's press list. If journalists raised the subject of the deaths in an interview, Spielberg refused to respond. Agitatedly waving his hands as if erasing them and their questions, he left the room. It was three years before he spoke about the case, and then it was to deflect the blame. 'No movie is worth dying for,' he told the Los Angeles Times in April 1983. 'I think people are standing up much more now than ever to producers and directors who ask too much. If something isn't safe, it's the right and responsibility of every actor and crew-member to yell, "Cut!"' The statement seemed to imply that the victims were somehow responsible for their own deaths.

Spielberg's first impulse had been to drop out of the film altogether, and he explored the possibility with Warners, but Semel insisted he abide by his contract. Without his name, the project was worthless. Though he remained, Spielberg took little active interest, except to scrap The Monsters are Due on Maple Street which, with its night-time violence, looked disagreeably like Landis's story. He replaced it with a soft-centred George Clayton Johnson episode, *Kick the Can*, set in a retirement home. One inmate, fearful of senility, proposes a midnight game of kick the can, bullying everyone but his oldest friend into playing the childhood game. When the friend returns with the home's supervisor, they find the whole group transformed into eight-year-olds. The friend begs to be included, but too late, as the new kids run off into the night.

Joe Dante had expected the entire film to be abandoned, and was surprised when Warners pushed him straight into *It's a Good Life*. Most people credit him with pulling *Twilight Zone* together. 'Without Joe, it would never have been finished,' Jerry Goldsmith says. The rewrites to his episode, dictated by its shifting position in the film, are a microcosm of the confusion that surrounded *The Twilight Zone*. Jerome Bixby ended his original story with the superbrat's tyranny continuing forever, but Matheson, having been told this episode would end the film, and wanting to offer some glimmer of a happy ending, closed his script on a slightly more optimistic note, with the house exploding and the boy's latest catch (Kathleen Quinlan) walking away – only to be offered a lift by the demonic Aykroyd in the ambulance. After the Indian Hills disaster, the ending became almost sunny, with Quinlan persuading the boy to accompany her on a voyage of discovery and education. As they drive away, the wasteland blossoms.

Shooting started on *Nightmare at 20,000 Feet* on 5 November. The same day, a Teamster named Carl Pittman told the Indian Hills inquiry that he'd seen Spielberg on the set on the night of the helicopter accident in July. Nobody ever corroborated the story, which Pittman later withdrew, but the police politely asked Spielberg if he had any comment. In a brief letter, he denied he had been anywhere near the location. Then, as later, however, neither he nor Terry Semel ever gave depositions to defence lawyers, nor offered corroborating witnesses; their legal staff insisted they were too important to be bothered. Forced to focus on the small fry, prosecutor Lea d'Agostino pressed charges against Landis, Folsey, and unit production manager Dan Allingham, all of whom, along with Warner Brothers, had already been fined $5000 for breaching child labour laws. Special-effects supervisor Paul Stewart and helicopter pilot

Dorcey Wingo were also indicted. The following year all were arraigned on charges of manslaughter. The politically ambitious d'Agostino told the press she wished it could have been murder.

George Miller finished his episode quickly and efficiently, but still Spielberg fidgeted. *E.T.* had been chosen for the Royal Command Performance and the whole team was going to London, an excursion that, in his present mood, appealed more than filming *Kick the Can*.

Hearing that Richard Matheson had been hired to adapt his story, a delighted George Clayton Johnson sent Kennedy and Marshall a new outline. Perhaps, he suggested, the children might not in fact run off, but opt to return to old age, though with new optimism and independence. He heard nothing more about it, but believes that, in the wake of the accident, Spielberg incorporated his ideas as a means of softening the film. Melissa Mathison, as 'Josh Rogan', rewrote Matheson's script to make the leader of the home's revolt a dapper Englishman named Agee with a Douglas Fairbanks complex. As Johnson suggested, the oldsters decide, after their midnight game, that they prefer decrepitude. Only Agee urges them to fly with him to a Never-Never Land of careless innocence and, when they refuse, goes alone.

Having seen veteran black performer Scatman Crothers in Kubrick's *The Shining* while he was shooting *Raiders* at Elstree, Spielberg inserted him into *Kick the Can* as a chuckling magician named Bloom who moves from one old folks' home to another, spreading the gospel of youth through play. The changes transformed a piece of Ray Bradbury-like whimsy into an evocation of another Spielberg preoccupation, Peter Pan. Despite this, Spielberg continued to take little interest in the film. He skipped pre-production meetings, delegating pre-production to Melissa Mathison and script supervisor Katherine Wooten. As the start date in late November approached, tension made him cantankerous. On the day after Thanksgiving, panic seized the office when it seemed he might be offered turkey for dinner two days running. A takeaway was demanded from his favourite Chinese restaurant, which, though it didn't make deliveries, was persuaded to do so in deference to their client. Even then, one dish wasn't to his liking, and the cry ran round the office, 'Steven must have snow peas!'

Shooting began the following Friday. The whole episode was filmed in only six days under Spielberg's perfunctory direction. More effort went into ensuring that the letter of the child labour laws was meticulously obeyed. Even the night scenes were shot 'day for night' on a sound stage to avoid keeping the children after 8 p.m. 'His heart just wasn't in it any more,' said first assistant Patrick Kehoe. Secretary Kathy Switzer agreed. 'He was just going through the motions.'

The result appalled everyone, especially Johnson. 'I was charmed in a couple of places . . .' he said, 'but the rest of it, making Scatman Crothers into the Tin Can Fairy or whatever . . . I called Richard Matheson and said, "What about all this? It's the damnedest script." He said, "Well, it's got nothing to do with what I wrote."' Celebrities like Clint Eastwood and Debra Winger crowded onto the set of Kick the Can on the last day in a show of solidarity engineered by Semel and Ross, but Spielberg thought only of putting the Atlantic between him and this nightmare.

In Paris, François Truffaut spent the day with him, taking him through the Cinémathèque Française's museum in the Palais de Chaillôt, like a dusty attic of film treasures. Nobody in Europe seemed very interested in the Twilight Zone disaster, but to keep himself at arm's length from the press, Spielberg moved to the St James's Club, a private hotel tucked away up a narrow cul-de-sac south of Piccadilly, with a side entrance inaccessible to paparazzi. It became his base for the five months during which he cast and prepared Indiana Jones and the Temple of Doom. The art deco penthouse suite, eventually renamed for him, became, in his own words, his 'home-from-home' for the next decade. He installed, at his own expense, a new stereo system and a large TV and video-game player in the guest bedroom. Later he would edit Temple of Doom in two other suites and audition for Empire of the Sun in another. The view over the roofs of the West End towards Big Ben also inspired early scenes in Hook.

The hotel staff soon learned of Spielberg's dislike of lifts and his inflexible rule never to accept packages, for fear of both bombs and unsolicited screenplays. They didn't reckon, however, on the persistence of screenwriters. A large aquarium was delivered to the club and, on the assumption that Spielberg had ordered it, installed in his suite. Only later was it discovered there was a script in a waterproof bag on its floor.

Once he returned to the US towards the end of 1983, Spielberg reluctantly picked up the reins again on *Twilight Zone*. A tenuous line of communication was re-established with Landis, through which he conveyed his feeling that the opening episode, even without the firefight, was too long. Landis trimmed a few seconds. Jerry Goldsmith's music did little to ameliorate the overall atmosphere of disillusion. Spielberg perfunctorily supervised the mix but, at the first screening, refused to watch Landis's episode, and loitered outside until it was over. The parents of both dead children named him in their lawsuits, as did the daughters of Vic Morrow, but Warners' lawyers effectively blocked the claims, and finally settled them out of court.

The Twilight Zone case damaged Spielberg's image in the film community, less because of the deaths, for which he could hardly be blamed, than for his weak, evasive, almost infantile response to the questions posed by the press and the law. Spielberg seemed to be playing at life, insulating himself from reality by means of a team of acolytes, from whom he demanded absolute obedience. 'Steven Spielberg,' writes Hollywood historian Paul Rosenfield, 'is shrouded by the most protective group of people in the club. He wants it both ways – he wants the creative stimulation of peers, yet he hires people who aren't his peers, and they become his armour.'

An unnamed ex-employee said of Spielberg at the time:

Steven has surrounded himself with people who tell him that he's God, and he believes he's God. You have to understand you're not dealing with adult, formed personalities. All these young directors are children, and they deal with problems like children. 'I'm not talking to him any more!' Steven's basic way of dealing with life is, if I don't like it, make it go away. And after making half a billion dollars, he can do that, in his own little world. After the *Twilight Zone* accident, John Landis happened to be one of the things he wanted to go away. It's as if he was saying, 'I don't want to hear about the case. I don't want to know about it. I don't care if he's guilty or not guilty. I'm playing in my back yard, and my back yard has *E.T.* in it. I don't want to hear about children being killed.'

The situation was not to improve. Even as Spielberg was poised to accept his first personal Oscar for *Schindler's List* in March 1994, another employee, forced to remain anonymous by the legal muzzle of the confidentiality agreement imposed on all Spielberg workers, described Amblin to the *Los Angeles Times* as 'a very dysfunctional place emotionally because Steven is perceived as a deity. He's not really the head of a company; he's sort of a god. He's protected at all turns from everything that will be unpleasant.'

13

Indiana Jones and the Temple of Doom

PRIME MINISTER: Doctor Jones, the eminent archaeologist?
WILLIE: Hard to believe, isn't it?

Dialogue from *Indiana Jones and the Temple of Doom*

INCREASINGLY DURING 1983 and 1984, Spielberg came under the influence of Steve Ross, 'a six foot three *E.T.*', in his words, who embodied his image of the ideal heroic father he'd fumblingly tried to create with the Identikit dad on which Puck was based. In response, Universal, realising they had to roll out their big guns if they were to hang onto him against Ross, proposed a lavish 'thank you' for *E.T.* Remembering Spielberg's pursuit of a bungalow, Wasserman and Sheinberg offered to build a headquarters for Amblin on the Universal lot at studio expense, and invited him to outline his requirements.

Until then, Spielberg had never shown more than a high-school student's interest in where he lived and worked, but, after seeing the private estates of old friends like Lucas and Coppola, as well as new ones like Michael Jackson and Steve Ross, he was changing his mind. The building he outlined to Universal, however, was, despite its 25,000 square feet of floor space, still more tree-house than corporate headquarters. Almost as important as its offices, conference rooms and private cinema were the kitchen with its own garden, and a crèche and playroom for kids of the staff. Amblin, Spielberg announced, would be 'like a Children's Crusade of film-makers. The only way you can get into this company is if you haven't made a movie before.' Unconvinced that New Age could be yoked to Old Hollywood, Paul Schrader noted dourly that the Movie Brats were turning into 'Movie Brats Inc.'

As Spielberg fiddled with the plans and Universal began bulldozing old bungalows to make room, Ross refused to surrender. Learning that Kathleen Carey had befriended a nine-year-old boy at the Holly Grove orphanage, he anonymously presented the home with VCRs, TV sets and other electronic gadgets at Christmas 1982.

Repeated visits to Ross's Long Island home had already persuaded Spielberg that he should have an East Coast residence as well as one in Los Angeles, and probably a New York apartment too. For men like Ross, and for the New York intellectuals who made it their summer hideaway, East Hampton, the leafy village on Long Island, was intimately associated with émigré painters like Francis Picabia and Fernand Léger, who discovered it in the forties, and those of the New York School, notably Jackson Pollock and Willem de Kooning, who'd followed them there. If its clapboard houses, groves of hardwoods and the tea-coloured expanse of Georgica Pond reminded Spielberg of any artist, however, it was Norman Rockwell, who set most of his paintings in such an archetypal semi-rural community.

Ross, hearing of a house coming on the market a few doors down from his own in East Hampton, purchased it through his company, confident Spielberg would take it off his hands. He did buy the 3.9-acre site from Ross in 1983, and started work with an architect on a design. New York writers and theatre people had regarded the Hamptons as their preserve for decades – Spielberg's new house had been the summer residence at various times of Neil Simon, Kurt Vonnegut and screenwriter Peter Stone – but during the late seventies film people had supplanted them. Spielberg's new neighbours were Alan Pakula, Michael Cimino and Sidney Lumet, and he had no compunction in levelling the old residence to build something more appropriate to his standing in this community. As a *pied-à-terre*, he also bought a double apartment in Donald Trump's glitzy new Trump Tower in Manhattan.

Through Ross, Spielberg had met Clint Eastwood, Barbra Streisand, record producer David Geffen and, initially most impressive, Quincy Jones. Christened Quincy Delight Jones Jr, the composer/arranger was almost fifteen years Spielberg's senior, and in every respect his antithesis. Black, Catholic, raised in Oregon as one of ten children, he was aggressively affectionate, hugging and embracing even relative strangers in extravagant expressions of affection. As a young man, he rocketed through two universities, supporting himself by playing jazz at night. While Spielberg was still howling in fright at *Bambi*, he was recording his first jazz album in Sweden. He wrote film scores, pursued his own racial agenda with works celebrating his African heritage, and worked with dozens of great artists, including Frank Sinatra, Ray Charles and Miles Davis. The pace caught up with him in 1974, when he had a massive stroke, but he bounced back, and by the early eighties was the close friend and adviser of Michael Jackson. Scarcely a night passed when Jackson didn't call Jones, just to talk things over.

Among the things Michael wanted to talk about was *E.T.* Jones had helped negotiate the deal through which Jackson assembled his *E.T. Storybook* album for MCA. When Jackson's regular recording company, CBS, sued MCA for $2 million over alleged loss of earnings for his new album, *Thriller*, as a result of the *Storybook*, Spielberg helped smooth the difficulty. By then he'd met Jackson, and been as awed as anyone by the charismatic young star. He visited his Encino estate, the grounds of which were furnished like a miniature Disneyland, and was startled by the lavishness of the singer's private world. 'If *E.T.* hadn't come to Elliott,' Spielberg said, 'he'd have come to Michael's house.' The singer gave him a signed copy of the issue of *Time* magazine which featured him on the cover. Spielberg framed it, and hung it in his office. Jackson also asked Spielberg to direct the 3-D quadraphonic 70mm short film *Captain Eo* he was preparing for Disneyland. Spielberg initially agreed but, finding the singer wanted little more than a giant rock video, passed the job to Coppola, who needed the work.

Jackson, who would later christen his private estate 'Neverland', shared Spielberg's enthusiasm for *Peter Pan*. Francis Coppola had planned a film about author J.M. Barrie's troubled relationship with the Llewelyn Davies family who inspired the play. When Zoetrope collapsed, he offered the project to Paramount, who asked Spielberg if he'd like to direct it. Spielberg refused. He visualised a live-action version of the original play, retaining the fantasy of Disney's cartoon but taking fewer liberties with Barrie's work. Paramount thought they could accommodate this, especially for Spielberg and Michael Jackson, but it proved easier to say than do, since a dozen producers were jostling for control of the story.

Barrie had presented the copyright in *Peter Pan*, and the books and stories which followed it, to Great Ormond Street Children's Hospital, which controlled them for fifty-two years. When this period expired in the late 1970s, Disney tried to arrogate the rights, only to be blocked by actor Mel Ferrer, who had his own remake plans. The Royal Shakespeare Company in London also mounted a revisionist stage production in 1982 which removed the whimsy accumulated over decades of pantomime versions and restored some of the original's darkness. Undeterred, Jackson, Jones and Spielberg began work on a musical, with songs by John Williams to a book by Leslie Bricusse.

Meanwhile, Jones interested Spielberg in another musical. Unlike 'Reel to Reel', this would be set in the streets of Manhattan or Detroit and made cheaply. 'We really want to do a no-holds-barred-dancing-in-the-streets-on-top-of-taxi-cabs motion picture,' Spielberg said. 'We're working on the story right now.' It never happened, though the project bears many resemblances to Alan Parker's 1980 *Fame*, which celebrated the youthful exuberance of young singers and dancers in much the way Spielberg envisaged, complete with dancers on top of taxi-cabs.

In the wake of *E.T.*, Old Hollywood struggled to make sense of Spielberg and to assess his importance in an industry that changed week by week. Studio bean-counters muttered about 'non-repeating phenomena'. Maybe Spielberg and his kind were a flash in the pan. After all, the percentage of cinema tickets bought by teenagers in the US had peaked at 47 per cent in the late seventies and begun to slide. (By 1995 it would hover around 20 per cent.) Memories of *1941*'s failure were still fresh, too. Old hands refused to accept that the interest and investment generated by film events like *E.T.* and *Star Wars* warped the traditional rule of thumb that out of any ten movies, one made money, two broke even, and the rest flopped. Wiser heads pointed out that Spielberg defied the rules. Only one of his films, *Sugarland Express*, had failed outright – *1941* would inch into the black with foreign and video sales – and the rest were the most successful in history. Exhibitors at least had no doubts. Teenagers might be staying away from other movies, but those of Spielberg and Lucas remained must-sees. When *Indiana Jones and the Temple of Doom* was announced early in 1984, the cinemas pledged a record $40 million in non-refundable guarantees, putting the film into profit before it was made, let alone released.

As he became aware of his new power, Spielberg initially hesitated to exercise it fully. Like Indy, he wavered between the roles of grave-robber and conservator, between fortune and glory, public adulation and private satisfaction. Nobody doubted after *Jaws* that he could be another engineer of mass-market hits like Victor Fleming, but the mantle of Kubrick and Lean seemed beyond his grasp. *E.T.*, however, had whispered to him that he might achieve the greatness of *all* the film-makers he admired, not simply the more facile of them. At first he hadn't been sure. The ease with which he pulled off his effects made him share the doubts of his critics about their validity. He believed *E.T.* to be a profound statement, but perhaps it was simply so skilful it fooled even him. Great communicator or consummate manipulator? In the twilight zone of Hollywood, not even he could tell. Gradually, however, Spielberg began seeking projects appropriate to the serious director he now felt he could become.

By example and precept, Steve Ross was teaching him the corporate game, confident that within a few years his protégé would be a major player. Before *E.T.*, Spielberg shared Lucas's dislike for boardroom manoeuvres, but Ross redefined his image of big business. 'I had typecast what a CEO was,' Spielberg said. 'I'd never met one before, and I wasn't far off, because I've met them since – and in my mind they looked like [they bought their clothes at the cheap chain store] J.C. Penney. And suddenly here was this older movie star.'

That he was beginning to enjoy his new authority became evident early in 1983. Just before leaving for Sri Lanka to shoot *Temple of Doom*, he and Harrison Ford, who would marry Melissa Mathison on 14 March, were flown to Las Vegas for the annual ShoWest exhibitors' convention, during which studios traditionally unveiled their films to the all-important cinema owners. With them was Paramount's top management and a contingent of creative people, including Jack Nicholson, Debra Winger and Martin Scorsese.

Michael Eisner's subordinate at Paramount, Dawn Steel, whose first production success, Adrian Lyne's frenetic dance movie *Flashdance*, hadn't then opened, was seething. Not deemed sufficiently important to rate an all-important seat on the dais at the inaugural dinner, she'd been relegated to the floor with other lesser players. At the preliminary cocktail party Frank Marshall introduced Scorsese to Steel, almost an adoptive member of the Amblin group because her paternal grandfather had been a Spielberg.

As they chatted, the banquet manager called for everyone to follow him to the dais. When Steel lagged behind, Spielberg turned and asked, loudly enough to embarrass the Paramount management, 'Dawn, aren't you sitting with us on the dais?' The gesture didn't get Steel her coveted spot in the limelight, but she won a useful consolation prize. After ten minutes, Scorsese left the dignitaries to join her. A few weeks later, they were living together.

In this rich medium, alliances grew like crystals, transcending race, education, fortune. The seeds of Spielberg's 1994 alliance with David Geffen and Jeffrey Katzenberg as 'DreamWorks SKG' were planted in these often casual encounters. Geffen, who was close to Sandy Gallin, personal manager of Michael Jackson and Neil Diamond, both of whom had dipped their beaks into the profits from *E.T.*, was also one of Steel's closest allies in the film business. 'Not only did David befriend me [in the early eighties],' Steel says, 'but he also befriended Jeffrey Katzenberg.'

The three made improbable confederates. Steel had launched her business career in 1975 with a mail-order company, Entrepreneuse Enterprises, to sell phallic Amarylis flowers with the rubric, 'The Penis Plant!', and toilet paper decorated with the ochre-and-green colours and 'GG' emblem of Gucci. Katzenberg, the personification of Budd Schulberg's hustling producer Sammy Glick from the 1941 novel *What Makes Sammy Run?*, was the son of a privileged Manhattan family. He'd dropped out of New York University to gamble in the Bahamas, from where he'd been ejected for trying to shade the odds at blackjack by counting cards. He gravitated to movies as assistant to Barry Diller, the

ABC executive who commissioned *Duel*, from whom Eisner hired him away.

Steel's lawyer Sid Davidoff described Katzenberg as 'four feet ten inches, ninety pounds soaking wet, a pit bull, tenacious as hell'. The height and weight were slightly off, but the rest was accurate. A mountain-climber and white-water rafter, his energy was legendary. The first time she met him, says Steel, 'I saw him run up the stairs, run into [studio head Frank] Yablans' office and then run out of Yablans' office down the stairs. I thought, This guy's like the Roadrunner. Beep. Beep.'

Geffen, Katzenberg and Spielberg, Steel, Michael Jackson and Quincy Jones, wove in and out of one another's orbits like captive moons, dominated always, however, by the gravitational pull of Steve Ross. Geffen and Katzenberg in particular became intimates. 'These two are probably inseparable today,' said Steel in 1994, 'and they have a relationship as peers, but Jeffrey was not David's peer when their relationship started.' Geffen, like Steel, came from the same East Coast background as Katzenberg (and Spielberg), and had also, like them, dropped out of college, but there the resemblance ended. The archetypal New Yorker, untidy but always in style, and effortlessly rich from pop music, Geffen floated above the daily grit of the film business – literally so on occasion, in his private jet. The 1981 drama about lesbianism in big-time athletics, *Personal Best*, was his first outing as a film producer, and the last for five years, though after that he would emerge as a studio owner and major Hollywood player.

Changes were taking place in Spielberg's private life too. The relationship with Kathleen Carey had cooled as she became more involved in her job, and early in 1983 she decided to leave him. Spielberg confessed:

> I cried for the first time in ages. The human being in me was pouring the tears out. But the doggone film-maker in me ran to the other room, grabbed my Instamatic, and took a picture of myself in the mirror. I had to have it on record.

He didn't cry for long. During the run-up to starting *Indiana Jones and the Temple of Doom* in Sri Lanka on 8 April 1983, he had a brief relationship with Barbra Streisand, an almost mythical alliance of titans more credible in a Jackie Collins novel than in real life. The affair may have had a more quotidian basis, since some people credited Spielberg with helping Streisand with her long-time project to direct and star in Isaac Bashevis Singer's *Yentl*. From Streisand, he took up with Kate Capshaw, who had played in *Best Defense*, the film Huyck and Katz wrote, and Huyck directed, before *Temple of Doom*, and who was being considered to play the lead in the new film. Born Kathy Sue Nail, the green-eyed blonde Texan had graduated from the University of Missouri with a master's degree in learning disabilities, and taught school for a while before, following the birth of her daughter Jessica, deciding on a career in showbusiness. Starting as a model for the Ford agency in New York, she broke into TV commercials, then graduated to soap operas like *Edge of Night*, and in 1982 launched a feature film career in Hollywood with *A Little Sex*, playing the aggrieved wife of philanderer Tim Mathison.

Capshaw was aggressive, giggly and, to some of Spielberg's friends, wearingly hectic, but he liked her *shiksa* vivacity, and she was soon his companion as well as a front-runner for the role of Willie, the nightclub singer in *Temple of Doom*. Capshaw, for her part, had decided that he was her man. Like a dog that recognises her own puppy by its smell, she knew, she said, simply from sniffing Spielberg, that they were destined to be together.

Shooting on *Temple of Doom* was delayed until after the Oscars on 11 April 1983. For once, the nominations made it hard to imagine Spielberg would fail to win handsomely. *E.T.* was in for Best Picture, Best Director, Best Screenplay, Best Cinematography, Best Sound, Best Score (for which Goldsmith's *Poltergeist* music was also nominated), Best Editing, Best Visual Effects and Best Sound Editing. The competition included Sydney Pollack's comedy *Tootsie* and Constantin Costa-Gavras's political thriller *Missing*, about an American father searching in Chile for his political activist son, apparently the victim of a death squad.

Missing was thought too weighty and controversial for Academy voters. Richard Attenborough's *Gandhi* likewise seemed a long shot after the success of the British *Chariots of Fire* the year before. But in the most studied insult imaginable, *E.T.*, the most successful and best-loved film in Hollywood history, was fobbed off with the Music, Special Effects and Sound Editing Oscars alone. Almost everything else went to *Gandhi*, even, to general astonishment, the Best Costume award. ('For what?' demanded columnist Rex Reed. 'Wrinkled sheets, burlap sacks and loincloths?') Attenborough was honest enough to be embarrassed by the obvious snub to Spielberg. As he went up to accept his Oscar, he paused to give him a consoling hug.

In public, Spielberg shrugged off the rejection. 'Look, we tried our best,' he joked. 'We stuffed the ballot boxes. We just didn't stuff them enough.' In the *Los Angeles Times*, he surmised that people felt the film had already won so many awards it didn't deserve more. Privately, however, he was deeply hurt, a fact he hid from his closest colleagues. It was a different matter with relative strangers. Jerry Goldsmith, who hadn't seen him since *Twilight Zone* and assumed that, like others connected with that debacle, he had 'ceased to exist' for the director, was astonished to get a call on the night following the awards ceremony.

'Can I come around?' Spielberg asked.

He arrived a few minutes later with his current cocker spaniel, Chauncey, and poured out his sense of hurt to a sympathetic but disconcerted Goldsmith. 'My wife came home and found us sitting there alone,' recalled the composer. 'It gave her quite a shock.'

Goldsmith's child took a fancy to Chauncey, so Spielberg later sent around a cocker puppy, a typically thoughtful gesture.

Why this sudden urge for rapport with someone he barely knew? Not so difficult a question to answer, perhaps. Spielberg would have deliberated, even if only in his subconscious, on the eagerness with which Hollywood scrutinised the acts of the powerful, and the advantage a friend might later take of any intimacy. The composer was older, and himself a loser in the same awards – though ironically to *E.T.* If Spielberg had spent weeks winnowing his acquaintances for someone, neither equal nor competitor, subordinate nor intimate, in whom to confide, he could hardly have chosen better than Goldsmith.

On 18 April 1983 Spielberg began shooting *Temple of Doom* in Sri Lanka while the second unit did the early car-chase through the streets of Macau. The two units would join up at Elstree. Aside from Capshaw and Ke Huy Kuan, an Angeleno new to movies who played ten-year-old Short Round, most of the casting had been done in England. Veteran Indian actor Roshan Seth played the oily prime minister of the evil palace, and David Yip, whose TV series *The Chinese Detective* had made him one of the few Asian actors to win fame in Britain, was Wu Shan, Indy's confederate in the opening nightclub scene who's shot before he really gets going.

Temple of Doom was even more extensively storyboarded than usual, and Spielberg arrived in Sri Lanka with albums containing four thousand images drawn up by Ed Verraux, Joe Johnson and production designer Elliot Scott. Reviving an idea he'd used on *Sugarland Express* and *Raiders*, he'd also had Scott model the Maharajah's mine, its rollercoaster-like railway line and the ore crusher where the villains meet their doom. He used these seventeen-inch maquettes and half-inch figures to plot out a sequence that duplicated all the vertiginous effects of a carnival ride.

The script had the usual in-jokes. Paramount's logo is moulded in grey metal on a giant gong, another homage to *Gunga Din*, which opens with a similar image. Dan Aykroyd, forgiven for his lapse at the Oscars, has a cameo as Weber, the officious dispatcher at Shanghai airport who puts Jones and his party onto a plane loaded with live chickens, and piloted by two henchmen of the villain. Spielberg also reprised the scene from *Jaws* where Brody's son imitates his father; here it's Short Round taking on Jones's worried gestures, underlining the degree to which Indy, Willie and Short Round, whose parents, in a foreshadowing of *Empire of the Sun*, were killed in the Japanese invasion of Shanghai, constitute a family.

After three weeks in Sri Lanka, where Elliot Scott built the village of lost children and the rope bridge on which Indy has one of his most taxing battles, the crew moved to India, and a fateful meeting for Spielberg. Amy Irving was playing an Indian princess in Peter Duffell's TV mini-series based on M.M. Kaye's romantic best-seller *The Far Pavilions*. Spielberg, ostensibly scouting locations, arrived in a light plane on their set. The years of separation from Spielberg had not been kind to Amy. Her career hadn't ignited as she'd hoped, either on Broadway or in Hollywood. *The Far Pavilions*, a British production with a cast of minor stars, was a substantial comedown even from her Hollywood films, none of which had been a hit. Nor had any white knight appeared to sweep her onto his charger and present her with the child she'd tearfully confessed to Emily Richard, backstage at *Amadeus*, she so desired. Her thirtieth birthday was approaching and, with it, some important decisions, both biological and professional. In their light, Spielberg looked much more attractive than he had a few years before.

'We saw each other across the runway,' Amy said later, 'and by the time we came together, I *knew*.'

She and Spielberg celebrated her birthday with a candlelit dinner *à deux*. Almost immediately, their relationship revived, to the chagrin of Kate Capshaw, who was dumped unceremoniously but forced to swallow her anger and keep working for her ex-lover. By June 1985, Amy would have a child. Kate, however, was not to be so easily ejected from Spielberg's life.

Doom's line producer Robert Watts had hoped to film many scenes in the Rose Palace of Jaipur in the Indian state of Rajasthan, but the local government, scandalised by the script's horror-comic character, demanded so many changes that he and Lucas decided suburban London would be safer. The Pankot Palace was built on the backlot at Elstree, and elephants hired from European circuses.

By the time Harrison Ford arrived in London, the mileage on his clock was beginning to register in his performance. Riding elephants in Sri Lanka had already strained his back and, as he began his stunts, a painful and deteriorating spinal condition manifested itself. British doctors diagnosed a ruptured disc. Ford flew back to California for treatment while

Spielberg shot around him. Rather than risk surgery, surgeons injected Ford's spine with a solution derived from green papaya, a well-known meat tenderiser. Used in concentrated form, it dissolved the herniated cartilege, and Ford was back to work within six weeks.

One result of the delay was that a large gathering in a hall in the north London suburb of Camden, arranged and announced some weeks before as an end-of-shoot 'wrap' party, became a 'getting-to-know-you' mixer for the actors and crew who would continue to work on the film for weeks. Spielberg arrived with Amy on his arm, the first intimation to many that she had returned to his life. Clearly in high spirits, he won everyone over with his charm.

He startled David Yip, who had never met him, by coming over to the actor almost immediately and saying, 'David, you must be wondering what's going on.'

'And for ten minutes,' says Yip, 'he talked to me about the film and what he was going to do. It was amazing. He either has an extraordinary memory or he's incredibly well-briefed.'

The following week, Yip started work in the Club Obi Wan sequence, an unrepentant repeat of the dance-cum-brawl in 1941. Indy is trading a giant diamond for an urn containing the ashes of a Chinese emperor, but an extra object is introduced when the three gangsters with whom he's dealing poison his champagne, and demand both the jewel and the ashes in return for a vial of antidote. In the resulting shoot-out, Yip is killed and the jewel and antidote fly across the floor, to be lost in a welter of balloons, dancing feet and spilled ice-cubes.

Spielberg shot the sequence for three days, assembling the action, as usual, to a mental plan. By this time, the script was beginning to crumble from repeated changes, many of them dictated by Ford's back. Spielberg stopped shooting a number of times, called for a typewriter and wrote new lines on the spot. At night he was on the phone to John Milius, who dictated dialogue from Los Angeles.

On the third day, with the club half-demolished, Spielberg arrived on the set and announced, 'Let's go back to the scene at the table. I know how to do it now.' When the assistant director pointed out that the table with its revolving 'Lazy Susan' centrepiece had been irretrievably smashed, Spielberg calmly told him to find another one, and for half a day reshot the by-play with jewel, urn and vial until even the dumbest teenager in Oatmeal, Nebraska could grasp it.

It was hard for Spielberg to keep his mind on the film. In June, *Twilight Zone: The Movie* opened across North America to hostile reviews. At the same time, John Landis and four others were indicted on charges of manslaughter. Two days later, a woman from the US Embassy arrived at the St James's Club where Frank Marshall and Kathleen Kennedy were staying, and where two suites had been turned into cutting rooms for *Temple of Doom*. She tried to serve Marshall with a subpoena to appear at the trial, but was told he would be busy all that day. In fact a Mercedes limo was even then speeding him to Gatwick airport, from where Amblin's private jet flew him to Paris. He never did testify in the case.

Back in Hollywood, Joe Dante was also shooting *Gremlins*, which Spielberg, technically at least, was producing, though, after the problems of *Poltergeist*, he remained at arm's length from the film. There had been wrangles enough during pre-production. First-time scenarist Chris Columbus's comedy about malevolent entities that take over the small town of Kingston Falls one Christmas was inspired by the years he'd spent living in a decrepit New York loft while attending film school. He had nightmares of mice nibbling his fingers as they dangled over the edge of the bed, and channelled his distaste into the film's villains – cuddly big-eyed creatures that metamorphose into monsters when exposed to water or fed after midnight. Even Dante was alarmed by the violence of Columbus's original script, in which, among other things, the gremlins decapitated the hero's mother, sending her head rolling downstairs.

Columbus equated the gremlins with man's misuse of technology. They're inadvertently unleashed by well-meaning inventor Hoyt Axton, whose gadgets always malfunction disastrously. When an ancient Chinaman arrives at the end of the film to remove the last gremlin from the ruins, he chides Axton, 'You do with this what you have done with all Nature's gifts. You are not ready.'

Spielberg, increasingly in thrall to technology, had no wish to produce a tract against it, nor against suburban values. From the outset, he told Dante and Columbus that he visualised *Gremlins* as something less like a satire and more an apocalyptic fable in the school of Hitchcock's *The Birds*, low-budget but realistic, shot in Utah or Oregon under authentic snow. Dante argued that real locations would render the puppet gremlins ridiculous. The story demanded stylisation. He saw it as a subversive *It's a Wonderful Life*, and persuaded Spielberg to let him shoot it on the Warners lot, in a Kingston Falls not too far from Capra's Bedford Falls, recreated in the image of Norman Rockwell – and Spielberg: its one cinema is even offering a double bill of *Watch the Skies* and *A Boy's Life*. He also had the star gremlin designed in the warm browns of Chauncey the spaniel. 'I know which side my bread's buttered on,' he joked sardonically. Dante's delight in misrule was never more effectively on show, but Spielberg remained nervous about the film, and unconvinced of its prospects for success.

The multitude of problems that faced Spielberg when he returned to Hollywood later in 1983 would have relegated lesser men to a rest home. Most visible was his revived relationship with Amy, which startled his friends. For once, news hadn't travelled fast, and the first many of them knew of her return was when Spielberg brought her to music-recording sessions for *Gremlins*. Those who'd regarded Kathleen Carey as a more desirable partner looked on Amy without warmth.

Amy was appearing in Shaw's *Heartbreak House* on Broadway, and Spielberg flew to New York every weekend to be with her. 'He watches me on stage,' she said, 'and I feel this energy of support come out of the audience. He's a sucker for me.' Anxious to appear a changed man, Spielberg began to take an interest in theatre, independently booking them seats for four shows in a row. 'Wow, did you do all this on our own?' Amy asked disbelievingly, which cannot have done much to bolster his confidence.

Builders had already sunk foundations for the East Hampton house, but after the break-up with Kathleen, Spielberg halted construction.

The house, he decided, risked becoming too much like a Beverly Hills mansion, and inconsistent with the Hamptons' history. When work recommenced, it was under Amy's influence. Steve Ross, quickly recognising a kindred spirit in her, and a route to Spielberg, introduced them to Charles Gwathmey of Gwathmey Siegel and Associates, among the country's most fashionable architects. Within a year, Gwathmey had hauled a late–eighteenth-century barn from New Jersey and reassembled it on Spielberg's site. With this foundation – an architectural 'quote', said Gwathmey glibly, as Spielberg's films were filled with quotes – he began the new house.

At the same time, Amblin Entertainment became a fully functioning private corporation, exclusively controlled by Spielberg and his subordinates, and he moved into the new headquarters Universal had built for him, with office space for thirty people. Amy's influence on the design was profound. The couple had toured her beloved New Mexico, taking more than five hundred Polaroids. These inspired a two-storey building in south-western style, slightly tapered, with burnt-pink adobe-look walls, built around a central courtyard with fountains. MGM producer Peter Bart spoke for many when he called it 'a Santa Fe modern palazzo'. Another visitor thought it 'an architectural fantasy [which] bears little relationship to the buildings nearby: industrial boxes housing sound stages and production offices'. John Milius tagged it 'the biggest Taco Bell in the world', then, lapsing into a parody of the portentous commentary to the *News on the March* report on Kane's mansion Xanadu in *Citizen Kane*, 'Its cost? No man can say.' Sid Sheinberg could. Universal put a book value on the building of $3.1 million, though later estimates, taking the cost of real estate into account, plus the continuing expenses of upkeep, which it also bore, were closer to $6 million.

A low adobe wall divided the building from the rest of the studio. Pressed into the clay was the silhouette of Elliott on his bike flying across the face of the full moon with Puck in a milk-crate on the handlebars. The image had become so famous that Spielberg adopted it as Amblin's trademark. The grounds were landscaped with fruit, olive and palm trees, and with beds of yellow daisies, lawns and ponds filled with multi-coloured Japanese *koi*, soon to become a Hollywood enthusiasm.

(Amused by their rhythmic mouth movements, Spielberg recorded the fish on video and matched the tape to excerpts from *Madama Butterfly*.) A kitchen that doubled as communal dining room served organic meals to the staff and their children, while the less health-conscious could snack on Oreo cookies, M&Ms and other candy, all free. There was a carpeted dog run, a basketball practice court, a barbecue pit, a tanning area.

Inside, there were no straight lines, no sharp corners. Even the beams were slightly rounded. The decoration favoured Navajo rugs, pre-Columbian pots and quarry tiles. Ceremonial Indian garments were framed in the entrance hall, next to movie posters. An open fire burned in Spielberg's first-floor office, which had two walls of windows looking down on the courtyard, and a tree-house ceiling of intertwined deep red salt-cedar branches from Santa Fe. His *Citizen Kane* sled was on display there, along with a call-sheet and a storyboard from Welles's film, and the original of Norman Rockwell's painting *The Connoisseur*. Opposite his desk, set into a wall next to alcoves for more rare Indian pots, was a portrait of Amy. And in case anyone forgot the source of these riches, framed cartoons about *E.T.* decorated one wall of the waiting area, and in the garden a willow shaded a wishing well from which jutted the gaping head of Bruce the Great White Shark.

Before the building went up, Spielberg had been expansive about his plans for fifteen to twenty Amblin productions, each funded at $15–$20 million. Once installed, however, he became more cagey. He said contentedly:

> Amblin insulates me from Hollywood, and that's why I love it. I don't have to play the musical studios game. I don't have to go to people. They come to me. What makes me a good businessman is that I always make other people pay for my movies. I never spend my own money.

His attitude to Universal became increasingly offhand as he learned to play it off against other companies eager to woo him. Asked in 1993 what Universal expected from Amblin, he said, 'Everything! They expect to get everything first, but, of course, they don't . . . I have no obligation to Universal, really, unless you want to look at this wonderful building and apply the word "guilt".'

Some in Hollywood, like David Brown, sneered at the new tycoon's unwillingness to spend a cent on the promised new productions. 'He works like *he*'s paying the rent,' said Brown, who persisted in doubting his old protégé's omniscience. For almost everyone else, however, Spielberg had become a sort of guru, regarded with a near-holy awe. Not for nothing was the Amblin building known in some quarters as 'The Vatican'. In 1983, John Landis inserted a scene in *Trading Places* where commodity trader Eddie Murphy is asked in a crowded restaurant about his opinion on the market in winter wheat. Instantly every table falls silent and the diners crane towards him, ears flapping. Spielberg's position was not dissimilar. 'When Steven Spielberg hires you,' says Mick Garris, one of his team on the TV series *Amazing Stories*, 'all the people who wouldn't even read your scripts find them brilliant.' Another director recalls, 'I've been to screenings where all the studio executives are sitting in the front, and Spielberg's alone at the back. And when the film ends, they turn around to look at him and see what they should think about it.' A story circulated around Hollywood of an unsuccessful producer who noticed Spielberg sitting alone on the beach at Malibu, contemplating the sunset. When he got up and left, the other slid into the hollow he'd vacated.

Spielberg's endorsement of a project was the next best thing to a guarantee of profit, and studios competed for it furiously. Cultivated by Terry Semel and Steve Ross, his near-symbiotic relationship with Warners continued and prospered, until he was referred to as 'our brother' in the studio's inner circles.

Joe Dante, having become friendly with producer Peter Guber during *Gremlins*, was offered Jeffrey Boam's script for *Innerspace*, in which a tearaway ex-astronaut is miniaturised and injected into the body of a feckless supermarket clerk: Dean Martin in the body of Jerry Lewis. Guber took the package to Warners, but had heard nothing until Spielberg casually told Dante that he was about to produce the script, with Robert Zemeckis directing. Dante protested to Warners.

'What can we do?' an executive responded. 'If Spielberg wants to take it to Zemeckis . . .'

'But you offered it to *me*!'

'Well, yeah,' shrugged the executive, 'but now that Steven's got it . . .'

The message was obvious. Spielberg finally let Dante direct *Innerspace* for Amblin, but the unpleasant taste remained.

Michael Crichton had a similar experience. After Spielberg's failure to float *Congo* with De Palma, the writer suggested it as an Indiana Jones episode. He pointed out that one of the book's most original inventions, a baby gorilla given the power of speech through a computer strapped to its back, was a perfect foil and sidekick for Indy.

'Steven . . . thought [the talking gorilla] could be done with a mechanical ape,' Crichton recalls. 'But I said that you can do that with *E.T.* because we've never seen anything like him, but everyone knows what a gorilla looks like – and if it looks fake, you're dead. It's in every scene.

'He said, "Well, I've had a lot of success with mechanical animals." I replied, "You sure have! I'm not going to argue with you, Steven, but I think you have to look carefully." And the next thing I knew, he wasn't doing the picture. So that presented a tremendous problem back in those days.'

In fact, the project was discussed at Lucasfilm, but Lucas preferred all Indy's adventures to be based on new stories. *Congo* would finally be made in 1994 for Paramount by Frank Marshall and Kathleen Kennedy, by then an independent producer/director.

Since the joint release of *E.T.* and *Poltergeist* had done nothing to injure either film, Spielberg and Lucas decided to issue both *Temple of Doom* and *Gremlins* in May 1984. Spielberg demanded absolute authenticity for all foreign versions. French, Italian and Spanish slang was used in the backchat between the gremlins. In the German version, they even sang authentic German beer-drinking songs in the bar.

The first cut of *Temple of Doom* was predictably violent, with a booby-trapped underground chamber with a descending spiked ceiling, human sacrifice, during which hearts are pulled out of living chests, and a palace banquet where guests gorge on bugs and monkey brains, but Lucas felt it still needed additional horrors. More violence was added, and the banquet scene augmented with some even more loathsome dishes: giant bugs filled with grey slime, milky soup swimming with bloody eyeballs, and 'Snake Surprise', a python stuffed with wriggling baby eels. (The added scenes are easily identified, since Ford doesn't appear in any of them.)

After the retakes, Spielberg and Michael Kahn fined down the film to 118 minutes, every one of which moved with the speed of the final rollercoaster ride through the Maharajah's mine. It was easier to understand than *Raiders*, but, perversely, this imposed a yammering energy that left audiences exhausted. By building *Raiders* in brief episodes, each with its climax and a respite before the tension built again, Kasdan had paced that film, but Huyck and Katz worked to a different and more agitated drummer. Where *1941* had been too loud, *Temple of Doom*'s machine-gun incident was too fast. Spielberg inserted pauses for laughs and toned down some effects, but the film would always give the impression of febrile motion.

Dante showed his finished version of *Gremlins* to Spielberg, who still disliked the film's misanthropy. Warners shared his doubts. In particular, they hated Phoebe Cates's revelation, typical of the film's abrasive vision of small-town American life, that she's hated Christmas ever since, as a child, she and her mother discovered her father's corpse, dressed as Santa Claus, in their chimney, where he'd died of a heart attack while trying to deliver gifts. Dante recalls:

That scene about daddy in the chimney was real controversial. It had been given to another character who was cut out, but I wanted it left in, so I gave it to Phoebe. But the studio, which hated the movie, said, 'Of course that scene has to go,' and I said, 'I don't think so. To me, this scene is the movie. The tone of this scene is the movie I wanted to make.' They made a big stink about it, so I had to go to

Steven. He had final cut. And he backed me up. But there was a lot of fallout from that scene.

The censorship board would have been happy to cut this and other sequences from *Gremlins* and *Indiana Jones and the Temple of Doom*. Lucas and Spielberg, however, backed by Warners and Paramount, who would see their profits slashed if the board imposed an adults-only certificate, badgered its members until they allocated a 'PG' rating. (Less lenient British censors made twenty-five cuts to *Temple of Doom* alone.) The films' violence did nothing to harm them at the box office. By 1989, *Gremlins* had made a profit of $80 million in US domestic cinemas alone. *Temple of Doom* grossed $180 million in the same market. In the wake of the films, however, a new certificate was established, Parental Guidance – 13.

On 9 April, Spielberg accompanied Amy to the Oscars. For once, he had nothing in competition. Amy, however, was up for Best Supporting Actress for her role in *Yentl*, one of the few nominations the film earned. (Feminists picketed the ceremony, pointing out that 273 men had been nominated for best director since 1927 and only one woman.) Amy's black velvet skirt from Ralph Lauren and antique black lace blouse were appropriately sombre, since she lost to Linda Hunt for her prodigious feat of playing a Chinese man in Peter Weir's *The Year of Living Dangerously*.

Once again, Spielberg was under pressure from Amy to marry her, and once again, he was resisting. Some of the tension surfaced in the press. On 8 November a columnist had noted, 'Amy Irving wishes Steven Spielberg would pop the question. So what did Amy get from the film-maker for her birthday? A diamond necklace and diamond earrings. Try a ring next time, Steve.'

A month after the Oscars, *Temple of Doom* and *Gremlins* opened to the predictable furore. Gary Franklin, reviewer for LA's KCBS-TV, claimed to be so sickened by *Doom* he couldn't attend Paramount's lavish lunch after the preview. In general, however, the film was greeted as a belated acknowledgement that teenage taste had changed, even if adults didn't entirely realise it.

Writing in *Vanity Fair* about the importance of *Temple of Doom* and *Gremlins* in the changing social attitude to screen violence, Steven Schiff quoted from *The Uses of Enchantment* by the since-discredited guru of child psychology, Bruno Bettelheim: 'Those who outlawed traditional folk fairy tales decided that if there were monsters in a story told to children, these must all be friendly – but they missed the monster a child knows best . . .: the monster he feels or fears himself to be.' Children were more ready to accept violence on screen than were adults, Schiff contended. 'It's useless to pretend . . . that *Indiana Jones and the Temple of Doom* isn't upsetting. And it's useless to pretend . . . that the people it upsets the most are children.' Joe Dante found the same to be true of *Gremlins*. 'I never saw a child upset by the movie. I remember a screening at Warner Brothers when a woman got up and started dragging a scream-ing child out of the movie. I remember thinking, "Shit, this kid is really scared." In fact the mother wanted to leave and the kid wanted to stay!'

To promote *Doom*, Lucas and Spielberg agreed to have their hand and footprints eternalised in cement in front of Mann's – formerly Grauman's – Chinese Theater on Hollywood Boulevard. Neither relished the event. When they stepped out of their burgundy limo in jeans, trainers and sports shirts, they were ninety minutes late and the quick-drying cement had begun to harden.

'This is the greatest honour I've ever been exposed to,' Spielberg said, ill at ease. Nudged by proprietor Ted Mann into saying something to 'sell some tickets', he went on awkwardly, 'We had snakes in the last picture and bugs in this picture. But supposedly man's greatest fear is public speaking, and that will be our next picture.'

At this point, Gary Franklin and his crew pushed to the front of the crowd and asked if *Temple of Doom* wasn't too frightening for its audience.

'Who do you think shouldn't see this film?' shouted the journalist.

'I think everybody can see this film except Gary Franklin,' Spielberg said shortly.

He and Lucas knelt down, pressed hands and feet into the cement and left in their limo, pausing only, like the canny merchandisers they had become, to scrape away the trademarks on their shoeprints. It would be some time before, metaphorically, Spielberg returned to this sleazy end of Hollywood with its whores, panhandlers and crazies. For the next few years he would breathe the rarefied air of Century City's tower blocks, not the fumes of Hollywood Boulevard, rub shoulders not with cinema owners but CEOs, not TV journalists but Pulitzer Prize-winners.

The Color Purple

Give me my robe, put on my crown; I have
Immortal longings in me.

William Shakespeare, *Antony and Cleopatra*

NOBODY EXPECTED recognition for *Temple of Doom* at the Oscars in
April 1985, and it received only two nominations, for Williams's
score and the visual effects of Dennis Muren and the team at George
Lucas's increasingly innovative special-effects studio, Industrial Light
and Magic (which won). This cleared the way for both Spielberg and
Amy to present awards. Amy refused at first, but changed her mind
when Spielberg agreed to appear. All this became further complicated
after they discovered in October 1984 that she was pregnant. Should an
expectant unmarried mother appear on national TV, especially on the
same stage, if not at the same time, as the baby's father? The Academy
agonised, then minimised the effect by having Amy and Gregory Hines
present Best Sound early in the show, keeping Spielberg almost to the
end, when he handed the Best Director statuette to Milos Forman for
Amadeus.

Before he did so, Spielberg said, 'This seems a fitting moment for us
to pay our respects to the French director François Truffaut.' Truffaut
had died of a brain tumour the previous October. It was both ironic and
sad that an audience of cinema professionals needed to be reminded
who Truffaut was. An aggregation of such solecisms made the telecast
depressingly memorable. To introduce David Lean's *A Passage to India*,
an elephant dressed in trappings from the film was coaxed on stage,
and Sally Field made her no-less-lumbering 'Now I *know* you like me'
acceptance speech for Best Actress in *Places in the Heart*. TV audience

figures were the lowest in years. Might this have been due, some wondered, to the cold shoulder turned to *Ghostbusters*, *Romancing the Stone* and *Beverly Hills Cop*, the year's big popular successes, and the Academy's warm embrace of the high-principled and challenging *Amadeus*, *Places in the Heart*, *The Killing Fields* and *A Passage to India*, which between them swept almost every major award? Their success seemed to give the lie to David Lean's gloomy accusation at a dinner for Best Foreign Film nominees that 'People at the studios ... can't or won't read,' and to lamentations like critic David Denby's that 'It is possible for a young man to gain control of a major studio film without ever having been to the theatre in his life and, even more amazing, without having read more than a few novels.' But Spielberg saw no inconsistency. It cost nothing to vote Oscars to prestige projects, but Old Hollywood wouldn't be caught dead *financing* them.

It was against this background that Spielberg, in a Pauline conversion bewildering to many, embraced literature. After years of professing, almost with pride, an antipathy to the written word, the man who transformed his high-school copy of *The Scarlet Letter* into a flip-book would buy the rights to three of the decade's most prestigious literary works, *The Color Purple*, *Empire of the Sun* and *Schindler's List*, and, with varying degrees of success, film all of them.

Like many mid-life conversions, his would be a case of 'too little, too late'. Within five years, he returned to fantasy, childhood and games. While the mood persisted, however, he pursued it with characteristic single-mindedness. Many asked why. He was no more a reader in 1984 than he had been in school, and, as his adaptations made clear, no more ready than he had been at the time of *Jaws* to respect the books he filmed. All the novels would be 'Spielberged', as his new friend 'Streisanded' a song.

The anticipated baby came into it: what new father has not vowed to create a heritage fit for his first child? So did his reunion with Amy, whose interest in literature and the theatre always exceeded his. Some friends whose opinions he respected were also voicing doubts about the lowbrow tone of his work. Even his early booster, Dilys Powell, had begun to fear that he was 'working beneath his own high standards. One looked vainly for themes,' she went on, 'not restricted by the age of the audience. One looked vainly for the unwavering devotion to the possibilities of film which one had seen in *Duel*.'

Steve Ross exerted the strongest influence of all. By now, Spielberg was thoroughly assimilated into a world which, feeding his love of chivalry, had assumed all the hallmarks of a capitalist Camelot. In 1985 Quincy Jones, Michael Jackson, Spielberg and David Geffen, with their partners and wives, spent a weekend in the Hamptons as the Rosses' guests. Afterwards, Courtney Ross, whose taste ran to the twee, sent each guest a set of five hand-illuminated books depicting the weekend in terms of a fairy story, and the participants as dukes and princes visiting a beneficent king and queen in their castle. Under the surface, however, ran powerful antagonisms. Geffen and Spielberg in particular competed for Ross's attention and favour. 'There was sibling rivalry,' Geffen agreed. 'I was jealous of [Spielberg] but I respected him and wanted his approval. And we were thrown together a lot.'

At these weekends, Ross discreetly encouraged Spielberg to lift his game. He would not have directly advised him to buy any one book with a view to filming it; that wasn't his style. 'Steve *never* talked Warner Brothers business with the stars,' says Terry Semel. 'He would never mix it. I used to say, "You have the best job in the world – you talk drivel to these people, and I'm the cheap sonuvabitch who's taking all their money."' But Ross provided a paradigm for Spielberg, who embraced literate cinema in pursuit of personal fulfilment, not out of a desire to educate the industry or the audience. Had Spielberg wished to further the cause of literature, there were better and more cost-effective ways of doing so. The budget of *Empire of the Sun* could have guaranteed distribution for three or four films by more appropriate directors, and his TV connections could have put literature into the homes of millions. Instead he 'collected' J.G. Ballard, Alice Walker and Thomas Keneally the way Ross collected de Koonings.

*   *   *

Spielberg took his first steps towards intellectual respectability at the end of 1983. During the scoring of *Gremlins*, he told Jerry Goldsmith, with the pride of a new son-in-law presented with a Chrysler dealership, 'Sid Sheinberg just bought a book for me.' It was *Schindler's Ark*, an account by Thomas Keneally of how gentile businessman Oskar Schindler rescued 1100 Jews from Polish concentration camps during World War II.

Keneally, a gnomish Australian of Irish extraction with a misleadingly leprechaun air, had begun his career as a Catholic brother, only to abandon the Church after eight years to become a novelist and screenwriter. Passing through Los Angeles in October 1980 on a promotional tour for his novel *Confederates*, he dropped into the Beverly Boulevard luggage shop of Leo Page to buy a briefcase. Chatting while he waited for Keneally's American Express card to clear, Page – real name Poldeck Pfefferberg, and one of the Jews saved by Schindler – discovered his client was a writer. 'Have I got a story for you!' he told him (as, it transpired, he told most novelists and screenwriters he met). Fascinated, Keneally cancelled his trip home and spent three weeks in Pfefferberg's home boning up on Schindler.

The story of Oskar Schindler was one of the most improbable to come out of the Holocaust. More successful as a philanderer than in business, the Czech was drawn to Poland in 1939 by rumours of enormous profits to be made in war supplies. In Krakow, he bribed and charmed his way into the circles of Nazi power, took over a failing enamelware factory, rented Jewish slave labour from the Germans, moved into a confiscated Jewish townhouse and started selling pots and pans to the Wehrmacht. Among the Nazis he bewitched was Amon Goeth, commandant of the camp being set up at Plaszow on the outskirts of Krakow as a staging point between the city's ghetto and Auschwitz. Partly for money, but mostly out of admiration for his friend, Goeth let him house his workers in a separate camp. From there, Schindler shipped them into Czechoslovakia and safety, bankrupting himself with bribes, mostly to Goeth.

Keneally wasn't the first writer to find Schindler's story interesting. In 1963, Page had brokered an MGM deal to produce a film from a Howard Koch screenplay. It fell apart when the lead, Sean Connery, dropped out, but Schindler's share of the option money for that project, $37,500, helped him survive a few more years in Paris. He'd died in 1974, after being recognised by Israel as a 'Righteous Gentile' and invited to plant a tree in its avenue of remembrance in Jerusalem.

Two years after he met Page, Keneally published his best-selling documentary novel *Schindler's Ark*. Spielberg hadn't actually read the book when Sheinberg bought it, only seen a TV documentary about Schindler and read an enthusiastic notice in the *New York Times Book Review*. Sheinberg saw the same notice and enquired about the rights, which had been snapped up by Warners.

Two screenwriters were assigned to do a treatment of the book. At a meeting with Keneally on a later visit, the executive in charge asked how they were going. They temporised. Had they at least read it?

'No,' they admitted. 'It's kinda thick.'

After this, Keneally had no objection to changing to Universal, and Sheinberg bought *Schindler's List*, with the idea of making it into a six-part series for TV. The purchase was announced in January 1983. Keneally received $500,000, a relatively meagre sum for a major book, shared with Schindler's widow, now living in Argentina, and her lawyer. Spielberg's role in the project was imprecise at first. He, Keneally, Sheinberg and Pfefferberg shared a riotous lunch to discuss it. Sheinberg mentioned that his father was from southern Poland and still lived there.

'Where? Where does he live?' Pfefferberg demanded. 'Get him on the phone. I want to talk to him.'

Sheinberg rang his father and Pfefferberg spent much of the lunch talking loudly to Sheinberg Sr in Polish.

Initially Spielberg saw the book in conventional terms, as a drama in the style of *Holocaust* or *Sophie's Choice*. Why not, he suggested, combine all the Nazis ranged against Schindler in a single incorruptible character determined to foil his plans? Keneally dismissed the idea. Spielberg commissioned a screenplay from him, but even before it was delivered, decided that if he was to plunge into intellectual film-making, it would have to be with something less demanding.

*   *   *

English writer J.G. Ballard had become one of the most highly regarded of all science fiction writers during the sixties with a series of dystopic novels like *The Drowned World*, *The Crystal World* and *The Drought* in which the remnants of mankind wander a world swept by natural disaster. In 1984, he revealed the roots of these fantasies in *Empire of the Sun*, an eerie and lightly fictionalised memoir of his childhood in a Japanese internment camp outside Shanghai. Before the book leaped into the bestseller lists, David Puttnam, producer of *Chariots of Fire*, had been set to acquire it for a peppercorn £10,000 as a project for director Roland Joffe, but lost it to Warner Brothers, whose Robert Shapiro bought it for British director Harold Becker (*The Onion Field*, *The Black Marble*, *Taps*).

Becker commissioned a script from playwright Tom Stoppard, who had made inventive adaptations of Graham Greene's *The Human Factor* for Otto Preminger and Vladimir Nabokov's *Despair* for Rainer Werner Fassbinder. An émigré himself, Stoppard had been a child in Singapore when the Japanese invaded. His mother took him to India, but his father remained, and died. Stoppard and Becker made a research trip to Shanghai, which they found had changed little since the war.

Meanwhile, interest in *Empire of the Sun* was bubbling up everywhere. David Lean became involved. At the British Academy of Film and TV Awards in London in 1985, Lean and Spielberg were seated at the same table. During the meal, Spielberg offered to produce anything Lean cared to direct. Lean suggested Ballard's book, and a delighted Spielberg opened negotiations with Warners. In the meantime he agreed to collaborate with Lean on restoring and re-releasing his original cut of *Lawrence of Arabia*. By the time Warner agreed to sell *Empire of the Sun*, Lean was busy preparing a version of Joseph Conrad's *Nostromo*, so Spielberg, while agreeing to act as executive producer on that film too, began to think about directing *Empire of the Sun* himself.

While Lean was in Los Angeles for the Oscars in March 1985, Spielberg also offered him part of his new TV project, just negotiated with Universal and NBC. *Amazing Stories* was Amblin's most ambitious enterprise yet, a series of fantasy stories by different directors, to run nationally every Sunday night at 8 p.m. for anything from thirty minutes to an hour. In an unexpectedly far-reaching deal for a chronically nervous and tight-fisted business, NBC's heads Grant Tinker and Brandon Tartikoff agreed to spend up to $1 million a programme, twice the budget of successful shows like *Cheers* and *Family Ties*, and committed themselves to forty-four episodes over two seasons, a guarantee that the series, even if it did poorly the first year, would have a chance to build a following. They also waived any network pre-censorship of scripts.

There was an element of the club about *Amazing Stories* and an unprecedented ease of access, both physically and intellectually. The young Mick Garris, whom Spielberg knew from his programme on LA's pay-TV station, the Z Channel, was shooting a film about the making of *The Goonies* when, on the first day, Spielberg said, 'Gee, you must do a lot of these documentaries.'

'I told him I was doing less of them because I was trying to make a go of it as a writer,' recalls Garris.

'He said, "We're looking for writers on *Amazing Stories*."'

'It turned out I was offered the [series'] first script,' continues Garris. 'When I delivered that one in three days, he asked me to do another one. Before I even finished the second one, he asked me to go on staff. I went literally from food stamps to a staff position as story editor on *Amazing Stories*.'

Spielberg had already outlined almost all the stories in the first series, combing his memory for half-recollected plots from old TV shows, science fiction magazines and comic books. These were passed to supervising producers Joshua Brand and John Falsey, the brains behind the successful hospital series *St Elsewhere*. As well as writing stories, reading scripts, checking rough cuts and approving the end product, Spielberg himself agreed, though not contractually, to direct five or six shows over the two years. (The series folded before he could do more than two, one of them the hour-long *The Mission*.) The rest would be divided between experienced directors like Martin Scorsese, Peter Hyams and Joe Dante, and interesting people on the fringe, such as Paul Bartel. Unable to afford big stars, he won their involvement by offering a chance to direct. Clint

Eastwood, Burt Reynolds and Danny De Vito all directed episodes – Clint a ghost story, *Vanessa in the Garden*, with a bit part for Spielberg's mother. Every director accepted union scale of $9964 for a six-day shoot, though most episodes took a day or two more. Lean, jokingly, also agreed to participate, providing he could have six months, to make sure he got the weather right. With visions of something as long and costly as *Lawrence of Arabia*, Spielberg reluctantly declined.

The opening episode, *Ghost Train*, which Spielberg directed from his own story, scripted by Frank Deese and shot by Allen Daviau, pointed up his new enthusiasm for the written word and the unmediated image. The main character escaped death on the crashed Highball Express as a child, and now awaits the arrival of the same train seventy-five years later, on a phantom track which, in a useful coincidence, runs right through his son's new house. The climax, with the train's arrival created physically, like a stage illusion, rather than cooked up in ILM's kitchens, gave notice that Spielberg had turned his back, for the time being anyway, on movie magic. He put equal effort into showing the affection of the boy, played by Lukas Haas, the child actor who had shot to stardom in Peter Weir's thriller *Witness*, for his 'Ol' Pa'. Roberts Blossom, Spielberg's favourite old fart, played the idealised granddad, striding about the fields like a Biblical patriarch, plucking rusted railway spikes from the soil and, a signal gantry turned human, sighting down long arms at the forgotten right-of-way. The film put all Spielberg's skills on show but it took no guru to foresee that it, and the series, were too unfocused to succeed in the world of *Star Trek*.

Quincy Jones coaxed Spielberg into the first of his literary adaptations to reach the big screen, a version of Alice Walker's 1983 Pulitzer Prize-winning novel *The Color Purple*. Both he and Kathleen Kennedy pressed copies on him, though Jones had an ulterior motive. He'd persuaded Peter Guber and Jon Peters, who owned the rights, to accept him as associate producer for a movie version which would celebrate the roots of black music. Guber and Peters hoped Jones could influence Spielberg to direct. Spielberg grumbled but agreed to read the book – 'Because it's thin,' he explained. But he was quickly won over. Later, he claimed to have wept over Walker's story.

The youngest of eight children, Walker, though only three years older than Spielberg, had battered her way to intellectual standing as a professional 'womanist'. Despite childhood brutality, partial blindness, abortion and divorce, she taught at Wellesley and Yale, edited the militant *Ms.* magazine, lived in Africa, and wrote, in addition to a biography of the black poet and leader of the 1930s Harlem Renaissance, Langston Hughes, a number of books of poetry, short stories and autobiographical works about feminism, the civil rights movement and dispossessed black women, especially in the rural South.

The Color Purple subsumed many of these interests in the story of two sisters separated in childhood, told through the letters they exchange from 1909 to 1946. Celie, who at fourteen already has two children, is given as housekeeper to a charming but violent and promiscuous older man, whom she calls throughout the book only 'Mr——'. Nettie comes to live with them, but, after a failed attempt at rape, the husband drives her away, and steals and hides the letters which reveal she has gone to Africa with a missionary group, taking Celie's children with her. Celie finds the letters years later, as she discovers her sexuality, through an affair with Albert's bisexual lover, blues singer Shug Avery, who forces her to confront and relish her life. 'God gets pissed off,' says Shug, 'if you walk past the colour purple in a field and don't see it.' Empowered at last, and emboldened by the examples she sees all around her of blacks terrorised both by whites and their own kind, Celie revolts against her husband's tyranny, and reclaims her letters and life.

The more deeply Spielberg dug into *The Color Purple*, however, the more worried he became. Some of its themes, like family violence and the tensions within a dysfunctional relationship, were familiar from his own childhood. But its black militancy and lesbianism troubled him. Walker was also known to be highly defensive about how her book should be treated on screen. When Jones pressed, he tried to pass the poisoned chalice. He had never devoted an entire film to dramatic relationships, he argued. They always existed simply as light relief. He had no confidence in his ability to film Shug and Celie's love scenes, nor the moment where Shug educates Celie about her body by encouraging her to examine her vagina minutely with a mirror. Why not get someone with a proven reputation in filming social problems, like Sidney Lumet, director of *Twelve Angry Men* and *Dog Day Afternoon*, to make it, or a black director, or, better still, a woman?

'You didn't have to be a Martian to direct *E.T.*,' Jones retorted.

Jones's argument was casuistic. A peripatetic childhood had taught Spielberg exactly how it felt to be a lonely misfit. But he constructed a tower of rationalisation on this flimsy foundation. Underpinning it was at least one firm point, the racial discrimination he experienced as a child. 'I felt I was qualified [to direct the film],' he told journalist David Hay, 'because of my own kind of cultural Armageddon.' Later, he would add, 'I wanted to do this book because I was scared I couldn't.' He asked Walker to write a screenplay, but after a first draft she told him, 'This is not my form. This is not the arena I enjoy working in. I really can't adapt my own book. Please feel free to get anybody you feel can adapt the book properly.' Spielberg put Menno Meyjes, one of Garris's discoveries from *Amazing Stories*, onto the job.

Spielberg's new intellectual ambitions didn't extend to Amblin, the first year's five-film production slate of which was defiantly pre-pubescent, with children as the main characters and an emphasis on games, treasure hunts and action sequences that imitated the rides he, and his audience, loved.

Before he moved into the new offices, he'd put *Gremlins*' scriptwriter Chris Columbus under contract to script his own story, *The Goonies*, about a group of misfit kids who negotiate a ghost train-like series of booby-trapped tunnels in the cliffs of the northern Oregon coast to discover a pirate ship. Eager for input and anxious to succeed, Columbus was the perfect collaborator, constantly popping into his office for advice. Spielberg bought more of his work, including a screenplay about Sherlock Holmes and Dr Watson as schoolboys uncovering a Victorian sect which worships in a wooden pyramid built in London's dockland. The resemblance of the menace in *Young Sherlock Holmes* to the Thugs in

Indiana Jones and the Temple of Doom raised some eyebrows. Some of the former's ideas might have found their way into the Indy film, though, if so, Columbus never complained of it. However, the effect was to undermine Barry Levinson's version of *Young Sherlock Holmes* when it was released some time after the larger production.

Columbus was to flourish professionally under Spielberg's influence, quickly becoming a highly successful writer/director of hits like *Home Alone* and *Mrs Doubtfire*. The price, however, was a loss of the combative energy that motivated *Gremlins*. Ten years later, British critic Adam Mars-Jones would complain of Columbus's work's descent into 'fuzzy warmth' with films like *Nine Months*. The script for *Gremlins*, he felt, 'still looks like Chris Columbus's only real achievement . . . Since then, Columbus has become alarmingly wholesome. It's like the revenge of Norman Rockwell, the return of the repressed Hallmark card.'

Amblin's first official development project was a script by Walter F. Parkes and Lawrence Lasker called *Wargames*, about a teenage computer hacker who breaks into the US missile system and nearly precipitates World War III. Though the story proved too abrasive for Amblin, its style was apparent in the eventual Warner Brothers production, which would be directed by Lucas's old friend John Badham, with Spielberg's lookalike Eddie Deezen in a bit role. Parkes became a frequent visitor to the company, which he nicknamed 'Amblin U', and would later take over as its manager.

An Amblin formula was already emerging. Like the company's headquarters, it had no sharp corners, no straight lines, and above all no kinks. Families in these films were dysfunctional, but not grimly so. Bankruptcy, unpopularity and divorce were the worst any child had to face. One boy in *The Goonies* has asthma. Another is overweight. Despite a plethora of skeletons, nobody nice gets killed, and the villains are bumbling enough to be almost loveable. Notwithstanding his own background and his often-expressed ambition to make a film about growing up in Arizona, Spielberg set most of Amblin's films in northern California, Oregon or, in the case of *Young Sherlock Holmes*, England: dripping, wooded landscapes that recalled the forests of Hans Christian Andersen and the Brothers Grimm. Anything might happen here, but none of it would have any relevance to the real world.

Amblin's willingness to cut deals, especially with people who Spielberg knew personally, drew scores of writers and directors to the company headquarters. David Giler, an old friend from the days hanging out with Guy McElwaine and Alan Ladd Jr at the time of *Sugarland Express*, proposed *The Money Trap*, an update of the forties classic *Mr Blandings Builds his Dream House*, about a Yuppie couple bankrupting themselves to renovate a house. Spielberg bought other scripts by Matthew Robbins and Hal Barwood, and would take on Joe Dante's *Innerspace*. He also bailed out Don Bluth when the ex-Disney animator's studio went broke in 1985, commissioning a cartoon feature about an immigrant mouse, *An American Tail*. For five years, Bluth, a perfectionist with a self-confessed stubborn streak, worked under Amblin's umbrella, though with increasing discomfort on both sides.

Pressed about the degree of his involvement in projects, like Bluth's films, where he acted as executive producer, Spielberg said, 'I did what the title implies – nothing.' This earned a hollow laugh in many quarters. Though the 'Executive Producer' credit had been debased into a short-hand acknowledgement to a writer or director who'd developed the project or a sop to a star who wanted to inflate his role in the making of the film, Spielberg's executive productions were aggressively hands-on. Pressed about his claim that he didn't interfere, Spielberg back-pedalled. He put his credit on films, he said, that he 'didn't want to direct but did want to see' – and, it went without saying, see them the way he believed they should be made. Richard Donner agreed that Spielberg was 'over my shoulder the whole time [on *The Goonies*]. But,' he continued diplomatically, 'he has so many good ideas you just want to grab them.'

At film school in Texas, Kevin Reynolds had written and directed the ambitious *Fandango*, about five college kids close to graduation who drive across the state in one wild weekend to dig up a bottle of Dom Perignon champagne ritually buried years before and drink it before dispersing, mostly for service in Vietnam. Impressed by the short, Spielberg underwrote Reynolds to direct a feature-length version at Universal. MGM also bought Reynolds's screenplay 'Ten Soldiers', a *Lord of the*

Flies-inspired thriller about a future Soviet/Cuban invasion of the US against which a guerrilla force of modern teenage Minutemen holds out in the mountainous south-west.

Reynolds made a pitch to direct it, but MGM head Frank Yablans wanted someone more bankable, like John Milius. Aware that Reynolds was Spielberg's protégé, Yablans' deputy Peter Bart visited Amblin to discuss his future. Bart recalls:

> Cordial and scrupulously tactful, Spielberg said he would gladly show me the as-yet-uncompleted *Fandango*. Listening to him discuss the project, however, I could detect he was less than thrilled with it. It wasn't as though he were knocking it – Spielberg would never 'knock' a colleague. But reading between the lines of his faint praise, I could surmise that Steven Spielberg was not in a mood to do battle on behalf of young Reynolds.

Word of Spielberg's reservations got around. Jerry Goldsmith refused to score *Fandango*, and though it gave an early push to the careers of Kevin Costner and Glenn Headly, its 1985 release through Warners with the slightly disdainful tag 'Amblin Presents', without Spielberg's usual credit as co-executive producer, was unsuccessful. Milius did direct 'Ten Soldiers', as *Red Dawn*, but it too flopped.

Amblin continued to seek and develop projects with untried directors and writers, but Spielberg's enthusiasm for new talent would diminish, and he'd work increasingly with experienced directors, like Richard Donner and Barry Levinson, or writers like Columbus who enjoyed his hands-on production style. However, the demands of this regime soon wore him down. 'I made a bet with myself,' he'd said in June, 'that I wanted to get into a small production company and try my hand at this for eighteen months, and I've done it eighteen months . . . It's just too darn much. And this is the last year I'm going to dabble in this sort of workload.'

Robert Zemeckis emerged as his heir apparent. Amiable, conciliatory, inventive but lacking Spielberg's virtuoso touch, the tall, burly Chicagoan who won Spielberg with his belief that *It's a Wonderful Life* was the most perfect movie ever made would come to represent for many people the acceptable and marketable face of New Hollywood; someone who could take the spikiest inventions of Industrial Light and Magic and adapt them to a Norman Rockwell fable like *Forrest Gump*.

Zemeckis's projects, deservedly in most cases, enjoyed the inside track at Amblin. One was a script from his and Gale's USC days, *Back to the Future*, which had been rejected by every studio in Hollywood before finding a home at Amblin. The paradoxes of time travel had made it the equivalent of crime fiction's locked-room mystery for sf writers. For half a century, they wrangled over intellectual puzzles like, 'Can a time traveller meet himself?' or, 'If you went back and killed your father as a child, would you cease to exist? – with its corollary, 'And, if so, how could you have killed him in the first place?' *Back to the Future*'s story of a 1980s teenager who returns to 1955 and retrospectively transforms his nerdy father and tippling mother into broad-minded and prosperous paragons added little to the mountain of existing invention, but it was the first film to streamline the often knotty speculations of sf writers for Hollywood.

Or *almost* the first?

Ray Stark, now operating his own unit at Columbia, was preparing another time-travel story, *Peggy Sue Got Married*. Though she hadn't signed a contract, Debra Winger had agreed to play the fortyish divorcee who's magically boosted back to 1960, where she tries to repair the biggest mistake of her life, marrying her high school sweetheart.

The film was set for production at the end of 1984, with a summer 1985 release, but in October Winger fell out with producer Paul Gurian over his choice of Jonathan Demme to direct. She preferred Penny Marshall of *Laverne and Shirley*, and when Gurian didn't agree, she left, as did Demme. Francis Coppola, just winding up his disastrous production of *The Cotton Club*, came in to direct Kathleen Turner.

It was at this point that Spielberg put *Back to the Future* into production. Shot in early 1985, it grabbed the summer spot TriStar had pencilled in for *Peggy Sue*, which was held back until October. Gurian, and others, complained that Spielberg had deliberately undercut Stark and Coppola, and were even more furious when Zemeckis's film grossed $207 million at the US domestic box office alone.

Given his competitiveness and preference for projects already 'certified' by the interest of someone else, it's conceivable that Spielberg revived an ancient script to beat out his old friend and rival. Winger and Penny Marshall were his friends, so he would have known about events inside the project. But it's more likely he acted simply on an instinct that urged him to produce more films for the wised-up and affluent teenage market which had made *Close Encounters* a hit. While Amblin films like *The Goonies* continued to appeal to the sub-teens, the company's productions, as well as the marketing spin-offs that had become increasingly important generators of income, were aimed at the older teenage audience, preoccupied with clothes, money, status and sex.

The pace of social and sexual change in the America of the eighties was dizzying to someone brought up in the repressive fifties. The failure of *1941*, the mockery of *King David* as a rip-off of *Raiders*, and the decision by Lucas, whose instincts Spielberg respected – 'SPIELBERG DEFERS TO PROPHET LUCAS' noted a *Variety* headline of 20 April 1983 – to shift *Temple of Doom* away from thirties nostalgia towards eighties violence, persuaded him his audience was evolving faster than he was. In 1986, fifteen-year-old River Phoenix, on location in Oregon for *Stand by Me*, Rob Reiner's adaptation of Stephen King's story about childhood friendships, would abandon his virginity with a friend of his hippy family. Rather than sneak into a motel, as Spielberg and many of his generation had done, the couple approached River's parents John and Arlyn (who'd re-christened herself 'Heart') and asked, 'Can we have your good wishes?' A special tent was pitched for them, festively decorated. Heart called their one-night stand 'a beautiful experience'. Her complaisance echoes that of Marty's parents in *Back to the Future*, who smile indulgently about his intention to spend a weekend in the wilderness with his girlfriend; the guiltless sexual freedom every teenager dreamed of.

Phoenix, who would play young Indiana Jones in *Indiana Jones and the Last Crusade*, could stand as an emblem of the emerging Hollywood to which all film-makers needed to accustom themselves. He shared none of their values or enthusiasms. He'd never seen a James Dean film, let alone one by Orson Welles, and when Peter Bogdanovich offered him what turned out to be the actor's last completed film, *The Thing Called Love*, the director of *Targets* and *What's Up, Doc?* had to explain who he was: Phoenix had never heard of him.

Back to the Future continued to have problems even after Amblin put it into production. Zemeckis had cast rising young performer Eric Stoltz as Marty McFly, the time-travelling teenager, but after a week's shooting he replaced him with Michael J. Fox, the star of the TV series *Family Ties*, who had been his first choice but who had been too busy to take the role. Spielberg himself was more preoccupied with an already troubled *The Color Purple*. A novel of letters risked turning into a recital of voice-overs, so he and Meyjes discarded Walker's form in favour of telling Celie's story as narrative. Even then, Terry Semel wasn't enthusiastic about a film which, with eleven principal roles and locations in Kenya and North Carolina, promised to cost a lot and earn little. He offered a budget of $15 million, and Spielberg, struggling to be conciliatory, agreed to accept the DGA minimum fee of $40,000 for directing it, waiving even that when he ran over budget. He could afford to, since his contract, like all he signed after *E.T.*, gave him between 10 and 15 per cent of the film's worldwide gross income.

The Color Purple might have had a bumpier passage had Steve Ross not backed it, even though the CEO was under attack from his own board. Herbert Siegel, his bitterest critic, shared the scepticism of many shareholders about the wisdom of WCI's expansion into cable TV and fibre-optics. As smoothly as he moved Rosenthal's mortuaries into parking lots, Ross had bought out American Express's 40 per cent share of a joint cable enterprise, financing it by selling off MCI's interest in the MTV rock-video chain and Showtime/Movie Channel. In 1985 he also brought David Geffen's record company under his umbrella. Ross's instincts proved correct when Geffen's operation prospered and WCI's cable arm became a $4 billion asset during the nineties, but Siegel thought these deals overstretched the company, and attacked them, both in the boardroom and in public. When Ross visited the set of *Color Purple* towards the end of shooting, Spielberg had the ten-strong gospel choir

of the film stand outside his window and sing, 'Drive Herb Siegel away!
Drive Herb Siegel away!'

Spielberg's commitment to consensus film-making almost buckled
under the weight of those individuals and groups who felt they had, or
should have, a role in making *The Color Purple*. With its sexuality and
singing, the role of Shug guaranteed a Best Supporting Actress Oscar
nomination. Tina Turner was offered the part but, amid much publicity,
turned it down. Diana Ross expressed interest, but Alice Walker was
adamant: 'We had to struggle to make it clear,' she said, 'that authenticity
means not having Diana Ross! No matter how interested she is in doing
it, or how much money they want to make, the final cast, though not
stars or widely known, must seem like they have stepped straight from
the book.'

Walker was indirectly responsible for the choice of the actress
to play Celie. With some backing from Mike Nichols, who produced
her one-woman Broadway show, Manhattan-born Caryn Johnson had
earned a reputation as a radical stand-up comedian under the name
Whoopi Goldberg. Not diffident about her enthusiasms, Goldberg, a
movie and TV fan who would later win a part in another of her
passions, the TV series *Star Trek: The Next Generation*, with the same
approach, sent Walker some reviews and a letter soliciting a role,
however, small, in the film. To her surprise, Walker wrote back that
she knew Goldberg's work and had passed on her submission to
Amblin.

Spielberg had read about Goldberg in *Newsweek* and been intrigued.
They met at a party, where Goldberg cheekily did a *shtick* on *E.T.*,
showing how, had Puck landed in laid-back and dope-friendly San Francisco, he might have been invited to a party and ended up stoned and
in jail. Spielberg set up an audition in Amblin's thirty-nine-seat screening
room, which Quincy Jones shrewdly packed with black opinion-makers,
including singing stars Lionel Richie and Michael Jackson. The audience
loved Goldberg, confirming Spielberg's enthusiasm. By putting a comic,
and a plain one, into the role of Celie, he also bypassed questions of sex
and glamour; the world was in no hurry to see the homely Goldberg in
a lesbian love scene, and this element of the story swiftly shrank to a

few playful kisses and a discreet pan away from the bed as Shug and Celie embrace.

Spielberg had to undergo something like an audition himself, visiting Walker in San Francisco with Jones and submitting his ideas over dinner. They got on well. Once approved, he started casting. Burly actor Danny Glover was a solid choice as Mr——, whom Meyjes renamed Albert Johnson, and for Shug, Spielberg remembered Margaret Avery, whom he'd directed fifteen years before in a commercial. Quincy Jones spotted plump, bustling Chicago TV talk-show hostess Oprah Winfrey and suggested her for Johnson's daughter-in-law Sofia, who, for refusing a domestic job with the white mayor's wife and punching the mayor when he attacks her, is jailed, emerging handicapped and prematurely aged.

Spielberg also offered a watching brief to black director, writer and still photographer Gordon Parks, whose 1969 film of his own autobiographical novel *The Learning Tree* many felt qualified him to make *The Color Purple* more than Spielberg. If Parks saw the gesture as a bribe, he was too diplomatic to say so, and carefully denied all creative involvement.

Steve asked me to come down on the set and create for him, and for myself, the world of Alice Walker as it was associated with *The Color Purple*. I don't normally do that sort of thing, but I thought it was a very fine novel and I realised what a departure it was for him. Steve was very anxious – and it was clear that he felt that it was the kind of movie he had to make just once in his life. At times he was almost apologetic about doing it. He didn't want me as a guide. At no time did I instruct his camerawork. He wanted me to draw together a body of stills that would excite people's imaginations at the promotion stage of it . . . I'd go and look at Steve's camera and he'd come and look at mine. It all worked pretty well.

Just in case it didn't, Alice Walker was also there for at least half the shooting, advising on dialect and the varieties of fruit and flowers Celie might have cultivated. Quincy Jones, who received co-producer credit, was even more intrusive. 'I need to feel what you're doing so I can feel the music better,' he told Spielberg, who reluctantly admitted him to Michael Kahn's cutting room every weekend of the editing period. Having failed to turn the film into a history of black music, Jones imposed his personality with an interminable and sentimental Copland-esque score. Spielberg never worked with any composer but John Williams again.

The baby was due in mid-June, and Amy had relaxed into classic motherhood. For the moment, her career went on hold. 'I'm totally unambitious now,' she told the *Los Angeles Times*. 'All I can think about is this child.' Orson Welles had offered her a role as his first wife, Virginia, in a film he was trying to float in Rome of Marc Blitzstein's left-wing musical *The Cradle Will Rock* and the furore when Welles tried to produce it on Broadway in 1937. He was even prepared to shoot while Amy was pregnant, since Virginia had also been pregnant in 1937, but a shortage of money kept delaying the start of photography. Welles asked Spielberg to finance the film, but he refused. Coppola, in this as in much else, was almost alone among the directors of New Hollywood in offering practical help to ageing masters. He had made Michael Powell 'director in residence' at Zoetrope, and Coppola and Lucas actively aided Akira Kurosawa to finance *Ran*. Spielberg confined his patronage to 'presenting' Kurosawa's last film, *Dreams*, and helping restore David Lean's *Lawrence of Arabia*. Idols belonged in their niche, not on the studio floor. Welles would die in October 1985, leaving *The Cradle Will Rock*, like many other films, unmade.

Spielberg and Amy were devoted parents-to-be, sharing Lamaze breathing practice, choosing names – Sophie Anne for a girl, Max Spencer (for Tracy) if it was a boy. They experienced the baby's first kick together, and Spielberg even protested when Amy did something as quotidian as buying a new maternity dress without asking him along. Spielberg, however, hadn't shed his adolescent sense of the child as a threat to his control of his life. 'I've been having these persistent dreams,' he said, 'that the baby comes out talking – being very articulate and opinionated and telling me where it wants to have dinner tonight . . . I won't know quite how to handle that.' Amy exacerbated Spielberg's anxieties by insisting on a pre-partum agreement making Spielberg legally responsible for the baby.

The Color Purple started shooting early in June 1985. Rather than miss the birth, Spielberg sent Frank Marshall to Kenya to direct the scenes of Nettie on her farm, and brought Amy with him to his location in Wadesboro, North Carolina. He was filming Celie giving birth when Amy went into labour. After twenty-three hours, during which she'd been visited by her own mother and sister, Spielberg's mother and various relatives, she rang from the hospital: 'Honey, now come and direct *my* delivery.' At 1.52 p.m. on 13 June, seven pound five ounce Max Samuel (not Spencer) was born. Spielberg cut the umbilical cord. They recorded the birth, and when he needed baby cries for Celie's child in the film, dubbed in those of little Max. Spielberg was delirious. 'I had my Peter and Wendy, my Michael and John,' he said. Peter Pan had grown up and could forget Neverland.

Universal re-released *E.T.* in cinemas on 12 July, squeezing the last drops of profit before the film went to video. Once again, it won huge audiences. Spielberg felt nostalgic for its relative simplicity. Making a film like *The Color Purple*, based on character, not action, demanded a massive overhaul of his narrative style. Storyboards were useless for actors who needed to feel a scene, not simply hit their marks and grimace winningly. He fell back on other directors for inspiration, in particular Ford, Lean, Welles and Wilder, whose work, fortunately, movie buff Goldberg knew well. Not able to articulate what he wanted, he would tell her, 'Give me a little of Ray Milland in *The Lost Weekend*,' and she would oblige.

The visual style had the same sense of the facsimile antique. Spielberg told Daviau to take another look at Ford's *The Grapes of Wrath* and William Wyler's *The Best Years of Our Lives*, both shot by Gregg Toland. Daviau's backlit vistas often seem staged for a Monument Valley background that doesn't exist, while the fields of flowers across which he tracks so deliriously would not be out of place in Zhivago's romantic visions of the Russian spring. Sofia's altercation with the mayor copies

Welles's abrupt cut from close-up to long-shot in the battle scenes of *Chimes at Midnight*. Even Spielberg's own original stylistic touches, like the dusty 'God Light' so appropriate to *Raiders of the Lost Ark*, look overwrought for scenes inside the house-cum-drinking club where Shug performs. Many people felt that the mélange of pastel colour, broad performances and idyllic Southern countryside turned Alice Walker into Walt Disney.

From its credits, written in cursive violet script, and the opening sequence of two children playing in a field of purple flowers, *The Color Purple* oozes the kitsch artificiality of a Hallmark greeting card. In this lacquered Georgia, every horse is sleek, every cow fat, every flower in bloom. Stormclouds gather and lightning flashes as theatrically as anything in *Bambi*, and frost on a windowpane frames Danny Glover as if in a daguerreotype. At 152 minutes, the film is too long for its frail narrative, and the character of Celie quickly deteriorates into a stoic observer or silent participant in the actions of others.

Seeing no value in waiting until summer, Warners set the release of *The Color Purple* for December, hoping it would share in the Christmas *gemütlichkeit*. Spielberg edited it in the glow of new fatherhood. Transient relationships and broken marriages being the norm and children still a relative rarity, New Hollywood welcomed Max with the mingled astonishment and formal respect the forest animals accorded Bambi. Brian De Palma, who had brought the couple together, stood godfather. Jerry Goldsmith composed a lullaby. Spielberg rang back with his thanks, and the crushing news that Michael Jackson had trumped him by writing no less than three original songs just for little Max.

Amazing Stories premiered on 22 September 1985. Even in North Carolina, Spielberg had the rushes flown in for checking. His attention to detail paid off in the series' polish, which lifted it above prime-time pap. Williams's whooping horn theme was a distinctive contrast to the brassiness of his *Raiders* music. Ron Cobb and Jim Bissel's fluid title sequence showed the role of the storyteller modifying from the shaman at the tribal campfire to the family gathered round the TV. However, the reviews were no better than respectful, and they got worse, as did the ratings.

Script editor Mick Garris was bombarded with scripts by people who 'thought they would write mini-Spielberg movies . . . All these space things and wild flights of the imagination, but [also meant to] make you cry.' If he'd accepted such stories, however, the series might have run longer:

> Its style changed a lot from week to week, and I think that may be one reason for its demise. One week you'd have an incredibly suspenseful thriller about a psychic and a serial killer, and the next week you'd have a silly little comedy about three aliens who come to earth because they like the TV shows. It was a very schizophrenic programme . . . and a television audience is used to growing to love a family and coming back to visit them in their living room every week. And I think those are a couple of problems that made for *Amazing Stories'* less than stellar success.

To give it a human face, the series needed Spielberg introducing each programme, as Disney and Serling had done, but he insisted on minimum involvement at a time when he was busy with *The Color Purple* and a new baby. He even ducked the traditional Hollywood cattle-call press conference and blow-out buffet to launch *Amazing Stories*, setting up instead a cumbersome ninety-minute coast-to-coast video hook-up where journalists, gathered at NBC affiliates around the country, tele-phoned questions to which he responded by satellite.

There was even less publicity when, at 1.30 p.m. on 27 November, Chief Judge Thomas A. Donnelly married him and Amy in a civil cere-mony in Santa Fe, New Mexico. Her sister and Saul Cohen, an attorney and friend of Spielberg, were the only witnesses. They left immediately for New York, then Paris, where they checked into the Crillon.

They never read the reviews of *The Color Purple*, but neither would have been surprised by them. The film was almost universally attacked – as racist by African-Americans, as anti-homosexual by lesbians who resented Spielberg's removal of that element of the book, and as saccharine by critics in general, who charged that Walker's indictment of inhumanity and racism had been turned into a New Age feelgood movie. Self-appointed African-American media groups picketed cinemas, accusing Spielberg of, among other things, showing blacks in the deep South as living in some comfort. When he returned from his three-month honeymoon, Spielberg pointed out that Walker's family weren't sharecroppers but middle class. He was howled down.

Audiences, however, turned out to see *The Color Purple*, if only from curiosity, and found its Old Hollywood style to their taste. It cleared $95.5 million in US domestic rentals, and made a further $47.5 million overseas. Its success softened for Spielberg the sense of anti-climax and failure. *Amazing Stories* hadn't taken off. *The Money Pit*, slammed by *Variety* as a film that 'begins unpromisingly and slides irrevocably downward from there', did such poor business over Christmas that Universal pulled it. *Fandango* failed too, and *Young Sherlock Holmes* had only modest success. *The Goonies* and the enormous hit of *Back to the Future* helped, but the year for Amblin ended ambiguously. Not so for Spielberg and Amy, however, who had eyes only for each other and for Max.

15

Empire of the Sun

> This is the primal genius of Spielberg . . . By now a billion
> earthlings have seen his films. They have only one thing in
> common. They have all, at some stage, been children.
>
> Martin Amis, 1982

WITH INTELLECTUAL respectability at least in prospect following
The Color Purple, Spielberg attacked the larger problem of his
image, both in Hollywood and nationally. At Amblin, the company's
corporate standing was underscored, the playground element de-
emphasised. There was no more talk of a 'children's crusade'. The free
candy counter became a salad bar, with raw vegetables instead of M&Ms;
E.T. would never have gone near the place. Aware that he was a prime
kidnap target, Spielberg tightened security. Signs pointing to the building
were removed, and a guard was stationed at the gate. In the wake of
some damaging leaks about Spielberg's difficult personality during the
fuss over *Twilight Zone*, all new employees were required to sign a lifetime
confidentiality agreement, swearing not to divulge anything seen or heard
while working for the company.

A series of discreetly publicised donations during 1986/7 launched
Spielberg II: The Sequel – sober, mature, responsible, with global, indeed
galactic concerns. He donated $100,000 to Harvard's search for life in
space, funded the Steven Spielberg-Warner Communications Gallery in
the new Norman Rockwell Museum at Stockbridge, Massachusetts, and
gave $850,000 for a studio in the George Balanchine School of American
Ballet in New York, a pet project of Courtney Ross. A $600-a-plate dinner
thrown by the American Friends of Jerusalem's Hebrew University, at
which Spielberg was honoured with its Scopus Laureate Award, raised

$90,000 for a Steven Spielberg Scholarship to the university and for the Steven Spielberg Archives on its campus to house its collection of historic films.

With a personal fortune approaching $200 million, Spielberg could afford almost anything he – or Amy – desired. In 1985 they bought a 5½ acre estate in the luxurious Los Angeles oceanside suburb of Pacific Palisades. Once the home of athletic silent-movie star Douglas Fairbanks Sr, it had belonged to David Selznick at the time he was making *Gone With the Wind*, and later to Cary Grant and his millionairess wife Barbara Hutton. Amy found the tile-roofed stucco house too small, so architect Harry Newman rebuilt it for $4 million as a 20,000-square-foot complex in Mediterranean style, with palm-shaded grounds that included a screening room and a guest house. Interior decorator Frank Pennino filled the house with Amy's favourite New Mexican artefacts and early American antiques, interspersed with art deco pieces and some serious art: a Modigliani and a Monet, bought by Spielberg with the encouragement of Steve Ross, and somewhat out of phase with his twenty-five original Rockwells. Max (and his father) were given a 'Hobbit Room', inspired by J.R.R. Tolkien's fantasy, with mushroom-shaped windows, a giant-screen TV, a soda fountain and a row of arcade-size video games. Spielberg moved his 'Rosebud' sled from the Amblin office, and hung it next to a coffee table where, under glass, original screenplays of *Citizen Kane*, *Casablanca* and Welles's radio broadcast of *The War of the Worlds* were displayed.

Pressure to crown his rehabilitation with an Oscar had been growing ever since *E.T.*, and in the run-up to the presentation of the awards on 24 March 1986, *The Color Purple* seemed the logical means for doing so. Others connected with the film were rolling their own logs too. Margaret Avery placed an excruciating advertisement in the trade press in the form of a letter to God in *faux naïve* Southern dialect. 'I knows dat I been blessed by Alice Walker, Steven Spielberg and Quincy Jones. Now I is up for one of the nominations fo' Best Supporting Actress alongst with some fine, talented ladies that I is proud to be in the company of.' (Academy voters, connoisseurs of *chutzpah*, nominated her performance, but gave the statuette to Anjelica Huston for *Prizzi's Honor*.) *The*

Color Purple also received ten other nominations, putting it in competition for Best Picture, Actress (Goldberg), Supporting Actress (Avery and Winfrey), Screenplay, Cinematography, Costumes, Art Direction, Original Score, Best Song and Make-up. *Back to the Future* was in for Best Screenplay, Sound and Sound Effects Editing, and *Young Sherlock Holmes* for Visual Effects. For Spielberg himself, however, there was nothing. Most of the major nominations were shared among Sydney Pollack's *Out of Africa*, John Huston's *Prizzi's Honor* and Peter Weir's *Witness*.

Spielberg was on Steve Ross's yacht when he got the news of the nominations. From there, both men authorised a Warner's press statement which, while thanking the Academy for honouring *Color Purple*'s technicians and cast, confessed itself 'shocked and dismayed that the movie's primary force – Steven Spielberg – was not recognised'. That shock and dismay were general. Goldberg slated the 230 directors in that division of the Academy who shunned Spielberg as 'just a small bunch of people with small minds who chose to ignore the obvious'. 'Omission Impossible' snapped the *New York Post*. *Newsweek* quoted an unnamed studio head: 'The only thing I can conclude is that it's personal jealousy and vindictiveness.'

Another anonymous executive countered that Spielberg 'didn't deserve' an Oscar because he was 'an extremely successful motivator of people's emotions, but not a great cinematic director'. Columnist Martin Grove suggested the Academy appoint a panel to root out any 'organised effort to dissuade voters from nominating Spielberg' among its members. Foremost among the suspects in such a conspiracy was John Huston. It was his grizzled face that *Newsweek* featured as a possible beneficiary of Spielberg's exclusion. Elsewhere, Huston growled to columnist Army Archerd that Spielberg 'had had so much success, he can afford to miss a beat'.

Spielberg's supporters on the Directors' Guild chose him as Best Director in their awards, but everyone recognised this as a consolation prize. Pointedly, neither he nor any of the *Color Purple* producers attended the traditional lunch for nominees, and he refused to present the Best Actor Oscar – contending that some of the mud being flung at him might stick to the award. Despite its many nominations, *The Color Purple* was to win not a single statuette. On Oscar night, when Sidney Pollack got up to accept his Best Film award for *Out of Africa*, he paused in his walk to the stage to shake Spielberg's hand. Backstage, the four hundred-strong international press corps which had applauded all the major awards greeted this one with silence.

Privately, Spielberg became convinced by his disappointment with *The Color Purple* that intellectual acceptance would elude him until a critic-proof project overwhelmed his detractors. When he found one in *Schindler's List*, everyone connected with the film denied such low motives, but Thomas Keneally says:

> He told myself and my daughter he delayed making this because he doesn't think he gets a fair run from critics. He said that if anyone else had made *The Color Purple* or *Empire of the Sun* they would have been treated more kindly by the critics. He certainly sees [*Schindler's List*] as a great opportunity, because he delayed in making it for that reason. He feels that if he's treated fairly he could do very well out of this in terms of critical acclaim.

In September 1984, as *Amazing Stories* premiered, *Variety* had announced that Spielberg would film a non-musical *Peter Pan* in London the following March, without Michael Jackson. 'Michael is a very close friend of mine,' said Spielberg, 'but he never was, and never will be, Peter Pan.' The relationship between Spielberg and Jackson would become increasingly distant and troubled, especially after accusations of child molestation against the singer. In 1995 there was an open break when Jackson included praise from Spielberg on the liner notes of his double album *History* that raged against his hounding by the press and greedy litigants. Phrases such as 'Jew me, sue me,' even though Jackson later removed them from the record, offended many old friends like Spielberg, who repudiated his notes in the letter column of the *New York Times*, claiming they'd been meant for a 'Best Of Michael Jackson' album, not this tirade.

Before *Peter Pan* started shooting, however, Spielberg thought better of the project. The heir to David Lean had no business with fairy stories. A planned version of *Tintin*, the Belgian comic strip, also went on hold. As a producer, however, he was more involved than ever in films for children, especially animation. Don Bluth was at work on *The Land Before Time*, humanising dinosaurs even more than Disney had in *Fantasia*. This made him unavailable to work on Amblin's most ambitious project, *Who Framed Roger Rabbit*, a co-production with Disney of Gary K. Wolf's book *Who Censored Roger Rabbit?*. Extending the combination of animation and live action begun in Spielberg's *Amazing Stories* episode *The Mission*, written by Menno Meyjes, in which a wartime bomber is saved when the cartooning waist gunner imagines a set of animated wheels for the crippled plane, *Who Framed Roger Rabbit* was a fantasy detective story set in a world where comic-strip characters – 'Toons' – co-exist with humans. Robert Zemeckis directed chunky English actor Bob Hoskins as the detective investigating the victimisation of a cartoon star and falling in love with his sultry *chanteuse* wife Jessica. Bluth nominated British animator Richard Williams to handle the integration. Spielberg, searching for ways to occupy Amy, had her dub Jessica's songs.

With diminishing ratings, *Amazing Stories* stumbled through its first series, but it was obvious to NBC that the show was a loser, so it negotiated premature termination. It survived into the 1986/7 season, but only twenty-six films were made. Though it failed to catch the popular imagination, the series proved important to Amblin. The press compared it to *The Twilight Zone* and *The Wonderful World of Disney*, but its true role, in terms of Amblin's development, was closer to the documentary short-subject series like *Crime Does not Pay* and *The March of Time* which studios in the thirties used as a training ground for new directors.

Eleven new directors and eighteen new writers were launched by *Amazing Stories*. Spielberg called it 'an incubator to give kids a chance to practically test themselves as film-makers. It was like a USC campus project.' Some of the new directors were ambitious friends of the company looking for a leg up, like Norman Reynolds, the production designer on *Raiders*, and cameraman Robert Stevens, director of photography on a number of episodes. Mick Garris started his directorial career with *Life on Death Row*, a moral fable about capital punishment in which a condemned killer is struck by lightning during a jail-break and becomes a healer. William Dear, a director of commercials who'd attracted Spielberg's attention with a low-budget sf feature, *Timerider*, about a motorcyclist kicked back into the past, was given *Mummy Daddy*, a jokey episode about an expectant actor father, unable to escape from his costume as an Egyptian mummy, racing to see his wife give birth. The series also helped mend fences. Tobe Hooper did an episode, *Miss Stardust*. Kevin Reynolds made a programme. So did Matthew Robbins, and Robert Markowitz, who'd directed Amy in *Voices*. Spielberg also offered one to Francis Coppola's son Gio, who had been his father's assistant on *Captain Eo*, but he was killed in a boating accident before he could do it.

The experience of Phil Joanou, who directed two episodes and was launched on his feature career by them, was typical of the newcomers who benefited. Just out of USC, he'd made a short called *The Last Chance Dance*. Spielberg heard about it, ran a cassette on the Warners executive jet en route to New York, and rang him.

'Can you meet with me next week in Los Angeles when I get back?' he asked. 'Is that convenient?'

'Any time in the rest of my life is convenient,' said an awed Joanou.

When he met Spielberg, Joanou confessed he'd admired *Jaws* so much that he took a still camera into the cinema, photographed every shot, recorded the soundtrack, then reassembled the film on his wall so he could play it over whenever he wished.

'I don't know if you should tell anyone about that,' Spielberg said. 'They'll say, "That's interesting, and did you have a little shrine to Steven in your room? With candles?" '

'Actually, there was only one candle,' Joanou admitted with embarrassment.

Amazing Stories was also the kitchen garden of Amblin. Interesting scripts were extracted and used as the basis for features. *The Mission* indirectly inspired *Who Framed Roger Rabbit*. Brad Bird and Tim Burton's

animated *Family Dog* became the pilot for a later series. Impressed with
Mummy Daddy, Spielberg backed William Dear in *Harry and the Hendersons*, a comedy about a family who encounter Bigfoot in the woods and
bring him home. With Garris, Spielberg also rewrote his own script
Grammy and Gramps and Company, about a group of inner-city oldsters
menaced by developers who are befriended by flying saucers. Extensively
revised by various hands, including its eventual director Matthew Robbins, it became Amblin's feature **batteries not included*. Clint Eastwood's
ghost story *Vanessa in the Garden* rehearsed some of the necrophiliac
preoccupations of *Always*. When his mistress and model Vanessa, played
by Sondra Locke, is killed in a coach crash, Edwardian painter Harvey
Keitel finds that she can return to life in any situation in which he has
painted her. As long as he continues to show her in his canvases, they
can be together. If he paints them together in bed, they can even make
love. After a triumphant gallery show (attended by Leah Spielberg, in an
outrageous hat), Keitel, well supplied with paint and canvases, embarks
with his imaginary muse on a grand tour of Europe.

Some people implied that Amblin was not always especially discriminating about where it found ideas. They cited parallels, for instance,
between Eric Luke's screenplay for *Explorers*, which Joe Dante released
through Paramount in 1985, and the story, credited to Spielberg, of *Fine
Tuning*, which Bob Balaban directed in the first series of *Amazing Stories*.
Brian De Palma wryly acknowledged, 'Secret Cinema* [Paul Bartel's first
film, made in 1977] played on a double bill with my second feature,
Murder à la Mode. I liked it so much, I was on a plane with Steven
Spielberg and I told him the story. He used it in an *Amazing Stories*' –
with, to be fair, Bartel again directing.

Praiseworthy as it was in its insistence on feature-film production
values at a time when technical standards in TV were declining, *Amazing
Stories* never satisfied either the fans, who wanted more sensation, or the
critics, who demanded more weight. Morally and intellectually, the series
hovered in a twilight zone which its model had avoided. Rod Serling,
the heir of Saki and the master of the ironic fantasy John Collier, had
relished ironies, biting off his final summaries with clenched jaw muscles,
like someone crunching a cyanide capsule. Spielberg, however, in *Amaz-*

Spielberg directs David Yip in the opening sequence of *Indiana Jones and the Temple of Doom* (1984).

Spielberg films Yip dying in Harrison Ford's arms.

Spielberg with director Barry Levinson on the set of *Young Sherlock Holmes* (1985).

Spielberg and Joe Dante at the time of *Gremlins*.

Spielberg and George Lucas immortalise themselves in cement in front of Mann's Chinese Theater, 1984.

Robert Zemeckis, Spielberg protégé and director of *Back to the Future* and *Forrest Gump*.

Spielberg and children: (*above*) with Henry Thomas on *E.T.*; (*left*) Raj Singh on *Temple of Doom*; (*below*) Cary Guffey on *Close Encounters*, and (*opposite*) Christian Bale (with John Malkovich) on *Empire of the Sun*.

'Give me a little bit of *Tobacco Road*...' Spielberg directs Whoopi Goldberg in *The Color Purple* (1985).

A dream of parental alienation. Richard Dreyfuss watches Spielberg's sometime girlfriend Holly Hunter with Brad Johnson in *Always* (1989).

Kevork Malikyan tries and fails to recreate a scene from
Alfred Hitchcock with Alison Doody in *Indiana Jones and the
Last Crusade* (1989).

Emily Richard with Christian Bale and Rupert Frazer during
the Shanghai location shooting of *Empire of the Sun* (1987).

Stan Winston's animatronic tyrannosaurus rex contemplates dinner from a can in *Jurassic Park* (1993).

Liam Neeson as Oskar Schindler, suave opportunist and unexpected saviour of his Jewish workers, in *Schindler's List* (1993).

Spielberg, in a White House baseball cap, directs *Schindler's List*.

ing Stories as elsewhere in his work, seldom resolved anything. Some stories in the series were fables, ending with a magic ring or phantom train carrying its cargo of disaster into someone else's life. Others, like *Life on Death Row*, in which jailers execute killer Patrick Swayze, only to see him revived by his newly-acquired ability to heal, posed Talmudically unsolvable problems, the story bequeathing the dilemma to another group of decision-makers, like an endless game of Pass the Parcel.

Empire of the Sun was a shrewd choice for Spielberg's next film. It straddled the worlds of science fiction and popular culture which he knew well, but trespassed also on the complexities of adolescence. It would, he told the *New York Times*, be 'a movie with grown-up themes and values, although spoken through a voice that hadn't changed through puberty yet'. The 'voice' he referred to was meant to be that of the young hero, Ballard's alter ego Jim Graham, but he might have been talking about himself.

Ballard, who was always careful to describe his book as a novel rather than autobiography, had re-ordered the events of his childhood for dramatic effect. The real Ballard was eleven when he was interned by the Japanese after Pearl Harbor with his parents, but in the book he's separated from them, and survives in the camp on his wits. He's taken under the wing of Basie, American head of a black-market gang, and doesn't meet his mother and father again until the end of the story, by which time his affection for the Americans and admiration for the Japanese and their chivalric codes has transformed his character.

Tom Stoppard wasn't surprised to find Harold Becker, the film's original director for whom he'd written his screenplay, suddenly out of the picture, and the project now with Spielberg. Trying to set up a film of his own play *Rosencrantz and Guildenstern are Dead* with *Rocky* producers Robert Chartoff and Irving Winkler, and watching Terry Gilliam floating his script for the sour futuristic fable *Brazil*, had educated him in the twists and turns of the movie business. He even doubted *Empire* would reach the screen at all, given that Warners had set Becker and Shapiro the task of budgeting the film under $25 million.

On their visit to Shanghai, Stoppard and Becker had found that while the mansions once occupied by Ballard and his parents still stood, fourteen or fifteen families now lived in each house. Since the architectural style was identical with that of English towns like Sunningdale, however, these scenes could easily be shot in or near London. The internment camp could also be recreated, in Spain. But there was no substitute for the Bund, Shanghai's pre-war business district, still largely intact. As Ballard says:

> The architecture of the camp was not an integral part of the experience of the people who lived in the camp, whereas the architecture of Shanghai, these great western banks, Midland Bank Classical, rolling down the Bund for two miles, absolutely expressed the peculiar nature of this city, the greatest city in China, created not by Chinese but by the British, the Americans and the French, a city created by my father and people of his generation.
>
> Shanghai is an important presence in the novel. Jim is forever hovering between his dreams of East and West; he's infatuated with the Japanese, but at the same time he can see the great apartment towers of the French Concession. He's obsessed with American cars which fill the streets of Shanghai and with the American style of life. The Chinese form a sort of ghostly background, as they did in my youth. I think it had to be established that the Shanghai created by the Americans and Europeans was a Western city, not a Chinese city with pagodas and so forth.

Norman Reynolds, once again production designer, was sent on another world trip, checking out possible alternatives to Shanghai like Buenos Aires, Liverpool, Vienna, Stockholm, Lisbon and Vienna. He found nothing sufficiently convincing, so Amblin knuckled down to horse-trading with the Chinese government. After the debacle of trying to set up a China shoot for *Indiana Jones and the Temple of Doom*, Universal fully expected years of negotiation, but by mid-1986 Amblin had won permission to shoot for twenty-one days in the spring of 1987. The China Film Co-Production Corporation and the Shanghai Film Studios would guarantee ten thousand extras, and police to keep them under control; everything else would have to be imported.

Spielberg and Amy were so plainly besotted with their young son that more footloose friends complained they seldom talked about anything else. 'Max is the centre of our world,' Amy said. 'Every night we have dinner with him and the whole evening is about whether we're going to watch a film with him, and what time the bath will be and who is going to tell the story.' The classic doting father, Spielberg changed nappies, played games, bought gifts, even took his boy to the office. When Don Bluth delivered *An American Tail*, Spielberg arranged for Max, then eighteen months old, to host the premiere. A cinema marquee in *Back to the Future* 2 featured *Jaws* 19, directed by Max Spielberg.

In December 1986, as a birthday gift to Spielberg, Amy promised to take six months off and become what she called, without much enthusiasm, 'a location wife and mother'. It was an easy promise to make. Even after *Yentl*, nobody was in a hurry to offer her interesting roles. She complained, 'I started my career as the daughter of Jules Irving. I don't want to finish it as the wife of Spielberg or the mother of Max.' Apart from a role in the TV film *Anastasia* and another beside her mother and stepfather in a version of *Rumplestiltskin* written by her brother David – Spielberg vetoed Max's appearance in the film – she'd had few offers, and when one did come, like the chance to recreate her Broadway role of Mozart's wife Constanze in Milos Forman's film of *Amadeus*, she had to turn it down because it would mean six months in Prague.

The tensions always implicit in their relationship began to surface again. In particular Amy resented Spielberg's pained reaction when she flirted with other men. Pleased with her ability to seduce, she enjoyed exercising her sexual appeal on their friends and guests, to Spielberg's embarrassment and anger. Matthew Robbins recalls:

It was no fun to go over there, because there was an electric tension in the air. It was competitive as to whose dining table this is, whose career we're gonna talk about, or whether he even approved of what she was interested in – her friends and her actor life. He really was uncomfortable. The child in Spielberg believed so thoroughly in the possibility of perfect marriage, the institution of marriage, the Norman Rockwell turkey on the table, everyone's head bowed in prayer – all this stuff. And Amy was sort of a glittering prize, smart as hell, gifted, and beautiful, but definitely edgy and provocative and competitive. She would not provide him any ease. There was nothing to go home to that was cosy.

After Christmas, Frank Marshall and Kathleen Kennedy, now married, flew with Spielberg to London and checked into the St James's Club. Spielberg still hadn't met Ballard, but the author dined with Kennedy and Marshall. 'I liked them very much,' he said. 'I felt the book was in the best possible hands.' Initially he'd been horrified to hear that Stoppard was writing the screenplay. 'It seemed to me like putting Oscar Wilde to work writing the screenplay of *Moby-Dick*. In fact I was completely wrong.'

For his part, Stoppard was even less sure of his role in this now vastly-expanded project, and in particular of his ability to work with Spielberg. Yet after some preliminary sparring the *echt*-American Spielberg and the brilliant, haughty Czech émigré, with his archetypally English love of cricket, London and its intellectual life, and his passion for the intricacies of his adopted language, became friends, to the extent that Spielberg asked Stoppard to act as Amblin's informal script editor. For a year after *Empire of the Sun*, the playwright read and commented on every project considered by the company. He also wrote yet another *Peter Pan* screenplay, which was never produced. Stoppard taught Spielberg something about precision in language; from Spielberg, the playwright gained a sense of narrative and the seductive impact of romance. 'I'm quite unsentimental,' says Stoppard of his collaboration with Spielberg on *Empire*, 'but Steven knows how to let the emotions out. My ending was cool. His was warm.'

Stoppard's script, with a few Menno Meyjes additions, radically redefined *Empire of the Sun*. Ballard's Shanghai was a city of the imagination. It belonged with the ruined futures of his novels, a surrealist world of deserted office buildings, drained swimming pools filled with debris and empty streets prowled by predatory warlords. For Spielberg, however, Shanghai became David Lean's London, and the story a modern retelling of *Oliver Twist*, with Jim as the abandoned waif and Basie as Fagin, half surrogate father, half employer, who both educates and corrupts him. Scavenging among the abandoned mansions from his headquarters in a rusting freighter on which he once served as steward, and running his network of toadies from behind a giant circular window that looks out on the camp as if on the entire world, Basie is like a deity to Jim: *Life* magazine and Norman Rockwell made flesh. Stoppard says:

> Steven's principal interest was in one axis in the book. In the book, Jim is really the centre of a wheel with a number of spokes, principally towards the English doctor. But Steven was really fascinated with the relationship between Jim and Basie. In Steven's mind it was connected with other stories of boys coming under the formative influence of experienced men: *Captains Courageous*, for instance, which he often mentioned.

In particular, Spielberg responded to Jim's chivalric vision of the war. To Jim, technology, especially that of aircraft, embodies a mystical power. The Japanese and American pilots are technocratic knights, sanctified by their machines. He reaches up to the nose of a Zero like a supplicant touching some holy statue, and greets the arrival of Mustangs over the camp with a delirious 'P-51! Cadillac of the skies!' When the atomic bombs explode over Hiroshima and Nagasaki, he sees the sky light up and is seized with a transcendent vision: God in the Machine.

Spielberg again cast in London. One of his first choices was Emily Richard, the actress whom Amy had met backstage at *Amadeus* and to whom she'd confided her ambitions to have children. Richard was six months pregnant, but so anxious to play Jim's mother that she kept her raincoat on for the interview and sat with a large handbag in her lap.

Nigel Havers, who had played one of the British athletes in *Chariots of Fire*, was the idealistic Dr Ransome, and Miranda Richardson the long-suffering Mrs Vincent who lets Jim share her and her husband's cramped quarters. Comic Leslie Phillips had a rare serious role as Maxted, a wealthy pre-war friend of his parents whom Jim meets again in the camp. The part of Basie went to John Malkovich. Jim Graham (Ballard's own first names) was an unknown Londoner, Christian Bale, and almost a lookalike for Anthony Wager, the young Pip of David Lean's *Great Expectations*. In the tradition of child performers, Bale was no plaster saint, but Ballard for one approved. 'He was like the character of Jim – a not-very-nice little boy.'

To process the children considered for Jim, and to read opposite them, Marshall hired a young Irish actor, commandingly tall, with a rumbling baritone voice and a phenomenal sexual aura, named Liam Neeson. He'd been Gawain in John Boorman's 1981 *Excalibur*, and had played in *The Bounty*, but at the time he was living with the actress Helen Mirren and working as a house-painter. At the end of the sessions, Spielberg anointed him with the sign that a performer had been noticed. He told him, 'We're going to do something special some day.'

After the near-scandal of the previous year, the governors of the Academy of Motion Picture Arts and Sciences, if not all its members, were ready to recognise Spielberg. The fact that he hadn't released a film in 1986 was no barrier, since some of the honours within its gift required no endorsement from the membership. Bypassing the Old Hollywood bloc among the directors who detested Spielberg, the Academy offered him the Irving Thalberg Award, presented since 1937 for 'a consistently high level of production achievement'. As an admirer of Thalberg, Spielberg accepted eagerly, not only as a belated acknowledgement of his standing but as a means of wiping away the last stains of *Twilight Zone*.

His appearance at the podium on 30 March 1987 was a public-relations coup. Its apparent spontaneity disguised extensive behind-the-scenes management. Richard Dreyfuss's introduction listed every film in Spielberg's professional career – except *The Twilight Zone*. (Landis, still awaiting trial for manslaughter, was in the audience, but he and Spielberg didn't speak.) Marilyn and Alan Bergman, Oscar-winning composers of 'Windmills of my Mind' and 'The Way We Were', helped Spielberg write the speech which he hoped would rehabilitate him in the eyes of the Academy. While he spoke, the bust of Thalberg kept toppling, so he rested his hand on it – as if fearing, some people joked, that the Academy would change its mind at the last moment and take it back.

He began by praising veterans like Cecil B. DeMille, William Wyler, Ignmar Bergman, Federico Fellini and Robert Wise, whom he labelled as his 'heroes'. The calculated gesture was meant to reassure Old Hollywood that he was one of them, not just an engineer of diversions for mindless teenagers. He went on:

> Most of my life has been spent in the dark. Movies have been the literature of my life. The literature of Irving Thalberg's generation was books and plays. They read the great words of great minds. And I think in our romance with technology and our excitement at exploring all the possibilities of film and video, I think we've partially lost something that we now have to reclaim. I think it's time to renew our romance with the word.

Leaving this promissory note to be redeemed later, he left immediately for Shanghai.

The location shoot on *Empire of the Sun* was a logistical *tour de force*.

Boeing 747s were chartered to fly lights and camera equipment, authentic pre-war American cars, Japanese tanks, plus the usual canned and preserved food. The Chinese government had outlawed rickshaws, so fifty of them had to be built and men trained to pull them. Nobody talked any longer about $25 million ceilings, and the film would eventually cost $35 million.

China daunted and exhilarated the crew, and Spielberg. Neither Frank Capra nor David Lean had never commanded such a mob of extras, nor addressed so gigantic a canvas. Faithful to Spielberg's Dickensian vision, Allen Daviau shot Shanghai like Limehouse, the Chinese quarter of nineteenth-century London. It's a city of evening windows glowing gold, bare trees, mansions looming from the fog. The misty river littered with the rusting hulls of freighters belongs in the opening of *Bleak House*. Determined to rival Lean, Spielberg shot a number of *Zhivago*-like set-ups copied from contemporary photographs: corpses of Chinese defenders littering rooftops above the main streets, beaming platoons of Japanese posing in the midst of chaos.

Even with strict crowd control, the mobs sometimes got out of hand. Shooting the scene during which Jim is separated from his parents in the panic after Japanese warships bombard the city and the army marches in, Emily Richard, still weak after the birth of her child a few weeks before, was knocked sprawling. In an instant, everyone froze, and a team of assistants swooped to pick her up and carry her to safety. Spielberg hurried to her side. Sensing her emotional fragility, he sat down beside her and said, 'Let's talk about our babies.'

From his wallet he took photographs of Max, and for ten minutes they chatted about children. Over his shoulder, Richard could see the first assistant director staring at the silent crowds of extras and, for Spielberg's benefit, pointing significantly at his watch. They didn't start shooting again, however, until she'd recovered.

The Chinese extras were docile, and painfully honest. Emily Richard was as impressed as anyone to find that, though all were issued with clothing and props, not one item was stolen during the entire shoot. By contrast, the cast and crew picked up so many souvenirs that their chartered 747 couldn't get off the ground when it tried to return to Europe. Some members of the crew had silk carpets and entire sets of porcelain. Richard herself nursed a large urn. A second plane had to be chartered for the loot, and the flight of the first to London took thirty hours, with frequent stops for refuelling.

In April 1987, production moved to Spain, where the camp had been built near Jerez. This was hallowed ground for anyone who loved cinema, since half the epics and westerns of the previous two decades had been shot here. One could top a hill over which Charlton Heston had strode in *El Cid* and scuff up left-over bullet casings from *Lawrence of Arabia*. Rainstorms delayed construction for five weeks, so Spielberg returned to the US, where the *Twilight Zone* case finally came to trial in May. While there was wide and sensational coverage in the papers, the outcome was never in doubt. Landis had consulted ace defence lawyer Alan Dershowitz, and finally retained James Neal, a Watergate prosecutor who'd successfully defended the Ford Motor Company against charges of criminal manslaughter. In a time-honoured Hollywood strategy, Neal's team overwhelmed the jury with technical evidence. Debris from the explosion could have disabled the helicopter, it was suggested, or its tail rotor may have delaminated in the heat. In either case, Neal argued, it was hardly negligence not to foresee a million-to-one chance. On 29 May 1987, Landis and the other defendants were acquitted.

The fact that Spielberg was never called upon to testify disturbed many in Hollywood, even among his friends. Did the ability to create a convincing artificial world mean that one was free then to retreat into it, absolved of all responsibility? Such a cavalier attitude to crime by the Hollywood hierarchy was to backfire on them in the nineties, when many showbusiness personalities were targeted by blackmailers, tabloid journalists and unscrupulous prosecutors, challenged by their apparent invulnerability.

Steve Ross was under attack at Warner yet again, this time over a new ten-year contract which would make him one of the highest-paid corporate officers in the world. His enemies on the board decided to make the annual general meeting of Warner Communications Industries the occasion of a proxy fight with which they hoped to oust him or at least curtail his spending.

The relationship between Ross and Spielberg had blossomed into a deep emotional attachment. Ross lavished his charm on Spielberg, inviting him and Amy on luxurious weekends, and even offering Leah a trip in Warner's executive jet, the interior of which he had redecorated, in honour of her restaurant, with Milky Way candy-bar wrappers. A *Wall Street Journal* report on Spielberg included an account of him signing off

from a conversation with Ross, ''Bye, I love you.' Ross, who told friends
he regarded the allegiance of showbiz personalities like Spielberg, Clint
Eastwood, Paul Simon and Barbra Streisand as his 'armour', shrewdly
included a copy of the article in a dossier he circulated to shareholders
in support of his salary demands. 'If Steven Spielberg is your friend,'
said Ross, 'you count yourself blessed.'

Spielberg, unexpectedly dapper in a white suit, appeared at the AGM
to make a pitch for Ross. 'I am here because I felt compelled that the
shareholders fully appreciate the driving force behind the company's
storybook success,' he told them. Revealing that he had resolved to work
for only two companies, MCA and WCI, he promised, 'as long as Steve
Ross remains skipper of this battlewagon, I will never leave my station.'
After this, he read a similarly enthusiastic letter from Clint Eastwood.
He concluded, 'There are thousands of creative people in my home town
who second everything that Clint and I have just said. We really do love
Steve Ross. We think Steve Ross is WCI.'

Ross retained control. In December 1987, he would ask the Warners
board to authorise granting 200,000 options on Warners stock to Spielberg and 100,000 each to Streisand and Eastwood. Enemies charged he
was paying off his showbusiness friends for their support, but doing so
with company funds. David Geffen was particularly annoyed at this sign
that Spielberg had supplanted him in Ross's affection.

Back in Britain, Spielberg and J.G. Ballard met at last. 'He was nothing
like the Spielberg I'd been led to believe,' says the writer. 'He was being
presented as a sort of suburban sentimentalist, and the man I met was
nothing like that. The man I met was adult, had a hard, mature mind,
was very thoughtful. As far as *Empire of the Sun* was concerned, he cut
no corners. He certainly wasn't trying to sentimentalise the book; quite
the opposite.'

Spielberg tried to involve Ballard in the production. He asked him to
speak the brief resumé which opens the film, sketching in the historical
background. Ballard recorded it, but another voice was used. Instead he
has a fleeting appearance as a guest at the fancy-dress party in Jim's

home. Initially, Spielberg offered him a costume of Roman armour, a subtle variation on the film's chivalric theme, but finding that it was made of plastic, Ballard chose an outfit as John Bull.

After Spielberg's assurance during the filming of *Temple of Doom* that they would work together again, David Yip had been confident of a role in *Empire*. When no call came, he asked his agent to check with Amblin. The agent rang back with the puzzling information that they were only using 'real Chinese' on the film. Yip, 100 per cent Chinese, protested, but the casting director insisted that, since they were shooting in China, they would hire only locals.

Convinced he had no hope of a job, Yip was surprised to be called some weeks later and told to fly immediately to Spain.

> They met me at the airport and told me they were going straight to make-up, because Steven wanted to say hello and look me over. I remember arriving on the location. There were thousands of people, and I don't see how he could have seen me come, but he turned around and said, 'Oh, hi, David,' and again you feel like a million dollars. It's an amazing gift he has. You feel instantly at home.

It was only when the costume department began fitting him that he found he was playing the man known only as The Eurasian, an opportunist who, in return for helping interrogate downed American aircrews, is rewarded with looted furniture, cars and valuables, stored in a stadium. Yip played his scenes with tongue in cheek, amused that, as one of the few Chinese among thousands of Spaniards, he alone was cast as someone of mixed blood. Perhaps his lack of conviction showed, since his entire role remained on the cutting-room floor.

Undeterred by Spielberg's minimum fee of $1 million to produce a film, plus 10 per cent of its gross income, Hollywood offered him most of its prestigious projects during the late eighties, whether appropriate to his talents or not. The flood didn't stop just because he was on location in Spain finishing *Empire of the Sun*. Peter Guber sent him Tom Wolfe's sprawling satire of the New York financial world, *The Bonfire of the Vanities*. Spielberg, weary of Significance, passed on it, and it went to Brian De Palma, arguably no less unsuitable as a director.

For almost two years, Dustin Hoffman had been fiddling with a film about an *idiot savant* and his hip brother, based on an original script by Barry Morrow. Originally visualised as two middle-aged men, the roles had been recast, at the suggestion of Hoffman's and Spielberg's agent Mike Ovitz, with Hoffman and Tom Cruise now playing the brothers. While Ron Bass rewrote Morrow's script, Martin Brest (*Beverly Hills Cop*) was signed to direct. By this time, however, Ovitz was having second thoughts. Brest resigned, and the script passed to Richard Price (*The Color of Money*) and finally Michael Bortman (*The Good Mother*). Ovitz asked Spielberg if he was interested in directing the film, now called *Rainman*. Although Spielberg acknowledged Hoffman as 'an icon' with whom he was 'hungry to work', he remained as leery of stars as ever, especially those with Hoffman's famous indecisiveness. He met Bortman but, after reading all the scripts, decided he preferred Morrow's original. Leaving Hoffman to develop a screenplay with his long-time collaborator Murray Schisgal, Spielberg went back to Spain. The script still wasn't finished when he returned, and as the deadline for the start of *Indiana Jones and the Last Crusade* approached, he dropped the project, passing his notes to eventual director Barry Levinson.

Amy joined Spielberg in Spain, but there was a nervous edge to her visits. With her promised six months' sabbatical at an end, she was chafing to work again. 'I tended to Max and lost out on roles to other flavours of the month,' she complained later, 'and I was going crazy.' Director Joan Micklin Silver visited her in Spain with the script of *Crossing Delancey*, about an upwardly mobile New York Jewish girl and her romance, arranged through a marriage broker, with a pickle merchant from her old neighbourhood. Otherwise offers were thin, especially from Broadway, where her real ambitions lay.

Amy did the Silver film, but with ill grace. '[I had] a chip on my shoulder,' she acknowledged. 'I had a baby and lost my place in line.' While she was shooting the film, she and Spielberg spent more time in the Hamptons than in Los Angeles. Spielberg was ill-at-ease, and uncomfortable with some of the new people lured to the house by Ross and Amy. Willem de Kooning, though already in the first stage of Alzheimer's Disease, was still working, and Amy and Spielberg, along with people like Richard Dreyfuss, whose wife Jeramie – a nurse whom he'd met in his detox clinic – was now Amy's close friend, met him and his wife Elaine at Ross's home. Spielberg neither liked nor understood de Kooning's work; the Hamptons house, furnished with Arts and Crafts pieces in oak, was mainly hung with folk art. De Kooning knew no more about movies. Dreyfuss once tried to explain the pressures of film-making, comparing it to painting on a railway line with a train approaching.

'Why would you want to make films on a railway line?' de Kooning asked.

Elaine's biographer Lee Hall described their reaction to a Ross party at which Spielberg was also a guest.

> Everything was quiet, conversation hushed, no arguments, and not much talk. At the end of the meal, they all went into a screening room and looked at a movie. Elaine was just amazed. She didn't know that people lived like that. They were so rich, they had everything, they didn't talk. This, to Elaine, was the strangest thing in the world. And, I think, not her idea of very much fun.

Amy loved the Hamptons, and would have been delighted to spend all her time there. Cosseting the egos of actors at Hollywood dinner parties and hiding her intellectual superiority wasn't her style. 'I felt like a politician's wife,' she said. 'There were certain things "expected of" me that definitely weren't me. One of my problems is that I'm very honest and direct. You pay a price for that. But then I behaved myself and I paid a price too.' She was already looking for a way out.

Empire of the Sun, 152 minutes long, opened in December 1987. Stoppard and Ballard met for the first time at the Los Angeles premiere when they were seated one in front of the other.

'Stoppard turned round,' says Ballard, 'and was shocked to find me there.'

'Perhaps I should find another seat,' Stoppard suggested diplomatically, but Ballard told him he was more than happy with his adaptation.

This was more than could be said for the public and the press. Many reviews compared the film unfavourably with *Hope and Glory*, John Boorman's memoir of a British childhood in the Blitz that had an authenticity they felt *Empire of the Sun* lacked. 'What surprised me,' says J.G. Ballard, 'and what I became aware of when I did a book tour around America before the film opened, and when I went to the premiere, was the degree of hostility of the American press towards Spielberg . . . Most of them seemed to have an almost knee-jerk negative reaction towards him. I remember someone saying, "Why did you allow him to film your book?" '

Spielberg had hoped that his speech when accepting the Thalberg Award would have won him acceptance from Old Hollywood and from the critics, but it became clear during the release of *Empire of the Sun* that both viewed him as scornfully as ever. 'I think Hollywood will forgive me once I'm fifty-five,' Spielberg told Adrian Turner morosely at the National Film Theatre, London, in 1978. 'I'm not sure what they'll forgive me for, but when I'm fifty-five they'll forgive me.' In the hope of salvaging something from the disaster of his attempt at reconciliation, he backtracked on his pious statements in his acceptance speech for the Irving Thalberg. 'Great words of great minds' weren't his sole interest, he insisted. Plain speaking from decent folks could be equally profound. Any comments to the Academy also needed to be seen, he said, less as personal promises than exhortations to Hollywood in general. 'I was talking about the future of the industry, and I was also talking to myself. I was sort of saying to myself, "You know, it's time to stop balls from rolling, and spaceships from landing, and the light shows. It's time to deal with what people say to each other when they have an emotional need to communicate." '

*   *   *

Few films offer so telling a demonstration of Spielberg's ability, indeed need, to 'Spielberg' a project as *Empire of the Sun*. Despite the contributions of Stoppard and Ballard, and its many tributes to David Lean, the film is permeated with Spielberg's sensibility. From the moment we meet Jim in the Gothic-style Anglican cathedral in Shanghai, singing, in an angelic treble, the hymn 'Suo Gan', its words Chinese but its music four-square English home counties, to the finale of the river carrying away the debris of the war as it has swept away coffins in the opening scenes, sentimentality and broadness of character defeat and betray the book's rot, grit and sleaze. Ballard meant Shanghai to be seen as a 'terrible city', frightening but sexy, and even edible, when a starving Jim imagines some distant buildings as confections spun from sugar. Spielberg turns it into a mildly alarming suburb, with a consoling Norman Rockwell on the wall.

'I was a bit surprised,' Spielberg said unemotionally of the negative reaction. 'It turned off a lot of people in America.' Elsewhere he complained, 'There are certain people in America who want to keep me young; that makes them feel safe.' As instant cultural analysis, this left something to be desired. Whatever Spielberg's subject matter, it would always 'film young', just as Norman Rockwell, if he had ever addressed a crucifixion, would have done so in well-contoured pastels. Style is more than a suit of clothes: it embodies decades of experience. Spielberg's influences run through *Empire* as the name 'Brighton' runs through a stick of rock. Break it anywhere, and there's the mark of the comic book in the emphatic low-angle splash of a foot into a puddle, or the influence of Hollywood classics in a crane shot over a crowd of refugees that recalls both *Gone With the Wind* and *Lawrence of Arabia*. To have become a different film-maker, Spielberg would have needed to go back to his childhood and not seen *The Greatest Show on Earth*, *Captains Courageous*, *Bambi*.

16

Indiana Jones and the
Last Crusade

... I said, 'I am not worthy of the quest,'
But even while I drank the brook, and ate
The goodly apples, all these things at once
Fell into dust, and I was left alone,
And thirsting, in a land of sand and thorns.

Alfred, Lord Tennyson, 'The Holy Grail', from *Idylls of the King*

SPIELBERG SOUGHT consolation from his troubles in fantasy. George Lucas felt the time was right for another Indiana Jones movie, as did Paramount, who had grossed $109 million on *Temple of Doom*. In the late summer of 1988, Lucas hired Jeffrey Boam, who had done a good job of Joe Dante's comedy *Innerspace* but a better one of adapting Stephen King's *The Dead Zone* for David Cronenberg in 1983, to pen the next episode in the Jones saga, basing the script on a story Lucas had written with Menno Meyjes. After the Jewish *Raiders* and a pagan *Temple of Doom*, *Indiana Jones and the Last Crusade* would have a Christian theme, nothing less than Indy's discovery of the Holy Grail, the cup used at the Last Supper and traditionally brought to Britain by Joseph of Arimathea after it caught Christ's blood on the cross. There it inspired King Arthur and the Knights of the Round Table.

Though he's battling his old enemies from *Raiders*, the Nazis, Indy is searching for himself in the new film, which reunites him with Sallah, the ebullient Egyptian played by John Rhys-Davies in *Raiders*, and Marcus Brody, Indy's scholarly colleague, again played by Denholm Elliott. In the past, Indy had hunted treasures like some demented tourist collecting souvenirs. With this film, Spielberg asked, 'Why does he bother?' Why search for lost temples and golden idols, then come home to a poky office cluttered with trophies, and students caterwauling outside the door? The answer comes from Jones Sr. He's devoted his life to looking for an artefact too, but it's the Holy Grail. *The Last Crusade* modifies the legend to make the Grail a source of eternal life. Anyone who drinks from it will never die. Here at last is a prize worth fighting for. To Spielberg, the film was an opportunity to reveal his unabashed enthusiasm for medieval chivalry, and the Grail legend in particular. The search for the Grail, says Lawrence Kasdan, 'is hugely powerful to Steven, and he sees most of his movies that way'.

At the beginning of the story, Jones Sr has disappeared after mailing Indy his diary containing a vital clue to the tombs of three crusaders who were the last to see the cup. After being sidetracked by the evil Donovan and a sexy Nazi spy, Elsa Schneider, Indy and Brody track the Grail to Venice, find a clue to its whereabouts in rat-infested sewers under an ancient library, push on to Germany, where Indy literally runs into Hitler, and race across Asia Minor, pursued by both Nazis and the Brotherhood of the Cruciform Sword, a group of zealots in red fezzes sworn to guard the Grail and its sanctuary. All of them end up at Petra in Jordan, where they find the Grail, guarded by a crusader. In the cataclysmic finale, Donovan shoots Jones Sr, who can only be saved if Indy brings him water in the Grail. He braves three booby traps to reach the sanctuary, and returns to heal his father. Donovan, however, chooses the wrong Grail for his drink, and instead of winning eternal life, ages a century in half a minute. The mountain caves in as the heroes escape, engulfing Elsa, the last knight and the Grail, but leaving Brody, the Joneses and Sallah to ride into the sunset.

Harrison Ford, smarting from his failure in Peter Weir's adaptation of Paul Theroux's novel *The Mosquito Coast*, a serious role which he'd hoped would release him permanently from action films, was willing to do another in the series to restore his box-office standing. To play his father, Lucas suggested someone venerable and scholarly: John Houseman, perhaps. Spielberg, however, preferred Sean Connery, whose stock had been rising ever since he began alternating James Bond films with character parts. Lucas pointed out that Connery was only twelve years older than Ford. Boam tipped the scales by suggesting that a virtue be made of Connery's potent image by characterising father and son as competitors. For instance, why not have them both share the bed of the sensual Elsa?

Though initially both Lucas and Spielberg fought shy of a plot twist so antithetical to conventional morality, both must have been secretly intrigued by it. The *Star Wars* films hinged on a combative relationship between Luke Skywalker and his father, a rivalry which Lucas's guru Joseph Campbell regarded as fundamental to any myth. As for Spielberg, son and father screwing the same woman evoked the Oedipal conflicts in his own life. Revealingly, he spoke of *Indiana Jones and the Last Crusade* as 'a movie I could stand naked on top of'. Connery liked the idea too. Keen to escape from a commitment to play a cameo in Terry Gilliam's version of *The Adventures of Baron Munchausen*, a project that had been bogged down for months with money problems, he provisionally accepted the role, his final approval dependent on the script.

Again casting by proxy from Los Angeles, Spielberg had screen tests made of prospective performers in London. Kevork Malikyan, who had impressed him in *Midnight Express* (and might have played Sallah in *Raiders* had he not arrived an hour late for his interview with Spielberg because of a traffic jam), was chosen for Kazim, leader of the Cruciform Sword zealots. Comic Alexei Sayle played a pasha with a taste for vintage automobiles. Robert Watts, executive producer on the earlier Indy films, suggested his London next-door neighbour, the Royal Shakespeare Company's Julian Glover, for the role of the Nazi finally played by Michael Byrne. Instead, Spielberg decided Glover had the right genial menace for Donovan, American Nazi-sympathiser and chief villain.

From his house in Spain, Sean Connery complained violently about the long delay in getting a script. Lucas stalled. He particularly wanted the film to open with an elaborate flashback to Indy's childhood in Utah in 1912. Young Indiana is a Boy Scout on a trip to Monument Valley who discovers a gang unearthing the legendary Cross of Coronado. Leading them is a man whose felt hat and leather jacket prefigure the later Indy; in fact he gives young Indy his greasy fedora. Cannily, Lucas and Spielberg hired River Phoenix, Hollywood's hottest young actor, who'd already won praise for his role opposite Harrison Ford in *Mosquito Coast*, to play young Indy. His casting, which would guarantee the teen audience who had begun to think of Ford as dangerously superannuated, was the production's best-kept secret. The script never even referred to the character by name; he was simply 'Boy On Train'. Once word leaked, Lucasfilm circulated a fallback rumour that Phoenix played Indy's younger brother. To allay Ford's fears that Phoenix might steal the movie, as he had almost done on *The Mosquito Coast*, the young actor was warned never to imitate Ford's mannerisms on screen, nor to suggest he had any interest in taking over the Indy role. Such was the success of the character, however, that Lucasfilm launched a TV series about his adventures.

Complex rewriting was needed to keep Jones Sr out of the story until young Indy was done and the mature Indy had established his hold on the audience. Boam solved this by inserting, in effect, a *second* opening sequence in which Indy as an adult retrieves the Cross of Coronado stolen from him as a boy. It's only then that we hear Jones Sr has disappeared, setting Indy the job of finding him, a prisoner of the Nazis, who covet his research into the hiding place of the Grail.

Connery, once he got the script, was furious about the erosion of his part. With time on his hands to consider the role, he'd imagined Jones Sr as a modern version of Sir Richard Burton, the swashbuckling Victorian explorer and sensualist who explored the sources of the Nile, secretly visited the Muslim holy city of Mecca and translated the *Arabian Nights* in all its rampant horniness. Tom Stoppard was again called in to beef up the character. Uncredited, he wrote the scenes in which Indy taxes his father with having abandoned him as a boy to go off on his own adventures. Their competition for Elsa Schneider was also emphasised, though Connery, not Stoppard, is credited with the revelatory exchange between father and son:

INDY: How did you know she was a Nazi?
JONES SR: She talks in her sleep.

Elsa was played by queenly blonde Irish unknown, Alison Doody. 'I can't play opposite someone called *Doody*,' an anguished Ford muttered to Julian Glover. 'You know what that *means*?' Ms Doody's career has not flourished.

With the additions to Connery's character, a part that had begun at page seventy of the script inched forward to page fifty, at the cost of roles like that of Kazim, so severely scaled down that many people were puzzled about what he and his companions were doing in the film.

Even though Spielberg's production plans were temporarily in abeyance while he prepared *Crusade*, Amblin continued to tick over. Warren Beatty and screenwriter William Goldman were developing a film about Howard Hughes. *Back to the Future* 2 and 3 were in production back-to-back under Zemeckis. Spielberg had also endorsed Gary David Goldberg's *Dad*, a lachrymose story from William Wharton's novel about a son trying to repair his relationship with his father after the latter's heart attack. Most people credited his support of this dim little drama to a residual guilt about Arnold Spielberg, now semi-retired and living in northern California. He earned a living producing sales videos, which he sent to Spielberg for his opinion on casting, though the two were only marginally closer than they had been during Spielberg's adolescence.

Spielberg's sister Anne had also gone into movies, working with Penny Marshall on films like *Big*, which she co-wrote with Gary Ross and co-produced. Spielberg had briefly been interested in directing this story of a boy who longs so passionately to escape childhood that he's transformed overnight into an adult, and a genius at designing toys. 'I flirted for a couple of months with Harrison Ford to play the part that Tom Hanks played,' he said, 'but . . . I felt [my sister] had been standing in my shadow long enough . . . This was Annie's chance to be successful – this was her coming-out party.'

Big was a major hit, but Annie Spielberg hasn't found her family connection of much value. 'He's a very tough bargainer,' she said of her brother, who accepted a couple of her projects for development. 'He's a hard man to deal with on those things. There are times I'd be tempted to take things other places, where I know that I'd get a better deal.'

It wasn't so much that Spielberg wasn't interested in his sister's films: he was feeling tired of producing in general. Strategically, his plans for Amblin as an independent studio hadn't worked out. He'd discovered the painful truth, already learned by Coppola but unnoticed by him in the first satisfaction of making films with other people's money: the major studios still ran Hollywood. They alone had the channels for promotion and distribution, and, via the multinationals which now owned them, the lines of credit with banks. He could only make films if one of these giants agreed. In retrospect, the late eighties and early nineties would be known as 'the decade when Hollywood went corporate.' Not even Spielberg's clout, nor a personal fortune estimated by *Business Week* magazine in May 1989 as being in excess of $250 million, bought him any more than a transient power.

Most people in the film business anticipated with satisfaction what they thought of as the end of New Hollywood, which now looked markedly middle-aged. Lucas had followed Disney, aiming each new *Star Wars* film at the same teenage audience, and godfathering TV series and low-budget children's features based on its canon. Coppola, who had tried to grow up and grow old with his audience, was a spent force, hiring out to any studio that paid his salary.

Spielberg's fall was regarded as imminent, indeed overdue. His films, with the exception of *Raiders* and *E.T.*, had not achieved classic status. Audiences weren't queuing to see reissues of *Jaws* or *Close Encounters* as they did for Disney's films, or Kubrick's, or even for Coppola's *Godfather* series, which had been reissued on TV with some of the cut scenes restored, to even greater acclaim. Not even a disastrous *Godfather* 3 dimmed their lustre. Increasingly, Coppola's and Scorsese's films, in particular *The Godfather* 2 and *Raging Bull*, Scorsese's brutal black-and-white portrait of the boxer Jake La Motta, figured in international polls as among the ten best ever made, while Spielberg's weren't mentioned. Even in financial terms, his films no longer dominated lists of the century's most successful productions. Corrected for inflation, *The Sound of*

Music at $790 million beat *E.T.* at $614 million, while both *The Sting* ($535 million) and *The Exorcist* ($550 million) were ahead of *Close Encounters'* $406 million.

The paternalistic practices of 'Amblin U' were no longer as popular with up-and-coming directors, some of whom resented having to 'Spielberg' their work. On *Harry and the Hendersons*, William Dear had bridled at what he saw as interference by Spielberg. The film's troubled history ended with Amblin dumping it on Universal and Dear going public with his complaints. After *The Land Before Time*, released in 1988, the relationship with Don Bluth, who had set up a new animation studio in Ireland, also cooled when Universal demanded a sequel to the successful *American Tail*, which had made $50 million in the US alone, generated a similar sum in spin-offs with McDonald's and the chain store Sears, and sold two million cassettes at $29.98 each. Bluth refused. The British company Goldcrest wanted him to make a film for them, and were offering 50 per cent of spin-off and character rights. He would also retain a 50 per cent ownership of the film, unlike *An American Tail*, which was totally the property of Universal, allowing them to use his Fievel character in the sequel *Fievel Goes West*, in which Bluth played no part and for which he was paid nothing.

Without any means of expanding into features, Spielberg's interest was shifting towards other media. He persuaded Universal to finance a new animation studio in London, Amblimation, to work on new projects over which he would have total control. Carole Kirschner was hired from CBS to head Amblin's TV unit and develop new animated series, including a spin-off from the *Amazing Stories* episode *Family Dog*, featuring the animal Tim Burton had invented while still a student at the Disney-funded college CalArts. Spielberg contracted with Universal to design rides for both the Los Angeles park and a new one being built in Florida. His plans included an elaborate multi-media evocation of *Back to the Future*.

He also approached composer Andrew Lloyd Webber, a fellow tenant of Trump Tower, to write a musical for him to direct.

'Tell me, Steven,' Webber responded, 'how much money do you make from your films?'

'Well,' said Spielberg, '*Close Encounters* and *E.T.* each netted me about $100 million.'

'One hundred million dollars,' mused Webber. 'That's about £50 million. It hardly seems worth the bother.'

At the end of 1987, weary of production, Spielberg passed creative control of Amblin to Kathleen Kennedy. 'She's going to select the movies we make,' he said, 'and I think you'll find them a little more mature and eclectic.'

In March 1988, *Empire of the Sun* opened in Britain with modest success. It was once again selected for the Royal Film Performance, but survivors of the Japanese occupation of China protested at their depiction as greedy, pusillanimous and despairing. Spielberg referred them to Ballard, who argued that the film was a child's view of the period, and therefore understandably partial.

Briefly in London for the screening, a muted Spielberg announced he had definitively shelved Stoppard's *Peter Pan*. He explained:

We were all ready to go. John Williams had already written nine songs. Then Max, my son, was born and the last thing I wanted to do was raise nine kids in London, hanging on wires against a blue screen, instead of being with my own child, raising him. And I think I lost interest in that theme of the boy who refuses to grow up. I was forty this year and I guess something changed. There's nothing I love more than making movies, but now there's another kind of love. If I had to give it all up for my son, I really believe I would.

Elsewhere he said, 'Peter Pan didn't have courage. I'm trying to grow up.' When the British Parliament waived copyright laws to allow Great Ormond Street Children's Hospital to continue to benefit from the rights to *Peter Pan* which Barrie had bequeathed to them, the hospital promptly endorsed an attempt by London-based entrepreneur Dodi Fayed to produce a film.

Significantly, Amy wasn't mentioned in any of Spielberg's statements about his family or his future. Rumours circulated of a separation, even divorce, though Amblin vigorously denied any such suggestion when it appeared in print. Spielberg's bitterness about his marriage emerged, however, in *The Last Crusade*, the female lead of which, in contrast to the other films in the series, is a treacherous and amoral liar who comes to an unpleasant end, toppling into the pit as her grasping fingers just fail to snatch the Grail.

Spielberg returned to Hollywood for the Oscars on 11 April 1988. As was becoming almost traditional, Amblin productions were well represented in the technical awards: *Harry and the Hendersons* was nominated for Make-up, and *Innerspace* won its Oscar for Special Effects. The year's big winner was Bernardo Bertolucci's *The Last Emperor*, ironically produced by David Puttnam, who'd been fired from his post as head of Columbia before it was released. Sean Connery won the Best Supporting Actor award for De Palma's *The Untouchables*, underlining once again Spielberg's instinct for casting.

That year's nominees offered another small consolation to Spielberg. Watching Albert Brooks's mordant picture of network TV, *Broadcast News*, which took out seven nominations but won none, he was struck by Holly Hunter. Watching her spunky performance, he realised he'd found an actress who could hold her own against comparisons with Irene Dunne in his remake of *A Guy Named Joe*.

Always moved from the bench into active play. Dreyfuss was now old enough for the Spencer Tracy role, and Spielberg had found an ideal foil for him in bulky TV comic John Goodman, who could easily carry Ward Bond's role as Al Yackey, the buddy left behind when Pete Sandrich dies. The script had been the rounds. Jerry Belson had updated it from World War II to the world of daredevil fliers who water-bombed forest fires in Colorado. After that, it passed to Diane Thomas, whose personal rags-to-riches tale of having written *Romancing the Stone* while working as a waitress ended tragically when she was accidentally killed in the sports car bought with her first pay cheque. Following her death, Spielberg sent the script to Stoppard, who – once again anonymously – did a number of rewrites.

In his spare time, Spielberg had kept his eye on the production of *Who Framed Roger Rabbit*. Originally budgeted at $27.5 million, it had ballooned to $45 million when Spielberg insisted, over the protests of his co-producers Disney, that they make the cartoon/live action interface even more inventive. Its release on 24 June 1988 would show that his instincts had not deserted him. The film grossed $153 million to become the year's box-office hit, and won Oscars for Editing, Sound and Visual Effects.

In May, shooting on *Last Crusade* began in Almería, Spain, the dusty plains of which stood in for Jordan, where Spielberg had received permission to film his climax at Petra, the 'rose-red city, half as old as time' hollowed out from the solid rock of the mountains. News of his domestic problems spread through the crew like a virus, but once again film-making erased his worries. 'He was on the set every morning, bright-eyed, fresh as a daisy,' said one actor. 'That went on throughout the production.'

After Spain, the unit moved to Venice. Amy and Melissa Mathison arrived with their sons, but only stayed a few days. 'Because of the heat spells,' Amy explained when she got to London, 'the canals are really in bad shape.' They decided to bring their 'little boys' to London and wait for the 'big boys' there.

The Brent Walker entertainment group had bought Elstree studios for £32.5 million in 1988, at the height of a property boom, visualising it as the cornerstone of a movie-making empire, but the company overextended itself, and was now trying to sell the studios. With MCA's backing, Spielberg tried to buy the complex. He visualised it expanding onto nearby Rainham Marshes to become a Universal-type movie theme park, but the local council refused permission for fear of environmental damage, and Elstree closed down. In 1993, half would be sold to the Tesco supermarket chain. The '*Star Wars* Stage' was dismantled and moved to Shepperton studios.

On the set of *Crusade*, Spielberg showed his usual skill in charming actors. Julian Glover was proud to be praised for his assumed American accent. 'It's one of the best I've heard,' Spielberg told him. 'You're going to get a lot of work after this film.' Bill Hootkins, who has coached many actors in American accents, including Laurence Olivier, laughed when he heard this. 'That's what you always tell someone when they're over the top. They relax then. They don't try so hard, and it sounds more natural.' Alison Doody was also manipulated, but more directly, by Harrison Ford. Kevork Malikyan says:

> He's a lovely man, but not all that concerned about the other people
> in the scene with him, but who didn't have any dialogue – like Alison.
> If he hits you, he *hits* you. And sometimes one foot would be up in
> the air, hitting Alison in the face. I found him very rough in that way.
> No nonsense. And no apologies either.

For the finale, Glover endured a punishing sixteen-second disintegration that took three days to shoot. It began with six takes with progressively older make-up, then another day with inflating pads taped to his forehead and cheekbones. As these were pumped full of air, his eyes seemed to recede into their sockets. To make him seem to grow instant long grey hair, he was fitted with a wig into which the hair was drawn back mechanically. Then the film was run backwards at higher speed. After that, they went to models.

Less work went into reconciling the loose ends of this finale. Having experienced what Elsa calls 'the healing power of the Grail', both Jones *père et fils* should be immortal, so a new twist had to be added in which the Grail's power to prolong life worked only within the sanctuary. Once one tried to pass the Great Seal with the Grail, the building crumbled – as did any fidelity to the myth, central to which is the need for someone to stay in vigil before it, guarding it from robbers like Indiana Jones. There were plenty of hints in Boam's script that either Indy or his father was being pencilled in for this task, relieving the crusader who'd been on the job for centuries. Such a conclusion would have ended the trilogy on the graceful irony of Indy, having hunted artefacts all his life, dis-covering his true reason for living in guarding the most important find of all. But the siren song of yet another sequel was too strong, and Indy lived to loot another day.

In August 1988, the first newspaper reports surfaced of a possible Spielberg/Irving divorce. These were instantly and comprehensively denied by Spielberg's lawyers, who quoted him as saying they were 'insulting, distressing, humiliating and embarrassing'. In fact, behind the scenes the same lawyers were hammering out a settlement. Inconveniently for these negotiations, Universal released E.T. for video sale and rental in October. Experts who had warned that the public would have no interest in paying $20 for a film they could rent for $2 were confounded when thirteen million cassettes were sold worldwide, without visibly diminishing the rental market. E.T. would finally gross a total of $300 million, of which Spielberg's share was $75 million, including $40 million from cassette sales alone. Hollywood radically revised its profit projections for future movies.

Led by the films of Spielberg and Lucas, the pattern of film distribution was changing, the American domestic market being overtaken by those of foreign countries, and by video, both in rentals and direct 'sell through' of cassettes. This growing sense of the movie-market tail wagging the Hollywood dog became institutionalised in October 1989 when the Japanese Sony Corporation, among the world's leading manufacturers of video- and music-playing equipment, bought the ailing Columbia and its feature-film production subsidiary TriStar from Coca-Cola.

The logic behind the move was seductive. Sony's Betamax video-recording system, despite its technical superiority, had lost out to Matsushita's VHS format, which most manufacturers of video equipment preferred. Determined to save face and retrieve the leadership it had won with products like the Walkman personal stereo, Sony's founder Akio Morita persuaded his more cautious heir apparent Norio Ohga that they should steal a march on their competitors by seizing the sources of artistic 'software' in the West. In 1987 Sony bought CBS Records for $2 billion, acquiring the contracts of Michael Jackson, Bruce Springsteen, Bob Dylan and a reluctant George Michael, who would sue the corporation in 1994, claiming that its refusal to renegotiate his deal constituted 'slavery'. After this, Sony went shopping for a film studio. Mike Ovitz and CBS chairman Walter Yetnikoff steered them to Columbia/TriStar. The purchase itself, the acquisition of producers Peter Guber and Jon Peters to run the company, and the subsequent capital investment in refurbishing MGM's old Culver City studio as a head-quarters, fitted out with the latest technology, cost an estimated $6 billion.

Hollywood viewed Sony's arrival with amused condescension. For the first time in its history, *Variety* ran a headline in Japanese. It said 'Buyer Beware!' They had just seen off British *wunderkind* David Puttnam, elbowed out as head of Columbia before the Sony takeover, and sent financier Gianni Nunnari back to Italy with a flea in his ear. After having been stuck with the ruins of MGM, the French bank Crédit Lyonnaise would also write off more than a billion dollars between 1992 and 1994 on its Hollywood adventures. 'It's nationalistic, in a weird way,' said one deal-maker of Hollywood's attitude to the newcomers. 'The feeling is: these fools, we took them down.' Another remarked, 'It's the Japanese this year – three years from now, who knows? We took the French out for a billion – we'll move on to the Chinese.'

Morita's poaching of Guber and Peters, who'd just signed a five-year deal with Warners, made Steve Ross furious. He sued Sony for $1 billion. The Japanese settled for $600 million, and agreed not only to relinquish Columbia's joint ownership of the Burbank studios, but all fifty projects Guber and Peters had in development. Ross's disapproval wasn't entirely selfish. He objected to 'selling the farm'. Control of national companies, he believed, should remain in America.

Spielberg agreed. When the Sony sale was announced, he was in Hawaii. On his return, he commented, 'Sony is giving the movie business a new chequeing account. Sony isn't pretending to become involved in the creative parts. Sony knows it's Americans who know the movie business, and the fact of Guber–Peters doesn't personally bother me.' Then the mask of industry statesman began to slip, triggered in part by the fact that, in hiring proved hit-makers Guber and Peters, Sony had fired Spielberg's friend Dawn Steel from her job as production head of the studio. 'But I'm wondering something,' he went on. 'The Columbia logo is the lady with the torch. So will she become a geisha? . . . And I'm trying to imagine what a compact movie feels like. Does a compact movie get great gas mileage?'

Since his estrangement from Amy, Spielberg was once again seeing Kate Capshaw. Frankly determined to grab the man she wanted, Kate made it clear she would embrace Judaism if asked, and was willing, indeed eager, to have children. Their relationship was an open secret. She'd taken a house towards the north end of Malibu, and Spielberg was often glimpsed strolling up the beach from his place in the afternoon.

Amy was in London promoting the highly successful *Crossing Delancey* with Max and her good friend, Richard Dreyfuss's wife Jeramie. Asked about reports of Spielberg's new romance, she said, 'I don't know anything about any other woman.' Not especially coherently, she rambled on:

 And y'know what? If we're not fine, sitting around reading about it isn't going to make my life richer. We don't let newspapers even come into our house. How would you like to open the papers and have reporters trashing your life? It's ugly. Oh, sure, I miss the papers, but we agreed that what you don't know – I mean, it's not as if we're totally innocent of knowing what's happening out there. We know. But we also know what's important, and we screen out negativity.

The reporter assumed that 'we' was she and Spielberg, but it's more likely she meant Jeramie Dreyfuss and her own new companion. In fact, the divorce settlement, giving Amy an estimated $100 million – half of everything Spielberg earned during their marriage – was already signed.

On 1 April 1989, the newly-formed American Cinematheque threw a Moving Picture Ball in Los Angeles, and chose to honour Spielberg. Connery, John Candy, Danny DeVito, Dreyfuss, Goldie Hawn all appeared. So, under protest, did Amy. 'Amy looked like she was in a straitjacket,' Paul Rosenfield said. When reporters asked Spielberg about his ambitions, he said one was 'to direct my wife in a movie'. Nobody missed Amy coldly turning away.

When *Indiana Jones and the Last Crusade* opened on 24 May 1989 in 2327 cinemas across America, Paramount, with pardonable pride, trumpeted the fact that it made more money in its first weekend than any film in history, $46.9 million. Not mentioned was the fact that the studio had raised seat prices by fifty cents for this hottest of hot tickets.

Spitefully, Amy's lawyers chose the same day to announce her petition for divorce on the grounds of 'irreconcilable differences'. On 30 June, divorce papers were officially filed. Amy and Spielberg had dinner together the following night, for all the world like the most civilised of splitting couples. Both had agreed not to reveal details of their settlement, but neither denied the estimate of $100 million. Also by agreement, Amy would have custody of Max.

By early May, Spielberg and Kate Capshaw were openly living together. Press reports claimed they would marry in November, but friends doubted that he would rush into another marriage so quickly. Behind the scenes, there was growing friction between the lovers. As Kate pressed for marriage, a nervous Spielberg insisted on a pre-nuptial agreement. He offered a lump sum of $2 million in the event of a divorce. Kate counter-demanded $2 million for each year the marriage lasted up to five years. In return she would waive any claims under the Californian community property laws which had given Amy her huge settlement. 'Kate spent months hammering out the details of what she wanted,' said a friend. 'Each time he was ready to sign, she'd think of something else she wanted in the papers. Steven finally got cold feet about marrying her.' A Spielberg spokesman quoted him as saying, 'I felt she was taking advantage of me and pushing me into something I wasn't ready for. She wanted a family, a career and my chequebook too!'

Kate moved out. Alone in the Malibu house, a chastened Spielberg rose each morning at 6.30 to eat a frugal breakfast of bran, juice and decaf – he'd just lost fourteen pounds – before driving to Burbank.

Friends observing his solitude and the back seat of his blue Porsche, poignantly fitted with Max's yellow baby chair, assumed him to be in despair. In fact his life was a good deal less dispiriting, since he already had another woman in his life, and a new movie to star her in.

Always and *Hook*

'What is it, Wendy?' he cried again.
'I'm old, Peter.'

J.M. Barrie, *Peter Pan, or The Boy Who Wouldn't Grow Up*

IN 1988, Tom Pollock, Lucas's old lawyer and negotiator of their *Raiders* deal, became president of Universal. 'One of the most important things I can do in this job,' he told the press, 'is to make sure Steven wants to work with us.' Spielberg immediately signed to do five films for Universal. The first would be his *Guy Named Joe* remake, *Always*.

As often before when his emotional life soured, Spielberg had turned to the undemanding arms of an actress. She was Holly Hunter, the tiny (five foot two), vivacious star of *Broadcast News*, in which her role as the TV news editor torn between her high intellectual standards and the temptation of romance with William Hurt's sports-reporter-turned-news-anchorman had won her an Oscar nomination, as well as both the New York and Los Angeles Film Critics' Prizes. With her background in theatre, where she created the lead roles in a number of Beth Henley plays, including *Crimes of the Heart*, Hunter had more in common with Amy than some of Spielberg's earlier actress romances – which, in the wake of the divorce, may have contributed to her appeal. The couple made no secret of their liaison, kissing and cuddling when Spielberg appeared on the TV show of British comedienne Tracy Ullmann, where he harmonised rustily with Ullmann on the Disney tune 'It's a Small World'. 'Holly is the funniest, warmest, most loving girl I've ever met,' he said. 'We'll see what tomorrow brings, but right now she's the one for me.' No doubt Amy got the message: Steve was doing just fine without her.

In *Always*, Hunter played the daughter-of-the-squadron role which had been Irene Dunne's in the original. Victor Fleming's *A Guy Named Joe* took place on US Air Force bases in wartime, a setting Spielberg initially tried to retain. After the negative reaction of British veterans to *Empire of the Sun*, however, he updated it to a group of aerial firefighters dumping water and fire retardant on forest blazes. Not that the differences are obvious. As John Goodman points out in the film, the airstrip in the woods with its A-26 Invaders and PBY Catalina flying boats has the air of a World War II base. All it needs to complete the picture is Glenn Miller.

The star pilot, Pete Sandich (Richard Dreyfuss), conforms to Spielberg's model of the dysfunctional hero, obsessed with his technical proficiency but blind to the emotional needs of those close to him, in this case his girlfriend Dorinda, the base air-traffic controller. Not herself at ease in the real world, Dorinda is another Spielberg tomboy, seldom seen out of a flying suit, hopeless at cooking but well able to fly and drink along with the pilots.

Pete can joke, charm, flirt, dance and sleep with Dorinda, but not declare his love. At the beginning of his last flight, he gets the words out, but they're drowned by his engines. A few minutes later, his plane explodes while saving his best pal, Al. If you love something too much, Spielberg seems to be saying, you will lose it.

Pete is returned to the world by a spirit guide named Hap. The first idea had been to have Dreyfuss wake up on a basketball court in a burned-out forest, shooting baskets with a long-dead uncle. The forest remained, but Hap became Audrey Hepburn, who gives Dreyfuss a haircut and some sisterly advice. Afterwards, they stroll through a field of grain – already, wrote critic Quentin Curtis, 'wading in corn'.

Pete's role, she explains, is to shepherd Dorinda through her grief and into the arms of his fated replacement, a hunk named Ted. Initially unable to wrench free of his feelings, Pete does what he can to impede the romance – little enough, since he is both inaudible and invisible to the living. He can only communicate by transferring vague hints or feelings, or through mediums like an old hermit whom Ted meets when he makes an emergency landing at an abandoned rural airport.

After bumbling about, doing more harm than good, Pete returns to Hap for clarification. She then explains he was mainly supposed to say goodbye to a pining Dorinda – difficult for someone in his incorporeal state. Still later, he receives yet another explanation: that he'd been sent back solely to rescue her when her plane crashes at the climax. The original script ended on the basketball court, with Pete, duty done, inducting yet another new arrival into his imprecise duties in the here-after. In the released version, he simply fades away, much as the film was to do.

The vividness of the impression left by Roberts Blossom as the hermit at the airfield emphasises the vacuum at the heart of *Always*. Characters at the periphery make the greatest impact, like Marg Helgenberger as Rachel, the good-natured mechanic doomed to play second string to Dorinda, and John Goodman's Al Yackey, a performance of extraordinary physicality by this winning comic. By contrast, former rodeo rider Brad Johnson, in Dorinda's words 'all twisted steel and sex appeal', plays Ted with charm school ineffectiveness. Nothing, from putting him in spectacles to having him resuscitate a stricken bus driver, can redeem his Chippendale/Wonderbread blandness.

The little that does work in *Always* is visual: the opening shot, of two drowsy fishermen on a lake diving in terror from their boat as a PBY appears out of nowhere to gulp a new load of water; the base bachelors, in a homage to John Ford's *They Were Expendable*, paying awed court to Dorinda when she descends in her new 'girl clothes'; Al being clumsily strafed by Ted with retardant as he watches student pilot practice from under an umbrella on a bluff; the incident at the abandoned airfield, where Pete's telepathic transmissions, garbled by Roberts Blossom, are fed back as exhortations to Ted to do just what Pete least wants him to do – return to the base, and Dorinda.

Pete reluctantly learns to say goodbye at the end of *Always*, but in ambiguous terms. As a sop to equality of the sexes, Dorinda (rather than Ted, as in the original) flies the final heroic mission, saving a group of firefighters (changed from the children of earlier versions) by water-bombing their way to safety. But a ghostly Pete remains with her in the cockpit, and it's he who forces her to save herself when she ditches in a lake. He's cut her loose, but only after proving she can't survive without him.

Spielberg had intended Dorinda to go off with Ted at the end of the film, but on the basis of Brad Johnson's tepid performance, not to mention the continuing bond with Pete which the script is unable to sever, his role in Dorinda's future was downgraded from lifetime love to brief diversion, not unlike Hunter's own relationship with Spielberg.

While the publicity sold *Always* as a 'romantic fantasy', its emotional tone is sombre, appropriate to a man in retreat from a damaging emotional experience. Spielberg said that Pete's presence as an unheard, unseen figure in the middle of emotional incidents reflected his own isolation as a child, when he watched his parents failing to communicate. The original had, he said, been only the second film, after *Bambi*, to move him to tears. *A Guy Named Joe*, he remembered, 'taught me how to make love to a woman [and] stuck with me all those years, and when I grew up and was short of girlfriends I used to think about it.' Given the sexual jealousy, impotence and isolation which pervade *Always*, however, it's more likely that Spielberg was replaying the last painful months of his marriage.

Reviewing *A Guy Named Joe*, in which Irene Dunne retains a comradely distance from Ted, played by Van Johnson, critic James Agee isolated the most disturbing element of the story, but agreed that, given the sexual innocence of forties Hollywood, it couldn't be shown. 'Pete and the audience are spared what might have happened if she had really got either frozen or tender with Mr Johnson, while Pete looked on,' he says. Amplifying this in a later review, he reflected that as 'the jealousy of a living lover for a dead man made one of Joyce's finest stories [i.e. 'The Dead', in *Dubliners*], the emotions a ghost might feel who watched a living man woo and cajole his former mistress seem just as promising to me . . . but to make such a film – above all at such a time as this – would require extraordinary taste, honesty and courage.'

Always circles this thorny theme, but loses its nerve. Spielberg has Pete watch in disbelief as the undomestic Dorinda fakes a home-cooked dinner for Ted, sees her resistance begin to crumble as Ted inveigles her into dancing, and agonises when they kiss, but at the last moment 'their' song oozes out on the stereo, and the moment passes in which he might have had to watch them make love. That night, Pete lies alert and adoring beside a sleeping Dorinda and pledges eternal but sexless love, like an Arthurian knight, while she composes shopping lists in her dreams. Is this Spielberg's vision of the perfect domestic relationship – with the sexes simply reversed?

At the National Jamboree in Arlington, Virginia, Spielberg, once a fumbling Boy Scout, was presented with the Distinguished Eagle Scout Award by the National Council of the Boy Scouts of America, which had recently, inspired by him, instituted a cinematography merit badge. 'It was the highlight of 1989 for me,' he said. 'The best memory from the entire year.'

The rest was depressing. *Always* was sickly from the start, in need of constant doctoring. Ninety-four-year-old composer Irving Berlin refused permisssion for his song 'Always' to be used as a theme. He 'had plans' for it, he said. Director Henry Jaglom also chose the same title for his low-budget comedy of a reconciliation with his ex-wife which would be released the same year. Spielberg contemplated calling his film 'I'll be Seeing You', since he was now thinking of this forties ballad as Pete and Dorinda's special song. Poor reaction at previews persuaded him, however, that the tune dated the story too much. He kept *Always* as his title but replaced the song with 'Smoke Gets in Your Eyes', which The Platters had revived and turned into a hit in 1959, the year he made his first boyhood film.

Always opened on 22 December to tepid reviews which made Tom Pollock wonder if his early faith in Spielberg was misplaced. It also inaugurated his tenure as boss of Universal on a low note. Things weren't to improve. Traits like sharing the lifestyle of the film-makers he'd once represented by living out of town and commuting to the studios in a van fitted with the latest in information technology, a travelling 'electronic cottage', marked Pollock in some eyes as trivial and indecisive. Even though he was technically in charge of production, Universal remained the studio of Lew Wasserman and Sid Sheinberg, now Hollywood's senior statesmen and major international players in the changing world of media.

If only because it was a Pollock project, nobody was in a hurry to embrace *Always*. When it was chosen for the Royal Command Performance in London in March 1990, Spielberg, Dreyfuss, Hunter and Goodman all pleaded pressing commitments elsewhere. Pollock and Brad Johnson were left to carry the can with Her Majesty in what one British paper called 'an unprecedented snub to the Queen' but which was more a rebuke by Hollywood of Pollock and his administration.

Spielberg had other things on his mind. The romance with Holly Hunter which had complicated the shooting of *Always* – after being coached a dozen times in a kiss, Dreyfuss acidly suggested to Spielberg that he demonstrate what he had in mind – didn't survive post-production, and by the start of 1990 he was back with Kate Capshaw. During their separation she had adopted Theo, an African-American boy, and by March she was pregnant with Spielberg's first daughter, Sasha, and undergoing instruction prior to being converted to the Jewish religion. There was no more public discussion of money. Whatever arrangements had been made remained blessedly private.

It must have seemed to Spielberg that everybody was making a movie but himself. Kate had achieved her most effective role to date opposite Michael Douglas in Ridley Scott's *Black Rain*, playing a Tokyo bar hostess, a characterisation of icy control. Frank Marshall, who'd cut his teeth shooting second unit for many Spielberg films, was directing the thriller *Arachnophobia*, for which Spielberg acted as executive producer and also filmed some sequences. Early in 1991, Marshall officially and amicably left Amblin, leaving Kathleen Kennedy behind in the newly-created job of head of production. It was understood she would follow him to their new company.

Another neophyte director, Tom Stoppard, was filming *Rosencrantz and Guildenstern are Dead* in Yugoslavia. Sean Connery had bought himself out of the role of the Player King the year before following a throat cancer scare, and Richard Dreyfuss replaced him. Stoppard and Spielberg were now friendly enough for Stoppard to ring him when he had a tricky directing problem.

Brian De Palma was shooting *Bonfire of the Vanities*, a project about which Spielberg continued to have doubts. Hollywood executives in general were in no hurry to censure corporate sharks, who were, in some cases, their friends or at least business acquaintances. Spielberg visited De Palma on the set a number of times, leading to some embarrassing moments that underlined their relative standing in Hollywood. The Warners restaurant was closed to De Palma when he tried to order a late breakfast, then abruptly open again once the manager glimpsed his companion, Spielberg. When the film was finished, it was rumoured that Warners had asked Spielberg to re-edit it in secret.

On 8 March, Spielberg and De Palma attended the banquet at which the American Film Institute presented its Lifetime Achievement Award to David Lean. For once the recipient was not, as Hitchcock and John Ford had been, so ill that he could barely do more than acknowledge the applause. Instead a testy Lean lashed out at the assembled film-makers for producing rubbish, and sequels to rubbish. Spielberg, as producer of *Back to the Future* 1, 2 and, eventually, 3, and *Gremlins* 1 and 2, had more reason to reproach himself than most, but he joined vigorously in the standing ovation.

A number of projects were announced as Spielberg's 'next film'. Dawn Steel, now an independent producer, did a deal to remake *La Fracture du Myocarde*, a French film by Jacques Fansten, as *Cross My Heart*. The plot, about a boy who covers up his mother's death for fear of being sent to an orphanage, seemed flimsy, but Universal, TriStar and Disney all made offers on the back of a rumour that Spielberg wanted to direct a 'little' movie. With his sister Anne, he discussed a film with a theme close to home. He said:

> It's about a brother and sister growing up, and it's really about when
> a brother and sister reunite after many years of estrangement and try

to make up those lost years in the forties – the years they lost in their twenties . . . I think it's a bittersweet film. It's probably the closest my sister and I both have come to talking much about each other and then making that public, which is always embarrassing.

Two more ideas came from Michael Crichton. Both he and Spielberg shared a dislike of anodyne medical shows – Spielberg since his days directing *Marcus Welby* and *The Psychiatrist* at Universal. Crichton proposed a hard-hitting super-soap set in the Emergency Room of a big-city hospital. Spielberg was tempted, and *E.R.* remained with Amblin, from which it emerged in the 1995 TV season as a hit NBC series.

'We were talking about changes [to *E.R.*] in my office one day,' says Spielberg, 'and I happened to ask [Crichton] what he was working on . . . He said he had just finished a book about dinosaurs, called *Jurassic Park*.'

The idea of genetically engineered dinosaurs had been with Crichton since 1981, when he'd tried to write a screenplay on the subject. In the intervening years, other writers had picked up on the growing evidence that dinosaurs weren't the ancestors of our reptiles, cold-blooded and slow-moving, but fast, hot-blooded precursors of birds. In particular, the 1984 novel *Carnosaur* by John Brosnan, writing as Harry Adam Knight, explored the idea so effectively that Roger Corman zoomed in ahead of Spielberg with a 1992 movie version.

Crichton had revived his script again in 1989 while his wife was pregnant and he, like many expectant fathers, began to stockpile stuffed toys. Some of those he bought were dinosaurs, which resonated with memories of a speculation by George Poinar, of the University of California's College of Natural Resources in Berkeley, that dinosaur DNA might be recovered from the bellies of mosquitoes preserved in amber. The screenplay quickly metamorphosed into *Jurassic Park*.

'You know,' Spielberg said, 'I've had a fascination with dinosaurs all my life, and I'd really love to read it.' He read the proofs, was as gripped by the story as millions would be when the novel was published in 1990, and offered to buy the movie rights for *Jurassic Park* before Crichton's agents put it out for competitive bidding.

'I'll give it to you if you guarantee me that you'll direct the picture,' Crichton said.

Spielberg stalled. Even so persuasive a concept as cloning dinosaurs and turning an island off the coast of Costa Rica into a prehistoric theme park posed fundamental problems for him, most particularly in the character of John Hammond, the eccentric entrepreneur who floats the project.

In part, Hammond was inspired by Crichton seeing *Fantasia* again, and reflecting on the contradictory character of its maker. 'Where's the other side?' he asked himself. 'The *evil* Walt Disney?' Hammond is his answer, a reckless obsessive determined, as was Disney, to impose his child-like vision of nature on the world. Crichton's dinosaurs are extensions of Hammond's twisted psyche. But Spielberg was himself too much a product of Disney to see dinosaurs as the poisoned creations of an unhinged mind. He preferred them to be simply behaving naturally when they turned on their keepers. 'Animals do what these animals do,' he argued. It was permissible for Hammond to be misguided, but he shouldn't be evil.

There were other problems in adapting the novel to the screen. A cliffhanging plot – will escaped velociraptors make it to the mainland and rampage across the world? – and some stock characters, in particularly Hammond's grandchildren, the boy a talky computer nerd, the girl an obnoxious whiner, always sneezing or screaming at the wrong time, betrayed the book's screenplay origins. However, in the relationship between his central characters, Grant, the middle-aged palaeontologist, and his assistant Ellie Sattler, Crichton had played against formula, making them colleagues with no sexual interest in one another – a problem for Hollywood, which still demanded a clinch at the finale. Other drawbacks included the book's lengthy polemic against uncontrolled genetic engineering, most of it articulated by mathematician and chaos theoretician Ian Malcolm, who exists mainly for this purpose. If the film was to inveigh against genetic pollution, it would have to do so in action and images, not words.

While Spielberg procrastinated, Crichton's agents put the book out to other companies, fanning their ardour by dropping the fact that

Spielberg was also interested. Fox bid, thinking of it for Joe Dante. Warners saw it as a Tim Burton film, and Sony thought it would suit Richard Donner. But Sid Sheinberg, convinced it was a natural Spielberg project even if Spielberg was not, snapped it up for $2 million, with an additional $500,000 to Crichton for a first-draft script.

Spielberg's interest in *Jurassic Park* was complicated by the continued presence of *Schindler's Ark* in the wings. It had been in preparation for eight years, and people were getting testy, not least the book's author. Thomas Keneally had already agreed to rename the book *Schindler's List* to satisfy his nervous American publishers, Simon and Schuster, who felt the word 'ark' might be taken as a suggestion that Hitler's victims had connived at their destruction by meekly 'going in, two by two' to the ovens. Now he was wondering what had happened to the film. Encountering journalist Richard Brooks on a plane en route to interview Spielberg, he snarled, 'Steven Spielberg, eh? Well, tell him I'd like to know what is happening to my script. He asked me to do a film script ages ago, but I never get an answer from him or anyone else in Hollywood. It's infuriating.'

There had been many times during the eight years when Spielberg would have been happy to be rid of the project. Periodically Poldeck Pfefferberg, who first got Keneally interested in Schindler, would ring Spielberg from his bag shop. 'I'm seventy-four years old,' he complained. 'I'm not getting any younger.' In 1985 the Polish government sent an envoy to Spielberg to ask when shooting would start, and offering its assistance. Unlike Warsaw, Krakow had not been razed by the Nazis, the representative explained. Schindler's factory still stood. So did his home. And though a monument had been erected on the site of the Plaszow camp, there was an identical quarry just half a mile away . . .

All this was acutely embarrassing. Spielberg had visited Poland and gone to all the sites of the story, but still he wasn't ready. Among other problems, Keneally's screenplay, even after two drafts, didn't work. If ever two people were on different wavelengths, it was Spielberg and the

Australian-Irish-Catholic Keneally, who employed a Jesuitical equivo-
cation in damning the director with faint praise.

> The screenplay compared to a novel is like a comic strip. But I don't
> use the term pejoratively ... We poor benighted novelists like to
> think that people who gross so much per day, like Spielberg, have
> to have an ultimately vulgar imagination. But I don't think that's the
> truth. Spielberg told me he saw Schindler as the third little pig in the
> Three Little Pigs story. Now, in a way, that's a laughable image, but
> in another way it's a grand focusing. It's not a bad image to write
> from, to pare down the complexity of a life like Schindler's to the
> clarity of a hundred-minute script. But I thought to myself: 'That's
> why you, Spielberg, are such a success – because in popular culture
> you're able to reduce everything to a fundamental one-line piece of
> mythology.'

In desperation, Spielberg offered the project to Sydney Pollack, who
asked Tom Stoppard to write a script. But Stoppard passed. Tom Pollock
then tried Kurt Luedtke, the Oscar-winning adapter of Isak Dinesen's
Out of Africa. As a German, he might clarify the elusive character of
Schindler. Luedtke spent four years on the project, but never got past
the first act, unable to explain why Schindler, the cynical womaniser
and rampant capitalist, had decided, literally overnight, to exhaust his
fortune and energy on saving his workers. The failure deeply upset
Luedtke and left Spielberg in despair. If so respected a writer couldn't
'lick the story', perhaps nobody could.

Later, Martin Scorsese became interested in *Schindler*. For a time it
seemed to Spielberg that having Scorsese make the film as an Amblin
production would solve all his problems. He'd see it on the screen, but
without the frustration and possible failure of doing it himself. Stuck in
bed with 'flu, he read the book again and underlined all the passages he
felt essential. After discussing the changes with Keneally, who had taken
a Californian teaching position, Spielberg sent the marked copy, at Robert
de Niro's suggestion, to Steven Zaillian, who'd adapted Oliver Sacks's
Awakenings. Penny Marshall had made a sentimental but successful film

from the script about a catatonic brought back to consciousness by a miracle drug, only to slip back again into coma. In the film, de Niro and Robin Williams had done little to address the moral complexities of using this medication, nor to plumb the character of Sacks, whom Williams showed as a genial nerd. All the same, Zaillian had at least succeeded in turning an uncinematic subject with unglamorous characters into a hit movie, so perhaps he could also resolve the questions raised by *Schindler's List*. The two of them took a trip to Poland together, and Zaillian started work.

By this time, Spielberg's imagination had been caught by plans for a remake for Universal of another adolescent enthusiasm, J. Lee Thompson's 1962 movie *Cape Fear*, about an ex-convict revenging himself on the small-town judge who had railroaded him into prison. Robert Mitchum had been an emblem of silent malevolence, every father's nightmare, and the ending, where Gregory Peck takes the law into his own hands, impressed Spielberg powerfully.

Wesley Strick had written an interesting screenplay, and when de Niro showed some interest in playing the villain, Spielberg's instincts as a producer overrode his normal territoriality. Strick and Spielberg went to New York to talk to de Niro. 'He seemed interested,' said Strick, 'though he hadn't really committed. He got Marty [Scorsese] involved. He and Steven together sort of twisted Marty's arm – relentlessly, from what I gather. In fact, they staged a reading of the script in New York, for Marty's benefit, which I attended.' Spielberg relinquished *Cape Fear* to Scorsese and de Niro, but not before extracting their promise that the judge's family would survive the film, giving Universal that *sine qua non* of box-office success, a happy ending. Scorsese reassured him they'd live. 'Well, then you can have anything you want up to that point,' Spielberg said.

With Scorsese now working on *Cape Fear*, Spielberg found himself with *Schindler's List* once again on his desk. He discussed it as a possible next film with Tom Pollock, but Universal was in no hurry to back another *Empire of the Sun*. The market had also been bombarded with World War II films like Herman Wouk's *War and Remembrance* miniseries, the controversial *Holocaust*, *Sophie's Choice* and Claude Lanzmann's monumental documentary of the Holocaust, *Shoah*, which was to leave an indelible impression on the eventual film of *Schindler's List*.

Many people also felt there were better directors to film the book. Billy Wilder made a pitch, citing his impeccable credentials: he'd fled Berlin in 1933. 'He made me look very deeply inside myself when he was so passionate to do this,' Spielberg said. 'In a way, he tested my resolve.' Fred Schepisi, Australian director of *Roxanne* and *Plenty*, well-oiled at a party, also told Spielberg he was 'the worst person to direct this film'. 'You'll fuck it up,' he said, 'because you're too good with the camera.'

'He was right,' Spielberg acknowledges, 'quite right, but he inspired me to do the film myself, the way I ended up doing it.'

While Sony basked in the honeymoon of its marriage to Columbia, Mike Ovitz brokered a similar deal in mid–1990 for Matsushita to buy MCA/ Universal for $6.6 billion. The sale left Wasserman and Sheinberg fabulously rich – Wasserman collected $327 million, Sheinberg $120 million – but still in charge of the studio, under Matsushita management. Out of loyalty to Sheinberg, who had been deeply humiliated when his eldest son Jonathan, himself a producer, blabbed about the deal to friends, bringing charges of insider trading from the Securities and Exchange Commission, Spielberg, increasingly regarded in the business as Sheinberg's surrogate son, soft-pedalled his opposition to the red sun rising above Hollywood's horizon. 'We can be jealous of the Japanese,' he said, 'but we've got to give them credit for turning out great cars and great entertainment tools like VCRs and television sets.' They were also pioneers of high-definition TV, which he saw as the wave of the future. The Matsushita sale, however, was to prove a disastrous misalliance. Wasserman and Sheinberg continued to act as if they still owned Universal, sniping periodically at Matsushita, which swiftly decided it had been sold a pup and began looking for ways to get out.

Over on the old Columbia lot, Sony had not yet lost its optimism. At the end of 1990, Ovitz approached Spielberg with an offer. Akio Morita was anxious to launch his new studio with a lavish vehicle for Christmas

1991. Paramount's *Peter Pan* project, so loaded with turnaround costs that no studio would touch it, had drifted for years. Now at last someone could see a reason for taking it on. Ovitz proposed it to Spielberg as the first big Sony film. Money, he implied, was no object, and he could take his pick of CAA's clients for the cast.

After five meagre years, the prospect of a near-guaranteed hit tempted Spielberg. And there was no doubting that Sony was prepared to pay. Having spent $100 million on refurbishing Burbank, tens of millions more were being invested in films like *Hudson Hawk*, *Bugsy* and *Geronimo*, all doomed to be expensive flops. While Jon Peters sent empty Falcon jets to London at $30,000 a time to pick up his girlfriend, and gave her and his ex-wife executive positions, Peter Guber was also trying to drum up interest in a Sonyland theme park.

The trough beckoned, but still Spielberg was uneasy. Though Guber and Peters were the creative force at Columbia Sony, studio management was in the hands of his least favourite executive, Frank Price. Ovitz reassured him: the film could be produced though Columbia's sister company TriStar, now run by Spielberg's old friend and ex-agent Mike Medavoy.

The subject of *Peter Pan* troubled him too. He had grown up with the fable of the boy who wouldn't grow up. To many, it seemed the central metaphor of his life and career. For twenty years, he evoked it – in *E.T.*, *Kick the Can* from *The Twilight Zone*, *Indiana Jones and the Temple of Doom* and *Empire of the Sun*. He had worked actively on the Michael Jackson version, then Stoppard's.

Now, however, as the chance came to make it, he hesitated. As he'd said in 1988, he no longer felt an identification with Pan or his milieu. He also found the character difficult to focus on. Peter's sexlessness, which had led to him usually being played on stage by women (and which probably underlaid the character's appeal to Michael Jackson), posed problems of identification. Asked point-blank if *he* was Peter Pan, Spielberg replied, 'No, no. I think my mom is the quintessential Peter Pan. She even looks like him. Seriously.'

Despite the sanitised versions made by Disney and presented on stage as Christmas pantomime fare, *Peter Pan* was fraught with problems. New biographies had revealed Barrie as sexually impotent and obsessed with his mother. He may even have tried to stunt his growth in order to remain as child-like as possible. *Peter Pan*, which he wrote in 1904, is a minefield of psychosexual obsessions.

In the original play, Peter is a little London boy who escapes from the real world the day he's born and hides in Never Never Land, an island inhabited by fairies and children who died at birth or who have fallen out of their prams and been forgotten by their nannies. The boys live in a tree-house, all sleep in the same bed and dress in the skins of bears. Protected by his friends the Picanniny Indians, and helped by the fairy Tinkerbell, Peter leads them in battles against the pirate Captain Hook.

Occasionally he returns to London where, disconsolate that his parents have forgotten him, he makes friends with Wendy Darling and her two younger brothers, luring Wendy back to Never Never Land to become his and the Lost Boys' mother. Wanting a mother too, Hook and his pirates kidnap Wendy. Peter rescues her, and in despair Hook throws himself into the sea. A crocodile bites off his hand and thereafter follows him, hungry for the rest. Wendy returns every day – a year to her – to clean Peter's house, tuck the boys in and tell them bedtime stories. But as she matures, she can no longer communicate with Peter. Some of the boys return with her to London, grow up and forget Never Never Land. Peter however remains locked in his fantasy, an enduring metaphor of the flight from adult reality.

Barrie continued to embroider the story until his death in 1937, turning it into a novel in 1911 and even a film script for Paramount, never shot. 'Never Never Land' was shortened to 'Neverland', and Peter became progressively more bloodthirsty. He killed fourteen pirates, cut off Hook's hand and fed it to the crocodile, which had swallowed a clock and thus gave warning of its approach. In recompense, Hook, the character with whom Barrie himself identified, and whom he played in charade versions of the story, was given a loveable sidekick named Smee.

Hollywood finally 'licked' *Peter Pan* by transforming it into an entirely different story.

In the early eighties, the young son of neophyte screenwriter James V. Hart had asked, 'Dad, did Peter Pan ever grow up?'

'Yes,' thought Hart. 'Peter Pan *did* grow up. We all did. We all ended our childhood, we became lawyers, bankers, movie producers, moguls, accountants, Wall Street bankers. We stopped believing in those things we believed in as children. An hour later we had our story.'

Hart visualised the adult Peter as Peter Banning, a tycoon in thrall to his mobile phone, taking calls in the middle of his daughter's school play (*Peter Pan*, of course) and too busy to make his son's Little League final, where he misses the crucial score. His life as Pan is totally forgotten.

Wendy is a nonagenarian philanthropist still sheltering an aged Tootles, one of the rescued Lost Boys, who has never recovered from the loss of Neverland. When Hook hears Banning is in London to attend a banquet in her honour, he kidnaps his son and daughter, determined to lure him back to his childhood haunt for a showdown.

In Peter's absence, the pirates have swelled to a mob, while the Boys have developed into a multi-ethnic tribe run by 'The Pan', at the moment a skateboarding New York street kid named Rufio. With Tinkerbell's help, Banning relearns the skills of imagination that allow him to fly, takes over the tribe and rescues his kids from Hook, who has almost seduced Banning's son over to his side.

Hart sold the script to director Nick Castle, whose major credit was *The Last Starfighter*. Castle took it to producers Craig Baumgarten and Gary Adelson. Once Spielberg showed some interest, however, Castle was out, and the script quickly passed to Sony and CAA, where Dustin Hoffman read it, and further changed the emphasis by playing down Peter's role and building up the one on which he had his eye – Captain James Hook. Spielberg, claiming that he knew nothing of Castle's involvement, and that he was 'horrified' to discover it, left Medavoy to cut a deal that defined ownership and cleared the air. In a complex trade-off, TriStar bought everyone's rights, including those of the Great Ormond Street Hospital's nominee producer, Dodi Fayed. Baumgarten, Adelson, Fayed and Hart (who gets co-screenplay and co-story credit) are all listed as 'executive producers' on the complete film, now called *Hook*. Castle was fobbed off with joint credit for original story.

*   *   *

Sony and Ovitz welcomed the new high-concept *Hook*, and in particular its scope, worthy of a great *zaibatsu*. 'we got Spielberg!' exulted Peter Guber. 'That's like being blessed by the Pope.' He was right to be confident. One investment house estimated *Hook* must gross $200 million to make a profit, but given the advance video and broadcast TV sales, merchandising profits, foreign sales and exhibitors' guarantees, *Hook* would, like many Spielberg films, be in the black *before* shooting started. Even if he never finished it, insurance would cover Columbia's loss. It was every studio head's dream, the sure thing.

At the end of 1990 Sony announced its multi-star cast: Robin Williams as Peter, Julia Roberts as Tinkerbell, and of course Hoffman as Hook. Only Sir Richard Attenborough evaded Spielberg: he was too busy directing *Chaplin* to play Tootles. Michael Jackson no longer figured in the equation, nor did John Williams's songs, though a couple crept into the film, along with echoes of Jackson in the character of Rufio, generically Hispanic/black/punk.

Richard Dreyfuss offered to play Smee, but Spielberg was too canny to allow two such giant egos as Dreyfuss and Hoffman in the same scenes, and chose Bob Hoskins from *Who Framed Roger Rabbit*. Asked if he was chagrined, Dreyfuss snarled, 'I'm not just jealous of Hoskins. I'm even jealous of Julia Roberts as Tinkerbell.'

After seeing her in Lean's *A Passage to India*, Spielberg cast eighty-four-year-old Dame Peggy Ashcroft as Wendy. When she had to pull out because of back trouble, Frank Marshall asked costume designer Anthony Powell, then in New York for Hoffman's fittings, to suggest someone.

'How about Maggie Smith?' Powell said, loyally proposing a friend, and letting it drop in passing that she'd played Peter on stage in 1973.

'How old is she now?' Marshall asked.

'Oh, I dunno,' waffled Powell. 'She must be in her early nineties now. Ninety-one . . . ninety-two.'

Smith got the role, and was more than credible in it. She was fifty-eight at the time.

*   *   *

Above anything, *Hook* needed to be big. 'We all have expectations for Neverland,' Spielberg said, 'so we needed to put our heads together to create a Neverland that you could believe in, that would look like Neverland and not just Laguna Beach.' Eventually he decided this could only be achieved by creating the entire fantasy element of the film on sets: except for the opening sequences in California, all of *Hook* takes place inside.

The budget was set around $40 million, most of which Spielberg, Hoffman and Williams would cream under the deal crafted by Ovitz which gave them 40 per cent of the film's gross income. Julia Roberts worked for a flat – and fat – $2.5 million. Great Ormond Street Hospital received £300,000, plus net – not gross – points, which, under the system of 'rolling breaks', was tantamount to nothing at all. 'We don't expect it to make millions,' the hospital administrator agreed phlegmatically.

The sets were by *Brazil*'s Norman Garwood, with the aid of 'visual consultant' John Napier, suggested to Spielberg by David Geffen. Napier designed the 1982 Royal Shakespeare Company production of *Peter Pan* and also conceived the eye-filling staging for *Nicholas Nickleby*, *Cats*, *Les Misérables* and *Miss Saigon*. The practical solidity of his sets brings the film closer to stage than screen, but it's more like a Disneyland ride than either. A skateboard track winds through the tree-house of the Lost Boys, which is riddled with secret panels and tunnels, as is the pirate headquarters. A complex of galleons, docks, store-rooms and Hook's sumptuous apartment, it's a Victorian stage entrepreneur's wet dream of trapdoors and reversible staircases.

Hook spilled over nine stages at Culver City, including, to Spielberg's great pleasure, Stage Twenty-Seven, where the Emerald City scenes of *The Wizard Of Oz* had been shot. There simply weren't enough performers to fill this vast space, so the pirate crew swelled with 150 extras drawn from the roughest end of Hollywood (and corralled separately from the high-priced talent when not on camera), and augmented still further with well-disguised cameos: Quincy Jones, rock musician David Crosby, even Glenn Close, lost in an impenetrable beard. In the London scenes, Phil Collins did a brief bit as a policeman.

*   *   *

Once Spielberg took on *Hook*, the script was further rewritten by his informal advisers. 'Steven tends to use writers like paintbrushes,' says James Hart. 'He wants this writer for this, this writer for that.' Carrie Fisher was credited with Tinkerbell's feisty dialogue, which turned the fairy into an improbably jealous suitor for Peter. In the most embarrassing scene of an often profoundly shame-making film, Tink magics herself to full size, slips into a Barbie-doll ball dress and makes a pass at her old playmate. Robin Williams, a sexless performer on screen, normally expresses his enthusiasms for women, as for everything else, in a flood of improvised comedy. He should have responded with an extended riff on this abrupt and deeply, if unintentionally, comic transformation. Instead, as through the rest of the film, he stands dumbfounded, then retires in dismay. Spielberg admits that suppressing Williams's comic invention was a fundamental error. 'I should have released Robin and let him go wildly in all directions. I contained Robin.'

One result of reining in Williams was to give Hoffman's devil all the best tunes. Once the film got going, the actor employed Malia Scotch Marmo, whose script for Lasse Hallström's *Once Around* with Dreyfuss and Holly Hunter was highly regarded, to rewrite Hook, whom he visualised as a bucktoothed Boston Brahmin with overtones of right-wing commentator William Buckley Jr. Some people compared his accent and style to a mix of Ronald Colman and James Mason, others to British comic Terry-Thomas. Critic Michael Coveney saw the 'gap-toothed, laboriously posh-vowelled rollicking swordsman with a gleaming silver mitt' as 'the ultimate cultural revenge on generations of English actors both flaunting their educated manners in Hollywood and adopting phoney American accents on the stage', but it's more likely that Hoffman, not for the first time, let his imagination get out of hand. The character he hung on Hook was the greasiest kind of ham.

Nothing about *Hook* was cheap and, since Sony seemed anxious to make their debut as splashy as possible, the cost continued to climb until it hovered around $75 million. There were no special disasters – simply the gradual erosion of a budget under the trickle of second thoughts.

The sole major glitch was occasioned by Julia Roberts. As shooting approached, the star, who'd just had her biggest hit as an improbably innocent prostitute in *Pretty Woman*, collapsed from 'exhaustion'. Abruptly calling off her marriage to actor Kiefer Sutherland, she flew to Ireland to see her new lover (and Sutherland's former best friend) Jason Patric. Spielberg contemplated filling the role with Kim Basinger or Michelle Pfeiffer, but Roberts finally reported for work. Since her contract had run out, however, Sony negotiated a new deal for $75,000 a day, and left the insurance companies to wrangle over who paid. Roberts did most of her scenes against a blue screen, which allowed them to be slotted into the film later by the special-effects wizards at ILM. A special make-up man was paid £2000 simply to keep her feet clean.

Hook, though technically a closed set, was *the* production to visit. Akio Morita toured the stages with his entourage, and was impressed, but painter David Hockney found the project grotesque, a creation without style, without imagination, that traded on sheer size. The exercise of technique in a vacuum produced nothing. Zero multiplied by seventy million remained zero.

Even Spielberg began to doubt. Each day he came on the set, he faced the nagging question, 'Is this flying out of control?' The year before, Jeffrey Katzenberg had circulated a twenty-eight-page memo to his staff at Disney suggesting it was time to 'blaze a path away from unreasonable salaries and participation deals'. Made in the shadow of scandals that racked American business, the film looked like being a valedictory for an era of Hollywood excess now ended. 'Maybe *Hook* is going to be the last show I put on,' Spielberg mused. 'A lot of my movies in the future are going to have to scale down.'

Not even this personal caveat prepared him for the miserable reviews *Hook* earned when it opened in 2197 theatres across the country for Christmas 1991. It grossed $14 million on its first weekend – not enough for a film that, if one took the costs of publicity and distribution into account, needed to make $200 million to break even. 'It has to rake in another $14 million this weekend,' said one exhibitor morosely. 'If it doesn't, there's a big problem.'

Variety found the film 'messy and undisciplined', while loyally pointing out that it 'splashes every bit of its megabudget ... onto the screen'. Exhibitors who'd paid a fortune were assured 'major hit status seems guaranteed'. Less partial critics were more savage. Many compared the film to the glutinous Technicolor confections the Lost Boys dream up to throw at one another, or a giant frosted cake that induced sugar shock. 'By the time this overstuffed epic comes to its conclusion,' said *Newsweek*, 'you feel like you've been watching the dance of an eight-hundred-pound elf.' Others were reminded of an amusement park ride. 'Peel away the expensive special-effects surface and there's nothing but formula,' wrote the *Washington Post*. For once, Spielberg ignored his rule and read the critics. 'Steven took it hard,' says one insider. 'Even my kids took it hard.'

In the self-critical moral climate that followed the junk-bond scandals of Wall Street, the ultimate responsibility for *Hook*'s failure was much-discussed. Many took the obvious route of blaming Spielberg for parading his pre-adolescent fantasies in public, but if there is a genuinely collabor-ative film in his career, an affirmation of his faith in consensus, it's *Hook*. He had refused the cup half a dozen times, but someone always passed it back. And once he accepted its particular mix of stars, money and expectation, the project assumed a life of its own over which he had little control.

He could console himself that the film, as anticipated, at least covered its costs on worldwide release. By early 1994 it had made $119.7 million in domestic rentals and $179.8 million overseas – respectable figures, but disappointing in the light of the original high hopes. It was nominated for five Oscars, all technical, but won none. Analysts had been almost hoping it would fail, as a corrective to the inflation that was driving production costs into the stratosphere. 'What the industry needs,' said one expert, Mark Manson of the investment house Donaldson Lufkin and Jenrette, while the film was still shooting, 'is for *Hook* to bomb so Sony can say "That's enough; we're not going to do this any more."'

The failure did colour the company's relations with Hollywood, but not enough to drive them out. For the next four years Sony haemorrhaged money and credibility as it struggled in a business determined to exclude it. In 1993 it plunged $124 million in the red on *Last Action Hero*, an

Arnold Schwarzenegger adventure which they'd hoped would save the film division. When it didn't, they began to negotiate to get out. Another foreigner had been put in his place – and Spielberg, in a roundabout way, was responsible.

18

Jurassic Park and Schindler's List

Nazis! I *hate* those guys.

Harrison Ford in *Indiana Jones and the Last Crusade*

THROUGHOUT THE early weeks of 1992, it became increasingly obvious to everyone that Steve Ross was dying. He'd flown back from Paris in the autumn of 1991 to attend Spielberg and Kate Capshaw's wedding in the Hamptons, but in October, after closing a huge new deal with Toshiba, back pain forced him into bed. A prostate tumour for which he'd been intermittently treated in secret had spread to the spine. Doctors started intensive chemotherapy, but without much hope. Spielberg was distraught. Another father was deserting him, and he was again powerless. Appointing himself unofficial jester, he dedicated himself to lightening Ross's last months. *Schindler's List* went onto the back burner again, and he took refuge in the reassuring technical challenges of *Jurassic Park*.

Michael Crichton had delivered a script which satisfied neither himself nor Spielberg. The author admitted he was tired of the story. Since, however, he knew better than anyone how to balance its factual detail against the needs of narrative, they agreed on a first draft which special-effects technicians could use in visualising dinosaurs and settings. In October 1991, on the set of *Hook*, Kathleen Kennedy, who would be producing *Jurassic Park*, asked Dustin Hoffman's scriptwriter Malia Scotch Marmo if she would be interested in rewriting Crichton's screenplay. By March 1992, she'd delivered her version. It removed Crichton's mouthpiece, the 'chaotician' Ian Malcolm, and transferred his anti-biotechnology dialogue to the palaeontologist Alan Grant, whom Scotch Marmo made a crusader against the commercialisation of science. By inserting scenes of plants overgrowing the park buildings and insinuating themselves into its mechanisms, she sought also to emphasise the book's message that man was powerless to contain nature. Spielberg didn't like this version either, and the project passed to David Koepp, who had been co-writing Robert Zemeckis's *Death Becomes Her*, a fantasy about cosmetic surgery gone mad.

Koepp's script for *Jurassic Park*, co-credited with Crichton, but written, Koepp insists, without his reading either Crichton's or Scotch Marmo's, became the one to be filmed. As usual, however, the real author was Spielberg. Like the sculptor who explained that, to turn a block of stone into a nymph, one merely cut away all the parts that didn't look nymph-like, a process of reduction which he micro-managed had revealed the film within Crichton's novel. British fantasy author Kim Newman itemised its elements, and their parallels in Spielberg's other work:

> The paring-down of a monster best-seller into a suspense machine (*Jaws*); the tackling of a popular-science childhood sense of wonder perennial with state-of-the-art effects that re-imagine 1950s B-science fiction (*Close Encounters of the Third Kind*); the all-action jungle adventure littered with incredible perils and gruesome deaths (*Raiders of the Lost Ark*); and big-eyed creatures who range from beatifically benevolent to toothily murderous (*Gremlins, E.T.*).

Ironically, the man who so tersely rejected the *politique des auteurs* two decades before had become its most successful exemplar.

Spielberg spent most weekends during the spring of 1992 with Ross in the Hamptons, reading scripts in the garden while the entrepreneur ran his business by phone, playing the power game with his usual vigour. A supporter of Bill Clinton, Ross even politicised the neutral Spielberg, who had once described himself as 'a Democrat with a Republican lining

... liberal about a lot of things but ... bullish about America'. Under Ross's influence, he become an active Democrat and Clinton enthusiast. The following year, Clinton would stay with the Spielbergs on visits to Los Angeles, and Hillary would jog on the beach with Kate. The world premiere of *Jurassic Park* took place in Washington DC, a benefit for Hillary's favourite charity, the Children's Defense Fund, and the President contributed a laudatory quote to a 'Special Spielberg Issue' of the *Hollywood Reporter* published on 10 March 1994.

When chemotherapy left Ross particularly low, Spielberg raked his memory for amusing incidents from their shared yacht cruises and fishing trips. Ross never lost his sense of humour. Once, when Spielberg and Courtney visited him in the Southampton hospital, Ross mentioned a report of people being poisoned by Louisiana oysters, and wondered where his lunchtime shellfish had come from, Long Island or Louisiana. Spielberg and Courtney were horrified when a doctor burst in, announcing that sixty patients were down with oyster poisoning. They were taken in until Ross started laughing.

Ross's impending death concentrated Spielberg's mind on his own future, both artistic and financial. The Hollywood he'd known when he entered the business at the end of the sixties had changed out of all recognition. MGM no longer existed. Sony Columbia was lurching from disaster to disaster under the erratic management of Guber and Peters. Disney was in its usual state of confusion, in part because of frequent clashes between Michael Eisner and the ambitious Jeffrey Katzenberg. Tom Pollock had not proved an assertive head of Universal, where Wasserman and Sheinberg still called the shots. But for how much longer? There was already friction with Matsushita over policy.

It was in this period of distraction that Spielberg did his most productive thinking about *Schindler's List*. He'd immersed himself in the period, watching documentaries about and reconstructions of the Holocaust until their texture was ingrained. In particular, he screened four times the entire ten hours of *Shoah*, released in 1985 by the French documentarist Claude Lanzmann, consisting mostly of testimony by survivors of Nazi pogroms. Documentaries, and in particular *Shoah*, inspired the look of *Schindler's List*. It was a style both realist and romantic, pioneered by thirties still photographers like August Sander but adapted by Lanzmann, as well as by German director Edgar Reitz, who exploited it for *Heimat*, the epic fifteen-hour reconstruction of life in Germany from the end of World War I to the economic miracle of the seventies that reached the cinemas in 1984.

As for the tall, commanding Schindler, effortlessly attractive to women and able to charm even Nazi generals, Spielberg saw him as a moral ancestor of Steve Ross. If Ross were an actor, Spielberg told him, he would put him in the part. Once he'd cast Liam Neeson as Schindler, he screened home movies of Ross for the actor. The film would also be dedicated to Ross.

Since he had worked for Spielberg during the auditions for *Empire of the Sun* in 1987, Neeson had had a patchy career, including a largely unsuccessful and nerve-racking year in Hollywood which almost ruined his health. An actor who lived on his nerves, he contracted diverticulitis and had 40 per cent of his colon removed. However he bounced back in 1988 with *Satisfaction* opposite Julia Roberts, who became one of his many lovers. Barbra Streisand, Brooke Shields, pop singer Sinead O'Connor and Jennifer Grey followed her to his bed. 'Women just go crazy over him.' says his friend, director Neil Jordan, sourly. 'He doesn't do anything to warrant it – or deserve it.'

In 1990 Neeson starred in Sam Raimi's horror film *Darkman*. He was seen by the actress Natasha Richardson, who was about to play Eugene O'Neill's *Anna Christie* on Broadway and needed someone for her seaman lover Matt Burke. Neeson accepted the role, and plunged into an affair with Richardson. Their attraction blazed on stage. Critic John Lahr called Neeson 'a sequoia of sex' and said, 'Not since Brando tossed meat up to Stella in *A Streetcar Named Desire* has flesh made such a spectacular entrance.' Neeson and Richardson later married.

Spielberg took Kate and her mother to see *Anna Christie*. Afterwards, they went backstage. When Mrs Capshaw told Neeson how moved she'd been, and wept, the actor impulsively hugged her. Later, Kate said to Spielberg, 'That's exactly what Schindler would have done.' With his bulk, his deep voice and his commanding profile, like pre-war German star Hans Albers, Neeson was also an archetypal thirties figure. Although

Harrison Ford, Robert Duvall, Mel Gibson, Kevin Costner, Australian actor Jack Thompson and Daniel Day-Lewis had shown interest in the part, Spielberg sent Neeson the script and shot a screen test before he left to start *Jurassic Park* in August 1992.

Universal's first $56 million budget for *Jurassic Park* quickly ballooned to $65 million as special-effects engineers began bringing Crichton's dinosaurs to life. One result of the three screenplays had been to slim down his prehistoric *dramatis personae*, which had included both a full-grown and an infant tyrannosaurus rex, a playful baby triceratops as well as its mother, some long-necked but cow-like brachiosaurs, taller than a tree, packs of procompsognathids, mild-mannered scavengers the size of small dogs, a stampeding herd of gallimimuses, and velociraptors, the most savage of dinosaurs, ranging from chicken-sized to a full-grown six feet.

As much in the interests of economy as art, the film dropped the babies, lost the procompsognathids, but built up the role of the velociraptors, literally 'fast grabbers', which became *Jurassic Park*'s true villains. First identified from fossils in 1924, velociraptors hadn't preoccupied palaeontologists much until a 1971 dig in Mongolia unearthed one which had died while tearing a protoceratops to pieces. Its six-inch-long razor-sharp claws indicated a born predator, but otherwise little was known about these animals and, of that, not much fitted the film. They probably hunted in packs, and might have communicated with soft hooting noises, like owls, two suppositions which the film turned into dramatically effective reality. On the debit side, however, they probably looked more like rats than lizards in real life. They also flourished fifty million years before the Jurassic era. In general, however, chronology went out the window on *Jurassic Park*, the creatures of which were dismissed by dinosaur expert Don Lessem as 'a hodgepodge of animals that have more to do with the Cretaceous period (135 to 65 million years B.P.) than with . . . the Jurassic period'.

To put these creatures on screen, *Jurassic Park* pushed out the envelope of special effects. Spielberg, with reason, disliked computer-generated images which, even in Robert Zemeckis's fantasy about cosmetic surgery, *Death Becomes Her*, where ILM used computer animation to melt holes in Meryl Streep and twist flesh like putty, were never 100 per cent lifelike. In particular, the T. rex, which had to attack, batter, tear open and overturn two four-wheel-drive vehicles, seemed to demand a full-sized twenty-foot creature.

Spielberg had seen such an animal at Universal's new Florida theme park, where the King Kong ride, a favourite of the Los Angeles tour, had been reconstructed and improved by Robert Gurr of GurrDesign. T. rex designs were commissioned from Gurr, but memories of the ridiculous $1 million King Kong built for Dino de Laurentiis's remake persuaded Spielberg to abandon the mechanical route and approach Stan Winston, whose realisation of H.R. Giger's innovative designs for the monsters in James Cameron's 1986 sf horror film *Aliens* surpassed those of Ridley Scott's seminal 1979 original. Winston contracted to create all the film's dinosaurs, including a full-sized T. rex, as electronically-controlled puppets. Model animator Phil Tippett would build smaller versions to be photographed in stop-motion animation, the traditional technique for dinosaur movies since the silent era. ILM were given the relatively minor task of creating vistas of the park with dinosaurs moving in the distance.

Actors had been in no hurry to play straight man to a T. rex. Richard Dreyfuss and Kurt Russell wanted too much money to play Grant. There were complaints again from some supporting players about Spielberg's tightness in imposing the so-called 'Pact Contract' which absolved the production from paying full SAG rates. 'There is no excuse,' said one, 'for a director like Spielberg to be paying actors with important roles $430 a week.' But given a gold-plated certainty at the box office like this, few declined. The job was made even more attractive when Crichton's ending, in which the island is fire-bombed, gave way to one in which the park and its animals remain intact for the inevitable sequel.

When William Hurt also turned down the role of Grant, it went to Sam Neill. Jeff Goldblum became Malcolm, Laura Dern was Ellie, and Briton Bob Peck played the white hunter Muldoon, a character who, like many in the film, became more 'actor-friendly' as the script evolved. Wayne Knight's obese Nedry, computer nerd and junk-food junkie, and Martin Ferraro as the lawyer Gennaro, a parody of corporate man with poor skin, baggy suit and unsuitable shoes, are in the story mostly to be eaten. Gennaro has the film's most humiliating end, perched, trembling, on a bush lavatory with pants round his ankles as the T. rex pauses for the laugh, then swoops to munch him like a hot dog.

John Hammond's children were off the hook – off the *Hook* in the case of nine-year-old Joseph Mazello, who had been up for the role of Robin Williams's son Jack in that film before being cast as Tim in *Jurassic Park*. Ariana Richards, shorn of the original's irritating mannerism, was a resourceful and grown-up Alexis. Richard Attenborough agreed to play John Hammond. At Spielberg's insistence, the crotchety, almost dwarfish curmudgeon of the book, greedy for profit and so indifferent to disaster that he's ready to start work all over again in another location with frozen embryos squirreled away in a secret cache, had metamorphosed into a jolly Santa Claus whose toys have got out of hand.

Script revisions also softened and romanticised Grant and Ellie. Now a couple, they nervously circle the idea of marriage and, more important, children, towards whom Grant is negative. In a new opening scene of surprising hostility for a Spielberg film, the palaeontologist scares a (inevitably fat) smartass kid by demonstrating with a fossilised velociraptor's claw the technique it would have used to gut him. In the course of saving Hammond's grandchildren from the dinosaurs, however, he comes to enjoy fatherhood.

Jeff Goldblum played Malcolm, also humanised in the script, at his most saturnine and satyr-like. Once again, location shooting fulfilled Spielberg's definition as the Rites of Spring when Dern and Goldblum became embroiled in a romance. As a consequence, Goldblum divorced Geena Davis and Dern her director husband Renny Harlin. Shortly afterwards Goldblum married Dern, and Davis married Harlin.

The pattern of *Jurassic Park* changed abruptly when, in mid-year, ILM decided to fight Spielberg's decision to rely on mainly corporeal creatures. Using new software that had just come on the market, they took Winston's designs for the gallimimus and the T. rex bone structure, laser-scanned them in three dimensions, fed them into their computers, and came up with fully animated skeletons. Replicating the gallimimuses into a herd, they shot them stampeding across an African background and sent the tape to Amblin.

Spielberg was astonished. This was a quantum leap beyond *Death Becomes Her*. The skeletons moved with absolute fidelity to life – something that always evaded stop-motion figures. He immediately cancelled his order for Tippett's puppets and handed everything to ILM. Except where the actors needed to interact physically with a creature, as in Winston's animatronic T. rex, a brachiosaur head, an ailing triceratops and the velociraptors, every dinosaur in *Jurassic Park* would be computer-generated.

After rejecting Costa Rica and Mexico as locations, Kathleen Kennedy decided to shoot the live-action sequences on the Hawaiian island of Kauai. Spielberg admitted this was less an aesthetic decision than a function of his age. He wanted to eat food that didn't give him dysentery, and to sleep each evening in a comfortable hotel. In late August, the 140-person crew rolled into the canyons of the island's interior, trailing their heavy equipment: not only Dean Cundey's cameras and lights but the generators to run them, and also the dinosaurs or part-dinosaurs they were to film.

These included the ailing full-sized triceratops. Winston's technicians worked round the clock to finish the animal which, in addition to being constructed to look convincing while lying on its side, had to have practical working eyes and a mouth with tongue, and to breathe realistically. But the use to which Spielberg puts this prodigy of ingenuity is a telling demonstration of Michael Arlen's suggestion that films were labouring under a 'Tyranny of the Visual'.

The visitors encounter the sick animal with the park's vet, Harding, and Dern decides, from its swollen tongue and dilated pupils, that it's been eating African lilac, which is poisonous. However, the enormous droppings yield no seeds. The solution – which the book provides – is that, like the birds into which they evolved, dinosaurs swallowed stones and retained them in their gizzards to grind food. From time to time, they replaced the stones. The Triceratops had been ingesting lilac seeds with the stones, but disposing of the evidence when it emptied its gizzard. This, or the concept of gizzard stones, isn't explained in the film, since Dern's explanation was cut from the released version. Now, she simply wanders off, chewing over the problem, and the tour moves on to its encounter with T. rex. One can see the reasoning. Gizzard stones are too complicated for teenagers to grasp. Then why not cut the whole sequence, not just the pay-off? And waste an animatronic triceratops? You know what those things *cost*?

Hawaii reserved its revenge for Hollywood's invasion until the last day of shooting. On 11 September Hurricane Iniki, the most severe of the century, raged across the islands with winds of 130 m.p.h. and gusts as high as 160 m.p.h. Twenty-foot waves crashed on the shore and the film crew took refuge in the ballroom of the Westin Kauai Hotel, specially armoured in concrete. Even as the storm ripped off its roof and water began to gush through the ceiling, Spielberg had time to think about movies. It was just like James Basevi's Oscar-winning special effects for John Ford's *The Hurricane*. Someone more philosophical might have reflected that, in real life as in the film, Nature would always triumph over the puny efforts of technology.

Even in Hawaii, Spielberg didn't forget Steve Ross. He dreamed up a private movie, a parody of *It's a Wonderful Life* which he filmed as soon as he got back.

We had Bob Daly and Terry Semel as hobos, looking for food in trashcans. Clint Eastwood, instead of being the legend, was a stunt man: an extra. ([Producer] Joel Silver shoots him – and actually kills him.) Quincy [Jones] was Clarence, the angel. Chevy Chase was God. I was in a mental institution, totally enclosed in a straitjacket, just my fingers free. I was putting together in shaving foam the face of E.T. and not quite knowing what I was trying to express. I said, 'He came to me . . . he came to me . . . he was a six foot three E.T.'

Ross died on 20 December. Courtney Ross insisted on a lavish ceremony in the Guild Hall in East Hampton, which was redecorated for the occasion. Even the paintings were taken down and replaced with a large de Kooning. A cameraman filmed everything: Courtney was a documentary producer. Spielberg and Kate led a contingent of celebrities that included Quincy Jones, Anouk Aimée, Nastassja Kinski, Paul Simon, Dustin Hoffman and Barbra Streisand. Delivering one of the eulogies, Spielberg said, 'For the last couple of days, I feel cold. I can't keep warm. I feel like there's a draught through my heart – and I know that Steve is up there, trying to figure out a way to plug up the holes.' Rather than being buried in the new Jewish cemetery, Ross was interred in the Green River Cemetery, near the graves of Jackson Pollock and Elaine de Kooning.

A numbed Spielberg continued supervising the special effects of *Jurassic Park*, scheduled for release in June 1993. ILM's computer brilliance hadn't worked out quite as well as he hoped. Their dinosaurs moved with precision, but they looked like robots: they couldn't 'act'. Phil Tippett, the specialist in stop-action, was called back to make them look more natural – and received an Oscar for his work.

Steven Zaillian had meanwhile delivered a script of *Schindler's List* which was the first to convey a comprehensible view of Schindler's character. The reductive process that had worked in turning *Peter Pan* and *Jurassic Park* into films finally trimmed the intractable story to a manageable size. It had taken longer, but some pieces of rock were more nymph-like than others. Spielberg sent the script to Tom Stoppard, who confirmed his opinion. Zaillian was, said Stoppard, 'the best screenwriter I had come across, almost ever'.

Zaillian's version, influenced by Spielberg, owes much to Robert Bolt's scripts for David Lean. Thomas Keneally, visiting Krakow for some of the filming, was reminded forcibly of *Lawrence of Arabia*. '[The film] had that authoritative feel, and even though it played with time and the literal facts, it was poetically accurate.' The characters in *Lawrence*, as in Spielberg's version of Keneally's book, 'don't have linear motivations'.

He went on: 'All of them operate from a mixture of self-image, opportunism and altruism. There's no one out there who can fully explain his or her motivation.' The parallels with Hollywood films of the thirties were even clearer than those with *Lawrence*. Schindler emerges from the film as a figure of glamour and charisma, like Steve Ross, and, also like Ross, larger than life. In dramatic terms, he stands at the apex of a triangle, at the other corners of which are Amon Goeth, the camp commander whom he cajoled, seduced and hypnotised into colluding in his plan, and Itzhak Stern, the Jewish accountant he chooses to run his company.

A simple man who understands only business and survival, Stern parallels Lawrence's mentor, master and cautious ally Feisal in *Lawrence*. Feisal is happy to use the fanatical stranger, but wary of him, and baffled by his motives. 'With Major Lawrence, mercy is a passion,' he says of Lawrence's obsession with caring for enemy wounded. 'With me, it is merely good manners.' Stern doesn't know why Schindler is always trying to share a schnapps with him, or thank him. He will be more than content if he can live till morning. Initially he sees little difference between Schindler and Goeth, except that one is on his side, the other his enemy. But his uncomplaining efficiency is a silent rebuke to his employer, and it's in trying to win the accountant's friendship that Schindler refines his own compassion.

The character of Stern, in which Zaillian conflated a number of Jews who managed Schindler's affairs, is one of the film's many concessions to Hollywood formula. Spencer Tracy played a similar role as the priest friend of club-owner Clark Gable in W.S. Van Dyke's 1936 *San Francisco*, a film which, structurally, *Schindler's List* much resembles. It was only through formula, tradition and consensus – his gizzard stones – that Spielberg could digest any subject, though these worked better on some elements of the story than others. 'Spielberg was very taken with Schindler's ambiguities,' says Keneally. 'That was the specific thing he liked about the man, this contradiction – the scoundrel/saviour, the rogue/ deliverer, the man who treated his wife badly but treated thousands of strangers well.' But such a contradictory personality didn't lend itself to stock characterisation, and, however interesting Spielberg found the contrasts in the book, he suppressed most of them in the film.

What both he and the audience most needed to have answered was what Spielberg called, after Charles Foster Kane's muttered word at the start of *Citizen Kane*, 'the Rosebud question'. What turned Schindler overnight from pleasure-loving opportunist to selfless benefactor? Keneally, with his theological background, felt no pressing need for an explanation. Such things happened; one took them on faith. Privately, he seems to feel that Schindler was a little mad, and his change of heart irrational – or, if one preferred a mystical explanation, transcendental. Spielberg knew his audience needed a more solid explanation. 'It wasn't to be a hero, I don't think,' he said, 'because he did have some modesty about him. That was part of his charm.' It may, the film implies, have been his fascination with the concept of power. As Schindler explains to Goeth, the emperor who spares the life of a transgressor is exercising more power than when he kills him. Finally, however, the question is unanswerable, since Schindler never answered it himself.

The film doesn't so much explain Rosebud as show Schindler at the precise moment of revelation. On the morning that the Krakow ghetto is destroyed and its inhabitants shipped to Goeth's camp, Schindler is out riding with his mistress. From a bluff about the city, they see soldiers ruthlessly emptying the houses, shooting people who resist, herding the rest into trucks. A little girl weaves expressionlessly through this nightmare, ignored by everyone. In a visual conceit as movingly appropriate as it is banal, Spielberg highlights her by tinting her coat a dusty red. Unnoticed, she slips through a door. The sequence should have ended there, but we see her climbing the stairs and hiding under the bed. Later, a smear of red in a handcart piled with corpses shows her fate.

Schindler's soul, we infer, has been so scalded by this image that he resolves to save the Jews under his protection. This is such a David Lean answer that Spielberg must have had as much to do with it as did Zaillian, who confirms that this scene, a major sticking point between them, was rewritten on the plane after a visit both made to Poland. The three or four pages of the ghetto sequence swelled to thirty, in which Spielberg documents the fate of everyone so far encountered in the story.

Lean's signature is even more apparent in the way Spielberg shoots Schindler's reaction. When, in a similar scene, Yuri Zhivago in *Doctor*

Zhivago watches Czarist cavalry cutting down demonstrators, Lean put the camera on Omar Sharif's face so that we sense his anguish. He did the same with Peter O'Toole in *Lawrence of Arabia* when, in order to save the expedition against Aqaba, he executes a man, and finds he enjoys killing. In both cases, there is something sexual in the revelation. Lean told Sharif to imagine, as he visualised the massacre, that he was fucking a woman but trying to hold back his orgasm. Schindler, too, on his horse, with his beautiful mistress, seems more excited than moved. Both he and Goeth are gripped by the pornography of violence. The Nazi casually murdering his prisoners, mostly unsuspecting women, with a rifle from his villa above the camp, is paralleled by Schindler standing at the top of the staircase to his factory and assessing the women who come to beg his protection. Unless they're pretty, they don't pass the doorman.

Ralph Fiennes, an English actor who'd caught Spielberg's attention playing Lawrence of Arabia in the British TV film *A Dangerous Man*, was cast as Goeth, and, though not Jewish, Ben Kingsley, an Oscar-winner for *Gandhi*, made an ideal Stern. When the film was already well advanced, Spielberg felt some supporting characters lacked dimension, and added scenes for the labourers in Schindler's factory, including the young Poldek Pfefferberg. Zaillian was directing his first film, *Searching for Bobby Fischer*, and too busy to do more rewrites, especially those with which, like these, he wasn't in sympathy, so Spielberg tried to bring in Stoppard again. Stoppard recalls:

> Steven sent me this version, and I thought it was in danger of becoming a script less good than the one I had read, and it turned out that Zaillian and I were fighting the same fight. Steven wanted me to have a pass on it, but it was still Zaillian's material. I was trying to take out stuff which had crept in which I didn't think was helping. There were certain logical problems in the narrative. I simply wrote Steven a long letter pointing out what the problem was, and what they should do about it, and why they should leave certain things alone and certain changes shouldn't have been made. Zaillian finished his film and came back on *Schindler*. And that was it, except for one day

when they were in Krakow – there was just one scene where Steven called me from Poland and I did a tiny thing overnight which he needed. But whatever my involvement with *Schindler* over the years, it is completely and absolutely Zaillian's script and nobody else's.

Spielberg decreed that the film would be shot entirely in Poland, with a Polish cameraman, Janusz Kaminski, and a Polish line producer, Branko Lustig, himself an Auschwitz survivor who carried a tattooed number. To design the production he hired Allan Starski, a Pole who as well as working for Andrzej Wajda had earned his Hollywood credentials with Alan Pakula's version of *Sophie's Choice*. In a reverse of his normal practice, which gave him gross participation from the first dollar, Spielberg told Sheinberg, 'I don't want any money until you guys make all your costs back.' Since he contemplated a film of more than three hours, with a largely unknown cast, and as surveys had shown that 60 per cent of American high school students, his primary audience, had never even heard of the Nazi extermination of the Jews, nobody had high hopes of profit anyway.

In February 1993, Steve Ross's memorial service took place in Carnegie Hall. Soprano Beverly Sills was the mistress of ceremonies at the two-and-half-hour event. New York's then mayor, David Dinkins, Hugh Carey, former governor of New York, and Caroline Lang, representing her father Jack, France's Minister of Culture, all spoke, as did Spielberg.

Also in February, *Jurassic Park* was unveiled for the retail companies licensed to tie in their products with the film. Increasingly, the deals which linked a new film to soft drinks, fast foods, clothing or toys were almost as important as selling seats. Universal and Amblin skimmed between 6 and 10 per cent of the wholesale price of every item. In particular, McDonald's were to launch a marketing effort of unprecedented proportions for *Jurassic Park*. In the Dinosaur Room at the Museum of Natural History in New York, the diplomatically-termed 'Marketing Partners' browsed on snacks, observed dispassionately by skeletons of the animals about to be seen in the flesh on screens across

the country, then trooped into the museum's giant-screen IMAX theatre
to goggle in understandable awe at some preliminary footage.

The seventy-five-day shoot of *Schindler's List* began on 1 March. The
intention had been to start in Auschwitz, where Spielberg hoped to
reconstruct the original crematoria, complete with chimneys, and use
1500 extras as prisoners. Despite signs warning visitors 'You are entering
a place of exceptional horror and tragedy. Please show your respect by
behaving in a manner suitable to the dignity of their memory,' both
Auschwitz and nearby Birkenau had been thoroughly, though discreetly,
commercialised, with restaurants, snack bars, exhibits and regular guided
tours. Despite this, and notwithstanding the fact that six other fiction
features, plus numerous documentaries, had been shot inside the wire,
the World Jewish Congress, which administered the camp, protested to
the Polish ambassador in the US about Spielberg's project, claiming to
fear a 'Disney version' of the Holocaust that would turn Auschwitz into
'a Hollywood backlot'. In fact, the real problem was procedural and
bureaucratic: Amblin had sought permission direct from the Polish
government rather than going through the Congress, the museum authorities and other Jewish organisations. Spielberg could have shot almost
anywhere else without anyone being the wiser, but Auschwitz had a
talismanic significance to him that he wasn't about to sacrifice. Since the
closest the administrators would let him to the real Auschwitz was
the front gate, he had Starski build a mirror image of the camp outside
the wire, the gate their only shared element. 'As far as I was concerned,'
Spielberg said truculently, 'we were shooting at Auschwitz.'

In the film, Schindler bribes Goeth into releasing 1100 workers into
his custody, and hires trains to ship them to Czechoslovakia. The men
arrive safely, but the women are diverted to Auschwitz and, with typical
despatch, stripped, shaved and herded into showers within an hour
of arrival. Normally they would be gassed, but Schindler, in an edgy
negotiating scene which underlines the fact that he is closer in temperament and sensibility to the Nazis than to the people he saves, bribes the
commandant with diamonds to release them. (It actually took Schindler
three weeks to get them out.)

These scenes were, for Spielberg, the most harrowing of the production. He wept as he looked through the viewfinder. 'It was a horrible, hysterical couple of hours,' he said of the shower sequence, 'and it was the kind of thing that I guess I could have humanely said, "Cut, we're all too emotionally involved to continue." But I thought it was important that we get it over with. We spent three or four horrible hours in that place, it was terrible for everybody.' To keep up his spirits meantime, he often rang Robin Williams, now a close friend, in Los Angeles. 'He made me laugh a lot,' Spielberg said. 'It was a great over-the-counter prescription.'

The fact that Spielberg, in the midst of recording the horrors of genocide, could supervise the completion of *Jurassic Park*, confirms his status as the most protean of contemporary film-makers. Initially, he didn't think it could be managed, and asked Richard Attenborough to take over shooting on *Schindler's List* for two weeks while he finished editing the earlier film. When Attenborough wasn't available, George Lucas handled day-to-day supervision of *Jurassic Park*, for which he receives a special credit at the end of the film.

Spielberg paid $1.5 million a week to a Warsaw TV station to reserve two satellite channels, one for image, the other for voice, and an additional $40,000 a week for permanent use of a satellite downlink machine through which his staff in Hollywood transmitted the *Jurassic Park* material. Every weekend and on one or two nights a week, he would download the dinosaur footage onto video, work on it with his editor Michael Kahn, then, at Kahn's insistence, spend two more hours on *Schindler*, so he could go to sleep thinking of that film. When *Park* was edited, he spent three consecutive Sundays in Paris, where Kate, now pregnant with their second son, Sawyer, was staying with the combined Capshaw/Spielberg family, to supervise the sound. His work was rewarded when, on its opening in June, *Jurassic Park* was the hit of the summer. Universal opened the film on 2842 screens simultaneously. It set new records for the first weekend, obliterating its biggest rival, Arnold Schwarzenegger's *Last Action Hero*, and went on to gross $900 million worldwide.

However much he fought his impulses, Spielberg couldn't help but make *Schindler's List* an entertainment: no *Jurassic Park*, but no *Shoah* either. His worst characters, even Goeth at his most loathsome, have charm. Nor could Spielberg close his eyes to the persistence of the human spirit. Even in the midst of atrocity, human beings will amuse themselves, do business, fall in love. Krakow Jews improvise a trading exchange in the last place the Nazis will look, the pews of a Catholic church during mass. A wedding is even held in the camp, and a light bulb crushed instead of the traditional glass. These scenes, and another in which men and women huddled round a brazier in the ghetto find time for a few chilly jokes, were to draw accusations that he had 'Spielbergised' the Holocaust.

In shooting the film, he avoided as far as possible all cinema's post-war developments in technique. 'We were aiming for a naturalistic look,' said his cameraman, Janusz Kaminski, 'not using things like bright lights. I'm trying to imagine myself being here [in Krakow] fifty years ago with a small camera without lights. We're favouring long lenses, doing a lot of hand-held shots. We want people to see this film in fifteen years and not have a sense of when it was made.' Yet nothing can put back the clock of innovation. The sharpness of modern lenses and the range of tones which new film stocks could resolve dictated that, even at its grittiest, *Schindler's List* should have a subliminal Hollywood sheen.

Spielberg also faced a moral and aesthetic choice when it came to shooting the ghetto. Krakow's real wartime ghetto was in relatively uninteresting Podgorze. But his eye was caught by the picturesque Kazimierz area, on the other side of the Vistula River, in the centre of the Old Town. Jews and Christians had lived cordially together there for centuries, but it was more like his mental image of a ghetto than the real thing, so he moved his cameras there. Today it's the high point of *Schindler's List* bus tours.

The film's set-piece, the attack on the ghetto, is a torrent of indelible images and thumbnail characterisations that only a film-maker of genius could have conceived and co-ordinated. As the Nazis surround the area and prepare for the raid, the families inside melt away under floors, above ceilings, inside beds, even into pianos. Some wad hoarded valuables into pieces of bread and swallow them. The Nazis, with typical thoroughness, hunt down almost everyone. A few are saved: some dive into the sewers, others find unexpected allies, like the boy collaborator in Nazi cap and armband who rescues the little girl from his school and her mother.

A true propagandist would show the Nazis as stock monsters, but Spielberg, here, as he was with Belloq in *Raiders of the Lost Ark*, half in love with his villains, can't help but be fascinated by the meticulousness with which they use a stethoscope to track down fugitives in the ceiling, or relish the surrealism of the moment where, as machine guns rip the walls of the tenements, a Nazi plays furiously but impeccably on an upright piano.

'Bach?' a soldier queries.

'Mozart,' says a colleague.

Goeth emerges as a more interesting character than Schindler, if only because his motives are more explicable. Instead of the stock Nazi beast Spielberg had visualised during early discussions of the project, Goeth is shown as a harassed bureaucrat who rationalises his brutality in the name of efficiency. Since he's convinced himself that his prisoners have no more humanity than sheep, he culls the weak, removes the children and disposes of troublemakers as casually as any modern farmer. Spielberg dramatises the degree of difference between Goeth and Schindler by giving both an almost identical scene with Helen Hirsch, the prisoner Goeth chooses as his housekeeper, and who lives in the cellar of his house. Played with supreme craft by little-known Embeth Davidtz, Helen shares some of Stern's breathless disbelief in continued survival. One has a sense that she knows every step may be her last. Her very subservience makes her attractive to Goeth, but he can't bring himself either to rape her or deny his attraction: she is, after all, as he explains distractedly to her, 'not a person in the strictest sense of the word'. In his scene with her, Schindler explains this, and reassures her that Goeth desires her too much to have her killed. Finally he saves her by winning her life from Goeth at cards.

Equally, we share Goeth's fascination with the suave Schindler. His first envious question is, 'Where did you get that suit? What is it? Silk?' They are genuinely friends. Schindler even tries to excuse Goeth to Stern as just a crook in a uniform, corrupted by the war. Dispassionately, the accountant, often the only person in the film to see reality, describes how this allegedly small-time middle manager randomly shoots prisoners, and Schindler falls silent. A climactic scene, which Liam Neeson says was, for him, the most moving in the film, made their affinity explicit.

> Amon Goeth comes back to the factory. He's been stripped of his uniform and imprisoned for marketeering and he goes to see what he thinks is his only friend, only to find out that Schindler was the one who fingered him. Schindler was called before the tribunal and what he said was, 'Goeth stole our country blind,' and that was enough to condemn him right there. I found that very touching, in a weird way, thanks to the power of Ralph Fiennes's performance. He gave a human face to this monster.

Spielberg shot the scene, but cut it out for the very reason Neeson gives: Goeth is already too sympathetic – an effect eradicated by his final appearance, perfunctorily hanged from a makeshift gallows. 'Heil Hitler,' he croaks as the guards kick to pieces the stool on which he stands.

Two sequences shot partly in colour frame the story. The first shows a family in an antique European interior lighting candles on Friday evening and reciting the prayers that precede the sabbath. In a series of dissolves, the candles burn down until only one is left. At the end, Spielberg brings surviving 'Schindler Jews', their relatives, and the actors who played them to their benefactor's grave in an inhospitable cemetery near Jerusalem. As they file by, each places a stone on the slab. (The last figure to do so, seen from a distance, appears to be Spielberg himself.) However, as Spielberg makes clear with the dedication which follows almost immediately, preceding his own credit and that to the actors, the life really being celebrated in this film is not so much Schindler's as that of Steve Ross.

With the editing mostly finished, Spielberg took time off for a European holiday. The Venice Film Festival offered him an Honorary Leone d'Or, and Spielberg attended the ceremony in September with a US contingent that included Harrison Ford, Robert de Niro, Robert Altman, Martin Scorsese, Michelle Pfeiffer, Tina Turner and Sydney Pollack. An Authors' Symposium had been arranged by left-wing director Gillo Pontecorvo to discuss the accelerating invasion of European cinema by American films. Spielberg, on the occasion of receiving his Leone d'Or, re-presented Pontecorvo with the Leone the Italian had won for *The Battle of Algiers* in 1966. He'd sold it at auction years before to raise money to fight for authors' rights, and Spielberg had bought it.

Spielberg and Scorsese in particular were outspoken in their sympathy for the plight of their European colleagues whose livelihood was being eaten away by massive American exports, but many in the audience were sceptical. Hollywood had shown little inclination to halt the flood of films that was wiping out national cinemas all over the world. Instead the studios complained about a quota that limited the number of imported films shown on French screens to a total of 50 per cent – ignoring the fact that the US imported only 2 per cent of movies shown on its screens. French director Bertrand Tavernier, one of the most vigorous campaigners against Hollywood domination, says, 'What we would like is that the percentage of non-American cinema shown in the United States would represent, say, 3 per cent instead of 2 per cent. That's our dream. When we met the people of the major companies and said, "Look, how can you accuse France of protectionism when foreign films don't even represent 2 per cent of your market?", we saw surprise in their eyes. You could see them thinking, "Two per cent? As much as that? How can we arrange things so that they have only 1½ per cent?"'

Some Europeans remained hopeful until Spielberg and Scorsese issued a press statement on 4 October opposing efforts by the French to exclude films from the free trade provisions of the General Agreement on Trades and Tariffs then being negotiated in Brussels. 'Closing the borders would not guarantee a rise in creativity in the local countries,' said Scorsese, 'or even a rise in interest on the part of local audiences. National voices and diversities must be encouraged and protected, but not at the expense of other film-makers.' A group of European film-makers including Pedro Almodovar, David Puttnam, Bernardo Bertolucci and Wim Wenders published an open letter in *Daily Variety* on 29 October attacking the statement as misinformed.

Schindler's List opened in the US in the first week of December 1993. At 195 minutes, it was not every exhibitor's dream film but, for once, in deference to the subject, most treated it with dignity and decorum, not to mention an unwonted lack of interest in profit. Many cinemas distributed a 'Code of Conduct' suggesting, among other things, that eating popcorn would not be appropriate during the film.

The overall tone of critical comment was reverent. Anxious not to give offence, the press leaned over backwards to welcome the film and praise Spielberg. Jewish critics were not so generous. Many agreed with the philosopher George Steiner that the only acceptable response to the Holocaust was silence. Some disliked it for the very things Spielberg had wanted to change in Zaillian's script: the emphasis on Schindler, Goeth and Stern rather than less central figures. Jay Hoberman in the *Village Voice* saw the Jews as 'relegated to supporting parts in their own cataclysm, hang[ing] around the Krakow ghetto . . . making Jewish jokes'. *Schindler's List*, he charged, was 'a feel-good entertainment about the ultimate feel-bad experience of the twentieth century'. Philip Gourevitch in the venerable Jewish paper *Forward* complained that 'powerful spectacle continues to be more beguiling than human historical authenticity – and the power of the Nazis a bigger draw than the civilisation of the people they murdered'. Novelist Howard Jacobson wrote patronisingly that, 'to do him justice, Spielberg cleans up more conscientiously than you'd think he'd know how,' but Claude Lanzmann, director of *Shoah*, scorned the film in toto. While not going as far as Steiner, he felt that the very fact of turning the Holocaust into fiction discredited Spielberg's project and everyone associated with it.

But the public was unaffected by the reviews. By March 1995, *Schindler's List* had earned a gratifying $45.9 million in domestic rentals. The Oscars gave it an added impetus. Of its eleven nominations, it won in seven categories. Neeson and Fiennes missed out for Best Actor and Best Supporting Actor, nor were the costume design, make-up and sound successful. But it won awards for Art Direction, Editing, John Williams's Original Score, Cinematography, Screenplay and, most important, both Best Film and Best Director. At last Spielberg, at the peak of his career, stood on the podium at the Shrine Auditorium with an Oscar in his hands.

How good is *Schindler's List* as a film? With hindsight, one can see that Spielberg's grounding in commercial Hollywood always made at least partial artistic failure inevitable. The film's best moments are those of tension, humour and pathos in which Neeson, Fiennes and Kingsley flash with the sort of sparks Spielberg wants to show us he can strike from good actors. But the very effectiveness of these scenes undercuts his attempts to show them or their historical situation in more depth. When, at the end of the film, the people Schindler has saved see him off into exile, the businessman's sudden explosion of remorse about not having rescued more of them – by selling his car, for instance – rings as false as Clark Gable's tearful prayer at the end of *San Francisco*. Hollywood heroes don't whine. 'You can make me the best man in the world,' John Wayne once told a director, 'or the worst, but never make me cheap.'

However much Spielberg tries to push his supporting cast into the foreground, they remain subsidiary to what is essentially a 'buddy' movie about two men from opposite sides of the ethical tracks, one of whom is forced finally to destroy the other. The film's vision of the Holocaust is equally suspect because of Spielberg's partiality for the Big Moment and the Flamboyant Gesture. As Pauline Kael said of *Queimada!*, made by Gillo Pontecorvo in 1968 and showing capitalism and Marxism at work during a slave revolt in the Caribbean, any attempt to portray history as film entertainment carries the seeds of its own destruction. 'When you personify a deterministic view of history,' Kael wrote, 'and don't stylise it but, rather, do it in natural settings, the leaders seem to be all that matter, so the method distorts the theory. It seems as if history were a melodrama made solely by heroes and adventurers.' Danielle Heymann, critic of *Le Monde*, while conceding that *Schindler's List* was 'a work of genius, made with precision, and remarkably well filmed', complained that 'Spielberg leads us down false paths. We see smoke and it's not a crematorium, it's a train. We see the showers and they spout not gas but water. All the cadavers we see we don't know and all the people we identify with are saved. And that's not how history goes.'

19

The Dream Team

Once again, Steven is surrounded by sharks and dinosaurs.

Tom Hanks, of the audience at the presentation of Spielberg's American Film
Institute Award for Cinematic Achievement, 4 March 1995

S PIELBERG WORE his honours lightly. The day after the 1995 Oscar
ceremony, he was on line with Robin Williams, playing the video
wargame Syndicate and hotly debating with him its merits in graphics
and sound. The achievement of his greatest dream left him empty. 'I
have no idea what to do next,' he said, 'and, more important, I don't
care.' He'd promised Kate to take a year's holiday from directing, a break
which, considering his personal fortune, estimated at $450 million, he
could well afford. With Wasserman and Sheinberg, he visited the Consumer Electronics Show in Las Vegas. Watching him stroll by, surrounded by the MCA retinue, a young game-player murmured to his
friend, 'Look, it's God.'

During his year's break, Spielberg had time to survey his future in a
changing business. Hollywood politics were replicating those of the
world at large. As blocs crumbled and great nations lost influence, smaller
ones tried to seize power. MGM was gone, Columbia belonged to Sony,
MCA to Matsushita. With Steve Ross dead, a struggle raged inside
Time/Warner. Newly-powerful media entrepreneurs like Ted Turner
manoeuvred for advantage, and while their interests extended into cable
and broadcast TV, magazines, computer bulletin-boards and even books,
their cockpit was often Hollywood.

Vanity Fair in October 1994 defined these *arrivistes* as 'The New

Establishment'. 'Call them swashbucklers of the Information Age,' said Elise O'Shaugnessy in her introduction to the piece, 'or the highwaymen of the infobahn; they are the leaders of the computer, entertainment and communications industries whose collective power and influence have eclipsed both Wall Street and Washington.' One of them was Spielberg. Others in the survey – Barbra Streisand, Mike Ovitz, Michael Eisner, Barry Diller, Oprah Winfrey and David Geffen – were either his friends or allies. A few more were about to impinge on his life, in particular Bill Gates of the software company Microsoft, and Edgar Bronfman Jr, head of the Canadian Seagram distilling company but ambitious to be a movie mogul. Significantly, *Vanity Fair*'s list didn't include either Lucas or Coppola, once thought of as indispensable members of New Hollywood. The Three had become The One.

Many of those in the survey, including Geffen, Ovitz, Diller and Jeffrey Katzenberg, were part of an informal inner circle of power-brokers who met every year at Sun Valley for a few days of networking under the aegis of investment banker Herbert Allen, who was a close friend of Ray Stark and an adviser to most big showbiz corporations, including Matsushita.

For the piece, America's most fashionable magazine photographer Annie Leibovitz shot these men and women with the appurtenances of their power. David Geffen circled Los Angeles in his private jet, Ted Turner rode his ranch on a horse, Michael Ovitz sat alone in a viewing theatre and Michael Eisner in the Disney corporate suite, regarded sardonically by a man in a Mickey Mouse suit.

Spielberg posed at sunset in rolled jeans and denim shirt, spotless trainers at his side, dangling bare feet in Georgica Pond, East Hampton, the eyes behind his Armani spectacles fixed on an indeterminate future. It was a bucolic vision worthy of Norman Rockwell: *Tom Sawyer in Middle Age*. With his personal world now totally under control, Spielberg was turning his mind to the image to which he would adhere for the rest of his life. It was, unsurprisingly, East Coast, not Californian; not innovative but reflective, a little saintly. Not abrasively Lean-like, but genial, courteous yet remote.

*   *   *

In Hollywood's fashionable restaurants, at Malibu, even on the white-water raft trips organised by major players like Jeffrey Katzenberg, the talk was always of Mike Ovitz. Everyone recognised him as the most potent threat to their power. The closed-mouth cat-like smile of the Universal Studios tour guide turned out to conceal sharp teeth. In a famous 1992 feud with the world's highest-paid scriptwriter Joe Eszterhas (*Basic Instinct*, *Sliver*), Ovitz had belied his pussy-cat image by reputedly warning him that CAA's 'foot-soldiers' patrolled Beverly Hills every day and would 'blow out the brains' of anyone who defied him.

Nobody doubted Ovitz could do just that, if he chose to. Through CAA, he spoke for most of Hollywood's major stars and film-makers: Dustin Hoffman, Warren Beatty, Kevin Costner, Robert de Niro, Barbra Streisand, Michael Douglas, Sean Connery, Tom Cruise, Robin Williams, Sylvester Stallone, Martin Scorsese, Francis Coppola, Robert Redford, Oliver Stone, Barry Levinson, Tim Burton, even Spielberg were all clients. Already a *de facto* producer, Ovitz assembled packages and sold them to studios, which refused the high price-tags at their peril. He had brokered the Sony and Matsushita deals and, in the case of Sony, turned down their offer to run Columbia. Now, as Lew Wasserman and Sid Sheinberg bickered with Matsushita over control of MCA, many speculated that the Japanese might install Ovitz as MCA/Universal's next boss. For his part, Ovitz confessed to friends and advisers like Herb Allen that he was weary of the competing egos of the agenting business, and might look favourably on a change.

An anti-Ovitz coalition among the New Establishment evolved almost before its members realised it. At its heart was David Geffen, whose dislike and distrust of the CAA boss was an open secret. Jeffrey Katzenberg became part of it, not only because of his friendship with Geffen but because he saw Ovitz's power as dangerous to the industry. Katzenberg also coveted Michael Eisner's chairmanship of Disney – and Eisner was Ovitz's best friend. Loyalty to Wasserman and Sheinberg, if nothing else, also persuaded Spielberg to oppose Ovitz. Nor did he want to find himself, as he had with *Hook*, reduced to just another component in a CAA package. Steve Ross had shown him his power and taught him something about using it. Though he remained dubious about

committing himself to any organisation over which he didn't exercise
total control, Spielberg could see the value of entering an alliance to
protect what he'd won, and to build on it.

With Kathleen Kennedy and Frank Marshall now flourishing in their
own company, management of Amblin passed to another married couple,
Walter Parkes and Laurie MacDonald. Parkes, who coined the 'Amblin
U' nickname for the operation, and whose association with Spielberg
went back to the first days of the company, when it backed preliminary
work on his script of *Wargames*, took over an enterprise which, at least
figuratively, had burst its walls. Amblin's permanent staff had swelled
from eighteen in 1983 to more than sixty, *Jurassic Park*'s production
team was hived off into trailers on the Universal lot, and a separate
building, called Movies While You Wait, was built to house directors
working on Spielberg projects, of which dozens were in development.

Animation, with its opportunities for total control, continued to pre-
occupy Spielberg. After *Fievel Goes West*, the Dinosaur feature *We're
Back!: A Dinosaur's Story* and the series *Family Dog* had all failed, he
moved Amblimation to Los Angeles, where he could keep an eye on it.
Work continued on an animated version of the musical *Cats*, and live-
action feature versions of *Casper the Friendly Ghost* (called simply *Casper*)
and the sixties Hanna-Barbera TV series *The Flintstones*.

For TV, Amblin launched *Tiny Toons*, a feature project that metamorphosed into a series, and *Animaniacs*, which Fox began running with
great success in 1994, but which transferred to Warners in 1995. Its
main characters, Yakko and Wakko, the Warner brothers, lived with
their sister Dot inside the water tower painted with the Warners shield
that is the most visible landmark on its Burbank lot, and descended to
engage with their friends in relentlessly self-referential adventures, often
with precise relationships to the movie business. Hollywood and Broadway in-jokes abounded. In one episode, an unsuccessful 'toon star and
his friend revenged themselves on two film critics, based on the popular
TV reviewers Gene Siskel and Roger Ebert. Lured to the premiere of
Jurassic Park, the critics were crushed by a T. rex that stepped out of the

screen and onto the front stalls, and for the rest of the episode were relentlessly blown up, mashed, doused and humiliated.

The main Amblin office now directed the massive marketing empire which pulled in a large part of Spielberg's income, estimated at $70 million annually. His investments included the British racing stable of ex-jockey Simon Sherwood, 20 per cent of Dennis Hoffman's Designer Donut chain, and a Los Angeles sub sandwich shop called Dive!, owned jointly with Jeffrey Katzenberg and a Chicago catering firm. Dive! Spielberged the eating experience. Every half hour, sirens sounded and the place exploded in a multi-media show. In 1995 a second restaurant, purpose-built this time, opened in Las Vegas, with half a cartoon submarine jutting from the façade, and glass walls down which water gushed during the show. Spielberg and Katzenberg announced imminent openings of six more, starting with one in Barcelona. 'The Japanese are building east to west,' joked Spielberg, 'so we're building in the opposite direction.'

On 3 April 1994, the helicopter of Disney president Frank Wells crashed in Nevada's Ruby Mountains while he was on a skiing holiday. The death of Michael Eisner's closest ally within the company threw Disney into turmoil. Katzenberg made a strong play for his post, citing his production of *Beauty and the Beast*, *Aladdin* (dedicated to Wells) and the forthcoming *The Lion King*, which would put Disney decisively back on top of the animation world. Eisner temporised. He was in poor health, and in July 1994 entered hospital for a quadruple coronary bypass. When he emerged, he told Katzenberg he'd decided not to promote him. Instead, Joe Roth, architect of John Hughes's hit 1990 comedy *Home Alone*, which launched the career of child star Macaulay Culkin, was being imported from 20th Century-Fox to share the studio's creative management. The insult was unignorable. In August, Katzenberg resigned.

As news spread of his departure, Spielberg called from Jamaica, where he was staying with Robert Zemeckis. He tried to be consoling about Katzenberg's future – which, given the executive's lack of a large personal fortune and his long-time identification with Disney, was not promising.

Quoting Christopher Lloyd's last line from *Back to the Future*, Spielberg told him, 'Where you're going, you don't need roads.'

'Why don't you guys do something together?' Zemeckis shouted from the background.

'We were teasing,' Katzenberg said later of the suggestion, 'but there was a moment when it went from a playful and fanciful idea to a great idea.'

He seized the hint like a life preserver and, within a week, pitched his plan to Spielberg. The two men already had a success with the Dive! restaurants. Now he suggested they start their own studio. As collateral, he offered his expertise, especially in animation. He could also deliver old friends like Gary David Goldberg, producer of *Family Ties* and other hit TV shows.

Spielberg was unconvinced. He was happy at MCA, and felt a personal loyalty to Sheinberg and Wasserman.

'You were *invited* to leave Disney,' he said, sensitive as always to the minute shifts in power by which Hollywood measures success and failure. 'I have no reason to leave MCA.'

Kate too was doubtful. Much as she liked Katzenberg, she didn't want Spielberg infected with his furious ambition and drive. The proposed alliance might have ended there but for a power shift inside MCA. Anxious to expand the company, Sheinberg and Wasserman asked Matsushita to approve the takeover of the innovative British–based recording company Virgin Records, plus the purchase of a TV network and the construction of a Universal theme park near Tokyo. Expecting a rubber-stamp acceptance, they were furious when the *zaibatsu*, paying back Sheinberg for his many sneering references to Matsushita, and his and Wasserman's oft-repeated threat to leave the studio when their contracts expired in 1995, refused. When both men made the fourteen-hour flight to Osaka on 17 September to discuss the projects, Matsushita's head Yoichi Morishita had underlings convey his decision, and only appeared at the meeting after two hours.

'I don't see any smiling faces,' he said serenely. 'I see you have been told.'

Seething, Sheinberg and Wasserman arrived back in Los Angeles to find the city alive with rumours that they were about to resign, and that Morishita might install Michael Ovitz to run the studio.

Suddenly Spielberg had a new incentive to think about leaving MCA. He got together again with Katzenberg, who had had his own second thoughts. Why not include David Geffen in the team?

'I've competed against David,' Katzenberg said, 'and I'm telling you, he has so completely put me away, so outclassed me in signing an act or a movie star or getting a script. We need him.'

Spielberg was unsure. From being his rival for Steve Ross's affection, Geffen had become Ross's outspoken critic. After selling his record company to WCI in 1985, Geffen was offended when Ross failed to tell him in advance of WCI's plans to merge with Time/Life. Not only did he dislike being left in the dark; he missed an opportunity to make a large profit. When ownership in his company reverted to Geffen in 1990 and Ross tried to buy it outright, Geffen sold it instead to MCA for $600 million and moved his headquarters to the Burbank lot.

The conflicts at MCA had also persuaded Geffen, a loner by nature, that an alliance with Katzenberg and Spielberg would protect him from any radical changes inside the corporation. Spielberg too had taken soundings, and found a surprising unanimity among financial advisers. A studio which institutionalised the advances made by New Hollywood could well be a good thing, both for the industry and its principals. Chemical Bank agreed to advance a $1 billion line of credit against an initial $250 million put up by the trio as seed capital – no problem for Geffen or Spielberg, but for Katzenberg a commitment that mortgaged him for eternity. A ritual visit was paid to Lew Wasserman to outline their plans. Once he approved, it remained only to think of a name and make the announcement.

On 28 September, Geffen, Katzenberg and Spielberg were in Washington DC as guests of Bill Clinton at a dinner for Russian president Boris Yeltsin. After the banquet, Geffen, an intimate of the Clintons, slept over in the Lincoln Bedroom while Spielberg and Katzenberg returned to the Hays-Adams Hotel, opposite the White House, to continue planning the new studio. By 1.30 a.m., they'd decided that, name or no name, they must announce their plans. They rang Geffen.

'Come over here *now*,' Katzenberg said.

'How do I get there?' asked a sleepy Geffen.

'Call a taxi.'

'You can't call a taxi in the White House,' he protested. At 6.30 a.m., he rang for a White House car and was driven to the hotel. After a brief discussion, he concurred with his partners that it was time.

A press conference was called for 11 October. Editors were told to hold space on their front pages. Ovitz was in the crowd that gathered to hear the news and, afterwards, Michael Eisner rang each of the partners separately to congratulate them. From first discussions to announcement, the alliance, known informally as 'the dream team', had taken seven weeks to form.

For the next month, little else was discussed in film circles. Was the trio about to take over MCA from Matsushita? Would other independents join them? Would they go public and issue shares? Was Amblin to be absorbed into the new company? What exactly would it produce? Where would the money come from? And what the hell was the thing to be called?

Some of these questions were soon answered. Wary of losing control, the trio vetoed ransoming themselves to shareholders. Instead, one-third of the company would be sold to individual corporate investors in return for $900 million in operating capital. As for the programme, twenty-four feature films would be released before the end of the decade. No titles were mentioned, except for an animated feature based on the Old Testament, which was to metamorphose into the TV series *Genesis*, fronted by journalist Bill Moyers. Within a year the group announced its backing for a film produced by Mick Garris from a script by Preston Sturges Jr, whose father had written and directed some of Spielberg's favourite films. Rumours also suggested that the trio might take over the next three *Star Wars* films, but as late at August 1995 George Lucas was claiming cagily that no discussions had taken place.

The division of power in the new group was spelled out in detail. Geffen would run the music division and Katzenberg manage the day-today running of the film studio. Spielberg agreed that Amblin would eventually become part of the new company, but for the moment he promised to honour all his commitments, and reserved the right to direct for anyone he chose. Given the six or seven films he owed under contracts to MCA/Universal and Warners, it could be some time before he made anything for his own company. On 10 October 1994 he announced Amblin's purchase for $2.5 million of an original script by Michael Crichton and his wife Anne-Marie, *Twister*, about scientists who track tornadoes. Wary as ever, Spielberg was keeping the door to independence open a crack.

The name, 'DreamWorks SKG', conflating the 'dream team' label and the initials of the three principals, was unveiled in early 1995. The cumbersome result of countless meetings, it proved, like a *cadavre exquise* confected by the Surrealists, with each person contributing to a drawing of a body without looking at what the others had drawn, to resemble nothing and satisfy nobody. Spielberg, however, was as proud as a new father – or a freshman president. In a slip of the tongue at the press conference, he referred to 'our new country', a concept he liked so much he began to call DreamWorks 'our sovereign state'.

By the end of 1994 the group was already shopping for real estate, pursued by half a dozen counties and Chambers of Commerce, all eager for this money-spinner to alight in their tax area. They decided finally on Howard Hughes's old aircraft factory at Playa Vista, a hundred-acre site on which the trio planned to build twenty sound stages, restaurants, schools and 13,000 homes sited on an artificial lake. 'We are hoping that productions that would have gone to the 007 stage in Pinewood,' said Geffen, 'will now stay here' – casting doubt on Spielberg's promise to support European cinema. The idea of taking over MCA had only briefly attracted the three. The studio carried too much dead wood, too many reminders of Old Hollywood. And what position, if any, in the new enterprise might Wasserman and Sheinberg occupy? Instead, the trio had informal discussions with Matsushita, proposing that DreamWorks distribute some of its products through MCA in return for a promise that Wasserman and Sheinberg remain in power.

In November 1994 Morishita asked Herbert Allen to fly to Osaka and advise Matsushita on their MCA options. In January 1995, the Japanese company authorised Allen to sell off 80 per cent of MCA. In April it passed to Seagram's Edgar Bronfman Jr. At the official signing ceremony handing MCA over to Bronfman, Ovitz, though he technically represented Matsushita, sat down opposite Morishita, next to Bronfman, while Allen, still dressed in the cowboy boots he'd been wearing on his ranch, stood out of the way, looking fondly from afar at the deal he'd helped bring about. To many people, it seemed as if Hollywood had once again seen off a foreign rival.

One of Bronfman's first acts was to negotiate a distribution deal with DreamWorks. He joined a long queue. ABC had already signed a production contract for $100 million in programmes. In March 1995, Paul Allen, the reclusive co-founder of Microsoft with Bill Gates, paid $500 million for an 18 per cent share of the company. A few days later, Gates put up $30 million, half the start-up capital, for DreamWorks Interactive, a subsidiary to make CD-Roms and other computer-related products. In May, the Korean company One World Media, part of the giant Samsung empire, pledged the final $300 million.

Disney couldn't sit by and watch such a radical realignment in the power structure, particularly one which placed the architect of its greatest recent hit films in the camp of a competitor with potentially unlimited resources. In the summer of 1995, it paid $19 billion for the media empire of Nebraska financier Warren Buffett. This included the ABC TV network and the ESPN cable sports channel. And to run the new operation, Michael Eisner, in a secret meeting on a forest trail near Aspen, Colorado, offered the job of Disney chairman to Mike Ovitz. Hardly a leaf had fallen before the news of his acceptance was all over Hollywood, and the jockeying for power began again.

Even working only part time, Spielberg was pushing ahead with half a dozen projects at Amblin. *The Lost World*, Crichton's sequel to *Jurassic Park*, was in preparation for Universal. British novelist Fay Weldon was writing *Assault on Bel Air*, a screenplay about the LA riots. Bruce Robinson, author of the successful comedy *Withnail and I*, was developing a script, and Carrie Fisher adapting her story *Christmas in Las Vegas*. Other projects included *Carnival*, an animated version of Leslie Caron's 1953 film *Lili*; Douglas Carter Beane's play *To Wong Foo, Thanks for Everything!, Julie Newmar*; a feature based on the British sf series *Doctor Who*; another about Zorro, directed by Mikael Solomon, Spielberg's cameraman on *Always*; and *Up River*, a new novel by William Harrison (*The Rollerball Murders*). In every case, Spielberg's involvement was hands-on. To Harrison, he suggested a climax with more action, and the author not only rethought the ending for the script but for the novel as well. Spielberg also bought *The Bridges of Madison County*, Robert James Waller's unexpected best-seller about a romance between a photographer and a rural housewife which her family discover only after her death. Widely tipped to direct it, he passed it to Bruce Beresford, but eased him out, with some resentment on Beresford's part, following a better offer of Clint Eastwood as both director and star. Even then, however, his control remained. He asked Eastwood and composer Lennie Niehaus to extend the song 'For All We Know' from a love scene between Eastwood and Meryl Streep into the succeeding scene where her children, via a letter, are discovering the liaison. Hearing the song, he reasoned, audiences would understand that the children had learned something new about their mother.

The Bridges of Madison County was a commercial success, as was the film of Crichton's *Twister* in 1996. However, *To Wong Foo, Thanks for Everything!, Julie Newmar* flopped, and even *Twister*, despite doing well at the box office, attracted accusations that the direction of ex-cameraman Jan de Bont, Hollywood's acknowledged expert in fast-paced car-crash thrillers after the success of *Speed* two years before, had disguised unconvincing special effects. 'Steven Spielberg Presents' had ceased to be a guarantee of quality and taken on, in the eyes of many, a tone of gimcrack sensationalism.

In November 1994 Spielberg launched the Survivors of the Shoah Visual History Foundation. He explained:

> When I was making the film in Poland, at least a dozen Holocaust survivors journeyed there using the film as a cushion to find closure

with their nightmare. They showed up, and often through tears began telling us their stories. I kept saying to them, 'Thank you for telling me, but I wish you could say this to a camera because this is important testimony.' I asked them if they'd be willing to do so, and they all said yes.

Within a year, the foundation had ninety full-time staff in nine offices around the world. They filmed interviews, maps, documents and photos, computerised and recorded them, cross-referenced, on CD-Rom. 'If you want to find out about where people slept,' said one of the team, 'what they ate, the kinds of latrines used, you type in a certain word – like "latrine" – and it takes you to exact points in interviews where people talked about it.'

$6 million of Spielberg's profits from *Schindler's List* were funnelled into the Righteous Persons Foundation which disbursed them to Jewish charities, artists and writers. It also funded projects like Synagogue 2000, an attempt to update and streamline Jewish religious observance. One of the first recipients was the Anne Frank House in Amsterdam. Spielberg pledged $250,000 towards its restoration. In 1996, it announced its first donation outside the USA; £65,000 to the University of Sussex to back a centre for German–Jewish Studies. After coaxing $1 million or more each from the Lew Wasserman Foundation, Time-Warner, NBC, Sony and Barry Diller, Spielberg unexpectedly went on the East Coast celebrity fund-raising circuit, showing himself at Manhattan and Hamptons cocktail parties to solicit contributions from financiers like George Soros. Over the next seven to ten years, Spielberg told them, he hoped that the foundation would hand out more than $40 million.

Spielberg's escutcheon, however, suffered an embarrassing stain in October 1995 when Dennis Hoffmann publicised their 1968 contract over *Amblin'*, and, claiming he'd been cheated out of the profits of a possible Spielberg feature, sued him for $33 million, his estimated gains from such a film. It was a sum he would have no trouble raising, should he choose to pay, since *Forbes* magazine in 1996 found that Spielberg was the United States' second largest show-business earner after talk-show host Oprah Winfrey, his combined personal income for the previous two years totalling $150 million.

Early in 1995, Spielberg was offered, in the centennial year of the cinema, an honorary Cèsar, the French equivalent of the Oscar. It was a controversial gesture by the French, in the light of his statements about French 'protectionism' at the time of the GATT talks. Spielberg had already back-pedalled, however, claiming to have been misled by the Hollywood studio lobby and the White House's mouthpiece on film policy, Jack Valenti.

On 25 February he stepped into the spotlight at the Théâtre de Champs-Elysées in Paris to face the *gratin* of French showbiz. The award was presented by Claude Lelouch, director of *A Man and a Woman*, who set the tone of the evening by assuring Spielberg that there was only one part of his films he didn't like: the words 'The End'. Spielberg smiled down at the front row which Kate shared with Gregory Peck and Jeanne Moreau, both also recipients of honorary Cèsars. The rest of the audience beamed back.

Stumbling through a list he took from his pocket, he thanked the French film-makers to whom he owed, he said, a debt of gratitude. Beginning with Jean-Luc Godard (whose influence on his work not even the most alert critic had noted), he cited twenty-nine others, from the Lumière brothers and George Méliès to Claude Lanzmann and, of course, Truffaut, whose advice about storytellers needing to live a life he quoted with obvious sincerity. 'Many of my films have been devoted to the craft of the imagination,' he went on, 'but I think because of *Schindler's List* and my wife Kate and my five children, I was able for the first time to leave form behind to live as a film-maker should.' He ended with a controversial promise to 'a country that is fighting for its cultural identity. I would like to say,' he told his audience, 'I will fight right along with you.'

This struck some listeners as absurd, given that films like *Jurassic Park* were, in their eyes, the very productions strangling the French industry. Of the $913 million earned by *Jurassic Park* by 1995, $556 million came from sales outside the US. Yet few could have been surprised, especially those who knew something of cinema's past. The history of the US is a history of cultural invasion and acquisition in which the cinema has traditionally played an active part. Before World War I, US consulates in China and Japan distributed American feature films as vehicles of political and social propaganda. Paramount and MGM bought up the bankrupt German cinema in the twenties, and invaded that of Britain and the Commonwealth in the thirties by gaining a monopoly of theatres and reserving them for Hollywood product.

Historically, Steven Spielberg and his films were inevitable. The McDonald's movie, the Coca-Cola cinema, mass-marketed to a waiting world, was 'an idea whose time has come'. Like Communism, the very strictness of its parameters may carry the seeds of self-destruction, but for the moment its continued success seems certain. Morality is on the side of an embattled Europe, but the profits lie elsewhere. And cinema is, above all, an organism whose medium is money.

What is Steven Spielberg's role in the new world order he has done so much to create? In its terms, he has nowhere else to go. Making more millions and winning more Oscars will prove nothing, either to himself or to the world. Historically the likelihood is that he will decline into a restless seeker of an achievement sufficiently great to top those already to his credit, and that, like his models David Selznick and David Lean, he will fail. Just as there could never be another *Gone With the Wind* or *Lawrence of Arabia*, there can be no more *Schindler's Lists*.

The alternative is honourable retirement and acceptance of his role as an icon of the mass market: a Jonas Salk if he manages his image well, a Colonel Harland Sanders if he doesn't. And if he should wish to retrieve his critical reputation by returning to the concise, economical style of what most people agree are his best films? The irony is that he has helped create a market where it has no place. For someone of such prodigious facility, this realisation in particular must be galling.

In assessing Spielberg's life as he reaches his fifties, one can't escape the parallels with those two archetypal American failures-in-success, Jay Gatsby and Charles Foster Kane. Coffined by the lives they have created with their labours, both listlessly wander their mansions. Their obituaries are already on file.

Welles, Spielberg and Fitzgerald fell victim, as did Gatsby, to the heartless scope of America, and what, in one of *The Great Gatsby*'s most moving passages, Fitzgerald calls Americans' 'capacity for wonder'. Americans are born with a hunger for novelty and divertissement which can never be satiated, and anyone who tries to do so exhausts himself in the effort. Kane and Gatsby with their lavish parties, like Spielberg and Welles with their films, gave themselves to their audience totally, and were devoured for their pains.

Their reward was a brief epiphany, a sense that, for a few years, they were at one with an ideal America. For an instant, its landscape and the works of those who inhabited it came briefly into focus, revealing visions so electric that they could enchant the world.

Just once, Spielberg and Welles shared an identical vision. In 1940 Welles and Herman Mankiewicz were writing *Citizen Kane* in a house in the Hollywood hills. Actor George Coulouris visited them, and Welles took him out onto the terrace. 'And we saw the whole city lit up,' Coulouris recalled. 'The war was on. "Look," he said, "one of the few cities in the world with the lights on." Then he described *Citizen Kane* to me, outlining the whole story, standing there with the stars above and the lights of Los Angeles below.'

More than thirty years later, Spielberg, on his way back from the Phillipses' after a brainstorming session with Paul Schrader, stopped on Mulholland Drive, perhaps only a few yards from the house where Welles had worked, draped himself dizzily over the bonnet of his car and, staring at the inverted web of light that was the San Fernando Valley, was seized by a presentiment of *Close Encounters of the Third Kind*, unaware that Welles too succumbed to the vision of order and optimism embodied in the lights of his adoptive city.

For Spielberg in 1973, the empire-builder and tycoon has not yet emerged. The pleasure in delighting others remains intact. He is simply, again to borrow a passage of Damon Knight, 'the isolated spark of consciousness, awake and alone at midnight . . . the grown-up child who still remembers, still believes'. At that moment, facing, as Gatsby had done, the special promise of America and sensing he could fulfil it, Steven Spielberg seems at his best.

Notes

Publication details of books frequently quoted, and mentioned here only by title, may be found in the select bibliography.

Pre-credit Sequence: *The Sandcastle*

'Two blood-letting years' is from interview with John Gallagher in *Grand Illusions* magazine Winter 1977 and 'I lost my sense of judgement' from *American Cinematographer* Spring 1990. 'I started out by asking myself', together with details of the sandcastle built by SS and Lucas, appears in *Newsweek* 15 June 1981.

Chapter One: *The Man Who Fell to Earth*

'The universe is stranger'. What J. B. S. Haldane actually said was, 'My suspicion is that the universe is not only queerer than we know: it is queerer than we *can* know:' Damon Knight's essay on Ray Bradbury, 'When I was in Kneepants, appears in *A Sense of Wonder*. Jules Feiffer's cartoon is in the *Village Voice* 27 January 1987. 'He has all the defects' is from *Outrageous Conduct*. 'There is no, "Nice try, guys"' quoted in the *Sun* 17 May 1989. 'I got the feeling' from author's conversation with Julian Glover, London, 1995. 'Steven Spielberg in his Adventures on Earth' appears in the American edition of *Premiere* magazine July 1982. 'It's a nice place' comes from *Michael Jackson: The Magic and the Madness*. Martin Amis quotes 'Some people look at the ground' in *The Moronic Inferno*. John Badham on Lucas is from *Reel Power*. Keneally on SS is from the Australian *National Times* 29 July 1983. 'Ronald Reagan was the strong father' is from 'The Last Crusade' in *Seeing Through Movies*. Arthur Schlesinger on John Kennedy is from the *New Yorker* 5 June 1995. Geffen on SS is in *You'll Never Eat Lunch in this Town Again*. 'He lacked social graces' is quoted in *Outrageous Conduct*. 'Directing is 80 per cent communication' is in *Reel Power*.

Chapter Two: *The Boy who Swallowed a Transistor*

This chapter draws on Spielberg interviews in *UK Penthouse* Vol. 13, No. 3, 1978 with Herbert Margolis and Craig Modderno, with Andy Warhol and Bianca Jagger in *inter/view* June 1982 and with Diane K. Shah in the *Los Angeles Times* 19 December 1993. Other details are from *Icons*. Ralph Rosenbaum is quoted from *When the Shooting Stops*, with Robert Karen, Viking, New York, 1979. 'I did begin by reading comics' quoted by Sheila Johnston, *Independent*, 23 March 1988. David Denby quoted from the *Australian* 2–3 August 1986. 'I don't like reading' is from an interview with David Breskin in *Rolling Stone* September 1985. David Halberstam from *The Fifties*. 'Have you ceased to exist yet?' is in *Outrageous Conduct*. SS's reminiscences on 'God Lights', TV 'snow', his fear of the dark, his shadow games and habit of staring at mirrors appear frequently in interviews. Most of these references are from *Icons*. SS described his high school theatrical experiences in *American Film* September 1978 and the meteor shower in numerous interviews, including *Penthouse* 1978. Leah Spielberg described SS terrorising his sisters in *People* magazine 20 July 1981. The description of seeing *The Greatest Show on Earth* is also often retold. In this case, it comes from *inter/view* June 1982. SS on goodbyes is from his interview with Michael Ventura, *Los Angeles Weekly* 11–17 June, 1982. 'I was hysterical' and 'He wasn't a good student' come from *Arizona* magazine 3 April 1983. SS on losing a footrace appears, among other places, in an interview with Michael Sragow in *Rolling Stone* 22 July 1982. 'I began wanting to make people happy' is from the *New Yorker* 21 March 1994. Dreyfuss on SS and suburbia is quoted in *The Movie Brats*. The quotes on Norman Rockwell are by Alan Rusbridger and Ugo Volli from the *Guardian* 11 December 1993. 'Some kids got involved in the Little League' is from interview with Mitch Tuchman, *Film Comment* January/February/1978. Leah Adler's 'My earliest recollection' and the story of burning the cardboard carton are from *Hollywood Reporter* 10 March 1994. 'Father chopping wood' is from *New York Post* 28 June 1975. 'My first film' is from the *New Yorker* 21 March 1994. 'But I knew I couldn't afford 16mm processing' is from interview with Steve Poster in *American Cinematographer* February 1978. SS on the experience of screening movies is from Gene Siskel's interview in *The Future of Movies* by Gene Siskel and Robert Ebert (Andrews & McMeel, New York, 1991).

Chapter Three: *Amblin' Towards Bethlehem*

William Manchester's remarks on anti-Semitism are from *The Glory and the Dream*. 'I felt I was qualified' is quoted by David Hay in *Sydney Morning Herald Magazine* 22 January 1994. Other details of SS's experience of anti-Semitism in Saratoga appear in the Melbourne *Sunday Age* 6 February 1994. 'Storefront kosher' is from *Icons*. Charles Moore commented on Los Angeles in *Los Angeles: The City Observed*. Merrill Shindler on the Dive! restaurants is from *Los Angeles Reader* 21 October 1994. 'Affirmative action' quoted in the *New Yorker* 17 January 1994. USC as 'a citadel of privilege' is from 'The Man Behind the Mask' by Teresa Carpenter in the American edition of *Esquire* November 1994. Paul Rosenfield on Hollywood is from *The Club Rules*. 'Bounced by the best' and other details of SS's early days in Hollywood from *Time* 23 June 1975. Spielberg's comments about avoiding the draft are from *Time Out* 10 November 1978. The first report on Spielberg's age was in the *Los Angeles Times* 8 March 1981. The second, including Marvin Levy's comments, appeared in the same paper on 24 October 1995. The account of being helped by John Cassavettes is from *Los Angeles Weekly* 11–17 June 1982. 'One day in 1969' and 'I never made any deals' are from *Hollywood Reporter* 13 April 1971. SS's account of *Amblin*'s preview is in *City of San Francisco* 2 December 1975.

Chapter Four: *Universal Soldier*

William Link is quoted in *The Club Rules*. Ray Bradbury on film studios appears in *A Graveyard for Lunatics* (Knopf, New York, 1990). 'I couldn't work outside Universal' is from *The Steven Speilberg Story*. SS on Joan Crawford and the problems of making *Eyes* come from *Icons*, *People* magazine 20 July 1981 and *Joan Crawford* by Bob Thomas (Simon & Schuster, New York, 1978). SS on Robbins and Barwood is from *Filmmakers' Newsletter* Summer 1974. John Gregory Dunne describes Richard Zanuck in *The Studio* (Farrar, Straus & Giroux, New York, 1969). Zanuck on his first impressions of SS from interview in *Cinema Papers* March–April 1976. 'A folly, a novelty item' is from *Time Out* 10 November 1978. 'Taking *Marcus Welby* seriously' is from *Millimetre* March 1975. SS on Jerrold Freedman is from interview with Mitch Tuchman, *Film Comment* January/February 1978. 'It's very very hard' is from interview with Diane Jacobs *Millimetre* November 1977.

Chapter Five: *Duel*

'We're old now, but when we were the New Hollywood' is from a 1995 BBC *Omnibus* profile of John Milius. The *International Film Guide* report appeared in the 1971 edition (Tantivy Press, London). 'In those times' is from an unpublished interview with Michael Pye on BBC TV. Joan Didion's comments *passim* come from 'In Hollywood', reprinted in *The White Album* (Simon & Schuster, New York, 1979). Gavin Millar's conversation is from an unpublished BBC TV interview. Quotes from Barry Diller *passim* are from Joyce Haber's column in *Los Angeles Times Calendar* 13 July 1975. 'I come from a family of beautiful women' and 'printed circuitry' are from interview with Jerry Tallmer, *New York Post* 28 June 1975. 'It begins on Sunday' is from *Time Out* 10 November 1978. 'I never mock suburbia' is quoted in *Time* 31 May 1982. George Lucas on SS is from *Hollywood Reporter* 10 March 1994. Tom Milne's review is from *Sight and Sound* Winter 1972/3. The Fellini lunch story is told in *Cue* 12 December 1974. Mal Karman's interview is in *City of San Francisco* 2 December 1975. SS to Iain Johnstone is from an unpublished BBC TV interview. Darrl Zanuck's recital of obscenities and Stephen Silverman on marketing blockbusters are in *The Fox that Got Away*.

Chapter Six: *The Sugarland Express*

Most technical details about the making of *Sugarland Express* are taken from SS's interview with Andrew C. Bobrow in *Filmakers' Newsletter* Summer 1974 (herinafter *Newsletter*). All quotes from Jerry Goldsmith, Emily Richard, Julian Glover, Tom Stoppard and Paul Freeman are from conversations with the author, London, 1995. SS's comments on sex and film-making *passim* are from the 1978 UK *Penthouse* interview and 'Steven Spielberg from Jaws to Paws' in *inter/view* May 1977. All Julia Phillips's quotes are from *You'll Never Eat Lunch in this Town Again* except 'We are equally intimate', which is from an interview with Larry Salvato in *Millimetre* September 1976. Aljean Harmetz on Alan Ladd Jr is from *Rolling Breaks*. Joey Walsh on writing *Slide* is from *Robert Altman: Jumping off the Cliff*. George Lucas's 'We are the pigs' is quoted in *Saturday Review* June 1981. Coppola's behaviour at the preview of *American Graffiti* has been much described. This version is based in part on Dale Pollock's in *Skywalking*. Joe Dante's remarks from an interview with the author, Hollywood 1989. 'The great gamblers are dead' is from an interview with Michael Ventura in *Los Angeles Weekly* 11–17 June 1982. Paul Schrader's 'That whole summer' is from *Esquire* July 1982. Martin Amis *passim* quoted from *The Moronic Inferno*. 'Relationships' is from Michael Ventura's interview (see above). 'Crying on a shoulder pad' is from *Rolling Stone* 22 July 1982. SS's Texas psychic encounter is described in *Icons*. SS on Victoria Principal is from *The Club Rules*. Details of how *Sugarland* was storyboarded appear in *Newsletter* (see above). Richard Zanuck on SS is from the *New Yorker* 21 March 1994. Interview with Wayne Knight by Bill Warren. SS on William Atherton from *Newsletter* (see above). Michael Sacks on Ben Johnson from *Boston Globs* 9 April 1974. 'We stole it' is from BBC TV *Omnibus* profile of Milius 1994. John Gregory Dunne quote from *Esquire* July 1982. Pauline Kael's review is in the *New Yorker* 18 March 1974.

SS on the affinities with *Ace in the Hole* and on Vilmos Zsigmond in *Newsletter* (see above). Summer 1974. Goldie Hawn on location shooting is from *San Francisco Examiner Chronicle* 7 April 1974. SS's discovery of *Jaws* is part of the mythology. 'I really found my faith' and SS's comments on Welles's *War of the Worlds* are from interview with Gail Heathwood in *Cinema Papers* April–June 1978. Schrader on negotiations with SS from *Schrader on Schrader*. 'I guess if I had *Sugarland* to do over' is from *Grand Illusions* magazine Winter 1977. Goldie Hawn's judgement of *Sugarland* is quoted by Peter Haining in *Goldie* (W. H. Allen, London, 1985). Richard Zanuck on the ad campaign is from *Filmmakers on Filmmaking*, edited by Joseph McBride (American Film Institute, Los Angeles, 1983). 'Wasn't there anything for the director?' is in *Marquee* magazine July/August 1982. 'We were aghast' is from *Filmmakers on Filmmaking*). *Newsweek*'s review appears in the issue of 8 April 1974. Billy Wilder on SS is from Joyce Haber's column in *Los Angeles Times Calendar* 13 July 1975. 'People thought' is from an interview with John Moran in *Cinema Papers* July–August 1975. Joey Walsh on 'Slide' is from *Robert Altman: Jumping off the Cliff*.

Chapter Seven: *Jaws*

SS's comments on *Jaws* are from his 15 March 1978 London National Film Theatre appearance. 'The book has a little *Peyton Place*', 'Carl Gottlieb and I', 'emasculating and cuckolding the sheriff' and 'the only likeable character was the shark' are from Monte Stettin's interview with SS in *Millimetre* magazine March 1975. 'I only have good memories' is from an interview with John Gallagher in *Grand Illusions* magazine Winter 1977. Ron and Valerie Taylor's attempts to shoot shark footage with Carl Rizzo described in SS's 1978 London NFT lecture. Richard Zanuck's comments about *Jaws* only making $31 million are quoted by SS in an interview with Barbara Paskin in the London *Film Review* February 1976. 'I like people who bring very little baggage' is from *The Club Rules*. 'No one crafts better deals' is from *Los Angeles Times Magazine* 19 December 1993. 'He's as close an actor' is from interview with Mitch Tuchman *Film Comment* Jan/Feb 1978. Dreyfuss's description of his religious background is from *The Jewish Image in American Film*. Dirk Bogarde on Robert Shaw is from *Snakes and Ladders* (Triad/Panther, London, 1978). Robert Shaw's criticism of the *Jaws* script is from *Time* 23 June 1975. Other details from *The Price of Success*. Gottlieb's comments *passim* from *The Jaws Log*. Other details from *The Making of the Movie Jaws*. Peter Benchley's tirade against SS is from the *Los Angeles Times Calendar* 7 July 1974. Roy Scheider on boats interrupting the shoot is quoted by Rex Reed from the New York *Sunday News* 15 June 1975. The union problems of *Jaws* are reported in *Variety* 10 July 1974 under the headline 'U's *Jaws* at Martha's Vineyard Snarled in IATSE Electioneering'. The Teamsters' threat to close the production down reported in *Woman's Wear Daily* 17 July 1974. Henry Hathaway's advice is from an unpublished interview for BBC Radio's *Conversation Piece* series, c.1989. Joe Dante's remarks from conversation with the author, Hollywood, 1989. Roy Scheider's criticism of the press is from Rex Reed's column, *Sunday news* 15 June 1975. Dreyfuss as 'a major energy output' is from *Millimetre* magazine November 1977. SS on Robert Mattey is in *City of San Francisco* magazine 2 December 1975. David Brown on reactions to *Jaws* from *Let me Entertain You*. There are many descriptions of the food fight at the Harbor View. This is from Joyce Haber's column in *Los Angeles Times* 11 September 1979. *Action*'s report on the making of *Jaws* is in the issue of July/August 1974. L. M. Kit Carson's account of being ejected from the set is in *Oui* magazine December 1974. 'Isn't there any more?' is from *Time* 31 May 1982. Diane Jacobs's comment is from *Hollywood Renaissance*. Pauline Kael reviewed *Jaws* in the *New Yorker* 8 November 1976.

Chapter Eight: *Close Encounters of the Third Kind*

Quotes throughout from Julia Phillips are from *You'll Never Eat Lunch in this Town Again* except for her comments on ancillary deals, from interview with Howard Maxford in *Starburst* Special Issue No. 9, 1991. The opening Chuck Jones quote is from *Chuck Amuck*. 'Making a sequel to anything' is from *Variety* 21 October 1975. Cohen on *Bingo Long* is from *American Film* July 1976. Sheinberg's 'I want to be the first to predict' is from Joyce Haber's column in *Los Angeles Times Calendar* 13 July 1975. SS on the *Jaws* backlash is from *Newsweek* 21 November 1977. Paul Schrader on SS's reaction to *Jaws* is in *Cinefantastique* Summer 1978. SS on Scorsese is from his introduction to *Martin Scorsese: A Journey* by Mary Pat Kelly (Temple University Press, Philadelphia, 1991). The account of Belushi's behaviour is from *Wired*. SS on Scorsese in from *Martin Scorsese: A Journey*. Dreyfuss on SS as scriptwriter is from *American Film* November 1977. Irving's remarks about her sexual experience appear in *Today* 3 April 1987. Martin Amis comments on SS's beard in *The Moronic Inferno*. 'All I can tell you' is from an interview with Monte Stettin in *Millimetre* magazine March 1975. Paul Schrader's remarks are from *Schrader on Schrader*. James Monaco on the script of *CE3K* is from *American Film Now*. Truffaut to Serge Rousseau is in *Letters*. 'In order to be a story-teller' was quoted by SS in the Cèsar ceremony, Paris, 1995. Bob Balaban's 'I spent nine months' is from *New York Times* 2 April 1995. Jeff Walker talked to Bill Warren, Los Angeles, April 1995.

Chapter Nine: *1941*

SS on the Begelman case is from *Variety* 22 February 1978. Quotes and descriptions of events leading up to the *Close Encounters* previews and premiere are from *Indecent Exposure*. Bill Warren on the *CE3K* previews from conversation with the author, Paris, October 1995. Michael J. Arlen's 'The Tyranny of the Visual' is reprinted in *The Camera Age: Essays on Television*. Alan Hirschfield on *CE3K* is from *Indecent Exposure*. Account of SS in London is from interview with Adrian Turner, 1994. 'Amy and I must have been together' is from *People* magazine 20 July 1981. Amy Irving's 'People who know you' from *Movie Star* magazine May 1981. Schrader's 'into a kind of Zen garden' is from *Cinefantistique* Summer 1978. Accounts of the conflict with Columbia over the 'Special Edition' of *CE3K* from *Variety* 24 October 1979. Interview with Barbara Paskin is in London *Film Review* February 1976. SS on Belushi is from *Film Comment* May/June 1982. Descriptions of Belushi's casting in and behaviour on the set of *1941* are from *Wired*. 'As tasteful an experience as reading *Mad* magazine' is from *New York Times* 9 December 1979. John Brosnan on *Raiders* is from *Starburst* Vol. 4 No. 1. 'Almost as innovative' is from *Los Angeles Herald Examiner*. Remarks by Julia Phillips and Dawn Steel are from *You'll Never Eat Lunch in this Town Again* and *They Can Kill You but They Can't Eat You*. Michael Eisner's 'We're supposed to be creative people' and 'We built in serious penalties' is from 'A Deal to Remember' by Ben Stein in *New West* February 1981. Kathleen Kennedy on SS's office is from *Wired*. Jeff Walker spoke to Bill Warren, Los Angeles, April 1995. 'I'll spend the rest of my life disowning this movie' is from *New York Times* 9 December 1979.

Chapter Ten: *Raiders of the Lost Ark*

All quotes from Joe Dante, Emily Richard, Paul Freeman, Bill Hootkins, Gordon Stainforth and Sir David Puttnam are from interviews with the author, Los Angeles 1989 and London 1994. The negotiations about *Continental Divide* are described in *Wired*. 'I can make this film for $2.5 million' and the description of seeing *Don Winslow of the Navy* are from *Film Comment* May/June 1982. Amy Irving on her feelings for SS and 'I know he's an incredible film-maker' are from *Los Angeles Times* 13 March 1979. 'The press loves to design its own failures' and 'earned the right to spend someone else's money' are from *Saturday Review* June 1981. 'I learned not to invite Universal and Columbia executives' is from *Variety* 24 October 1979. 'I thought I was immune to failure' is from *Time* 31 May 1982. 'I'll be pregnant by April' and 'Life has caught up with me' are from interview with Leo Janos *Cosmopolitan* June 1980. The report on Columbia's production plans, including quotes from John Vietch and Frank

Price, appears in *Variety* 21 April 1980. SS on Kathleen Carey is from *Time* 31 May 1982. Frank Marshall on working with Bogdanovich is in *Starburst* September 1982. Jeff Walker talked to Bill Warren, April 1995. Philip Noyce on Harrison Ford is from *Sydney Morning Herald* 20 August 1994. 'I got it right down to the bones' is from *Marquee* magazine July/August 1982. SS's encounter with Karen Allen is documented in *Rolling Stone* 25 June 1981.

Chapter Eleven: *Poltergeist* and *E.T.: The Extraterrestrial*

Quotes from Jerry Goldsmith are from conversation with the author, London, 1995. 'E.T. made me yearn' is from *American Cinematographer* Spring 1990. Details of Begelman's conviction and exoneration appear in *Indecent Exposure*. 'They're scared of little pictures' is from *Variety* 30 May 1980. 'A deal is a work of science fiction' is from *Time* 31 May 1982. 'A sense of poised dynamism' is from *Final Cut*. Interview with Thelma Moss in *New York Post* 2 June 1982. All quotes by and about Steve Ross and those of Terry Semel appear in *Master of the Game*. 'I couldn't write alone' is from interview with Michael Ventura *Los Angeles Weekly* 11–17 July 1982. 'My revenge on TV' is from *Time* 31 May 1982. Anthony Goldschmidt on the poster design is from *New York Times* 20 April 1984. Martin Amis on *ET* is from *The Moronic Inferno*. SS at Cannes reported in *Variety* 20 April 1983. ET's 'plucking your heartstrings' is from BBC1 report on the film's release.

Chapter Twelve: *The Twilight Zone: The Movie*

'They've hired Kathleen Carey!' is from *Master of the Game*, as are SS's remarks about Steve Ross and Charles Paul's account of the E.T. videogame deal. 'I think Kathleen and I will have kids' is from *People* magazine 23 August 1982. 'Machiavellian risks' is from *New York Times* 10 June 1981. Brian Gibson recounts his experience with *The Tourist* in the BBC TV series *Naked Hollywood* 1994. 'His *Annie Hall*' is from *Film Comment* May/une 1982. Dee Wallace's comments on secrecy on the set of *E.T.* is from *People* magazine 21 December 1981 and on her alleged blacklisting from *Outrageous Conduct*. J. G. Ballard's comment about *The House on Haunted Hill* is from a conversation with the author 5 August 1994. Wesley Strick on *Cape Fear* is from *Martin Scorsese: A Journey*. The account of the genesis of Joe Dante's and George Miller's episodes for *The Twilight Zone* is taken from conversations with Joe Dante in 1990 and further discussions between Dante and Bill Warren in 1995, and with Richard Matheson. The negotiations for SS to join Disney were reported by Marilyn

Beck in the *New York Daily News* 28 June 1982. Other information is from *Storming the Magic Kingdom*. Joe Dante and Bill Warren supplied details of the production of Landis's episode of *The Twilight Zone*. Carol Serling's 'Rod's stories were about people' is from *The Twilight Zone Companion*. Much of the background and many of the quotes in the section on the aftermath of the disaster and SS's reaction are from *Outrageous Conduct*. The conversation between SS and John Landis is part of an unpublished interview with Landis by Bill Warren. SS's 'I think people are standing up much more' is from his interview with Dale Pollock, *Los Angeles Times* 13 April 1983. 'Without Joe, it would never have been finished,' is from a conversation with Jerry Goldsmith, London, 29 January 1995. 'I was charmed' appears in from *The Twilight Zone Companion*. Details of SS's residency at the St James's Club were supplied by its manager Michael Lucas in a conversation of January 1995. Paul Rosenfield is quoted from *The Club Rules*. 'Steven has surrounded himself' is from *Outrageous Conduct*. Amblin 'a very dysfunctional place' is from *Los Angeles Times*, reprinted in the *Guardian* 22 March 1994.

Chapter Thirteen: *Indiana Jones and the Temple of Doom*

All quotes from David Yip, Joe Dante, Mick Garris, Julian Glover and Jerry Goldsmith in this chapter are from conversations with the author, except Dante's remarks about *Innerspace*, which appear in Hillier's *The New Hollywood*, and 'I know which side my bread's buttered on,' from *New York* magazine 24 March 1986. Quotes from SS about Steve Ross are mostly from *Master of the Game*. 'Like a children's crusade' is from *Film Comment* May/June 1982. Jack Mathews on SS's corporate colleagues is quoted by Kirk Honeycutt in 'The Art of the Deal' in *Hollywood Reporter* 10 March 1994. SS on Michael Jackson's house is from *Michael Jackson: The Magic and the Madness*. 'We really want to do' is from *inter/view* June 1982. Dawn Steel's account of the ShoWest incident is from *They Can Kill You but They Can't Eat You*, as are details of her career and quotes about Jeffrey Katzenberg. Details of the press and trade reaction to the rejection of *E.T.* are taken from *Inside Oscar: The Unofficial Story of the Academy Awards*. Details of Amy Irving's reconciliation with SS and their life together thereafter are from *McCalls* June 1985, *Ladies Home Journal* March 1989, *US* October 3 1988, *People* magazine 27 March 1978 and 7 August 1989, and *Los Angeles Times* 17 April 1984. Peter Bart's comment on the Amblin headquarters is from *Final Cut*, 'an architectural fantasy' from 'Steven Spielberg in Black and White' by David Hay (*Sydney Morning Herald Good Weekend* 22 January 1994). SS on his relationship with Universal is from *Los Angeles Times Magazine* 19 December 1993. David Brown's comments appear in *Let Me*

Entertain You. Steven Schiff's review appears in *Vanity Fair* September 1984. The report on SS and Lucas at Mann's Chinese Theater is from *Los Angeles Reader* 25 May 1984.

Chapter Fourteen: *The Color Purple*

All quotations from J. G. Ballard, Tom Stoppard and Mick Garris from interviews with the author as previously cited. David Denby on studio heads in the *Australian* 2–3 August 1986. 'Steve *never* talked Warner Brothers business' is from *Master of the Game*. Thomas Keneally quotes 'It's kinda thick' and describes the lunch with Sheinberg and Pfefferberg in the Australian *National Times* 29 July 1983. SS's remark by David Hay is in *Sydney Morning Herald Magazine* 22 January 1994. 'Scared I couldn't' is from *Los Angeles Times Magazine* 19 December 1993. Gordon Parks's quotes from *Stills* magazine October 1985. SS on the 'executive producer' credit is from *Millimetre* magazine July 1982. Peter Bart's remarks from *Final Cut*. 'I made a bet with myself' is from *New York Times* 29 December 1990.'Spielberg Defers' is from *Variety* 20 April 1983. River Phoenix's story from *Independent on Sunday Magazine* 5 December 1993. 'I'm totally unambitious' is from *Los Angeles Times* 14 April 1985. 'I've been having these persistent dreams' is from *Icons*. 'I had my Peter and Wendy' is from interview with George Perry in *Sunday Times Magazine* 15 June 1986.

Chapter Fifteen: *Empire of the Sun*

All quotes in this chapter from J. G. Ballard, Tom Stoppard and David Yip from interviews with the author. Details and quotes about the campaign to deny SS an Oscar are from Jack Kroll's report in *Newsweek* 17 February 1986. Thomas Keneally's 'He told myself' is from the *Melbourne Age Weekend Review* 26 September 1984. Phil Joanou is in *Hollywood Reporter* 10 March 1994. Irving's 'I started my career' is from *People* magazine 3 April 1989. 'It was no fun to go over there' is from the *New Yorker* 21 March 1994. 'If Steven Spielberg is your friend' is from *Business Week* 29 May 1989. Amy Irving's 'I tended to lose out' is in *Today* 21 August 1987. Elaine DeKooning's reminiscences are in *Elaine and Bill: Portrait of a Marriage*. 'I was talking about the future' is from *American Film* June 1988. 'There are certain people' is from *Steven Spielberg: The Man, the Movies and their Meaning*. Christopher Hampton on *Nostromo* quoted in *David Lean* by Kevin Brownlow (Richard Cohen, London, 1996).

Chapter Sixteen: *Indiana Jones and the Last Crusade*

All qutoes from Julian Glover, Kevork Malikyan and Bill Hotkins are from interviews with the author, previously cited. Lawrence Kasdan on the Grail legend is from 'Kasdan on Kasdan' in *Projections 3* (Faber & Faber, London, 1994). Anne Spielberg on SS as negotiator is from the *New Yorker* 21 March 1994. The profit figures of famous films were cited by Francois Velde in a letter to the *New York Times* 4 June 1995. SS's conversation with Andrew Lloyd Webber reported in the *Guardian* 25 January 1991. SS on cancelling *Peter Pan* is from interview with Sheila Johnston, *Independent* 23 March 1988. SS on his hopes for an Oscar quoted in *Inside Oscar*. SS's plans for Elstree were reported in the *Daily Mail* 1 July 1988 and elsewhere. Both quotes about Sony's purchase of Columbia and SS's comments are in the *New Yorker* 28 February 1994. Paul Rosenfield on Irving is from *The Club Rules*. 'Kate spent months' appears in *Today* 25 September 1989.

Chapter Seventeen: *Always* and *Hook*

Tom Pollock on SS is quoted in *Business Week* 29 May 1989. SS on Holly Hunter is quoted in *Today* 25 September 1989. 'Wading in corn' is from *Independent on Sunday* 23 May 1993. James Agee's comments on *A Guy Named Joe* are reprinted in *Agee on Film* (McDowell Obolensky, NY, 1959.) Details of SS's involvement with *The Bonfire of the Vanities* are in *The Devil's Candy*. 'It's about a brother and sister' quoted by Gene Siskel in *The Future of Movies*. 'I'm seventy-four years old' and SS's negotations on *Schindler's List* detailed in *Boston Globe* 12 December 1993. Keneally's remarks on SS's adaptation of *Schindler's List* appear in *Sydney Morning Herald* 16 November 1985. Details of the *Cape Fear* project, including Wesley Strick's remarks, are in *Martin Scorsese: A Journey*. Fred Schepisi's 'You'll fuck it up' is quoted in the *Melbourne Age Weekend Review* 3–4 April 1993. Details of Guber and Peters management of Sony come from James B. Stewart's article 'Sony's Bad Dream' in the *New Yorker* 28 February 1994. An account of the MCA sale to Matsushita and Jonathan Sheinberg's involvement appears in the *New Yorker* 17 January 1994. News of the purchase of the Hughes factory and DreamWorks' plans for the site is in *Screen International*, 5–11 January 1996.

Chapter Eighteen: *Jurassic Park* and *Schindler's List*

All quotes from Tom Stoppard are from interview with the author. Most details of Steve Ross's last months are taken from *Master of the Game*. Kim Newman on *Jurassic Park* is from *Sight and Sound* August 1993. SS on his political beliefs is from *Rolling Stone* September 1985. Material and quotes about Liam Neeson, including those of Neil Jordan and John Lahr, taken from *New York Times Magazine* 4 December 1994 and *Sydney Morning Herald* 4 February 1995. 'A hodgepodge of animals' appears in 'Designing Dinosaurs: How to Bring *Jurassic Park* to Life' by Don Lessem, *Omni*. July 1993. Many technical details are about the planning of *Jurassic Park* are from *The Making of Jurassic Park*. The attitude to children in *Jurassic Park* is interestingly discussed by William Paul in *Laughing, Screaming: Modern Hollywood Horror and Comedy* (Columbia University Press, NY, 1994). 'We had Bob Daly and Terry Semel as hobos' is in *Master of the Game*. Thomas Keneally's comparison of *Schindler's List* and *Lawrence of Arabia* is from *Sydney Morning Herald* 8 February 1994. The problems of shooting at Auschwitz were reported by the *Guardian* 29 November 1993. Liam Neeson was interviewed for the *Paris Free Voice* by Lisa Nesselson June 1994. Scorsese and Spielberg's statements on the GATT talks reported in *Variety* 8 November 1993. Bertrand Tavernier's remarks from an interview with the author, Paris, 1995. Reviews of *Schindler's List* were summarised in the *Melbourne Age Weekend Review* 5–6 February 1994. Daniele Heymann's review quoted in *Paris Free Voice* June 1994.

Chapter Nineteen: *The Dream Team*

'I have no idea what to do next' and account of SS's visit to the Consumer Electronics Show are from the *New Yorker* 21 March 1994. SS on Dive! restaurants from CNN report 29 August 1995. Account of the Matsushita meetings with Wasserman and Sheinberg from *Los Angeles Times Magazine* 21 May 1995. The potential sale of MCA and its relationship with Matsushita was detailed in *Los Angeles Times* 3 April 1994. Details of the formation of DreamWorks SKG were assembled from too many sources in the trade and general press to detail, though much information, including that on the initial telephone conversations between SS and Katzenberg, and Zemeckis's comment, as well as the White House phone call to Geffen came from 'A Hollywood Recipe: Vision, Wealth, Ego' in the *New York Times* 16 October 1994. Other quotes and facts came from the *Los Angeles Times* Business Pages, in particular the issues of 13 October ('Merger of the Moguls: Dream Team Trio Outline Plans for Studio'), 14 October 1994 ('Hollywood Trio's Options: Buy MCA or Build a Dream'), by Alan Citron, 21 October ('Big News, But Where are the Big Plans?') by Robert W. Welkos,

25 October, ('Dream Team's 1st Project: Mastering Spin Control'), 21 March 1995 ('Paul Who? Dream Team's New Benefactor') and ('Dream Team May Get New Player: Bill Gates'), both by Alan Citron and Claudia Eller, 23 March 1995, 'A High-Tech Hollywood Alliance' by various writers. 'When I was making the film in Poland' and 'If you want to find out where people slept' from New York Times 10 November 1994. SS's comments from the Cèsar telecast TF1 25 February 1995. Damon Knight's quote (about Ray Bradbury) is from In Search of Wonder.

Filmography

SHORT FILMS

1968

Amblin'
Produced by Dennis Hoffman. Screenplay and editing by Steven Spielberg. Director of photography. Allen Daviau. Starring Pamela McMyler and Richard Levin.

TELEVISION EPISODES AS DIRECTOR

1969

Eyes (Rod Serling's Night Gallery)
Starring Joan Crawford, Barry Sullivan, Tom Bosley.

1970

Daredevil Gesture (Marcus Welby MD)
Starring Robert Young and James Brolin.

1971

Make Me Laugh (Rod Serling's Night Gallery)
Starring Godfrey Cambridge. (Part of this episode was directed by Jeannot Szwarc.)

LA 2017 (The Name of the Game. LA 2017)
Starring Gene Barry and Barry Sullivan.

The Private World of Martin Dalton (The Psychiatrist)
Starring Roy Thinnes and Jim Hutton.

Par for the Course (The Psychiatrist)
Starring Clu Gulager and Joan Darling.

Murder by the Book (Columbo)
Starring Peter Falk, Jack Cassidy and Martin Milner.

Duel (NBC World Premiere Movie)
Duel was shown at seventy-four minutes in its TV debut and eighty-five minutes in cinemas. For full credits, see listing under Cinema Features.

1972

Something Evil (CBS Friday Night Movie)
Starring Sandy Dennis, Darren McGavin, Ralph Bellamy, Johnny Whittaker.

Savage (NBC World Premiere Movie)
Starring Martin Landau, Barbara Bain, Will Geer and Barry Sullivan. Also known as *Watch Dog* and *The Savage Report*.

1985

Ghost Train (Amazing Stories)
Starring Lukas Haas, Roberts Blossom.

1987

The Mission (Amazing Stories)
Starring Kevin Costner, Casey Siemaszko, Kiefer Sutherland.
Spielberg also produced and contributed the original stories for most of the episodes of *Amazing Stories* 1985–7.

FEATURE FILMS AS DIRECTOR

1973

Duel
Produced by George Eckstein. Script by Richard Matheson from his short story. Editor: Frank Morriss. Director of photography: Jack A.

Marta. Production designer: Robert S. Smith. Music: Billy Goldenberg. Assistant director: James Fargo. Stunt co-ordinator: Carey Loftin.

Starring Dennis Weaver (David Mann), Jacqueline Scott (Mrs Mann), Eddie Firestone (Cafe owner), Lou Frizzell (Bus driver), Gene Dynarski (Man in café), Lucille Benson (Snakearama lady), Shirley O'Hara (Waitress), Alexander Lockwood (Old man in car), Amy Douglass (Old woman in car), Dick Whittington (Radio call-in man), Carey Loftin (Truck Driver), Dale van Sickle (Driver of Mann's car).

The Sugarland Express

Produced by Richard D. Zanuck and David Brown. Script by Matthew Robbins and Hal Barwood from Spielberg's story. Editors: Edward M. Abroms, Verna Fields. Director of photography: Vilmos Zsigmond. Production design: Joseph Alves. Music: John Williams. Assistant director: James Fargo. Starring Goldie Hawn (Lou Jean Poplin), William Atherton (Clovis Poplin), Ben Johnson (Captain Tanner), Michael Sacks (Officer Slide), Harrison Zanuck (Baby Langston), Gregory Walcott (Officer Mashburn), Louise Latham (Mrs Livvy).

1975

Jaws

Produced by Richard D. Zanuck and David Brown. Screenplay by Peter Benchley and Carl Gottlieb from Benchley's novel (plus, uncredited, Howard Sackler and John Milius). Editor: Verna Fields. Director of photography: Bill Butler. Additional underwater photography: Ron and Valerie Taylor, shot by Rexford Metz. Production design: Joseph Alves. Special effects: Joseph A. Mattey. Music: John Williams. Starring Roy Scheider (Brody), Richard Dreyfuss (Hooper), Robert Shaw (Quint), Lorraine Gary (Ellen Brody), Murray Hamilton (Chief Selectman Vaughn), Carl Gottlieb (Meadows), Peter Benchley (TV reporter), Susan Backlinie (First shark victim).

1977

Close Encounters of the Third Kind

Produced by Julia and Michael Phillips. Screenplay by Spielberg (plus, uncredited, Paul Schrader, Matthew Robbins, Hal Barwood, Jerry Belson and others). Editor: Michael Kahn. Director of photography: Vilmos Zsigmond. Additional photography: William A. Fraker, Douglas Slocombe, John Alonzo, Laszlo Kovacs (plus, uncredited, Allen Daviau).

Production design: Joseph Alves. Special effects: Douglas Trumbull.
Starring Richard Dreyfuss (Roy Neary), Melinda Dillon (Jillian Guiler),
François Truffaut (Claude Lacombe), Teri Garr (Bonnie Neary), Cary
Guffey (Barry Guiler), Bob Balaban (David Laughlin), J. Patrick
McNamara (Project Leader), Shawn Bishop, Adrienne Campbell,
Justin Dreyfuss (Neary's children), Roberts Blossom (Farmer),
Alexander Lockwood and Amy Douglass (Implantees), George
Dicenzo (Major Benchley).

The first version of *Close Encounters* ran 135 minutes. The 'Special
Edition' released in 1982 ran 132 minutes. The Special Edition deletes
the appearances of Blossom, Lockwood, Douglass, Dicenzo and others.
Later, for US TV, Spielberg re-inserted some of the cut footage plus
earlier out-takes to create a 145 minute version.

1979

1941

Executive Producer: John Milius. Produced by Buzz Feitshans. Script
by Robert Zemeckis and Bob Gale from a story by Zemeckis, Gale
and Milius. Editor: Michael Kahn. Director of photography: William
A. Fraker. Production design: Dean Edward Mitzner. Art director:
William F. O'Brien. Special effects: A. D. Flowers. Visual effects
supervisor: Larry Robinson. Music: John Williams. Starring John Belushi
(Wild Bill Kelso), Dan Aykroyd (Sergeant Tree), Ned Beatty (Ward
Douglas), Lorraine Gary (Joan Douglas), Tim Mathison (Birkhead),
Nancy Allen (Donna), Warren Oates (Maddox), Treat Williams
(Sitarski), Robert Stack (General Stilwell), Murray Hamilton (Claude),
Toshiro Mifune (Mitamura), Christopher Lee (Von Kleinschmidt), Slim
Pickens (Hollis Wood), Penny Marshall (Mrs Fitzroy). Also Patti
LuPone, Elisha Cook Jr, Dub Taylor, Lionel Stander, Lucille Benson
and Susan Backlinie.

1981

Raiders of the Lost Ark

Executive producers: George Lucas and Howard Kazanjian. Producer:
Frank Marshall. Script by Lawrence Kasdan from a story by Lucas
and Philip Kaufman. Editor: Michael Kahn. Director of photography:
Douglas Slocombe. Production design: Norman Reynolds. Art director:
Leslie Dilley. Visual effects: Richard Edlund, Kit West, Bruce Nicholson,

Joe Johnstone. Music: John Williams. Starring Harrison Ford (Indiana Jones), Karen Allen (Marion Ravenswood), Paul Freeman (Belloq), John Rhys-Davies (Sallah), Denholm Elliot (Marcus Brody), Alfred Molina (Satipo), Ronald Lacey (Toht), Wolf Kahler (Dietrich), Bill Hootkins (Major Eaton), Vic Tabian (Barranca and Monkey Man), Anthony Higgins (Gobbler).

1982

E.T.: The Extraterrestrial

Produced by Spielberg and Kathleen Kennedy. Line producer: Frank Marshall. Script by Melissa Mathison from an idea by Spielberg. Editor: Carol Littleton. Director of photography: Allen Daviau. Production design: James D. Bissell. Visual effects supervisor: Dennis Muren, Kenneth J. Smith. Special effects co-ordinator: Dale Martin. ET design: Carlo Rambaldi. Spaceship design: Ralph McQuarrie. Music: John Williams. Starring Henry Thomas (Elliott), Dee Wallace (Mary), Peter Coyote (Keys), Drew Barrymore (Gertie), Robert MacNaughton (Michael), K. C. Martel (Greg), Sean Frye (Steve), Tom (C. Thomas Howell), Erika Eleniak (Pretty girl). Uncredited: Pat Bilon, Tamara de Treaux, Matthew de Merritt (ET), Debra Winger (voice of ET).

Poltergeist

Produced by Spielberg and Frank Marshall. Associate producer: Kathleen Kannedy. Directed by Tobe Hooper. Script by Spielberg, Michael Grais and Mark Victor from Spielberg's story. Editor: Michael Kahn. Director of photography: Matthew F. Leonetti. Visual effects supervisor: Richard Edlund. Set designer: Bill Matthews and Martha Johnson. Special effects make-up; Craig Reardon. Music: Jerry Goldsmith. Starring Craig T. Nelson (Steve Freeling), JoBeth Williams (Diane Freeling), Beatrice Straight (Dr Lesh), Dominique Dunne (Dana), Oliver Robbins (Robbie), Heather O'Rourke (Carol Anne), Zelda Rubinstein (Tangina), James Karen (Teague).

1983

The Twilight Zone: The Movie

Executive producer: Frank Marshall. Produced by Spielberg and John Landis. Spielberg directed one episode, Kick the Can. Script by George Clayton Johnson, Richard Matheson and 'Josh Rogan' (Melissa Mathison) from Johnson's story. Editor: Michael Kahn. Director of

photography: Allen Daviau. Music: Jerry Goldsmith. Starring Scatman
Crothers (Mr Bloom), Murray Matheson (Mr Agee), Bill Quinn (Mr
Conroy), Martin Garner (Mr Weinstein), Selma Diamond (Mrs
Weinstein), Priscilla Pointer (Miss Cox).

1984

Indiana Jones and the Temple of Doom

Executive producers: George Lucas and Frank Marshall. Line producer:
Robert Watts. Script by Willard Huyck and Gloria Katz from a story by
Lucas. Editor: Michael Kahn. Director of photography: Douglas
Slocombe. Production design: Elliot Scott. Special visual effects:
Dennis Muren, Michael McAlister, Lorne Peterson, George Gibbs.
Music: John Williams. Starring Harrison Ford (Indiana Jones), Kate
Capshaw (Willie Scott), Ke Huy Quan (Short Round), Roshan Seth
(Chattar Lal), Amrish Puri (Mola Ram), Philip Stone (Captain Blumburtt),
Roy Chiao (Lao Che), David Yip (Wu Han), Raj Singh (Young Rajah),
D. R. Nanayakkaru (Shaman). Uncredited: Dan Aykroyd (Weber).

1985

The Color Purple

Executive producers: Joan Peters and Peter Guber. Produced by
Spielberg, Frank Marshall, Kathleen Kennedy and Quincy Jones.
Script by Menno Meyjes from Alice Walker's novel. Editor: Michael
Kahn. Director of photography: Allen Daviau. Production design: J.
Michael Riva. Art director: Robert W. Welch. Special effects supervisor:
Matt Sweeney. Music: Quincy Jones. Starring Whoopi Goldberg
(Celie), Danny Glover (Albert Johnson), Margaret Avery (Shug Avery),
Willard Pugh (Harpo), Oprah Winfrey (Sofia), Rae Dawn Chong
(Squeak), Akosua Busia (Nettie), Adolph Caesar (Old Mr), Dana Ivey
(Miss Millie), John Patton Jr (Preacher), Larry Fishburne (Swain), Desreta
Jackson (Young Celie).

1987

Empire of the Sun

Executive producer: Robert Shapiro. Produced by Spielberg, Frank
Marshall and Kathleen Kennedy. Script by Tom Stoppard (and Menno
Meyjes, uncredited) from J. G. Ballard's novel. Editor: Michael Kahn.

Director of photography: Allen Daviau. Production designer: Norman Reynolds. Music: John Williams. Starring John Malkovich (Basie), Christian Bale (Jim Graham), Miranda Richardson (Mrs Victor), Nigel Havers (Doctor Rawlins), Joe Pantoliano (Frank), Leslie Philips (Maxton), Robert Stephens (Mr Lockwood), Emily Richard (Jim's mother), Rupert Frazer (Jim's father), Paul McGann (Lt Price), Takitoki Kataoka (Kamikaze boy pilot), Masato Ibu (Sergeant Nagata), Bert Kwouk (Mr Chen).

1989

Indiana Jones and the Last Crusade

Executive producers: George Lucas, Frank Marshall. Line producer: Robert Watts. Script by Jeffrey Boam from story by Lucas and Menno Meyjes. Editor: Michael Kahn. Director of photography: Douglas Slocombe. Production designer: Elliot Scott. Visual effect supervisor: Michael J. McAllister. Music: John Williams. Starring Harrison Ford (Indiana Jones), Sean Connery (Professor Henry Jones), Denholm Elliot (Marcus Brody), Alison Doody (Elsa Schneider), Julian Glover (Walter Donovan), John Rhys-Davies (Sallah), Michael Byrne (Vogel), Kevork Malikyan (Kazim), River Phoenix (Young Indiana Jones), Richard Young (Fedora).

Always

Produced by Spielberg, Kathleen Kennedy and Frank Marshall. Script by Jerry Belson (and Diane Thomas, uncredited) from Dalton Trumbo's screenplay for *A Guy Named Joe*, based on a story by Chandler Sprague and David Boehm, adapted by Frederick Hazlitt Brennan. Editor: Michael Kahn. Director of photography: Mikael Solomon. Production design: James Bissell. Music: John Williams. Starring Richard Dreyfuss (Pete Sandrich), Holly Hunter (Dorinda Durston), John Goodman (Al Yackey), Brad Johnson (Ted Baker), Audrey Hepburn (Hap), Marg Helgenberger (Rachel), Roberts Blossom (Airport hermit).

1991

Hook

Executive producer: Jim V. Hart. Produced by Kathleen Kennedy, Frank Marshall and Gerald R. Molen. Script by Jim V. Hart and Malia Scotch Marmo from story by Jim V. Hart and Nick Castle. Production design: Norman Garwood. Music: John Williams. Songs by Williams and

Leslie Bricusse. Starring Robin Williams (Peter Banning/Peter Pan),
Dustin Hoffman (Captain James Hook), Maggie Smith (Wendy
Darling), Julia Roberts (Tinkerbell), Charlie Korsmo (Jack Banning),
Bob Hoskins (Smee), Dante Basco (Rufio). Uncredited: Glenn Close,
David Crosby (Pirates), Phil Collins (London Bobby).

1993

Jurassic Park

Produced by Kathleen Kennedy and Gerald R. Molen. Script by Michael
Crichton and David Koepp from Crichton's novel. Editor: Michael
Kahn. Director of photography: Dean Cundey. Production designer:
Rick Carter. Dinosaur effects: Stan Winston, Phil Tippett, Michael
Lantieri, Dennis Muren. Music: John Williams. Starring Sam Neill (Alan
Grant), Richard Attenborough (John Hammond), Laura Dern (Ellie
Sattler), Jeff Goldblum (Ian Malcolm), Bob Peck (Robert Muldoon),
Jerry Molen (Harding), Wayne Knight (Nedry), Joseph Mazzello
(Tim), Ariana Richards (Lex), Martin Ferrero (Donald Gennaro).

Schindler's List

Produced by Spielberg, Gerald R. Molen and Branko Lustig. Script by
Steven Zaillian from Thomas Keneally's novel. Editor: Michael Kahn.
Director of photography: Janusz Kaminski. Production design: Allan
Starski. Music: John Williams. Starring Liam Neeson (Oskar Schindler),
Ralph Fiennes (Amon Goeth), Ben Kingsley (Itzhak Stern), Embeth
Davidtz (Helen Hirsch), Jonathan Sagelle (Poldek Pfefferberg),
Caroline Goodall (Emilie Schindler), Dominika Bednarczyk (Little girl
in ghetto).

FILMS AS PRODUCER

In addition to his credit as producer of films he directed, Spielberg received
producer, executive producer or co-executive producer credit on *I Wanna
Hold Your Hand* (1978), *Used Cars* (1980), *Continental Divide* (1981), *Gremlins*
(1984), *Back to the Future, The Goonies* and *Young Sherlock Holmes* (all 1985),
The Money Pit and *An American Tail* (both 1986), *Innerspace* and **batteries
not included* (1987), *Who Framed Roger Rabbit* and *The Land Before Time*
(1988), *Back to the Future II* and *Dad* (1989), *Back to the Future III, Gremlins
II: The New Batch, Joe Versus the Volcano* and *Arachnophobia* (1990), and *An
American Tail II: Fievel Goes West* (1991).

He is credited for original story for the script of *Ace Eli and Rodger of the Skies* (1973) and *The Goonies* (1985), as co-producer, co-screenwriter and for original story on *Poltergeist* (1982) and as co-producer with John Landis on *The Twilight Zone: The Movie* (1983).

Spielberg also appears by proxy in the credits of the following films which carry the credit 'Presented by Amblin Entertainment', 'Amblin Presents' or 'An Amblin Entertainment Production': *Fandango* (1985), *Harry and the Hendersons* (1987), *Akira Kurosawa's Dreams* (1990) ['Steven Spielberg Presents'] *Cape Fear* (1991), *Noises Off* (1992), *A Far-Off Place* (1993), *The Flintstones* (1994) ['Steven Spielrock Presents'], and *The Bridges of Madison County*, *Casper* and *To Wong Foo, Thanks for Everything!, Julie Newmar* (all 1995).

Select Bibliography

Amis, Martin, *Invasion of the Space Invaders: An Addict's Guide to Battle Tactics, Big Scores and the Best Machines*, Introduction by Steven Spielberg, Methuen, London, 1982

Amis, Martin, 'Steven Spielberg: Boyish Wonder' in *The Moronic Inferno and other Visits to America*, Jonathan Cape, London 1986

Arlen, Michael J., 'The Tyranny of the Visual' in *The Camera Age: Essays on Television*, Farrar Straus Giroux, New York, 1980

Bach, Steven, *Final Cut: Dreams and Disaster in the Making of Heaven's Gate*, Morrow, New York, 1985

Balaban, Bob, *Close Encounters of the Third Kind Diary*, Paradise Press, New York, 1978

Belushi, Judith Jacklin, *Samurai Widow*, Carroll & Graff, New York, 1990

Bergan, Ronald, *Dustin Hoffman*, Virgin, London, 1991

Blake, Edith, *The Making of the Movie Jaws*, Ballantine, New York, 1975

Brown, David, *Let Me Entertain You*, Morrow, New York, 1990

Brode, Douglas, *The Films of Steven Spielberg*, Citadel, New York, 1995

Bruck, Connie, *Master of the Game: Steve Ross and the Creation of Time-Warner*, Simon & Schuster, New York, 1994

Buzzell, Linda, *How to Make it in Hollywood: All the Right Moves*, HarperCollins, New York, 1992

Callan, Michael Feeney, *Sean Connery: The Untouchable Hero*, Virgin, London, 1993

Cash, William, *Educating William: Memoirs of a Hollywood Correspondent*, Simon & Schuster, New York, 1993

Clinch, Minty, *Harrison Ford: A Biography*, New English Library, London, 1986

Coveney, Michael, *Maggie Smith: A Bright Particular Star*, Gollancz, London, 1992

Crawley, Tony, *The Steven Spielberg Story: The Man Behind the Movies*, Quill Press, New York, 1983

Farber, Stephen and Green, Marc, *Outrageous Conduct: Art, Ego and The Twilight Zone Case*, Morrow, New York, 1988

Farber, Stephen, and Green, Marc, *Hollywood Dynasties*, Delilah, New York, 1984

Friedman, Lester D., *The Jewish Image in American Film*, Citadel, New Jersey, 1987

French, John, *Robert Shaw: The Price of Success*, Nick Hern Books, London, 1993

Goodwin, Michael and Wise, Naomi, *On the Edge: The Life and Times of Francis Coppola*, Morrow, New York, 1989

Gottlieb, Carl, *The Jaws Log*, Dell, New York, 1975

Hall, Lee, *Elaine and Bill: Portrait of a Marriage. The Lives of Willem and Elaine De Kooning*, HarperCollins, New York, 1993

Harmetz, Aljean, *Rolling Breaks and Other Movie Business*, Knopf, New York, 1983

Harris, Marlys, J., *The Zanucks of Hollywood: The Dark Legacy of a Movie Dynasty*, Virgin, London, 1990

Hillier, Jim, *The New Hollywood*, Studio Vista, London, 1993

Horricks, Raymond, *Quincy Jones*, Spellmount, London, 1986

Jacobs, Diane, *Hollywood Renaissance*, Delta, New York, 1980

Jones, Chuck, *Chuck Amuck: The Life and Times of an Animated Cartoonist*, Introduction by Steven Spielberg, Avon, New York, 1990

Kahn, James, *Poltergeist* (A novel based on the story by Spielberg and the screenplay by Michael Grais and Mark Victor), Warner Books, New York, 1982

Kleinfelder, Rita Lang, *When We Were Young: A Baby-Boomer Yearbook*, Prentice Hall, New York, 1993

Knight, Damon, *In Search of Wonder*, Advent Press, Chicago, 1956

Litwak, Mark, *Reel Power: The Struggle for Influence and Success in the New Hollywood*, Morrow, New York, 1986

McClintick, David, *Indecent Exposure*, Morrow, New York, 1982

McGilligan, Pat, *Robert Altman: Jumping off the Cliff*, St Martins Press, New York, 1989

McKenzie, Alan, *The Harrison Ford Story*, Zomba Books, London, 1984

McNeil, Alex, *Total Television: A Comprehensive Guide to Programming from 1948 to the Present Day, Second Edition*, Penguin, London, 1984

Madsen, Axel, *The New Hollywood*, Crowell, New York, 1975

Manchester, William, *The Glory and the Dream*, Little Brown, Boston, 1974

Miller, Mark Crispin (editor), *Seeing Through Movies*, Pantheon, New York, 1990

Monaco, James, *American Film Now*, New American Library, New York, 1984

Moore, Charles, *Los Angeles: The City Observed*, Vintage, New York, 1984

Mott, Donald R. and Saunders, Cheryl McAllister, *Steven Spielberg*, Twayne, Boston, 1986

Pollock, Dale, *Skywalking: The Life and Films of George Lucas*, Harmony Books, New York, 1983

Pye, Michael and Myles, Linda, *The Movie Brats: How the Film Generation Took Over Hollywood*, Faber & Faber, London, 1979

Rosenfield, Paul, *The Club Rules: Power, Money, Sex and Fear; How it Works in Hollywood*, Warner Books, New York, 1992

Salamon, Julie, *The Devil's Candy:* The Bonfire of the Vanities *Goes to Hollywood*, Jonathan Cape, London, 1991

Schrader, Paul, *Schrader on Schrader and Other Writings*, edited by Kevin Jackson, Faber & Faber, London, 1990

Serling, Rod, 'The Monsters are Due on Maple Street' in *Stories from the Twilight Zone*, Bantam, New York, 1986

Shay, Don and Duncan, Jody, *The Making of* Jurassic Park, Ballantine, New York, 1993

Silverman, Stephen, M., *The Fox that Got Away: The Last Days of the Zanuck Dynasty at Twentieth Century-Fox*, Lyle Stuart, Secaucus, 1988

Spielberg, Steven, *Close Encounters of the Third Kind*, Fotonovel, Sphere, London, 1978

Spielberg, Steven, *Close Encounters of the Third Kind*, A novel based on his original screenplay, Sphere, London, 1978

Steel, Dawn, *They Can Kill You but They Can't Eat You: Lessons from the Front*, Simon & Schuster, New York, 1993

Taraborrelli, J. Randy, *Michael Jackson: The Magic and the Madness*, Birch Lane Press, New York, 1991

Taylor, Derek, *The Making of* Raiders of the Lost Ark, Ballantine, New York, 1981

Taylor, John, *Storming the Magic Kingdom: Wall Street, the Raiders and the Battle for Disney*, Knopf, New York, 1987

Taylor, Philip M., *Steven Spielberg*, Batsford, London, 1992

Truffaut, François, *Letters*, edited by Gilbert Adair, Faber & Faber, London, 1989

Wicking, Chris and Vahimagi, Tise, *The American Vein: Directors and Directions in Television*, Dutton, New York, 1979

Wiley, Mason, and Bona, Damien, *Inside Oscar: The Unofficial Story of the Academy Awards*, Ballantine, New York, 1988

Woodward, Bob, *Wired: The Short Life and Fast Times of John Belushi*, Simon & Schuster, New York, 1984

Worrell, Denise, 'The Eternal Childhood of Steven Spielberg' in *Icons: Intimate Portraits*, Atlantic Monthly Press, New York, 1989

Yule, Andrew, *Enigma: David Puttnam, The Story so Far*, Sphere, London, 1989

Yule, Andrew, *Sean Connery: From 007 to Hollywood Icon*, Donald I. Fine, New York 1992

Zicree, Marc Scott, *The Twilight Zone Companion*, Bantam, New York, 1982

Index

The World According to Mike Leigh

Michael Coveney

'There are few critical biographies as deeply felt as Michael Coveney's superb study ... a book which combines a lucid account of the lugubrious Jewish Salfordian's life and times with a truly powerful championing of Leigh's place at the forefront of contemporary English culture ... there is an enormous amount of insight into this very complex, troubled and obsessively brilliant man whose work will be seen and talked about long after we are all out of print.'   STEVE GRANT, *Time Out*

Mike Leigh is widely recognised as one of the great mavericks and creative geniuses of British stage, cinema and television. Since his first film, *Bleak Moments*, burst on an unsuspecting public in 1971, he has produced a body of work (*Secrets and Lies* won the Palme D'Or and International Critics' Prize at Cannes, as well as Best Actress Award for Brenda Blethyn) that is idiosyncratic, controversial, often hilarious and always acutely sensitive to the human condition.

Written with its subject's full cooperation, *The World According to Mike Leigh* is the first major critical evaluation of Leigh's career. It illuminates his northern Jewish background, the evolution of his working methods, his tenacity, humour, seriousness and bloody-mindedness. Michael Coveney has followed Leigh's work closely, on screen and in the theatre, for over twenty years, and has had unrestricted access to Leigh's papers and records in the telling of this remarkable story.

0 00 638339 4

Stanley Kubrick

A Biography

John Baxter

'In this superbly readable biography, John Baxter traces Kubrick's career from the day this spoilt Jewish boy from the Bronx was given a camera for his thirteenth birthday to his present situation as an eccentric hiding away in a remote Hertfordshire mansion.'

GERALD KAUFMAN, *Sunday Telegraph*

'John Baxter's highly readable biography makes Kubrick maddening, endearing and paranoid in equal proportions . . . Many of the stories are riveting.'

NIGEL ANDREWS, *Financial Times*

'Judicious and well-researched.' PHILLIP FRENCH, *Observer*

'John Baxter's superb biography sets out with enormous relish to unravel this mystery [of Kubrick's reclusiveness]. His earlier biographies, of Buñuel, Fellini, Ken Russell and Spielberg, are among the best in their field, and his account of Kubrick's somewhat tortured soul is written in the same vivid prose.'

J.G. BALLARD, *New Statesman*

'*Stanley Kubrick* is the sharpest book on cinema since Jake Eberts and Terry Ilott's *My Indecision Is Final*, the history of Goldcrest Films.' BRIAN ALDISS, *Daily Telegraph*

ISBN: 0 00 638445 5

Quentin Tarantino
The Man and His Movies

Jami Bernard

Worshipped like a film star by fans of his ultra hip, ultra violent movies, reviled and condemned by the self-appointed guardians of morality, Quentin Tarantino has become the cult hero of the nineties.

Using exclusive material from her interviews with Tarantino and those close to him, Jami Bernard traces this fascinating rise from high school dropout and B-movie junkie to the darling of Hollywood, and explores the philosophy and the mythology of the writer and director who has, with just a few explosive films, turned the movie world on its head.

With the furore over *Reservoir Dogs*, the triumph of *Pulp Fiction* and the bitter conflict over *Natural Born Killers*, Tarantino's meteoric rise has been turbulent and headline-grabbing. Through the unique inside knowledge of those who have worked, played and done battle with him, Jami Bernard looks beyond the media icon and reveals the man.

0 00 255644 8